The Eventful Years
— Memoirs of Chen Jinhua

I would like to thank the following for their care and support in the publishing of this book:

Sheng Huaren

Xu Kuangdi

Wang Chunzheng

Gao Shangquan

Su Shulin

Wang Jiming

Xie Qihua

Long Yongtu

Zhang Yanning

Li Deshui

Wang Tianpu

The Eventful Years
— Memoirs of Chen Jinhua

Chen Jinhua

Foreign Languages Press

First Edition 2008

Website: http://www.flp.com.cn
Email Addresses://info@flp.com.cn
sales@flp.com.cn

ISBN 978-7-119-05191-8
© Foreign Languages Press, Beijing, China, 2008

Published by
Foreign Languages Press
24 Baiwanzhuang Road, Beijing 100037, China

Distributed by China International Book Trading Corporation
35 Chegongzhuang Xilu, Beijing 100044, China
P.O. Box 399, Beijing, China

Printed in the People's Republic of China

Preface to the English Edition

During the last 30 years of the 20th century, China ended the "Cultural Revolution," adopted the policy of reform and opening up to the outside world, the focus of the work of the state shifted to socialist modernization, came into one with the times and participated in the cooperation and competition of economic globalization. It was a period of great changes, one in which the Chinese people opened a new chapter in their history.

Compared with the first 30 years of the 20th century, China is now in a completely new era. In that period, China was becoming a semi-feudal, semi-colonial society due to the successive invasions and oppressions of foreign powers. The state was weak and people lived in misery. Faced with the impending collapse of the state, some renowned politicians and thinkers of the late Qing Dynasty (1644-1911) and the early Republic of China (1911-1949) anxiously called for "unprecedented change," for "change of the heaven and earth," "historically unprecedented change," "change of the universe," and so on. They worried about China's future and fate, and were utterly dismayed by the contemporary situation. When China entered the second 30-year period, the Chinese people began to advance change for the sake of national salvation and revival. When one fell, others stepped into the breach; millions upon millions of Chinese people fought heroically for liberation, national independence and a prosperous nation, finally won victory over the Japanese invaders and successfully carried out the New Democratic Revolution. After another 30 years, China entered the final 30 years of the 20th century. With unparalleled courage, insight and resolve, China entered a new era of national invigoration, the building of socialism with Chinese characteristics and a well-off society. China developed itself on a larger scale and at a more rapid rate by means of profound reform so as to face changes both within and beyond China.

In the final nearly 30 years of the 20th century, the Communist Party of China (CPC) and the Chinese Government together holding the reins of a China undergoing huge changes, engineered, promoted and created a new situation by making a number of major decisions. I was fortunate enough to take part in implementing some of those decisions, personally felt the power of and witnessed the historic changes brought about by those decisions. Starting from the gradual market-oriented reform to the establishment of the continuously self-improving socialist market economy, China has greatly tapped and promoted the growth of production. Within a short period of 30 years—a single generation—China's overall economic output increased by a factor of 5.6, with an annual growth of 9.67 percent. Its international economic ranking improved from 11th place to fourth. China's foreign trade ranking rose from 27th place in 1978 to third in 2006. Shortages of food and clothing, which had plagued the Chinese people for over a thousand years, were beginning to be properly solved. The poverty-stricken population in China fell from over 250 million in 1978 to 20 million in 2006. Chairman Mao Zedong said in the late 1950s that in 30 to 50 years' time, China's world citizenship would be revoked if its steel output should fail to reach 200-300 million tons. Now his prediction has been realized. In 2006, China produced 420 million tons of steel, 11 times of that of 30 years ago. China is the only country in the world whose annual steel production has exceeded 200 million tons. *The Eventful Years—Memoirs of Chen Jinhua* gives a quite comprehensive account of some major decision-making, describing the background, implementation and results of those decisions.

The changes in China are tremendous. *China 2020*, a report issued by the World Bank in 1997, states: "China is the fastest-growing economy in the world, with per capita incomes more than quadrupling since 1978, achieving in two generations what took other countries centuries." This achievement belongs to China as well as the world. China's development draws world attention, and has the world's support and cooperation. China's development also supports the sustained growth of the world economy, and has gradually become a major world factor. China's experience during its rapid economic growth has aroused the interest of experts and specialists of many countries. China's experiences, whether positive or negative, China's successes and setbacks, are all useful for the exploration of human progress. The large-scale exploration and implementation of extensive and profound reforms by a large developing country with a population of 1.3 billion are most significant in all aspects. For developing countries in particular, the problems encountered by China might be what they have today or might have in future. China's experiences could well serve them as reference. The accounts in this book provide first-hand materials for the study of Chinese development. In this book, I do not cover up errors in the making or implementation of decisions, do not conceal difficulties and problems, but do admit the gap between China and the world advanced level.

I am delighted by the translation and publication of this English edition of *The Eventful Years—Memoirs of Chen Jinhua*. The Japanese-Chinese Economic Association and Mr. Akira Chihaya, former President of the Association, decided to translate the book into Japanese, and the Japanese edition was published and distributed last August. The Olympics Museum has included this book in its permanent collection. Such actions, in my opinion, reflect not merely the value of the book itself, but admiration for China's development, a confirmation of mutual benefit and cooperation between China and relevant countries, enterprises and friends, an expression of respect for a record that tracks the footprints of China's development.

I am most grateful to the Sinopec Group and the Foreign Languages Press for their excellent work in translating, publishing and distributing the English edition of my book.

Chen Jinhua
August 2007, Beijing

Contents

Chapter X Recalling the Visits to China of Russian, Japanese, Cuban and American State Leaders / 519

Preface

In the history of the development of the People's Republic of China (PRC), the Communist Party of China (CPC) and the Central Government have made a number of important decisions. I had the good fortune to participate in the implementation of some of these decisions, including New China's second round of large-scale importation of complete sets of technology and equipment in the early 1970s; in the Work Team of the Central Committee of the CPC sent to Shanghai after the fall of the "Gang of Four" (a name coined by Mao Zedong to refer to the anti-Party clique comprising Jiang Qing, Zhang Chunqiao, Wang Hongwen and Yao Wenyuan—all members of the Political Bureau of the CPC at that time) in October 1976; in the third round of large-scale importation of complete sets of technology and equipment and the construction of the Shanghai Baoshan Iron and Steel Works in the late 1970s; in the establishment of China National Petrochemical Company for the purpose of better exploitation of domestic oil in 1983; in the adoption of a socialist market economy system, a decision made in 1992; in the exercise of macro-economic adjustment in a bid to prevent overheating of the economy in 1993; and in the establishment of the Boao Forum for Asia in Hainan Province, China as proposed by former government leaders of the Philippines, Japan and Australia in 1999. In making decisions for these major events, as well as for the second and third rounds of large-scale importation of complete sets of technology and equipment, the Party and the state leaders of past generations, in particular Zhou Enlai and Deng Xiaoping, demonstrated their wisdom and strategy in bringing the advantages of the socialist system into full play and in handling major events with concentrated efforts and showed their ambitious blueprint for China's future; these have had a far-reaching influence on China's industrial modernization and the building of its national strength. In the process of implementing those important decisions in which I was personally involved, I could feel the great physical power of those decisions and witnessed the historical changes to China that they brought about.

The Party History Research Office of the Party School of the Central Committee of the CPC asked me to write down my experiences in implementing those major decisions. After a long period of consideration, I agreed to do so. I think this might be meaningful for the study of the history of the rule by the CPC and the history of the development of the PRC. As one of many witnesses personally involved in those major events during the past score of years, I feel it is a kind of historical duty to recall the causes and results of some decisions, the details of their implementation and their great achievements, to study their important functions and far-reaching impact on China's modernization drive.

The 30-odd years of the development of the PRC from the early 1970s to the early 2000s is a remarkable chapter in the history of CPC rule. These 30-odd years of pioneering history were full of glories and dreams, victories and setbacks, struggles and hardships. Today, history has turned over a new page; however, the task of speeding up development of the People's Republic still requires tenacious effort. It still needs a pioneering and enterprising spirit, needs people to go all out in building this country. All the activities recounted in this book indicate that it was the efforts of millions of devoted people that changed history and pushed China to advance. China is still in the middle stage of industrialization. To build a well-off society in an all-round way, to basically materialize the goal of achieving modernization by the middle of this century, there is still a long way to go, and we need to continue our struggle. Therefore, we must have our targets and make use of our predecessors' experience. History is handed down generation-to-generation and always moves ahead. China needs development; therefore it needs to inherit, to take the experience of predecessors as reference.

My experience related in this book may be of some use in studying the leading role of the CPC in promoting all undertakings in China, and in studying the history of the development of the Republic. These days, more and more publications on the study of the development of the Republic have appeared, some of them original and profound in their view. However, the recounting of an author's own experiences is rare. This book may help to fill the gap. In certain books I have read, some historical facts are inaccurate, and there are errors in figures too. I have given my account based on historical facts that I witnessed myself. For certain important historical facts, I have checked the relevant archives, consulting colleagues, officials, scholars and specialists in the know; tried my best to make sure that everything that happened in history is truthful, accurate and will not mislead those studying the development of the Republic.

History is a mirror. It should truthfully reflect reality. Implementation of all the major CPC decisions covered in this book was not all plain sailing. There were twists and turns and setbacks; there were joys and woes. There existed correctness and errors, successes and failures. I believe all these things are most valuable. Based on my own experience and what I witnessed, I have written about the twists and turns and setbacks in the process of implementation of relevant decisions, summed up experiences and lessons. This is an authentic historical record telling readers how duties were performed.

I have always believed that one generation can only do what is within its capability and fulfill its obligations. A renowned Qing-dynasty scholar Zhao Yi once wrote these lines of poetry: "Poems of Li Bai and Du Fu have been passed from lip to lip / And they are no longer fresh

/ Heroes emerge generation after generation / Each shining for centuries." In the long river of history, people of different times may write only the chapter of their own times' history. People of my generation are fortunate to have lived in the eventful years of the late 20th century. Time and tide have pushed people such as myself into the limelight of the historical stage, to perform different roles and write our own chapter of history. Speaking of achievements, to be honest, historical opportunities happened to fall into our laps. It was our luck. Speaking of setbacks and errors in work, to say we were limited by the times is not being defensive. To examine a brief period of dozens of years in history from such a perspective, I feel peaceful in mind. Similarly, if readers could look at those stormy years in history from the same perspective, they would feel peaceful too.

Chapter 1

New China's Second Round of Large-scale Importation of Complete Sets of Technology and Equipment

- Background to the Decision-making
- Expansion and Approval of the Importation Plan
- Implementation and Construction of Projects
- Important Role and Far-reaching Influence

The first half of the 1970s saw a new peak of large-scale importation of complete sets of technology and equipment after the first round of large-scale importation of technology and equipment from the Soviet Union and East European countries that took place in the 1950s. With the support of Chairman Mao Zedong and led by Premier Zhou Enlai, this second round of importation by New China was planned and organized directly by the Business Leading Group of the State Council, blazing a new trail for China's economic cooperation with foreign countries. It was a turning point. The pioneering effort in solving several key problems in the national economy accelerated the development of related industries, narrowed the gap between China and the world advanced level, and established and developed trade and economic cooperation relations with Western developed countries, ushering in a period of opening-up to the outside world and taking part in the cooperation and competition of economic globalization.

At that time, I was working as Deputy Director of the Planning Group of the Ministry of Light Industry (A merger of the Ministry of Textiles, No. 1 Ministry of Light Industry and No. 2 Ministry of Light Industry in July 1970), and concurrently Deputy Head of the Office for Importation of Complete Sets of Technology and Equipment under the Ministry of Light Industry. Therefore I was directly involved in New China's second round large-scale importation of complete sets of technology and equipment. During this round, we actually signed 26 project contracts with foreign countries. I was personally in charge of the execution and implementation of five project contracts, namely Shanghai Petroleum & Chemical Plant, Liaoyang Petroleum & Chemical Fiber Plant, Sichuan Vinylon Plant, Tianjin Petroleum & Chemical Fiber Plant and Nanjing Alkylbenzene Plant. In terms of technology, all five projects were of world advanced level in the early 1970s. The total amount of investment in these five projects represented 35.39 percent of the total amount of investment into all 26 projects. In addition, there were 13 projects concerning chemical fertilizers, which were vital for tackling the problem of food shortage. Among those 18 projects, 13.68 billion *yuan* was used for solving food and clothing problems, representing 63.8 percent of the total investment. The principle of "solving several key problems in the national economy in a down-to-earth manner" was earnestly implemented and produced good results.

Background to the Decision-making

One day in early January 1972, when I was attending a national planning conference in the Jingxi Hotel, Gu Xiulian of the State Planning Commission (SPC) came up to me and said that the Party Central Committee had decided to introduce complete sets of technology and equipment for production of chemical fiber and chemical fertilizer, and asked me to draft a memorandum. Qian Zhiguang, Minister of Light Industry, immediately invited Cao Lu, Jiao Shanmin, Li Zhengguang, Wang Ruiting and others to discuss the issue, believing that it was a most important decision and that we must go into action right away. Before I prepared the memorandum, Li Xiannian and Hua Guofeng called special meetings to deliberate the issue. On the basis of those discussions, I drafted "The Report on Importation of Complete Sets of Technology and Equipment for Production of Chemical Fiber and Chemical Fertilizer," which was then handed over to Gu Xiulian. On January 22, the Report, bearing the signatures of Li Xiannian, Hua Guofeng and Yu Qiuli of the Business Leading Group of the State Council, was submitted to the higher-ups. On February 5, Premier Zhou Enlai wrote these words on the Report: "I tend to agree. Please submit it to Chairman Mao for examination and instruction." Pretty soon, Chairman Mao and some other leaders of the Party and the state gave their approval. Two days later, Li Xiannian gave back the Report to Yu Qiuli, Qian Zhiguang and Bai Xiangguo (Minister of Foreign

Trade and Economic Cooperation) to take care of the work.

Why was the decision made in early 1972 to import complete sets of technology and equipment? And why focus on technology and equipment for chemical fiber production at the very beginning? Here is the background.

One: changes of political climate and policy adjustment. On August 31, 1970, Chairman Mao announced "My Opinions" at the Second Plenary Session of the Ninth Central Committee of the CPC, which lay bare the illicit activities of Chen Boda. The political campaign "Criticizing Chen and Carrying out Rectification" was thus launched throughout the country. On September 13, 1971, Lin Biao betrayed the Party and fled. This event, later known as the "September 13 Incident," was an important turning point of the "Cultural Revolution." It was tantamount to announcing the failure of the "Cultural Revolution" both in practice and in theory. After this, the domestic political climate changed considerably. As of October 1971, with the support of Mao Zedong, Premier Zhou Enlai took charge of the day-to-day work of the Party and the state. He made an effort to modify policies towards cadres, the economy and other matters. At a number of national conferences later convened on professional subjects, efforts were made to remove the destructive economic consequences inflicted by the "Cultural Revolution" by way of criticizing the ultra-left trend of thought and anarchism, including some "Leftist" practices *vis-a-vis* foreign-related affairs, and to restore normality to political life and the national economy. Speaking of the widespread tendency of cadres not daring to engage in production and people not daring to work hard as a result of Lin Biao's advocating "putting politics first," Premier Zhou said that "ultra-leftism is nothing more than trumpeting meaningless, abstract and metaphysical stuff. It exaggerates and goes to extremes." He emphasized that "political movement and production must not be in opposition," and encouraged cadres at all levels to focus on production and profession in a right-minded way. In accordance with Premier Zhou's instruction, on October 14, 1972, the *People's Daily*, organ of the Party, devoted a whole page to three articles, including "Anarchism Is a Counter-revolutionary Tool of Sham Marxists—a Study Note," to criticize the ultra-left trend of thought and anarchism. This provoked a great response nationwide. The criticism drive led by Premier Zhou was hailed by the great majority of cadres in and outside the Party, intellectuals and the broad masses. The domestic situation took a marked turn for the better. In those days, the Gang of Four willfully accused innocent people with political charges, criticizing so-called "slavish comprador philosophy," "traitorous policy," etc. In this atmosphere, the criticism of ultra-leftism and policy adjustment led by Premier Zhou paved the way for the introduction of complete sets of technology and equipment.

Two: exchanges between China and foreign countries were restored and expanded, and Western developed countries were anxious to do business with China. In October 1971, by an overwhelming majority of votes, the 26th General Assembly adopted the resolution to restore all legitimate rights of China in the United Nations (UN) and accepted China as a member of the UN Security Council. This was a major sign of the improvement of China's position in the world since the launch of the "Cultural Revolution." Another major sign was the visit to China of US President Richard Nixon in February 1972, thus melting the 20-odd years of icy relations between the two countries and marking the beginning of the normalization process between China and the USA. With those events as basis, China and the USA constantly expanded and deepened their mutual exchanges. When he met President Nixon, Mao Zedong criticized the wrong practice of the "closed-door" policy in foreign trade during the "Cultural Revolution," saying, "You were interested in personnel exchange and doing a little bit of business, yet we were dead set against it. For a dozen years, we insisted that if major issues were not solved, we would not bother with trivial things.

I was one of them. Later on, we realized that you were right, hence the ping-pong diplomacy." The China-USA Shanghai Communiqué states explicitly that "economic relations based on equality and mutual benefit are in the interest of the peoples of the two countries." Both sides "agree to facilitate the progressive development of trade between their two countries." The resumption of the legal seat of China in the UN and relaxing of relations between China and the USA greatly improved China's international environment, helped to bring about a new tide in diplomatic relations between China and other countries. Western developed countries, in particular Japan, Canada and some countries of Western Europe, successively established diplomatic relations with China. The diplomatic breakthrough brought about new opportunities for foreign trade and economic cooperation. The Western countries were faced with a grave economic crisis in the 1970s. Problems caused by surplus productivity became more acute. Products, equipment and technology were all anxious to find a way out. Therefore, there was a great eagerness to do business with China. This provided favorable conditions for China for the importation of complete sets of technology and equipment.

Three: the inadequate supply of materials for the textile industry in China was growing more acute by the day, which hampered the growth of textile products. Shortage of clothing for the people had long remained unsolved. At the time, raw materials for the Chinese textile industry were primarily natural fibers, among which the most important was cotton. But the level of cotton output had remained at a little over 40 million *dan* (a Chinese unit of weight, about 50 kilograms) [two million tons] per annum for a long time. Mao Zedong once said: "It's been so many years since the Liberation, how can we face the people if the problems of shortage of food and clothing are not properly solved?" He gave the instruction: "Work hard for the growth of grain and work hard for the growth of cotton." In the 1970s, there was an annual cotton conference attended by cadres at all levels. Local Party secretaries and governors of the major cotton producing counties were all called to such conferences. Premier Zhou usually chaired the conference in person and required all localities to grow more cotton and sell more cotton to the state. At one such conference, I remember Premier Zhou personally asking each Party secretary of the major cotton producing counties about the cotton growing situation in their county. He told the cadres to keep in mind a picture of the whole country rather than caring just for the piece of land under their own jurisdiction. One must make one's own fields fertile, yet not forget the fields of others. He urged local officials to grow more cotton. Even so, the total output of cotton in 1971 in China was, in fact, merely 43 million *dan* [2.15 million tons], 7.6 percent less than in 1970. After deducting the cotton needed by farmers themselves, army and urban residents, only 31 million *dan* [1.55 million tons] of cotton was left for the textile industry. Whether growing cotton or grain, there was a problem of land shortage. To increase cotton production, land used for cotton must expand at the cost of reducing the amount of land for grain. That would result in shortage of grain, which was vital to the country. After all, grain was of the greatest importance to the people. Difficulties in cotton production would lead to under-production in the textile industry, which meant less clothing for the people.

China exercised a cloth ration coupon policy for as long as 30 years—from adoption of the "Order on Planned Purchase and Supply of Cotton Clothes" at State Council Meeting No. 224 in September 1954 to the announcement of the abolition of cloth ration coupons in 1983. Each year, the quantity of cloth ration coupons to be issued was meticulously calculated. Once approved by the Party Central Committee and Chairman Mao, it was then announced in the form of a formal document of the Party Central Committee. The quantity of cloth ration coupons issued varied from place to place according to the local climate. Generally, each person was granted 16, 18 or 20 *chi* (unit of length equaling one third of a meter) of cloth. It is now almost 60 years since I began my working life. I spent half my career in the Ministry of Textiles. I served as secretary to the minister, director of the Research Office, deputy director of the Planning Group, etc. I understood thoroughly how important clothing was to a family. Such things are incomprehensible to the young people of today. We used to say: "A garment is new for three years, old for three years, used for another three years by re-sewing and re-patching," "The eldest child wears the new clothes, the second child wears the old clothes and the third child wears the patched clothes." This is unheard of nowadays. It is all past history. But it is indeed what we personally experienced. It was no wonder that the clothing problem was a concern of the top leaders as well as each family. Those countries that had accomplished industrialization had solved this problem through development of the chemical fiber industry. They replaced raw materials from agriculture with raw materials from industry. Chemical fiber represented 40 percent or more of raw materials for their textile industry. To solve the problem of raw materials shortage in China's textile industry so as to solve the clothing problem, the Ministry of Textiles submitted a memorandum to the Party Central Committee, citing the experiences of industrial countries as reference and proposing a "twin-track" policy, namely, to make use of both natural and chemical fibers. The policy was approved. But the issue of chemical fiber production technology, primarily of synthetic fiber, could not be solved domestically. The only way out was to develop cellulose fiber, i.e., viscose fiber. Later, we developed some vinylon fiber, but it was poor quality and products made of such fiber were limited. People did not like it. What they most liked was terylene and acrylic fiber. But we had little of these. So the clothing problem still remained. In the early 1970s, it became even more acute. The Party and state leaders went all out to crack this nut, which had to do with people's livelihood. Mao

Zedong once said that we must think of the people who are still suffering from inadequate clothing and bedding. It was urgent to put the importation of complete sets of equipment for production of chemical fiber on the agenda.

Four: breakthroughs made in domestic oil production made it possible for China to develop petrochemicals. In 1959, China's oil output was 3.73 million tons, supplying only 40.6 percent of domestic demand. In 1965, thanks to the discovery and successful exploitation of the Daqing Oilfield, China's oil output reached 11.31 million tons, adequate to satisfy domestic needs. In 1972, great changes took place in China's oil industry. Oil output that year reached 45.67 million tons, more than required by the country. It was still the period of the "Cultural Revolution," of strife between different factions and anarchy rampant, with the coal industry in some provinces and cities in a state of collapse. Without coal, power plants were seriously affected and some of them had to turn to oil for power generation. It was most wasteful and an entirely wrong practice. But it indicated that China had surplus oil that could be used, not only for fuel, but also for the production of chemical fibers. This prepared the ground for the large scale importation of complete sets of technology and equipment for chemical fiber production.

These four factors made it the right time for China to embark on large-scale importation of complete sets of technology and equipment from abroad. Just imagine, had any of the four factors been absent, it would have been difficult to import foreign technology and equipment. Thanks to Premier Zhou's far-sightedness, China caught the right opportunity. It had been impossible to do so earlier, and would have caused losses to the country had it been done later.

As well as the above four factors, an incident around that time had a great impact on the decision to import. I learned about it from Li Xiannian and Yu Qiuli. It was in August or September of 1971, when Mao Zedong was making an inspection tour in southern China. He had a habit, or rather a way of doing things, that wherever he went, he would send his secretaries and others on his staff to go to local communities, factories, villages and other grassroots entities to find out how things were and what was on people's minds. When he got to Changsha, Mao Zedong granted a day off to his people, asking them to go around the city, do some shopping, and find out what things were like. A woman worker returned in high delight, and when Mao asked her what had come over her she replied: "I bought a pair of terylene trousers after standing on line for ages." Young people of today may be unaware, but those over middle age certainly know that in those days it was smart to wear trousers with smartly pressed straight creases. Such trouser creases will not last long in cotton trousers, but terylene will retain the creases long and fast. Furthermore, it does not wrinkle. However, terylene was difficult to get hold of. Mao was quite surprised by her reply. One day after the "September 13 Incident," Mao brought up the subject with Zhou Enlai and asked: "Why can't we produce more polyester fiber? Standing on line for a little while might be OK but never 'for ages.'" Zhou said: "We have not mastered the technology, and are unable to produce the material." Mao asked again: "Can't we buy the technology?" "Of course." Then Zhou went to Li Xiannian and Yu Qiuli and asked them to buy it. Though I have seen no original written record about this, it was reflected in "The Report on Importation of Complete Sets of Technology and Equipment for Production of Chemical Fiber and Chemical Fertilizer" which I drafted in January 1972. It is stated in the Report that if China imported four sets of equipment for production of chemical fiber, the total output of terylene would reach 1.9 billion *chi*. That would largely satisfy the needs of the rural and urban residents. That Report was full of theoretical analysis, and many issues were addressed in a broad-brush manner. There was no mention of any specific measures, with the exception of terylene, for which detailed figures were given. Obviously the story I had learned was not groundless, for terylene was specially added to the Report.

I came across an article titled "My First Terylene Shirt" by Liu Xin'ge in the magazine *Zong Heng* (No. 3, 2004). He relates a vivid story about how he tried hard to buy six *chi* of terylene in order to make a shirt. People who had experienced that period would be easily moved and the article could be a historical proof demonstrating people's urgent demand for terylene.

Expansion and Approval of the Importation Plan

The second round of large-scale importation of complete sets of technology and equipment lasted about a year—from the initial plan representing a US$ 400 million investment to import four sets for chemical fiber production and two for chemical fertilizer production, to the final US$ 4.3 billion decision to import 26 large-scale projects. During this period, the State Planning Commission submitted four major reports.

The first of these, "The Report on Importation of Complete Sets of Technology and Equipment for Production of Chemical Fiber and Chemical Fertilizer," drafted by myself and submitted on January 16, 1972, pointed out: "In order to fully utilize China's resources of oil and natural gas to rapidly develop chemical fiber and chemical fertilizer, we are planning to import complete sets of facilities for production of chemical fiber and chemical fertilizer and some related key equipment. For chemical fiber, we are planning to import four facilities from France and Japan at a cost of US$ 270 million. When these facilities are completed, the annual output of synthetic fiber will be 240,000 tons, roughly equivalent to five million tons of cotton. It can be used to produce four billion *chi* of textiles, of which, the output of terylene (polyester), including the current production output (referring to those processed domestically from imported materials), would amount to 1.9 billion *chi*. That would largely satisfy the needs of rural and urban residents." The four facilities were planned to be located in Sichuan, Liaoning, Shanghai and Tianjin. For chemical fertilizer, we planned to import two sets of 300,000-ton large-scale facilities for production of synthetic ammonia, the plants to be located in Sichuan and Daqing. The Report also raised the issue of building a 300,000-ton capacity synthetic ammonia plant using coal as raw material in the south of Shanxi Province. At the same time, US$ 90 million was needed to speed up the construction of 25 synthetic ammonia plants throughout the country, and to import key equipment, components and steel for expansion and renovation of existing plants. In addition, a further US$ 40 million was needed for importing some single machinery items, and materials for production of synthetic materials. In total, it would come to US$ 400 million. The Report proposed the immediate formation of three specialist groups to go abroad to carry out technical investigation; that domestic support facilities be included in both long-term and current year economic plan; and to aim for completion of the construction of these facilities by 1974 and for production capacity to be in place by 1975.

On February 7, following approval by Chairman Mao Zedong, Premier Zhou Enlai and other Party and state leaders, the plan was put into practice. Then the Ministry of Light Industry, which was in charge of the importation, and the Ministry of Fuel and Chemicals, which was closely connected with the related work, sent specialist groups to western Europe and Japan to investigate suitable facilities to import. In May, two months later, they submitted to the State Council a report on their findings and suggestions for the importation of chemical fiber equipment. On May 24, Li Xiannian approved the plan and appointed Chai Shufan to chair negotiations with foreign businesses. Chai, who had been working in a cadres school[1], was urgently recalled to the capital by Zhou Enlai. Chai, an expert in foreign affairs, was an upright man. At the end of 1975, the so-called "Counter-attacking Rightist Trend to Reverse the Verdict" political campaign was in full swing. At a State Council meeting to repudiate "foreign comprador philosophy," Wang Hongwen, then Vice Chairman of the Party, was present. When someone criticized Chai Shufan saying that the Ministry of Foreign Trade was selling out China, Chai rejected this on the spot, saying that though the Ministry had made many mistakes, to accuse it of "selling out China" was utter nonsense. This silenced the whole conference hall. His argument was forceful, and the critics could produce no evidence. Wang could do nothing about it but keep a sullen silence. But all this was yet to happen. Anyway, after a month of negotiations, Chai submitted a memorandum "Report on the Progress of Negotiations on Import of Chemical Fiber Equipment" to the State Council. On September 2, Zhou Enlai read the report and sent it to Li Xiannian and Yu Qiuli. Zhou asked them: "Is it possible to first import a set of Japanese chemical fertilizer equipment, a set of petrochemical equipment from Mitsubishi and a set from Asahi Kasei Corporation? Are the raw materials all extracted from oil?" On September 19, Li Xiannian wrote on the "Report on the Importation from Japan of Equipment for the Production of Chemical Fertilizer and Chemical Fiber Ahead of the Plan" submitted by the State Planning Commission and the Ministry of Foreign Trade and Economic Cooperation: "Tend to agree. Send it to Hua Guofeng and Ji Dengkui for examination and approval. (This Report has been submitted to the Party Central Committee.)" Thus the decision to import the first batch of equipment for production of chemical

---

1. Referring to May Seventh Cadre School, farm-school for government officials, staff of public institutions, teaching staff of colleges and universities, etc. to do manual labor in rural areas for the purpose of remolding their outlook and values in accordance with Mao Zedong's "May 7 directive" issued during the "Cultural Revolution."

fiber and chemical fertilizer was finalized.

While I was drafting the Report, the national development planning conference was held. News of the Report being drafted spread among the conference delegates and people from local governments vied with each other to request that the imported facilities be sited in their areas. A preliminary decision was made that the four sets of chemical fiber equipment would be placed in populous areas where the textile industry was relatively developed, but short of raw materials—places such as Shanghai, Tianjin, Liaoning and Sichuan. Later a work team comprising people from the Ministry of Light Industry, State Construction Commission, ministries of Fuel and Chemicals, Communications, Water Resources and Power was set up under the leadership of Vice Minister Jiao Shanmin and sent to various places in Liaoning, Shanghai, Tianjin and Sichuan to choose sites for the future plants. After preliminary selection and comparison of local conditions, the sites were determined. They were Jinshanwei of Jinshan County in Shanghai, Liaoyang in Liaoning Province, Beidagang in Tianjin, and Changshou County in Sichuan. The work team submitted a brief report about the sites chosen for future chemical fiber equipment to the SPC, Li Xiannian and Hua Guofeng.

After six months' preparation, including negotiation and selection of sites, the issue of the importation of four sets of chemical fiber equipment and several sets of chemical fertilizer equipment together with components was smoothly solved. This was the first step for China's importation of complete sets of technology and equipment. In the wake of our success in foreign negotiations, overseas investigation and selection of sites, many other ministries followed suit, including the ministries of Metallurgy, Fuel and Chemicals, Machinery, Telecommunications, Civil Aviation, Water Conservancy and Power, Railway, No. 3 and No. 4 Machinery Industry. They took the opportunity to introduce advanced technology. They submitted memos requesting permission to dispatch delegations overseas to study technology levels in developed countries; to learn about the latest developments in the international market in order to get the best deal, and then import those technologies that were advanced, reasonably priced and suitable for China. This was the internal factor for later expanding the scale of importation of complete sets of technology and equipment from abroad. At that time, Western countries were showing great enthusiasm for China's importation of technology and equipment. The Liaoyang chemical fiber project was introduced from France. Because of a difference of US$ 10 million in price, execution of the contract was delayed. When the then President of France Georges Pompidou visited China, he tried to persuade China in person, inviting Premier Zhou Enlai to a dinner at the French embassy in Beijing to discuss the issue. I learned from Premier Zhou's entourage that the French President said that the signing of the contract would arouse great interest among the international community and that he hoped the Chinese Government would concede the price. In consideration of the overall situation, Premier Zhou finally agreed and the two sides signed the contract at last. Indeed, this was warmly received throughout the world. Many Western countries regarded it as a signal and began doing business with China. This was the external factor for expanding the scale of China's importation of complete sets of technology and equipment.

The second report concerned the importation by Wuhan Iron and Steel Works of 1,700 mm continuous sheet rolling mills. On August 6, 1972, the SPC submitted to Li Xiannian, Ji Dengkui, Hua Guofeng and the State Council a memorandum titled "Report on the Import of 1,700 mm Continuous Sheet Rolling Mills." This illustrates the introduction of complete sets of technology and equipment from abroad spreading from the petrochemical industry to the iron and steel industry. Iron and steel had long been a major industry in China. But the quality and variety of iron and steel were unable to satisfy domestic demand. High quality steel sheet had to be imported. In an effort to solve the problem, as early as 1959 and 1964, the Ministry of Metallurgy had twice submitted memorandums asking to install 1,700 mm hot and cold steel sheet rolling mills at Wuhan Iron and Steel Works. In 1971, the Ministry of Metallurgy submitted a third memorandum, asking to buy 1,700 mm rolling mills. The SPC agreed the request and submitted it to the State Council. The report stated: "Inadequacy of steel rolling capacity, lack of a complete variety of steel, particularly inadequate supply of steel sheet and tube, are quite an outstanding problem in the current development of the national economy... Therefore the Ministry of Metallurgy requests to import a set of 1,700 mm continuous rolling mills, including hot continuous rolling mill, cold continuous rolling mill, zinc-coating units, tin-coating units, silicon-steel sheet units, etc., so as to increase rolling capacity by about two million tons of steel sheet, including about 800,000 tons of cold-rolled steel sheet." This report also said that while manufacturing more rolling mills in China, it was necessary to import a small number of key rolling mills. The price of a continuous rolling mill facility was quoted at around US$ 200 million, which, although representing a large sum of foreign exchange, was worthwhile when compared to the US$ 300 million a year for the import of three million tons of steel sheet. The report proposed that a special team comprising people from the Ministry of Metallurgy, No. 1 Ministry of Machinery Industry, Ministry of Foreign Trade and the State Planning Commission be organized to be in charge of the work. Premier Zhou wrote these words on the memorandum: "I tend to agree with the plan. Submit the report to Chairman Mao and other members of the Political Bureau in Beijing for examination and approval." On August 21, the Party Central Committee and the State Council approved the importation of 1,700 mm rolling mills from the Federal Republic of Germany and Japan, which were to be placed in the Wuhan Iron and Steel Works.

The third report "Request for the Importation of Complete Sets of Chemical Equipment" was submitted to the State Council by the SPC on November 7, 1972. It proposed the importation of 23 sets of chemical equipment at a cost of US$ 600 million. At the same time, industries such as coal, oil, chemicals, machinery, defense, water conservancy, power, communications and forestry had, after overseas investigation tours, also submitted memorandums to import technology and equipment from abroad. Thus, the scope of introduction kept expanding. As a result, three batches of import of technology and equipment, including newly suggested import projects, landed on the desk of Premier Zhou. Zhou found the import plan somewhat bitty, holding the view that it was a good opportunity to go the whole hog and should be further expanded. He asked the Business Leading Group of the State Council and the SPC to group together all requests for technology and equipment imports. He said: "Be prepared to adopt a larger-scale importation plan."

The fourth report was named the "Four-three Plan," for the reason that it needed US$ 4.3 billion. On January 2, 1973, in line with Premier Zhou's instruction and the opinion of the Business Leading Group of the State Council, the SPC submitted a report entitled "Request for Increase in the Importation of Equipment and Expansion of Foreign Economic Exchange" to Li Xiannian, Ji Dengkui, Hua Guofeng and Zhou Enlai. This was the "Four-three Plan." Li Xiannian soon handed the report to Premier Zhou. After deliberation and amendment, the State Council approved the report in principle on March 22. The report stated: "As a result of research, we plan to import a batch of complete sets of equipment and single machinery within the next three to five years, and hope to make this equipment play a full role in the Fifth Five-year Plan (1976-1980) period. The goal is to introduce new technology, support agriculture, strengthen basic industries and light industry, and speed up the socialist construction of China. The initial proposal for the import calls for US$ 4.3 billion." Later, a further US$ 880 million was added, making the total outlay in foreign exchange US$ 5.18 billion.

This report raised six principles in the introduction of foreign technology and equipment. One, adherence to the principle of independence and self-reliance. "We must muster our efforts and solve several key problems in the national economy in a down-to-earth manner." Two, combining learning and innovation. The "Leftist" approach of "repudiation first, transformation second, and utility third," advocated by some was criticized by Premier Zhou as inappropriate; he stressed that we should adopt an approach of "learning first, utility second, transformation third, and creation fourth," meaning that innovation and transformation come after digesting and absorbing. Three, import and export should be balanced. Four, combining old and new, be economical in foreign exchange expenditure. The imported facilities should as far as possible be placed in existing plants, allowing the use of existing public utilities and accommodation facilities in order to reduce expenditure. Five, keep a good balance between present tasks and future goals. Six, most of the imported equipment should be sited in the eastern coastal areas, with a small proportion sited in the interior. Those six principles became the guiding principles for China's second round importation of complete sets of technology and equipment. The report also suggested that the SPC and relevant ministries and commissions set up an "Equipment Importation Leading Group."

There were altogether 26 import items in the second round large-scale importation of complete sets of technology and equipment. They were as follows: Four sets of chemical fiber equipment—for Shanghai Petroleum & Chemical Plant, Liaoyang Petroleum & Chemical Fiber Plant, Sichuan Vinylon Plant, Tianjin Petroleum & Chemical Fiber Plant; three sets of petrochemical equipment—a 300,000-ton ethylene facility for Beijing Petroleum & Chemical Plant (today's Sinopec Beijing Yanshan Chemical Corporation), a 115,000-ton ethylene and support facilities for PetroChina Jilin Petrochemical Company, and a set of vinyl chloride equipment for Beijing No. 2 Chemical Plant; 13 sets of chemical fertilizer equipment with annual production capacity of 300,000 tons of synthetic ammonia, or 480,000 or 520,000 tons of urea—placed respectively in Cangzhou of Hebei Provine (Cangzhou Chemical Fertilizer Plant), Liaohe of Liaoning Province (Liaohe Chemical Fertilizer Plant), Daqing of Heilongjiang Province (Daqing Chemical Fertilizer Plant), Nanjing of Jiangsu Province (Qixiashan Chemical Fertilizer Plant), Anqing of Anhui Province (Anqing Chemical Fertilizer Plant), Zibo of Shandong Province (Qilu No. 2 Chemical Fertilizer Plant), Yichang of Hubei Province (Hubei Chemical Fertilizer Plant), Dongting of Hunan Province (Dongting Chemical Fertilizer Plant), Guangzhou of Guangdong Province (Guangzhou Chemical Fertilizer Plant), Chengdu of Sichuan Province (Sichuan Chemical Plant), Luzhou of Sichuan (Luzhou Natural Gas Chemical Plant), Chishuihe of Guizhou (Chishuihe Natural Gas and Chemical Fertilizer Plant), and Shuifu of Yunnan Province (Yunnan Natural Gas Chemical Plant); one set of alkylbenzene equipment for Nanjing Alkylbenzene Plant (It has been reported, incorrectly, that there were ten sets, but it was decided from the outset to import only one); three large-scale power stations, sited, respectively, in Beidagang of Tianjin, Douhe of Tangshan, Hebei Province, and Yuanbaoshan of Chifeng in Inner Mongolia; two sets of iron and steel equipment—1,700 mm rolling mills for Wuhan Iron and Steel Works, and one set of equipment for pellet chloridizing for Nanjing Iron and Steel Works. In addition, there were 43 sets of comprehensive mechanized coal mining units, single items such as a world advanced turbine compressor, combustion turbine, industrial steam turbine, etc. Every one of the above 26 items cost over 100 million *yuan* apiece. Items priced at more than one billion *yuan* include the equipment given to Liaoyang Petroleum & Chemical Fiber Plant (2.9 billion *yuan*), 1,700 mm rolling mills to Wuhan Iron and Steel Works (2.76 billion *yuan*), equipment for Daqing Chemical Fertilizer Plant (a

Japanese Yen loan, due to the fluctuation of the exchange rate, the price was increased to 2.67 billion *yuan*), equipment for Shanghai Petroleum & Chemical Plant (two billion *yuan*), Tianjin Petroleum & Chemical Fiber Plant (1.35 billion *yuan*). Only two items were relatively small, namely the vinyl chloride production equipment for Beijing No. 2 Chemical Plant, and the equipment for production of pellet chloridizing for Nanjing Iron and Steel Works.

Table 1 lists the 26 complete sets of facilities for importation in the "Four-three Plan"

Item	Site	Place of Origin	Production Capacity (1,000 tons per annum)	Date of Execution
Tianjin Petroleum & Chemical Fiber Plant	Tianjin	Japan West Germany	paraxylene (PX), 64; benzene, 20; dimethyl terephthalate (DMT), 90	1975
Liaoyang Petroleum & Chemical Fiber Plant	Liaoyang, Liaoning Province	France Italy West Germany	ethylene, 73; catalytic reforming feedstock, 155; aromatics extraction, 123; ethylene oxide (EO) / ethylene glycol (EG), 44; PX, 58; DMT, 88; polyester (PET), 87; EO, 45; nylon 66 salt, 46; hydrogen, 4 × 106,000 cubic m per annum; nitric acid, 54; hydrogen-added gasoline, 40; polypropylene, 35	1973
Shanghai Petroleum & Chemical Plant	Jinshanwei, Shanghai	Japan West Germany	ethylene, 115; polyvinyl alcohol (PVA), 33; acrylonitrile, 50; treatment of waste liquid of acrylonitrile, 8; PET, 25; aromatics extraction, 100; high pressure polyethylene, 100; ethanol, 30	1973

Sichuan Vinylon Plant	Chang-shou, Sichuan Province	France Japan	vinyl acetate, 90; carbinol, 95; acetylene, 28	1973
Beijing Petroleum & Chemical Plant	Fangshan, Beijing	Japan West Germany	ethylene, 300	1972
Jilin Chemical Industry Corporation	Jilin	Japan West Germany	ethylene, 115; synthetic alcohol, 100; styrene-butadiene rubber (SBR), 80; octyl alcohol, 50; butyl alcohol, 6.95	1975-1976
Beijing No. 2 Chemical Plant	Jiulong-shan, Beijing	West Germany	vinyl chloride, 80	1973
Cangzhou Chemical Fertilizer Plant	Cang-zhou, Hebei Province	USA Holland	synthetic ammonia, 300; urea, 480	1973
Liaohe Chemical Fertilizer Plant	Panshan, Liaoning Province	USA Holland	synthetic ammonia, 300; urea, 480	1973
Daqing Chemical Fertilizer Plant	Daqing, Hei-longjiang Province	USA Holland	synthetic ammonia, 300; urea, 480	1973
Qixiashan Chemical Fertilizer Plant	Nanjing, Jiangsu Province	France	synthetic ammonia, 300; urea, 520	1974
Anqing Chemical Fertilizer Plant	Anqing, Anhui Province	France	synthetic ammonia, 300; urea, 520	1974

Qilu No. 2 Chemical Fertilizer Plant	Zibo, Shandong Province	Japan	synthetic ammonia, 300; urea, 480	1973
Hubei Chemical Fertilizer Plant	Zhijiang, Hubei Province	USA Holland	synthetic ammonia, 300; urea, 480	1973
Dongting Nitrogen Fertilizer Plant	Yueyang, Hunan Province	USA Holland	synthetic ammonia, 300; urea, 480	1973
Guangzhou Chemical Fertilizer Plant	Guangzhou, Guangdong Province	France	synthetic ammonia, 300; urea, 520	1974
Sichuan Chemical Plant	Chengdu, Sichuan Province	Japan	synthetic ammonia, 300; urea, 480	1973
Luzhou Natural Gas Chemical Plant	Luzhou, Sichuan Province	USA Holland	synthetic ammonia, 300; urea, 480	1973
Chishuihe Natural Gas & Chemical Fertilizer Plant	Chishui, Guizhou Province	USA Holland	synthetic ammonia, 300; urea, 480	1973
Yunnan Natural Gas Chemical Plant	Shuifu, Yunnan Province	USA Holland	synthetic ammonia, 300; urea, 480	1973
Nanjing Alkylbenzene Plant	Nanjing, Jiangsu Province	Italy	normal paraffin, 50; linear alkylbenzene, 50	1975
Dagang Power Plant	Beidagang, Tianjin	Italy	2 × 250,000 kw	1973
Tangshan Douhe Power Plant	Tangshan, Hebei Province	Japan	2 × 320,000 kw	1973
Yuanbaoshan Power Plant	Chifeng, Inner Mongolia	France Switzerland	1 × 300,000 kw	1974

Wuhan Iron and Steel Works (1,700 mm rolling mill project)	Wuhan, Hubei Province	Japan West Germany	cold-rolled sheet 1,000; hot-rolled sheet, 3,000; silicon steel, 70	1974
Nanjing Iron and Steel Works (pellet chloridizing project)	Nanjing, Jiangsu Province	Japan	hydrogenised sulfuric slag pelletization, 300	1976

In 1972, when China decided to import complete sets of technology and equipment from abroad, China's total amount of imports and exports stood at US$ 4.84 billion, of which imports were US$ 2.2 billion. According to the "Four-three Plan," the importation of this technology and equipment would cost US$ 4.3 billion and with interest included, this figure would come up to US$ 5 billion, equivalent to 21.4 billion *yuan*. In those days, it was a large sum. In 1972, the total investment in infrastructure construction throughout China was a mere 41.2 billion *yuan*. In fact the cost of the 26 projects was in excess of 21.4 billion *yuan*. Those two figures indicated the great resolve of the CPC Central Committee and the State Council in the introduction of foreign technology and equipment. Only leaders like Premier Zhou had the courage to make such a decision, a decision that has been proved correct by later developments. It manifested the profound insight of Premier Zhou and other leaders who were on top of trends in world economic development, science and technology. Without the resolve and farsightedness possessed by Premier Zhou, it would have been impossible to raise a proposal to import foreign technology and equipment on a large scale. Even if such proposals had been made, they would have got nowhere.

Implementation and Construction of Projects

The implementation of China's second round of large-scale importation of complete sets of technology and equipment was managed perfectly. By the end of 1979, contracts concerning all 26 projects had been executed at a cost of US$ 3.96 billion, 300 million less than the estimate in the "Four-three Plan." In the conditions that then prevailed, it was a great success to have made such a good bargain. The construction of the 26 projects was on the whole sound. According to statistics, as of the end of 1979, 20 of the 26 projects had been completed and put into operation. The average construction period for each project was three years and eight months, the longest being five years. In the same period, for home-grown large and medium-sized projects, the average construction period was as much as 11 years. There was a telling rhyme about the construction of the Tianjin Tractor Factory: "Tianjin Tractor Factory is delayed day after day, even girls have grown into grannies. It took us eight years to defeat the Japs, but after ten years of construction there is still no sign of the Tianjin Tractor Factory." It circulated widely, even reaching the ears of Chairman Mao. Once he quoted these lines to criticize the sluggish construction of some domestic projects. The reasons for this phenomenon were complicated. As China was in the chaotic period of the "Cultural Revolution," interference, sabotage and troubles were rife. Furthermore, funds were inadequate. There was no guarantee of supply of raw materials and equipment. People employed to build a project turned into people living on the project. Year in year out, it lingered on, reliant on funds granted by the state. If no funds were forthcoming, they waited. Naturally, construction of the project kept being delayed. Clearly, domestic projects were constructed far more slowly than those imported from abroad. Besides, the scale of the large and medium-sized domestic projects was much smaller. For instance, the annual production capacity of the 13 chemical fertilizer projects imported under the "Four-three Plan" was 300,000 tons of synthetic ammonia, 480,000 or 520,000 tons of urea, with an average construction period of three years and four months. By contrast, the 19 projects of medium-sized chemical fertilizer plants with annual production capacity of 100,000 tons of synthetic ammonia invested and constructed domestically between 1971 and 1979 took an average of five years and ten months to complete. In terms of capacity, the domestic plants were one-third the size of the imported plants but construction took almost twice as long.

Table 2 details the construction of each of the imported projects in the "Four-three Plan":

Project Name	Construction Commencement	Production Commencement	Accumulated Investment (unit: 1 million *yuan*)
Tianjin Petroleum & Chemical Fiber Plant	09/1977	08/1981	1,358.19
Liaoyang Petroleum & Chemical Fiber Plant	08/1974	09/1981	2,904.23
Shanghai Petroleum & Chemical Plant	01/1974	05/1978	2,091.75
Sichuan Vinylon Plant	08/1974	12/1979	961.31

Aggregate investment for chemical fiber projects and its percentage of the total investment for 26 projects			**7,315.48 34.14%**
Beijing Petroleum & Chemical Plant	08/1973	12/1976	2,614.17
Jilin Chemical Industry Corporation	12/1976	12/1983	688.07
Beijing No. 2 Chemical Plant	10/1974	07/1977	124.73
Aggregate investment for petrochemical projects and its percentage of the total investment for 26 projects			**3,426.97 15.99%**
Cangzhou Chemical Fertilizer Plant	07/1973	12/1977	243.12
Liaohe Chemical Fertilizer Plant	06/1974	12/1977	343.42
Daqing Chemical Fertilizer Plant	05/1974	06/1977	2,674.47
Qixiashan Chemical Fertilizer Plant	09/1974	10/1978	321.28
Anqing Chemical Fertilizer Plant	03/1974	12/1978	405.26
Qilu No. 2 Chemical Fertilizer Plant	04/1974	07/1976	263.03
Hubei Chemical Fertilizer Plant	10/1974	08/1979	298.75
Dongting Nitrogen Fertilizer Plant	04/1974	07/1979	313.29
Guangzhou Chemical Fertilizer Plant	12/1974	10/1982	507.39
Sichuan Chemical Plant	05/1974	12/1976	160.12
Luzhou Natural Gas Chemical Plant	04/1974	03/1977	206.42
Chishuihe Natural Gas & Chemical Fertilizer Plant	01/1976	12/1978	171.85

Yunnan Natural Gas Chemical Plant	01/1975	12/1977	187.59
Aggregate investment for chemical fertilizer projects and its percentage of the total investment for 26 projects			**6,095.99 28.45%**
Nanjing Alkylbenzene Plant	10/1976	12/1981	268.75
Aggregate investment for the alkylbenzene project and its percentage of the total investment for 26 projects			**268.75 1.25%**
Dagang Power Plant	12/1974	10/1979	458.73
Tangshan Douhe Power Plant	12/1973	03/1978	586.72
Yuanbaoshan Power Plant	09/1974	12/1978	371.94
Aggregate investment for power projects and its percentage of the total investment for 26 projects			**1,417.39 6.62%**
Wuhan Iron and Steel Works (for the 1,700mm rolling mill project)	03/1972	12/1978	2,768.00
Nanjing Iron and Steel Works (for the pellet chloridizing project)	01/1978	12/1980	136.11
Aggregate investment for steel projects and its percentage of the total investment for 26 projects			**2,904.11 13.55%**

The successful construction of those imported projects was due largely to the guidance, care and support of leaders of the Party Central Committee and the State Council, including Premier Zhou Enlai, Deng Xiaoping, Chen Yun, Li Xiannian, Yu Qiuli and Gu Mu. They personally exerted much attention and gave practical support to the importing, implementing and building of those projects. Whenever any problems occurred and were addressed to them, they would solve them promptly. For instance, Premier Zhou stressed time and again that we had to follow the contracts, carry them out in good faith and take care that nothing went awry.

The Shanghai Petroleum & Chemical Plant was built on a soft layer of land reclaimed from the sea, at Jinshanwei, Shanghai. In the initial period of construction, Japanese businessmen complained that the foundations were not solid enough. For fear of accident, piles were driven much deeper into the earth than elsewhere. Premier Zhou was most concerned and anxious about it. He gave instructions, talked to people, requiring that measures must be taken to ensure the safety of the project. We could feel in our work that Premier Zhou and other leaders of the Party Central Committee and the State Council were shouldering a great risk. If there were an accident, the Gang of Four would seize the opportunity to make trouble, criticize and even slander them.

Deng Xiaoping showed great concern and gave active support to the importation of those facilities. In June 1973, shortly after being rehabilitated and beginning to work, he went to the Shanghai Petroleum & Chemical Plant and made an on-site inspection. Construction there had progressed quickly and, within six months, 7.08 sq km of land had been reclaimed from the sea at Hangzhou Bay. The imported facilities would be sited there. After being briefed on the project, Deng asked a range of detailed questions—from the progress of negotiations, estimated returns, investment, annual interest, plant site, living quarters, sewage treatment and pollution solutions to the transportation of the imported equipment. He also toured the plant. In the summer of 1975, two years later, Deng Xiaoping returned to Shanghai, accompanying some foreign dignitaries. Having seen them off, on the way back to Beijing he made a detour to visit the plant construction site at Jinshan, leaving all his luggage in the coach. It happened to be raining, but despite the rain, he toured the construction site. Noticing the rapid progress of construction, he said cheerfully: "I was here in June 1973. Now two years have passed. At that time, there was nothing here." At the briefing meeting, he asked various very detailed questions. The plant was importing nine large-scale facilities, and Deng wanted descriptions of each of them, to know their place of origin and the price in foreign exchange. One imported facility was as high as a three- or four-story building and extremely heavy. In those days, there were no trucks with large flat-bed trailers. "How was the equipment transported to the construction site?" Deng asked. He was told that the staff and workers of Shanghai Communications and Transport Bureau were very smart and experienced, particularly those old workers who knew how to make bamboo rafts. They had devised an ingenious transport plan whereby the large, thick and tall cylinders were put onto bamboo rafts and floated from the Huangpu River to Zhangjing River, thus being delivered to the construction site on time. Deng praised those workers for their cleverness, saying that their experience should be given high attention in engineering construction. After seeing the trial run of wastewater treatment facilities, he emphasized the importance of pollution control. Before leaving the site, he said he was delighted to see the rapid progress of the construction work and he had nothing more to say. At that time, Deng's work focused on rectification, and capital construction was one major field for rectification. On his return to Beijing, he told Gu Mu about the rapid progress of construction of Shanghai Petroleum & Chemical Plant and asked him to call an on-site meeting in Jinshan to publicize its experience, thereby promoting rectification in the field of capital construction. Gu Mu told him that the SPC convened a meeting every year at which the Shanghai Petroleum & Chemical Plant was invited to tell attendees its experiences over the year, so perhaps an on-site meeting was not necessary. Deng said firmly that the on-site meeting must be held, and that it should be held in the name of the State Council. All provinces and ministries should send people to attend the meeting. So a preparatory group was set up with Gu Mu as its head. In the group were Song Yangchu, Li Jingzhao, Li Hou, Li Hao, Li Mengbai, Jiao Shanmin, myself and Niu Diyi. The meeting was held in August 1975 at the Shanghai Petroleum & Chemical Plant. Present at the meeting were leaders in charge of capital construction of all ministries, commissions and provinces, and those in charge of the projects for importation listed in the "Four-three Plan." Gu Mu made a speech on behalf of the State Council. It was a successful meeting, one that played a great role in promoting rectification work in the field of capital construction at that time.

However, implementation and construction of the importation of complete sets of technology and equipment provided for in the "Four-three Plan" met with much interference and disruption from the Gang of Four and its local followers, causing some serious consequences. Almost all the contracts for the imports were signed in 1973 but, in early 1974, the Gang of Four called a meeting titled "Repudiating Lin Biao and Confucius," launching another national political campaign. Jiang Qing personally cooked up the "Snail Incident" and the "*SS Fengqing* Incident." Her rebuke of and interference with the Daqing Chemical Fertilizer Plant seriously disrupted the plan of introduction of complete sets of foreign technology and equipment.

The "Snail Incident" refers to the import of color tv cathode ray tubes. At that time, China was studying color television technology, but was hindered by technological issues. I remember that we were having a national planning conference at the Qianmen Hotel and the SPC required delegates from every province to bring along their television sets to be shown at the conference. I saw those sets and found them

Old cloth ration coupons

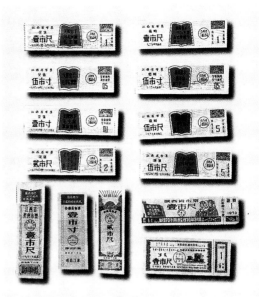

Cold-rolled silicon-steel sheets are produced by the 1,700 mm continuous sheet rolling mills of Wuhan Iron and Steel Works.

Chen Jinhua (first right) accompanied Yu Qiuli (second right) on his inspection tour of the Shanghai Petroleum & Chemical Plant in October 1982.

Deng Xiaoping pictured during the Rectification Campaign of 1975

The *SS Fengqing* is launched.

Li Xiannian (center) inspecting the Shanghai Petroleum & Chemical Plant

The Sichuan Vinylon Plant started with imported equipment from France and Japan.

A 1976 photo of Su Zhenhua (sixth left), Peng Chong (eighth left) and Ni Zhifu (ninth left) with comrades of the Work Team of the Party Central Committee and the Shanghai Municipal Party Committee (Lin Hujia, fourth left, Yan Youmin, second right and Chen Jinhua, first right)

The people of Shanghai celebrate the downfall of the Gang of Four.

The people of Beijing rejoice at the victory over the Gang of Four.

The front page of the October 30, 1976, issue of the *People's Daily*

The Special Court trying the two anti-Party cliques hands down its judgment.

Shipyard workers in Shanghai denouncing the crimes of the Gang of Four

After the downfall of the Gang of Four, a number of artists returned to the stage. This is a photo of Deng Yingchao with Xie Tian, Yu Yang, Yuan Wenshu, Bai Hua, Sun Daolin, Zhao Dan and some other famous performers at the Capital Theater.

Chen Jinhua (third left, front row) and Seiji Sudou, Vice Chairman of Hitachi, Ltd, cut the ribbon at the ceremony for the checking and acceptance of a color television assembly line introduced from Japan to the Shanghai No. 1 Television Factory in July 1982.

保存

工 作 记 事 本

揭批"四人帮"工作日记

郑定铨

1976. 10. 12.
至
1977. 4. 29

于上海半

中华人民共和国轻工业部

The front page of the work diary of a member of the Work Team sent to Shanghai by the Party Central Committee terrible in quality. Blue was not blue, red was not red and the three primary colors were mixed in a chaotic way. So as to improve the situation and solve the technical problems with Chinese color televisions as soon as possible, the No. 4 Ministry of Machinery Industry organized a delegation comprising people from enterprises including Xianyang of Shaanxi Province to go to the US to study the issue, in preparation to import a color tv tube production line. At the end of their US visit, the glass producer Corning gave a glass snail to each member of the delegation as a gift made by the company itself. When Jiang Qing learned about this, she seized the opportunity to make trouble. She made a point of going to the No. 4 Ministry of Machinery Industry and said that the Americans had insulted China by giving snails, that they were ridiculing Chinese industry crawling at snail's pace. "We must not yield to the pressure of the imperialists." She accused the State Council of "worshiping things foreign and fawning on foreigners," and called the purchase of foreign technology and equipment an "act of treason," a manifestation of "slavish comprador philosophy," etc. She demanded that the Ministry return the glass snails to the US Liaison Office in China and issue a protest. She also said: "We don't need the US production line." Premier Zhou wisely asked the Chinese Liaison Office in the United States to find out the truth and give a report on American customs. They discovered that in the US glass snails were often used as gifts or artistic exhibits, symbolizing happiness and peace. Corning had had no malicious intention. When the facts were clear, the Political Bureau of the CPC decided to retract Jiang Qing's speech in the No. 4 Ministry of Machinery Industry. However, because of this fuss, the importation of the color tv tube production line was delayed for several years. The importation of other projects was also affected.

The "*SS Fengqing* Incident" happened as follows: In order to accelerate China's ocean transport industry, in 1964, Premier Zhou made a decision to put ship-building and ship-purchasing on the same level of importance. Chairman Mao gave his consent. In 1970, Premier Zhou instructed: "We should strive to stop leasing foreign ships within next few years and base ourselves on domestic shipbuilding. When ships built in China cannot meet our needs, we may appropriately purchase a few vessels. We should have a good mastery of ocean transport." The *SS Fengqing* was one of nine freighters with a displacement of 10,000 tons designed and built by China at that time. It was built by the Shanghai Jiangnan Shipyard for Shanghai Oceanic Transport Branch Company under the Ministry of Communications. The Ministry had worried whether ships with five major components made domestically, including engine and radar, were good enough for ocean voyages and, in the interests of safety, stipulated that vessels such as the *SS Fengqing* with five major components made domestically should operate only along the coast. In early 1974, instigated by the Gang of Four, workers of the Jiangnan Shipyard and some of the *SS Fengqing* crew put up *dazibao* (big-character posters, prevalent during the "Cultural Revolution") during the "Repudiating Lin Biao and Confucius" political campaign saying, "We want to make revolution and the *SS Fengqing* must sail on the high seas." That year, the *SS Fengqing* sailed to the Mediterranean, and the Ministry of Communications sent Li Guotang and Gu Wenguang to help in the voyage. The ship returned to Shanghai port before October 1, China's National Day, but followers of the Gang of Four fabricated some facts to frame Li and Gu and detained them for denunciation in Shanghai. Seeing her chance, Jiang Qing said: "It is true that a few people who worship things foreign and fawn on foreigners and with strong bourgeois comprador mentality exercise dictatorship over us in the Ministry of Communications." She accused the State Council and the Ministry of Communications of following the "slavish comprador philosophy," "worshiping things foreign and selling out China" on the issue of shipbuilding. Their direct target was Deng Xiaoping, who was then in charge of the work of the State Council. They raised the issue to embarrass Deng at the Political Bureau meeting but Deng rejected it categorically. Unbeknownst to Zhou Enlai and Deng Xiaoping, they secretly sent Wang Hongwen to Chairman Mao in Changsha to make complaints against Zhou and Deng. Wang Hongwen said to Mao: "A row over the *SS Fengqing* broke out between Jiang Qing and Deng Xiaoping at the Political Bureau meeting. It was very bad. It looks like Deng still sticks to his old fallacy of 'building a ship is not as good as purchasing a ship; purchasing a ship is not as good as leasing a ship.'" He also said that the reason for Deng Xiaoping's recent bad mood must have something to do with the recent consideration of candidates for the post of chief-of-staff. "At present, Beijing is reeking with explosives." On hearing all this, Chairman Mao rebuked Wang Hongwen, telling him that if he was unhappy with certain things, he should talk to the people involved directly. It was no good going about things in such a way. Mao asked him not to mix with Jiang Qing. When Premier Zhou learned about this, he called Ji Dengkui, Hua Guofeng, Li Xiannian and Deng Xiaoping to the hospital ward where he was being treated and asked what had actually happened at the Political Bureau meeting and the "*SS Fengqing* Incident." Later, he twice met Wang Hairong and Tang Wensheng, recounting what he had learned and put in a good word for Deng Xiaoping; he then asked them to convey his opinion to Chairman Mao that from what he had heard from attendees of the Political Bureau meeting, Deng Xiaoping had not left the meeting without permission as claimed by Jiang Qing. It was Li Xiannian who had persuaded Deng to leave. After Deng left, Zhang Chunqiao said that he had long known that Deng would throw down the gauntlet sooner or later. Jiang Qing also said that she had deliberately raised the question with Deng. Obviously, they had prepared to attack Deng in advance. Later, as Chairman Mao showed himself to be on the side of Deng Xiaoping, the issue of the "*SS Fengqing* Incident" petered out. With this the Gang of Four's political conspiracy to denounce the importation of complete sets of foreign technology and equipment as "following slavish comprador philosophy" was shattered.

In 1975, Jiang Qing could wait no longer and meddled directly in the importation of the chemical fertilizer equipment by Daqing Chemical Fertilizer Plant. She said that since Daqing Oilfield was a model of China's self-reliance policy, why should such a plant import things foreign? She threatened to find out who was behind it all and advocating the "slavish comprador philosophy." She ordered construction of the plant to stop and the demolition of buildings already built. Under such pressure, Kang Shi'en discussed with Sun Jingwen to find a way of handling the situation. They asked Zhou Taihe to look in the Central Archives for the original documents approved by the central leadership. The document they found had Chairman Mao's script of a circle drawn around his name with red pencil, signifying agreement[2], Premier Zhou Enlai's script "Agreed," and Li Xiannian and Ye Jianying's "circles" around their names, all indicating agreement. They made a copy of the document and sent it to Jiang Qing, thus shutting her up.

The Gang of Four's interference with and disruption of the importation of complete sets of technology and equipment had a serious impact on progress of the importation work. At that time, I was the deputy head of the Foreign Equipment Import Office of the Ministry of Light Industry and monitored progress on a daily basis. But for a long time after the launch of the "Repudiating Lin Biao and Confucius" campaign, local governments were up to the neck in political activities and too busy to make regular reports. So-called "on-site denunciations," "criticisms of those in leading posts and their grassroots henchmen" were happening everywhere. From leaders in the State Council to con-

---

2. Formal documents submitted to the top leaders of the CPC and the Central Government usually have a list of names authorized to examine issues in question printed on the top of the document. Those authorized persons may make a circle on his or her name to indicate he or she has read the document and has no objection, or write his or her comment on the margin of the document.

struction site foremen, many came in for criticism sessions. This made the construction work extremely difficult. The construction site of Liaoyang Petroleum & Chemical Fiber Plant collapsed for a period at the high tide of the political campaign.

Such interference and disruption also affected the engineering quality of the construction. Before Wang Hongwen left Shanghai for Beijing on his promotion to the top leadership of the CPC, he bragged that he would bring with him some "heavy artillery," i.e. citing a few examples to justify the necessity of the political campaign. The Shanghai Petroleum & Chemical Plant was one. He instructed Shanghai Municipal Revolutionary Committee, (as the municipal government was then called) and the Shanghai Petroleum & Chemical Plant to break construction convention in order to set a good example. As mentioned before, in August 1975, the State Council called an on-site meeting in Jinshan, the site of the Shanghai Petroleum & Chemical Plant. People at the meeting were impressed by the construction speed of the plant and voiced their admiration. But, as professionals, they also noticed a number of flaws in engineering quality. They were also concerned about production safety, as some flaws were very serious. For instance, the plant had installed a large number of pipes, and pipe welding is a most demanding job. After pipes are jointed, each part of the weld should be X-rayed to make sure it is perfect. However, the plant had failed to do a thorough job on this. Some valves had been installed without pre-polishing, which might cause leakage in the future and lead to unimaginable consequences. Those worries were reflected in the bulletin for top leaders (not for ordinary representatives present at the meeting). On September 20, the State Construction Commission (SCC) reported to the State Council about the on-site meeting in Jinshan, Shanghai and mentioned the problems that had caused concern among some of the participants. In particular, it pointed out that if examination of components and installation were not carefully executed, there could well be accidents in the future. On hearing this, Li Xiannian was very worried too. He studied the issue with Yu Qiuli and Gu Mu and decided to send a team to Shanghai to inspect the engineering quality of the construction, appointing me to head the team. Members of the team came from the SCC, Ministry of Light Industry and Ministry of Fuel and Chemicals. Furthermore, Li Xiannian stressed that I should invite along some experienced workers from Daqing Oilfield and engineers from the Ministry of Fuel and Chemicals. In those days, Chairman Mao called on everyone to learn from Daqing, particularly their "three honesties and four strictness" (the "three honesties" refer to being an honest man, honest words and honest working; the "four strictness" were strict requirements, strict set-up, strict attitude and strict discipline). If we brought along experienced workers from Daqing, followers of the Gang of Four in Shanghai would not dare to mouth off and openly challenge us. This might be called a kind of political savvy.

On September 27, I arrived in haste at Shanghai, carrying with me a personal letter written by Li Xiannian. I met with Tang Guangxuan and Lu Jihua of the Industry and Communications Department under the Shanghai Municipal Revolutionary Committee. After some discussion, we decided to form a work team and go to Jinshan before October 1, China's National Day. At the time, whilst the Shanghai Petroleum & Chemical Plant undoubtedly paid great attention to the progress of the project construction, quality was, however, being neglected. We discovered a number of quality problems. In those days, an intangible belief seemed to exist that an emphasis on quality was an implicit denial of achievement. Some people were very sensitive about this. We were there to inspect quality, correct errors, and must not give people the impression of being there to find fault and to deny their achievement. This was really a tricky situation. The Command Office of the plant proposed lighting up the ethylene cracker on September 28 as a sign of a gift to National Day. This would of course spur everyone in the plant to greater efforts to expedite the progress of the project, and all entities concerned would join the concerted effort. But from a quality and safety standpoint, the conditions were not right for the lighting-up. We were on the spot and knew for sure that lighting-up would surely cause an accident—not later but right away—and that it would be catastrophic. But the Shanghai Municipal Revolutionary Committee was adamant, believing it would show that their bosses—the Gang of Four— had also paid great attention to industry. The press and radio in Shanghai had already prepared to cover the event. *Jiefang Daily* and *Wenhui Bao*, leading newspapers in Shanghai, even had their galleys ready. But we were of the view that this was simply showing off and had no actual significance. It had to be stopped. At once we called and reported the issue to Qian Zhiguang, Minister of Light Industry. Qian agreed with us and asked us to persuade the Command Office to postpone the lighting-up. Seeing we were firm on the issue, and had the specific instruction of the minister, the Command Office people reluctantly accepted our opinion and changed the "lighting-up" to "drying" the cracker. Actually, it was too soon even to dry the cracker. As the Party Central Committee emphasized "rectification," and pushed by the Work Team, the Shanghai Party Committee of the CPC and Shanghai Municipal Revolutionary Committee had to hold an on-site meeting a few days later. At that meeting, the person in charge of the Command Office made a speech, as did a veteran worker from Daqing. But we were not given a chance to speak. In short, due to interference and disruption by followers of the Gang of Four, the problems raised at the Jinshan on-site meeting called by the State Council were not properly solved; quality improvement was not given its deserved attention. On July 15, 1976, the lighting-up of the ethylene cracker took place and production began. But it failed because of quality problems. It was not until December 30, 1976, by which time the Gang of Four had been arrested, that the third "lighting-up" succeeded. There were no serious problems with the equipment as regards raw material feed, production and technology. However, there were quite a number of problems with public utilities; water and gas leakages caused by burst pipes were frequent. Had we not insisted on the quality of the project, there would have been more problems, which might have posed more serious threats to subsequent production safety.

Facts show that, for a modern, sophisticated project with strict requirements of systematic and integrated parts, compliance with rules and regulations, and supervision of construction and production are essential; otherwise catastrophe would be inevitable. It should be said that during the second round importation of complete sets of technology and equipment, the Shanghai Petroleum & Chemical Plant did fairly well in terms of project construction. Nevertheless, there existed some serious quality problems. This was a consequence of anarchism and ultra-leftist ideas running rampant, as well as the "breaking conventions, breaking the rules of capital construction" advocated by the Gang of Four. It is my belief that without the interference and disruption of the Gang of Four, the project construction for the imported equipment would have been better executed.

Important Role and Far-reaching Influence

Many achievements were made in the importation of foreign technology and equipment under the "Four-three Plan." I think the most important achievements are in the three aspects described below.

First, the principle of "solving several key problems in the national economy in a down-to-earth manner" was implemented in the large-scale importation of complete sets of equipment. This was the first of the six principles for the importation work laid down in the "Four-three Plan." At that time, China faced many problems in the national economy. Of these, the toughest was how to feed and clothe 870 million people. Chemical fertilizer, chemical fiber and alkylbenzene, all closely related with people's food, clothes and daily necessities, accounted for 18 of the total 26 projects. The total investment for these projects was 13.68 billion *yuan*, accounting for 63.84 percent of the total investment for the imports stipulated in the "Four-three Plan." Their importance is obvious.

Food. China's first Five-year Plan gave priority to heavy industry, to the neglect of agriculture and light industry. Naturally their development was slow. 1958 was the first year of the second Five-year Plan. That year saw the launch of the "Great Leap Forward" campaign with steel in paramount position. The balance of the national economy was seriously jeopardized and agriculture and light industry were further marginalized. In the wake of this campaign, China suffered from three consecutive years of natural calamity and following wrong policies. As a result, the Chinese people suffered great hardship. To reverse the situation, the Party Central Committee decided to adjust the national economy and put forward the new economic order of priority—"agriculture, light industry and heavy industry." When making the overall economic plan, the needs of agriculture and light industry would be the first to be considered and met. The meeting of the Secretariat of the CPC held on December 2, 1961 adopted a decision to implement a ten-year economic development plan, which was divided in two periods. The problems of food, clothes and daily necessities had to be solved before 1967 (i.e., within the third Five-year Plan period). At the end of April, 1964, the SPC formulated "Preliminary Outlines of the Third Five-year Plan (1966-1970) (Outlines)," laying out the basic missions. Firstly, striving to develop agriculture, basically solving the problems of food, clothes and daily necessities of the people. Li Fuchun said: "China is a country of poverty. The problem of food, clothes and daily necessities for a population of 600 to 700 million people is a big challenge. Only when the people's daily needs are in order will we be able to better develop our country." Li gave the following analysis: "The industrial plan must embody support to agriculture, galvanize agriculture, light and heavy industry, and all aspects of food, clothes and daily necessities. What is our focus? Is it primarily chemical industry? Chemical industry is rich in products, all of them related to the support of agriculture; agriculture, light industry and heavy industry; food, clothes and daily necessity; improvement of quality and increase of variety of industrial products; as well as strengthening of national defense. Once the issue of chemical industry is solved, all the above five issues are solved." During this period, the SPC asked all ministries and commissions to report their work. The first was the Ministry of Chemical Industry. The Party

Group of the ministry reported its long-term plan for the development of chemical industry. Li Fuchun also instructed that the targets for chemical fertilizer and chemical fiber must be prioritized to be included in the Outlines.

From May 10 to 13, 1964, Mao Zedong heard the report of the SPC. In his view, the international situation had further changed, China's surrounding environment was showing signs of tension, and the danger of war was still present. This weighed on him heavily. Several times, he said that we must prepare against war. At the working conference of the Party Central Committee held ten or so days later, Mao Zedong formally instructed the starting of "Construction of the Third Line Area" in China's far interior. Hence, the ideas for solving the problems of food, clothes and daily necessities stipulated in the third Five-year Plan were totally ignored. Mao also put forward the concept of "two fists" (the agriculture and national defense industries) and "one backside" (basic industry), criticizing the plan formulated by the Commission on the grounds that "the backside is not properly placed on the seat." "We must drive up basic industry. Don't pay too much attention to other aspects. Be appropriate." In this way, the principle of the new economic order of agriculture, light industry and heavy industry was in fact changed. Solving the problems of food, clothes and daily necessities was out of the question. Before long, the "Cultural Revolution" had begun, with ultra-leftism and anarchism rampant. Agriculture and light industry were disrupted. People's lives got worse. During the period spanning the "Great Leap Forward," three consecutive years of natural calamities and the "Cultural Revolution," the output and supply of grain and cotton remained static or even fell. Circumstances gradually improved after the importation of four sets of equipment for chemical fiber production and 13 sets of equipment for chemical fertilizer production. These imported facilities laid an effective foundation for finally solving the problems of food and clothing in the 1980s.

As for grain production, because of its limited arable land, China has for many years striven to raise per-unit yield. This requires many conditions, one of the most important factors being the use of chemical fertilizer. The saying "with ample fertilizer, crops will blossom like flowers" indicates this truth. China's chemical fertilizer industry, led by the renowned scientist Hou Debang, developed technology to "manufacture ammonium bicarbonate via synthetic ammonia carbonization process" with equipment capacity of 2,000 tons per annum. This is what we often refer to as "small chemical fertilizer facilities." Some 1,533 facilities with such technology and equipment were built. The number of facilities was quite high but product quality was poor. The effective nutrition rate of fertilizers thus produced was only 17.7 percent and some failed to reach even this level. The effective nutrition rate of urea produced by large chemical plants in many developed countries at that time was up to 46.3 percent, nearly three times that of our "small chemical fertilizer facilities." According to some agricultural departments, application of one kg of urea could raise rice output by four or five kg. Therefore, urea was greatly welcomed by peasants.

As I mentioned before, the earliest import prescribed in the "Four-three Plan" included four sets of production equipment for chemical fiber and two for chemical fertilizer. Facts showed that those chemical fertilizer facilities were very advanced and very efficient in urea manufacture. Therefore, pretty soon more facilities for chemical fertilizer were imported to bring the total to 13 sets. After that, import of such equipment continued to increase. In total, we had 33 sets of equipment for chemical fertilizer, supported by domestic ancillary facilities, producing an annual output of 15.93 million tons of urea. Based on the ratio of 1:4-5, 15.93 million tons of urea meant an extra 65-80 million tons of rice, representing 14-17 percent of China's total rice output of 462.18 million tons in 2000. This increase was most encouraging. Solving China's food problem, apart from implementing the household responsibility system with remuneration linked to output in rural areas, depended on two major factors: one was the high-yielding hybrid rice invented by Yuan Longping; the other was urea. Without these two things, there would have been no way of coping with the ever-increasing demand for rice. Sun Jingwen, Minister of Chemical Industry, told me that by the end of 1977, it had imported 13 sets of equipment for chemical fertilizer, of which seven had already been put into production. By June 1978, those facilities had produced a cumulative total of 3.61 million tons of urea. Had we imported such quantities of urea, it would have cost US$ 520 million at the prevailing price on the world market—or more than double the cost of importing those seven facilities. Therefore, financially it was a good deal. The fact that China has been able to feed 22 percent of the total world population from less than 10 percent of the world's arable land, must be attributed in part to the import of chemical fertilizer equipment.

Clothes. Shortage of raw materials for clothing production was solved by the importation of complete sets of equipment for the production of chemical fiber. New China lacked a foundation for chemical fiber industry. In 1957, it had only a small experimental factory, producing a mere 200 tons of chemical fiber per annum, which went into the production of artificial silk. In 1972, i.e., before the import of foreign technology and equipment, after years of efforts, China's output of chemical fiber was only 137,000 tons, accounting for 5.5 percent of domestic demand for raw material for the textile industry. This proportion was far less than the 40 percent of chemical fiber in the textile industry of the developed countries in the West, and was unable to solve the problem of raw materials shortage for textiles. The four imported sets of equipment for chemical fiber played the role of a "hen" that went on to lay many "eggs"—raw materials for textiles. Pushed by later implementation of reform and opening-up, China's chemical fiber industry developed rapidly. In 2003, China's output of chemical fiber reached 11.61 million tons, representing one third of the world total output, and more than that of the USA. Thus, China became the world's largest producer of chemical fiber. In 2003, China's total amount of textile raw material exceeded 17 million tons, of which chemical fiber accounted for 11.81 million tons, over two thirds of the country's total fiber production. This greatly eased pressure on agriculture, enriched the variety of clothes for the people, and satisfied need among all walks of life. One third of the chemical fiber was used for clothes, one third for household furnishings and one third for industry, proportions similar to those in the USA and other developed countries. This also indicated the speed of development of China's chemical fiber industry, and especially the important role of chemical synthetic fiber in structural transformation of textile raw materials. In less than 20 years, China was transformed from being a country short of "clothes and quilts" to one of the largest textile producers in the world. This was an unprecedented world record. Today, Chinese textiles can meet not only domestic needs, but can also be exported in large quantity. The export value in 2003 exceeded US$ 80 billion. Today, the Chinese people have a rich variety of clothes. In my view, of the problems of "food, clothing, housing, daily necessities and transport" the most satisfactorily solved problem was that of clothing. Today, as far as clothes are concerned, the gap between the most developed and the less developed regions of China is not great, whilst in food, housing, daily necessities and transport there are still big differences. In terms of clothing, there is no difference between high-income people in China compared with those of advanced countries in the West, such as the USA and some European countries, nor are there any between low-income people of China and those of the West. In my view, the import of foreign technology and equipment for chemical fiber played a great role. Without it, people's clothes would not be in such great shape today.

Daily Necessities. Let us take the example of alkylbenzene, a raw material for the production of washing powder. Washing powder is a daily life necessity in rural and urban areas alike. In the past, it was rationed and available to buy only on production of a special coupon. Mostly people used soap to wash clothes. Soap is made from the interaction of fats and oils with alkali. During the three hard years from 1959 to 1961, people had little to eat, so where could they find fat or oil to make soap? Li Xiannian asked the Ministry of Light Industry to look into and solve the problem. A number of small factories were established to produce soap from synthetic fat acid, but, due to technological problems, soap produced this way had a bad smell. Once Li Xiannian told us a joke: "Coal miners' wives refused to go to bed with their husbands since their faces were black with coal, the men having no soap to wash their faces after work. Later on, soap made of synthetic fat acid was provided, but still the wives refused to go to bed with them, this time because their faces reeked." That was all true. Later on, dozens of such technically backward factories were closed down. This was because the Nanjing Alkylbenzene Plant equipped with the imported equipment had gone into production. When the equipment was first imported, it had a production capacity of 52,000 tons per annum; following later plant renovation and expansion, the annual capacity reached 93,453 tons in 2003. Then it established a joint venture enterprise with a Taiwan investor and built a further two plants. The aggregate output of the three plants in 2003 amounted to 146,000 tons. In addition to meeting domestic demand, they exported 14.4 percent of their production.

As early as in 1964, Li Fuchun, when researching the third Five-year Plan, had the idea of focusing on chemical industry development so as to push forward the industry in a bid to solve the problems of shortage of food, clothes and daily necessities. His idea was undoubtedly correct. It was also the successful experience of industrialized countries: they had all followed the line of developing heavy chemical industry first and made great achievements. Unfortunately, Chairman Mao did not accept his idea. Ten years later, masterminded and led by Premier Zhou, this idea was put into practice and bore remarkable fruits. History has proved that developing heavy chemical industry in a concentrated manner is indispensable to the industrialization process. It is particularly so for a large country with a 1.3 billion population and an acute problem of shortage of natural resources.

Secondly, through this large-scale importation of complete sets of equipment, we began to learn about the outside world, particularly about the Western developed countries. The first large-scale importation of equipment in the early days of New China had been from the Soviet Union and Eastern European countries. Though they sold us their relatively advanced technologies, those technologies were themselves limited since they were mostly American technologies from before World War II. By the 1950s, they could no longer be considered as world-leading. Since the Soviet Union adopted the theory and policy of "two blocs," it and the Eastern European countries had their own and exclusive system. Their knowledge of the West was limited; and they were not keen on international exchanges and giving help to us.

The second large-scale importation of complete sets of technology and equipment was the first time since the founding of New China that we had had extensive exchanges and cooperation with the developed countries in the West. Our cooperation partners were mainly from Japan, Germany, France, Italy, the Netherlands, Switzerland and the USA. As early as January 1964, Mao Zedong said after hearing the report at the industry and communications conference: "I shall consider allowing the Japanese to come to China to open factories and mines when the time is appropriate, and learn from their technology." But this never happened, as later he believed that the international situation was getting tense; moreover, the "Cultural Revolution" was launched. It was not until eight years later in 1972, that his idea was implemented.

The importation not only brought to China advanced technology and equipment of the developed countries of the West; it also introduced advanced management concepts and expertise, extensive and current market information. It also made us see the development of the outside world, understand advanced technology, highly developed industry, high efficiency and productivity. It made us realize the gap between China and the developed countries in the West. Without the importation, I would not have had a deep understanding of what road China should take for its industrialization. Let me give you an example. At the time, a medium-sized synthetic ammonia plant in China with an annual production capacity of 100,000 tons needed several hundred workers. But a large plant equipped with the imported equipment with an annual production capacity of 300,000 tons needed only a hundred or so workers. It was a more than ten-fold difference in productivity. When Li Renjun of the SPC examined the size of all plants concerned at that time, people of various departments and localities insisted on retaining the original payroll numbers. They argued that they needed people for offices, kindergartens, schools, canteens, etc. This is not difficult to understand. We had only book knowledge about modern large-scale production, and well-provided social services and cooperation in the West. However, for a long time, we stuck to the practice of having everything in a plant, no matter big or small the plant. This practice only increased the burden on our state-owned enterprises and saddled them with a difficult situation for a long time.

Thirdly, the large-scale importation of complete sets of equipment helped China train many people, nurture a contingent of people familiar with foreign affairs, and gain experience. This prepared the ground for later implementation of the policy of opening-up to the outside world, cooperation and competition in the process of economic globalization. The first round of importation had trained a large number of specialists and management personnel. But their limitations were obvious. Such limitations were manifested primarily in the areas of technology and management. Only through the second round of large-scale importation of complete sets of equipment, did we truly acquire advanced technology and management expertise, accumulate experience in exchanges with Western countries, learn methods of doing business with them, particularly how to raise funds by making use of the international capital market, how to introduce software, how to carry out cooperation at a higher level, etc. To my knowledge, many key leading figures involved in the third round of large-scale importation were trained in the second round process.

Credit for the achievements we have made since adopting the policy of reform and opening-up, achievements that took Western developed countries half a century or even a century to accomplish, should go to Deng Xiaoping Theory, the Party's basic line and the basic economic system, and the Chinese Government's opening-up policy. In addition, in my view, the second round of large-scale importation of complete sets of equipment played a positive role. The experience gained then must not be overlooked. It served as a link between past and future, and played a pioneering role. It made us turn, at the right time, away from the Soviet Union and Eastern European countries towards the Western developed countries, and participate in economic globalization in an active and all-around manner. Without the foundations laid and conditions prepared by that large-scale importation, we would have had more difficulties later, and the cost of solving those difficulties would have been much higher.

Chapter 11

The Work Team Sent to Shanghai by the Party Central Committee Following the Downfall of the Gang of Four

- Background, Formation and Principal Mission of the Work Team
- Exposing, Repudiating and Investigating the Crimes of the Gang of Four and Its Followers
- Rectifying the Leading Bodies and Implementing the Party's Policies
- Making Revolution, Promoting Production, Work and Combat Readiness

On October 6, 1976, the Party Central Committee detained the members of the Gang of Four, thus ending the "Cultural Revolution." The most worrying concern of the Party Central Committee was the stability of Shanghai, the Gang of Four's major base in usurping the power of the Party. It was in Shanghai that lackeys of the Gang of Four made a vain attempt to stage an armed insurrection after the fall of their masters. In consideration of the situation in Shanghai, the Political Bureau of the Party Central Committee decided to send a Work Team headed by Su Zhenhua, Ni Zhifu and Peng Chong to Shanghai on October 12 to take over power from the local Party and government. The members of the Team came from many Party and government departments, Beijing Municipality and the People's Liberation Army (PLA). At its peak, there were 226 team members, including 17 officials of ministerial level. If news reporters and service personnel are included, the total number was as high as 250.

On October 10, 1976, Vice Premier Gu Mu had a talk with me. He asked me to go to Shanghai to find out the true situation there under the camouflage of preparing for compilation of the 1977 economic plan. When Su, Ni and Peng arrived in Shanghai, they appointed me as head of the Culture and Education Group under the Municipal Party Committee, to be in charge of the campaign to expose and denounce the Gang of Four and to carry out rectification in the fields of culture, education, publishing, film, drama, public health, sports as well as in schools of higher learning.

Under the leadership of the new Shanghai Municipal Party Committee, the Work Team seized back the power of the Party and the government, reshuffled the leading bodies, smoothly carrying out the campaign against the Gang of Four. Thus, things became clearer and society was kept stable. Shanghai embarked on a road to a new development stage. On the eve of May Day 1977, apart from a few who were requested to work in Shanghai, most of the Team went back to their own organizations.

The Party Central Committee's dispatch of the Work Team to Shanghai after the downfall of the Gang of Four was a major historical event, which is worth recounting.

Background, Formation and Principal Mission of the Work Team

On the evening of October 6, 1976, Wang Hongwen, Zhang Chun-qiao, Jiang Qing and Yao Wenyuan, members of the Gang of Four, were detained and the Political Bureau called an emergency meeting at the residence of Ye Jianying at Yuquan Hill in the western suburbs of Beijing. It was announced at the meeting that the Gang of Four had been detained. Hua Guofeng was unanimously elected Chairman of the Communist Party of China (CPC), and of the Central Military Commission of the CPC, which would be approved retrospectively at the Plenary Session of the CPC Central Committee to be held later. The meeting also decided to publish the fifth volume of the *Selected Works of Mao Zedong* as soon as possible, to prepare publication of the *Complete Works of Mao Zedong*, to build the Mao Zedong Memorial Hall in Beijing, and to set up a special case group to further investigate the crimes of the Gang of Four. The Political Bureau would convene a number of meetings of leading members of provinces, autonomous regions and municipalities directly under the central government and the military area commands; members of the Political Bureau would talk to them group by group so as to brief them about the detention of the Gang of Four, learn about the responses of various places, and exchange views. The meeting gave particular attention to Shanghai since it was the strongest bastion of the Gang of Four. It was in Shanghai that the Gang of Four had attempted to set up a second military force and hatched a plot to usurp the power of the Party and the government. The Political Bureau members were particularly worried about the stability of Shanghai and feared that anything might happen there. As early as September 21, when Ye Jianying went to see Hua Guofeng at his home, Ye pointed out that there might be some kind of trouble but nothing serious could happen. Such troubles might occur in Shanghai which, at that time, was controlled by the Gang of Four.

October 7. The Political Bureau members first invited leaders of Jiangsu and Zhejiang provinces and the Nanjing Military Command to go up to Beijing. They briefed them on the detention of the Gang of Four and asked them to be on special alert for anything suspicious in Shanghai. After that, they called to Beijing Ma Tianshui, Secretary of Shanghai Municipal Party Committee, and Zhou Chunlin, Commander of the Shanghai Garrison. What was unusual this time was that Ma received notification of the meeting via the Shanghai Garrison. In the past, it had always been the other way round when such a meeting had been called. Ma's nose told him that something was wrong. With palpitating heart, he talked to the two other municipal Party secretaries Xu Jingxian and Wang Xiuzhen. They compared notes and worked out a liaison method that Ma should call back two hours after reaching Beijing. When Ma got to Beijing, he was told by the Political Bureau that the Gang of Four had been detained for investigation. Ma was a close crony of the Gang of Four and stuck to his stand, voicing his opposition to the detention. Many books and articles published these days say that Ma called it a coup d'état, a palace coup. I don't think this was true. I knew Ma well: he was a cunning man, and in a situation like that he would not have been so straightforward. According to the reminiscences of Wu De (member of the Political Bureau, the First Secretary of the Beijing Party Committee, who was present at the meeting), Ma opposed the detention of the Gang of Four, and said it was a mistake to detain them. I find this version more convincing.

That very day, Xu Jingxian and Wang Xiuzhen tried every which way to find out how Ma was faring in Beijing. As the Political Bureau had made it a rule that no one should make calls during the short stay in Beijing, Ma did not have the guts to break the rule. Of course, Shanghai could not discover Ma's whereabouts: they tried calling the offices of Zhang Chunqiao, Wang Hongwen and Yao Wenyuan, but could not get through. They then tried their friends in Beijing, such as Zhu Jiayao of the Ministry of Public Security, Yu Huiyong of the Ministry of Culture and Lu Ying of the *People's Daily* but got no news of Ma. It was not until 11 pm that Yu Huiyong called back to say: "This afternoon, Wu Qingtong, head of the General Office of the State Council, notified me that the overseas visit of the Chinese cultural delegation had been cancelled. He also said that the decision was made by Premier Hua Guofeng." Hearing this, and mulling over the events of the day, Xu Jingxian believed that something must be wrong. Xu was a clever man. When I was assigned to work in Shanghai later, he had a talk with me. We talked for four hours, and he was very careful about his wording. In 2003, his memoir *A Dream of Ten Years* was published in Hong Kong. I read the book and found his account very clear. I imagine he had no access to archives and other important files, so it was all probably from memory.

October 8. Xu Jingxian and Wang Xiuzhen kept on calling all sorts of people in Beijing. Finally, through their friends, Xu got through to the switchboard of the Jingxi Hotel and made contact with Ma's secretary Fang Zuoting. Fang said that Ma was under the weather with another attack of gastric disease. Xu immediately sent for Ma's wife and asked whether Ma had this disease before. When she replied that Ma had had no such disease, Xu realized right away that something indeed was amiss. Xu and Wang Xiuzhen began to plot an armed insurrection.

On the afternoon of October 8, Xu and Wang called four meetings in succession, studying and planning the insurrection.

The first meeting was called at 2 pm. Present at the meeting, besides Xu and Wang, were three members of the Standing Committee of the Shanghai Municipal Party Committee, namely Zhang Jingbiao, who was the head of the General Office of the Shanghai Municipal Party Committee, Wang Shaoyong, who was in charge of procuratorial, judicial and public security organs, Feng Guozhu, who was in charge of foreign affairs, and two of their close cronies from the Shanghai Garrison. Xu told them he had been unable to get in touch with Wang Hongwen, Zhang Chunqiao and Yao Wenyuan; that probably a coup had taken place in Beijing and they had all been arrested, and that Ma Tianshui was probably under house arrest. He asked them to discuss whether Beijing would take any dragnet action to trap them all. After deliberation, they concluded that they must not wait to be arrested but must put up a fight. Wang Xiuzhen asked the two men from the Shanghai Garrison about the troops, asking how many troops could be mobilized if they were to take action. Their reply was that the number of troops that could be mobilized was limited; it was militiamen they should rely on. Without militiamen, they would get nowhere.

The second meeting was called a little after 3 pm. Xu and Wang invited Shi Shangying and Zhong Dingdong, commanders of the Shanghai Militia, and Xue Ganqing and Xu Chenghu from the Municipal Bureau of Public Security. The meeting decided to prepare the insurrection under the camouflage of a combat readiness inspection. Wang Shaoyong asked Shi Shangying how many militiamen he could muster, how many weapons and bullets they had. The reply was that 2,500 militiamen with four million bullets were available, but that there was a cache of eight million bullets in two military warehouses. The meeting particularly went into the issue of command of the militiamen. Shi Shangying said that he would carry out the orders of Xu, Wang Xiuzhen and Wang Shaoyong.

The third meeting was called at 4 pm. Xu invited the heads of the *Jiefang Daily* and *Wenhui Bao* newspapers and of the radio center, telling them there had been a coup in Beijing with many arrests. He asked them to follow Chairman Mao's behest, and not to relay any news from the Xinhua News Agency concerning the arrest of Wang Hongwen, Zhang Chunqiao and Yao Wenyuan without first reporting it to the Shanghai Municipal Party Committee.

The fourth meeting was called after 5 pm. It was a Standing Committee meeting of the Shanghai Municipal Party Committee. The meeting also invited Zhu Yongjia (head of the history section of the Municipal Writing Group), Chen Ada and Ye Changming. Xu gave a brief account of how he had tried to gather information from various sources to establish what had happened. All the signs indicated that something was wrong with the Party Central Committee, so Shanghai must be on guard. A little after 7 pm, Liao Wenquan, secretary to Jin Zumin, a right-hand man of the Gang of Four posted in the All-China Federation of Trade Unions, called to tell Xu Jingxian: "My mother is suffering a heart attack." From this secret code, Xu was now sure that his assumption was turning out to be true. Zhu Jiayao, posted by the Gang of Four in the Ministry of Public Security as Vice Minister, called from Beijing, saying "People are all assembled. The door is locked, and no one can move." Liu Qingtang of the Ministry of Culture also called, saying: "Disease has occurred. We have all fallen ill." All those calls indicated that every one of the Gang of Four had been arrested. So Xu and others decided to plan the insurrection in detail. Xiao Mu, secretary to Wang Hongwen, said at the meeting: "Problems at the top have been solved. Now Beijing is homing in on us." Zhu Yongjia said it must have been Hua Guofeng and Wang Dongxing who masterminded the coup. His remarks made the meeting more heated. "What shall we do?" asked Xu Jingxian. "We must be prepared for a fight," said Zhu

Yongjia. "We'll set up a Paris Commune. It shouldn't be difficult to hold out for a couple of days. We can publish a public announcement to the whole city, to the whole country. Or we can give out some pamphlets first, entitled 'How Khrushchev Seized Power'." Then Wang Zhichang of the Writing Group added: "We must put up some slogans, like 'Give us back Hongwen!' 'Give us back Chunqiao!' 'Give us back Jiang Qing!' and 'Give us back Wenyuan!'" When looking into specific actions to take, Wang Xiuzhen said that the militiamen had been mobilized. There would be 2,500 of them available initially, followed soon by a further 31,000, and that weapons and bullets must be made ready to issue to them. She proposed that Zhu Yongjia should oversee the news media and publicity. After discussion, Xu made four decisions: (1) preparation for the rebellion should start right away; (2) to prevent any accident, he and Wang Xiuzhen should work in two different places; Wang and Feng Guozhu should work in the office of the Shanghai Militia headquarters while he himself would work in Dingxiang Garden; (3) to do some work on winning over the army stationed in Shanghai; (4) Zhang Jingbiao should remain on duty in the office of the Shanghai Municipal Party Committee. The meeting also decided that Zhu Yongjia should go to the *Jiefang Daily*, *Wenhui Bao* and the radio center after the meeting to convey the decisions made by the Standing Committee of the Shanghai Municipal Party Committee in preparation for the rebellion.

On the evening of October 8, as Xu, Wang, and others were plotting their insurrection, Ma Tianshui returned to his room in the Jingxi Hotel after meeting the members of the Political Bureau and immediately told his secretary Fang Zuoting: "We should prepare a false statement. When we get back to Shanghai, we'll discuss whether we should put up a strong or a weak fight. Once we start, we'll suffer heavy losses. We can't turn the tide and taking action won't work." Those words from Ma were confessed by his secretary later. Judging from what Ma said, he was clearly in a dilemma. It was difficult for him either to voice or not to voice support for the detention of the Gang of Four. If he voiced support for the Party Central Committee's decision, how could he face his "little brothers" when he got back to Shanghai? Those "little brothers" of his were difficult to rein in. If he kept silent, that would imply refusal to support the decision of the Party Central Committee and he feared he might not be allowed to go back. This reflected Ma Tianshui's real thoughts at that time.

October 9. The Xinhua News Agency announced the decision of the Party Central Committee to publish the fifth volume of the *Selected Works of Mao Zedong* and to prepare publication of the *Complete Works of Mao Zedong*; also, the decision of the Party Central Committee, the Standing Committee of the National People's Congress (NPC), the State Council and the Central Military Commission to build the Chairman Mao Memorial Hall. In the wake of this news, a wave of support for the two decisions swept the country.

That same day, Huang Tao, a member of the Standing Committee of the Shanghai Municipal Party Committee, was urgently called back from Jinan to Shanghai to prepare details of the insurrection with Liao Zukang, secretary to Wang Hongwen. Zhang Chunqiao thought highly of Huang. He was a front-liner in the struggle against the State Council. After discussion, they proposed to prepare organizations such as the Trades Unions, the Women's Federation, the Youth League and major factories for the insurrection. They believed the time was not yet right to announce the slogans suggested by Wang Zhichang, rather that they should incite the people by neutral-sounding slogans that could hoodwink ordinary people such as "Proletariat and the revolutionary people unite and fight to the finish against careerists like Khrushchev!"

That day, the Shanghai Militia Command called a meeting of leaders of 10 districts and five militia divisions under the direct leadership of the Command, arranging detailed steps for the insurrection, preparing all manner of rifles and pistols and vehicles, and amassing materials and food. In a secret room in his office building, Ma Zhenlong of the Light Industry Bureau began to store auto plates, hard tack, etc. for use in the insurrection. People of the Shanghai Militia Command went to China Textile Machinery Plant to look into setting up a radio command there. Intense work was going to prepare for insurrection.

October 10. At this critical moment, the Party Central Committee summoned Xu Jingxian and Wang Xiuzhen to attend a meeting in Beijing, greatly jeopardizing their plot to stage an insurrection. Since Ma Tianshui had not made clear his stand, the Party Central Committee believed that keeping Ma alone in Beijing would not work, and so decided to summon Xu and Wang to Beijing too. Before Xu and Wang set off, they told their "little brothers" to take extra care and to go to Wang Shaoyong, Feng Guozhu and Zhang Jingbiao for instruction in case of anything important. The other three members of the Standing Committee of the Shanghai Municipal Party Committee were all senior people, experienced in political struggles. From various sources, they had learned about the fall of the Gang of Four. They simply ignored the decisions made at the Standing Committee meeting on October 8, on the pretext that they should wait for Ma, Xu and Wang to return before taking action. However, there were some fishy things happening that day: for instance, fire fighters and traffic police held an emergency exercise at midnight. But now there was no one in charge of the work preparing for insurrection.

On the morning of October 10, Vice Premier Gu Mu had a talk with the Director-General Xie Hongsheng of the Machinery Department of the Ministry of Light Industry and myself, requiring us to go to Shanghai as soon as possible to find out how things were there. At that time, I was working as deputy head of the Planning Group of the Ministry of Light Industry and was quite familiar with Shanghai. As previously related in Chapter I, in August 1975, Deng Xiaoping had asked Gu Mu to call an on-site meeting in Jinshan, Shanghai. After that meeting, Li Xiannian, Yu Qiuli and Gu Mu decided to ask me to head a 20-strong team to go to Shanghai Petroleum & Chemical Plant to assist and supervise work to improve the quality of the project. I went to Shanghai, bearing a letter written by Li Xiannian in person. At first, despite differences between people in Shanghai and ourselves, our work went quite smoothly and fruitfully. However, towards the end of November, as the campaign of "Repudiating Deng Xiaoping, Counter-attacking the Trend to Reverse the Verdict of Rightists" was hotting up, Wang Xiuzhen said at a meeting that the team was in Jinshan only to find fault with their work with the aim of nipping something new in the bud. Our work became more difficult and with the consent of Qian Zhiguang, Minister of Light Industry, the team withdrew to Beijing.

In early 1976, I went to the May 7th Cadre School of the Ministry of Light Industry in Gu'an, Hebei Province, for tempering through labor, and worked as Party branch secretary. I returned to the Ministry shortly before October 1, China's National Day. After the festival, I went to work in Tangshan, as it was an important city for light industry. My job was to study how light industry was recovering after the disastrous earthquake there. On the morning of October 8, I received a call from the Ministry, asking me to get back to the Ministry immediately. I asked why but got no answer. I got back that same evening. In the office building, I came across a female colleague whose husband worked in the General Staff Headquarters of the PLA; she whispered to me that Jiang Qing had been arrested. "Is this why I was called back?" I wondered. The next day when I got to my office, I was asked to remain in the city since a certain higher-up wanted to talk to me. The following day, Gu Mu summoned us and, sure enough, it had to do with the fall of the Gang of Four. As soon as he saw us, he came straight to the point: "I'm here to talk to you on orders. The Party Central Committee has detained Wang Hongwen, Zhang Chunqiao, Jiang Qing and Yao Wenyuan for further investigation. What the Party Central Committee is most concerned about is the situation in Shanghai. So it has been decided to dispatch a few people from various ministries to go to Shanghai under cover of preparatory work for formulating next year's national economic plan." He asked us to see as many people as possible and find out how things stood in factories and society, and to keep an eye on the Gang of Four's followers. "Send information collected back to Beijing by letter. The address is No. 9 Lixin Street, North Huangchenggen. There are people to handle those mails." After the meeting, it was too late to get air tickets to Shanghai for the next day, so we set off for Shanghai on October 12. Our eight-strong team arrived at Shanghai's Hongqiao Airport at 8.20 pm. There were already people waiting for us at the airport. On the way in to downtown Shanghai, I saw many such slogans "Forever follow the behest of Chairman Mao!" in large black characters on the walls. Small groups of militiamen patrolled the streets, rifles slung across their shoulders. Tension was in the air. We settled in at the Park Hotel. So as to have more news sources, we tried to order some newspapers, but we could not obtain *Reference News*, a paper carrying many foreign releases. According to our later analysis, the hotel must have been pre-warned to cut us off from news sources from abroad.

The next day, we went to the Industry and Communications Department, the Textile Industry Bureau and the Light Industry Bureau under the Shanghai Municipal Revolutionary Committee. We were received by Tang Wenlan, Director of the Revolutionary Committee of the Textile Industry Bureau, and Ma Zhenlong, Deputy Director of the Revolutionary Committee of the Light Industry Bureau. These two bureaus had the most Gang of Four followers: Tang and Ma were "little brothers" of Wang Hongwen. Talking to them, we detected that they were somewhat distracted. However, we did not discover anything untoward; people were just coming and going in a normal way. Afterwards, we wrote three or four letters to Beijing with the somewhat superficial information we had collected. We posted the first letter in Suzhou, two hours drive from Shanghai in those days, just in case.

October 11. The Command of the Shanghai Militia sent people to China Textile Machinery Plant to reconnoiter. They reported that there were seven gates and the plant could hold 10,000 people.

October 12. In the morning the Political Bureau of the Party Central Committee held a meeting at the residence of Ye Jianying, discussing the dispatch of a Work Team to Shanghai to take over power there. Hua Guofeng said: "Obviously, those working in the Shanghai Municipal Party Committee cannot possibly continue their work. They are stubbornly on the side of the Gang of Four and oppose the Party Central Committee. They are even hatching a plot to stage an armed insurrection. The faction suppressed by the Gang of Four in the past is also a branch of the rebels. It is now busy mustering people. Local residents have also taken action off their own bat. They need proper guidance. The Party Central Committee should send people to take power in Shanghai immediately, or there could be big trouble." Ye Jianying voiced his agreement with Hua, adding: "In order to rein back those people from going to extremes and starting an insurrection, we must send a veteran to Shanghai, one whose high prestige both in the army and among civilians will be able to control the situation. In my view, Su Zhenhua is the right man. He is a veteran revolutionary and has suffered a great deal from the persecution of the Gang of Four. He is a man of determination. At the critical moment in the fight against the Gang of Four, he played an important role. From the war years, he gained rich experience in directing battles. In the early days of New China, he worked as the Party Secretary of the Guizhou Provincial Party Committee and was praised several times by the Party Central Committee and Chairman Mao. Besides, Shanghai has the East Sea Fleet Naval Base. If Su

Zhenhua goes to work in Shanghai, there are things that will favor him." Chen Xilian added: "I agree with Ye's nomination. Su Zhenhua is a member of the Standing Committee of the Central Military Commission. Once both he and I were responsible for routine work of the Commission. When the leading members of the Military Area Commands were reshuffled in 1974, he did a lot of coordinating work and played an important role. All these will be beneficial to coordinating relations between the Nanjing Military Area Command, the Navy and the Air Force. In particular, Liao Hansheng and some other veterans cruelly persecuted and suppressed by Lin Biao and the Gang of Four are on very good terms with Su Zhenhua, and he will surely get their support. He is a most appropriate choice to take a Work Team to Shanghai." Then Li Xiannian said: "Ye's idea is well thought through. Shanghai is where the Gang of Four started. Cracking down on the lackeys of the Gang of Four is an integral part of the struggle against the Gang of Four. It is one of the most important measures of the Party Central Committee. The stability of Shanghai will have a special significance for the whole country. Therefore, the issue of who goes to Shanghai to take over power—in particular who heads the Team—is extremely important. Su Zhenhua is all for the arrest of the Gang of Four. He is resolute in the fight against the Gang of Four. Chairman Mao once said that we needed him in command of the Navy. This time, we also need him to head the team to go to Shanghai to fight the lackeys of the Gang of Four. He is able to play a leading role. So I agree with Ye's proposal." Then Hua Guofeng said: "I agree with Ye's nomination. Su Zhenhua is politically sound. He is active and resolute in the struggle against the Gang of Four. Given the actual situation of Shanghai, which has been under the control of the Gang of Four and its followers, the people whom the Party Central Committee sends to Shanghai should be able to take over the positions of Zhang Chunqiao, Yao Wenyuan and Wang Hongwen and work in Shanghai for some time into the future.

The Gang of Four and their followers claim that Wang Hongwen is the 'leader' of the working class, don't they? What kind of leader is he? We should send a real leader of the working class to Shanghai. I therefore propose that Ni Zhifu goes to Shanghai too." Li Xiannian said: "I agree. Ni Zhifu is a native of Shanghai, a working class role model in terms of technical inventions. He is very popular among workers. What's more, he has experience in governing a city. He is truly a leader of the working class." Ye Jianying added: "He is a man of principle, and is most thoughtful when tackling problems. He is an outstanding representative of the working class. We need a doctor to accompany him since he is not in good health." Hua Guofeng came in again: "Conflicts between Shanghai and Jiangsu were very sharp in the past, but relations between them, both politically and economically, are now very close. We had better send someone from Jiangsu too." Li Xiannian suggested: "Peng Chong is a good choice. He is very good in handling conflict, and is doing well in Jiangsu. The Gang of Four did everything possible to persecute him, and he is dead against them. His going to Shanghai would help ease conflicts between the two places. If Shanghai has any difficulties and problems, Jiangsu will surely give help." All present agreed that Su Zhenhua, Ni Zhifu and Peng Chong should go to Shanghai to seize back power. Ye Jianying said: "We may also select a few people from the Party Central Committee and ministries and commissions to join the Team. The Party Central Committee and the State Council have already sent some people to Shanghai to find out the true situation there. Su Zhenhua and Ni Zhifu may take some people to go with them. Peng Chong may also take along a few people to assist. They should be part of the Work Team headed by Su Zhenhua, Ni Zhifu and Peng Chong." The meeting spelt out the task for the Work Team of the Party Central Committee: Solve problems, stabilize Shanghai. Later on, this became a major guideline for the Work Team. The meeting also pointed out: "The mission of the Work Team is to lead the struggle in exposing and repudiating the Gang of Four, and it should by no means engage in specific administrative work. Of course, production must not be affected; the situation must be brought under control." At the meeting, Ye Jianying time and again stressed the important position of Shanghai in the country, and the great impact on the whole country that would result from doing a good job in fighting against the Gang of Four by exposing, repudiating and investigating its crimes. Ye emphasised: "Breaking the old and establishing the new. Breaking the old must be done thoroughly, and establishing the new must be conducted in a correct way. Solve problems and stabilize Shanghai."

The decision made, all the members of the Political Bureau had talks with Ma Tianshui, Xu Jingxian and Wang Xiuzhen. They expressly demanded that the three of them make a clean break with the Gang of Four, give up any insurrection attempt, change their political stance, and do a good job in managing Shanghai affairs. Ye Jianying said: "Shanghai is where the Communists started the Revolution. The people of Shanghai, particularly the workers, have high political awareness. The Gang of Four hoodwinked them in the past, but now they are awaking. You must no longer stand on the side of the Gang of Four. If you stick to your wrong stand, you will have no future. You must stand on the side of the majority of the people, and do a good job in managing Shanghai affairs." This was the gist of the talk. Of course, the Political Bureau members also used conciliatory words, hoping to put them at ease and prevent them taking extreme action.

On the evening of October 12, in Shanghai Wang Shaoyong and Zhu Yongjia called a meeting to plan a general strike, stage demonstrations, take control of the radio center, and blackout information from Beijing. They prepared to publish an "announcement to the whole city, the whole country," raising such slogans as: "Give us back Jiang Qing!" "Give us back Hongwen!" "Give us back Chunqiao!" and "Give us back Wenyuan!"

A little after 10 pm that night, I got a call from Zhang Xiu, Party Secretary of China Textile Machinery Plant. He warned us to be on the alert and to stay together. His words were vague, but his meaning was clear. We learned later that the Shanghai Militia Command had set up a radio station in that plant. It was a back-up radio station; the main one was in the Jiangnan Shipyard. At breakfast time, I met Qin Zhongda who had come to Shanghai with us. He was the Head of the Planning Department of the Ministry of Chemical Industry at the time and later went on to become the Minister of Chemical Industry. Since people of his group had no close contacts to pass on any inside information from the chemical industry sector in Shanghai, I urged him to take extra care and not to go out alone; they should stick together. "In case of any emergency, get in touch with us," I said.

October 13. As soon as Ma Tianshui, Xu Jingxian and Wang Xiuzhen returned to Shanghai, they first met the other three members of the Standing Committee, namely Wang Shaoyong, Feng Guozhu and Zhang Jingbiao. They were anxious to know how things stood in the city. They also conveyed to them the message from their meeting in Beijing with the Political Bureau. Finally they decided to convene a Standing Committee meeting at 3 pm, but since they could not agree the time for the meeting, it was postponed until 4 pm. At the meeting, Ma told the members of the Standing Committee what the Political Bureau members had said at the Beijing meeting. Then Xu added Chairman Mao's criticism of the Gang of Four and said that he agreed with the Political Bureau's decision. Wang concurred, saying that after hearing what Mao had said, she was beginning to realize what was right and what was wrong. But Huang Tao argued: "How can they arrest them on such meager evidence?" His words threw the meeting into chaos. Some members even called Ma, Xu and Wang traitors.

News of the downfall of the Gang of Four spread quickly. The people of Shanghai learned the news from all kinds of channels. Men in the street, civil servants and educated people in particular, were very excited about it. At first, people put up big-character posters and took to the streets to hail the two decisions made by the Political Bureau. On October 14, the day after the return of Ma, Xu and Wang, remnants of the Gang of Four attempted to do something within the legal framework. But local residents began taking action, surrounding the office buildings of the Shanghai Municipal Party Committee at Xujiahui and Kangping Street. They rushed into the buildings and put up big-character posters. In the streets, we could see for the first time slogans denouncing Wang Hongwen, Zhang Chunqiao, Jiang Qing and Yao Wenyuan. Under such pressure, the Shanghai Municipal Party Committee made an emergency call to the Political Bureau in Beijing, saying: "Many slogans have appeared in the Xujiahui and Kangping Street area where the offices of the Shanghai Municipal Party Committee are located. Also around Yan'an Road West and Huaihai Road where motorcades of foreigners pass. They were put up by students of Jiaotong University. The slogans are mainly 'Down with the Gang of Four.' They name the names of Wang, Zhang, Jiang and Yao. There are also such slogans as 'Smash the lackeys of the counter-revolutionary clique!' We are afraid that if such slogans keep increasing, particularly those naming the Shanghai Municipal Party Committee, people who have not changed their stand will put up big-character posters defending the Gang of Four and targeting the Party Central Committee. If anyone dares resort to violence, we will take resolute action to suppress it." This call informed the Political Bureau that people in Shanghai had risen up. But at the same time it was a threat.

October 15. The front pages of *Jiefang Daily* and *Wenhui Bao* both carried articles about how Shanghai workers had begun a new wave of studying the works of Marx, Lenin and Mao Zedong; that they upheld the basic principle of "three dos and three don'ts" (i.e. practice Marxism, not revisionism; unite, don't split; be open and aboveboard, don't intrigue and conspire), declaring a fight to the finish with anyone betraying Marxism, Leninism or Mao Zedong Thought, tampering with Chairman Mao's behest, practicing revisionism, splitting the Party and hatching conspiracy. For the first time, newspapers in Shanghai denounced the Gang of Four but without naming them as individuals.

October 18. The Party Central Committee issued a notice to the whole Party (Document No. 16 of the Party Central Committee), setting out the crimes committed by Wang Hongwen, Zhang Chunqiao, Jiang Qing and Yao Wenyuan, and their anti-Party activities aimed at usurping the Party leadership, as well as Chairman Mao's criticism of the four since 1974. It announced the decision of the Party Central Committee to detain the four of them for further investigation. The Notice called upon the whole Party to carry out resolute struggle against the anti-Party clique. The Notice said that Wang, Zhang, Jiang and Yao had conducted anti-Party activities and that their crimes were most serious. They had refused to listen to Chairman Mao, willfully tampered with Marxism, Leninism and Mao Zedong Thought, and opposed Chairman Mao's proletarian revolutionary line on a number of issues both in and outside China. They had practiced revisionism under the name of Marxism. They had ganged up and engaged in sectarianism in a bid to split the Party and usurp the power of the Party. They had resorted to conspiracies, set up secret liaison offices, and stealthily gathered a so-called "black dossier" on leading members of the Party. They had tried to meddle in everything, hoodwinked and incited people to topple leaders of the Party, central government and the army both at the top and the grassroots level. With the media under their control, they had distorted facts, called white black, manufactured rumors, cheated people, given themselves the limelight, and shaped public opinion to justify their activities to usurp the power of the Party and the state. Chairman Mao had sternly criticized them and reasoned with them several times, but they had turned a deaf ear. The Notice also stressed that the struggle against the anti-Party clique of the Gang of Four was a life-and-death struggle between proletariat and bourgeoisie, between socialism and capitalism, between Marxism and revisionism. The Notice pointed out the policies that had to be observed in the struggle against the Gang of Four: firmly trust the majority of the people, learn from past mistakes and avoid future ones, free most of the hoodwinked people, reduce the number of people for punishment, distinguish between those who had made mistakes from those who were involved in conspiracy.

October 19. The Work Team held a meeting at the residence of Su Zhenhua at the Yuquan Hill in Beijing. Besides Ni Zhifu and Peng Chong, the other team members present were: Lin Hujia, Vice Minister of the SPC; Yan Youmin, Vice Minister of Public Security; Mao Lianjue, Deputy Secretary-general of the Beijing Party Committee; Che Wenyi, Bureau Chief of the Xinhua News Agency in the Navy; Zhang Shouhua, Deputy Head of the Publicity Department under the Political Department of the Navy. The meeting discussed the major issues concerning the takeover of power of the Party and government in Shanghai. After the meeting, everyone went to prepare for the mission.

In the afternoon of that day, students of 16 universities held a mass meeting at Culture Square in Shanghai. The square swarmed with many workers and Red Guards who had learned the news of the fall of the Gang of Four. The gathering totaled over 30,000 people. Representatives from Shanghai's Jiaotong University, Fudan University and Music Conservatory, etc., made speeches denouncing the crimes of the Gang of Four. That was the first mass meeting denouncing the Gang of Four ever held in Shanghai.

At midnight, the Shanghai Municipal Party Committee made a second urgent call to the Political Bureau, saying: "We had planned to hold a mass meeting denouncing the crimes of the Gang of Four at Culture Square in the name of the Shanghai Municipal Party Committee;

but 300,000 people from over 100 units will be holding a mass meeting tomorrow (20th) at People's Square led by Jiaotong University. The meeting sponsors have called us, saying that the mass meeting to be held by the Municipal Party Committee was a conspiracy and they would crash the meeting site to disrupt the meeting. We are unable to order any forces to protect our mass meeting, and so have no choice but to cancel it. We are prepared to participate in their meeting and to expose and repudiate the Gang of Four together with the broad masses of the people, and to accept whatever criticisms the people at the meeting direct at us. The work of the Municipal Party Committee has entirely collapsed, and we urgently need instructions from the Party Central Committee." This second call gave a true picture of Shanghai. The Shanghai Municipal Party Committee had lost control of the city. This tallied with what we had learned.

October 20. Su Zhenhua chaired a formal meeting of the Work Team in Beijing. He said at the meeting: "Though the members of the Gang of Four have been put in prison, the power of the Party and the government in Shanghai is still in the hands of their followers. They are restless and about to create big disturbances. If such disturbances did erupt, this would have a bad impact throughout the country. For this reason the Political Bureau has decided to send a high-powered Work Team to Shanghai immediately to take over the power of the Party and the government. This is most urgent: please get prepared and we shall depart at once."

As a precaution against any accident, the Political Bureau did not notify the Shanghai Municipal Party Committee about sending a Work Team to Shanghai. A special plane took the Team to Shanghai, where they installed themselves in the Naval Base. It was not until midnight that the Political Bureau notified the Shanghai Municipal Party Committee that, in consideration of the situation in Shanghai as reported by the Shanghai Municipal Party Committee, a Party Central Committee

Work Team headed by Su Zhenhua, Ni Zhifu and Peng Chong was to arrive in Shanghai that night and would contact the Shanghai Municipal Party Committee after arrival. Shortly after Su Zhenhua and the others had arrived and entered the hostel of the Shanghai Naval Base, Su sent for Ma Tianshui. Su said to Ma: "In consideration of the situation in Shanghai and your request, in order to stabilize Shanghai and carry out the struggle against the Gang of Four, the Party Central Committee decided to send this Work Team to Shanghai. We three are in charge of the Team. We hope that you will muster together, relay and implement the message of the Beijing meeting and Document No. 16 of the CPC." Su then asked Ma what he had done since his return to Shanghai and how he viewed the situation. Ma stuttered: "Since we returned to Shanghai, we relayed the gist of the Beijing meeting to the members of the Standing Committee and the leading members of the districts, counties and bureaus. Now the people have risen up and demonstrated in front of the offices of the Municipal Party Committee. We are unable to work. With the Work Team here, we will surely do better. We guarantee to obey your leadership." Su told Ma in a serious tone: "Ours is a Work Team only, and our major work is to learn about the situation here. The routine work of the Municipal Party Committee is your responsibility and you should just carry out your duty. You were deeply involved in the activities of the Gang of Four in the past. Now you should pull yourself together and make amends for your faults. If anything serious happens in Shanghai, you will be held responsible!"

October 21. In the morning Su Zhenhua, Ni Zhifu and Peng Chong talked to Liao Hansheng, Political Commissar of the Nanjing Military Area Command and Zhang Ting, Deputy Chief-of-Staff of the Nanjing Military Area Command, who had arrived from Nanjing. They exchanged views and discussed the task. Su Zhenhua said that in view of the fact that the followers of the Gang of Four in Shanghai had not given up their plot to stage an insurrection, the Nanjing Military Area

Command should maintain high vigilance; in particular, the troops on duty in Jiangsu and Zhejiang should be on high alert. The Navy should keep watch on any activities at sea. The two army men working in the Shanghai Garrison were involved in the insurrection conspiracy and should be recalled to Nanjing immediately. Su also requested Nanjing to send people to Shanghai to assist the Work Team. The goal was to keep Shanghai stable. I heard from Su later that there had been another proposal at the time, to carry out a military exercise by the field army stationed in nearby Wuxi City so as to threaten Shanghai. However, Ye Jianying squashed the idea, saying there was no need for it and that we had to trust the workers and peasants of Shanghai. Any army maneuver would cause immediate panic.

While Su talked with leading members of the Nanjing Military Area Command, Lin Hujia and Yan Youmin called another meeting of those who had arrived earlier and we briefed them on the situation in Shanghai over the previous ten days. After that, Lin said to me: "Su Zhenhua's thinking is that you should go to the Municipal Writing Group, and thoroughly lay bare the conspiracy of the Gang of Four to usurp the Party leadership by creating counter-revolutionary propaganda." I had thought I might be assigned to departments like the Light Industry Bureau whose work was familiar to me as a subordinate agency of the Ministry of Light Industry. It came as quite a surprise to be sent to a cultural entity. So I told Lin I was not mentally prepared for this. "I'd like to find out the situation there first, and then talk to you," I said. The Shanghai Municipal Writing Group was one of the two propaganda bases of the Gang of Four. It had originally been a writing group of the Municipal Party Committee established after Chairman Mao's instruction to intensify class struggle in the field of ideology. From its inception, it had been led by Zhang Chunqiao. Xu Jingxian was the branch Party secretary of this Writing Group. It had several sections, namely Literature Section using the pen name Ding Xuelei; History

Section using the pen name Luo Siding, with Zhu Yongjia as its head. There were also sections of Philosophy, Dialectics of Nature, etc. Its first article, engineered and organized by Jiang Qing, had been "On the Newly Composed Historical Drama *Hai Rui Dismissed from Office*." The article had criticized Wu Han, author of the drama, a famous historian and Vice Mayor of Beijing, thus raising the curtain of the "Cultural Revolution." Since then, this Writing Group had kept on cooking up this kind of article, denouncing Liu Shaoqi and Deng Xiaoping, and attacking Premier Zhou Enlai by innuendo. It served as a vanguard of the Gang of Four in its attempt to usurp the Party leadership. For over a decade, it had ridden roughshod in the field of ideology and culture, willfully attacking people. I had a relative working as section chief on the newspaper *Jiefang Daily*, and after Lin asked me to go to the Writing Group, I went to see him, trying to find out the truth about the Group. I asked him some roundabout questions and he told me that the Writing Group played the leading role in mass media. It numbered scores of people. Fudan University and Shanghai Normal University, both strong in liberal arts, helped them in finding materials, preparing drafts, etc. It had also mustered researchers, such as scholars in the field of theory, and, in this way, had formed a large network. It was perhaps the next day, before I had learned much about the Writing Group, that Lin Hujia instructed me to go to the Culture and Education Group of the Municipal Revolutionary Committee rather than to the Writing Group.

On the evening of October 21, Su Zhenhua, Ni Zhifu and Peng Chong had a talk with Ma Tianshui, Xu Jingxian and Wang Xiuzhen in the conference room of the hostel of the Shanghai Naval Base. The main purpose of this meeting was to notify Ma, Xu and Wang that Beijing was going to hold a rally of one million people on October 24. Such meetings should also be held throughout the country. As arranged by the Party Central Committee, Su and Ni would go back to Beijing to attend the rally there, and Peng would return to Nanjing to attend the Jiangsu Province rally. "Shanghai used to be the base of the Gang of Four," said Su, "so to hold such a rally here is very important and will have great impact on the whole country. You must stand on the side of the people of the whole country and make the rally a success. This is also a test for you." Right after the talk, Su and Ni returned to Beijing, Peng to Nanjing.

October 23. The Work Team of the Party Central Committee held a formal meeting at which the list of its members was announced. Lin Hujia chaired the meeting. He said: "Originally we planned to send you to the various bureaus which are subordinates of the ministries and commissions you yourselves come from. For instance, those from the Ministry of Light Industry to go to the Textile Industry Bureau in Shanghai, those from the Ministry of Machinery Industry to go to the Electro-mechanics Bureau, to work as liaison. But we have noticed that a handful of people on the Municipal Party Committee are trying to hamper our work, playing tricks through various Party and government agencies. It seems difficult for the time being to bypass those agencies to go to the grassroots units. After much deliberation, we have decided that we should first go to those offices, bureaus and groups of the Municipal Party Committee and the Revolutionary Committee to investigate the crimes of the Gang of Four, break up its network, and seize back the power of the Party and the government. Once you have got installed in those agencies, then go to the grassroots units when necessary." Lin also told us we should all go in the name of the Work Team of the Party Central Committee, and that our principal mission was to expose, repudiate and investigate the crimes of the Gang of Four and their lackeys so as to thoroughly root out this anti-Party clique. Su, Ni and Peng approved the list of members of the Work Team. They had also prepared a letter of introduction to the Municipal Party Committee for us. The members were:

General Office of the Municipal Party Committee: Xu Liangtu (Deputy Head of the Production Group, SPC, later its Vice Minister, Cao Dacheng (State Construction Commission), Chen Feizhang (SPC)

Organization Group of the Municipal Party Committee: Li Ximing (Vice Minister of Water and Power, later Secretary of the Beijing Municipal Party Committee), Wang Xiping (later Vice Minister of Communications), Li Feng (Director-general of the Planning Department, Ministry of Fuel and Chemicals), Liu Han

Industry and Communications Group: Li Jingzhao (member of the leading group of the State Construction Commission, later its Vice Minister), Gan Zhijian (later Vice Minister of the SPC), Zhou Li

Planning and Statistics Group: Cao Weilian (Director-general of the Science and Technology Bureau of the No. 1 Ministry of Machinery Industry, later Vice Minister of the Ministry), Wang Deying (later Vice Minister of the State Construction Commission, Deputy Secretary of the Central Commission for Discipline Inspection of the CPC), Xie Hongsheng (later Vice Minister of Textile Industry, Vice Minister of the State Machinery Commission)

Finance and Trade Group and Suburbs Group: Guo Shirong (Vice President of the All-China Federation of Supply and Marketing Cooperatives)

Culture and Education Group: Chen Jinhua (Deputy Head of the Planning Group, Ministry of Light Industry), Lu Wanzhang (Director-general of a bureau under the Ministry of Light Industry), Wang Jinguang (Director-general of another bureau under the Ministry of Light Industry)

Writing Group: Che Wenyi (Bureau Chief of the Xinhua News Agency in the Navy)

Public Security and Militia Group: Yan Youmin (Vice Minister of Public Security)

Foreign Affairs and the United Front Work Group: Qin Zhongda

(Head of the Planning Group of the Ministry of Chemical Industry, later Minister of the Chemical Industry)

There were also 14 people assigned to the Special Case Investigation Group, including Gu Linfang (later Vice Minister of Public Security)

Based on the accommodation registration forms of the Work Team, there were 226 people at its peak, of whom 17 were officials at provincial and ministerial level, 59 at bureau level. If those working directly for Su, Ni and Peng and media people were included, the total number would come to about 250. Obviously, it was a powerful task force comprising many excellent caliber people. Later on, some of them became leaders of the Party and the state, ministers, ambassadors, general managers of the key state enterprises, etc.

After the announcement, Lin Hujia gave five guidelines for our work. (1) The mission of the Work Team was to learn about the situation and solve problems in accordance with the No. 16 document of the Party Central Committee, and to ensure that the campaign to fight against the Gang of Four was carried out in a planned way. (2) The Party committees of all bureaus, groups and offices under the Municipal Party Committee and the Revolutionary Committee were to rally closely around the Party Central Committee headed by Hua Guofeng, have a clear-cut political stand, stand in the forefront of the struggle, earnestly study and implement Document No. 16 of the CPC, fully arouse and rely on the people in the struggle against the Gang of Four, thoroughly expose and repudiate the crimes committed by the Gang of Four and its followers, help those who had followed the Gang of Four in doing evil to separate themselves from the Gang of Four and convert to the side of the correct line of Chairman Mao and pass the test given by the Party and the people in the great struggle. (3) All officials, staff and workers were to man their posts, making revolution while engaging in production, work and combat readiness and do their job well under the unified leadership of the Party committee. (4) Any important meeting or activity held by the Party committees of all bureaus, groups and offices of the Municipal Party Committee and government was to be reported to the members of the Work Team, and, if necessary, the members might attend such meeting or activity. Any important information in the political campaign was to be promptly reported to the members of the Work Team. (5) All members of the Work Team were to be on high alert, guarding against any trouble or sabotage conducted by the class enemy. All documents and archives were to be properly kept, not to be disposed of without authorization, not to be transferred or destroyed. Any violation of this rule was to be duly punished. Lin also stressed that the "little brothers" of the Gang of Four were mostly posted in the sectors of industry and communications, therefore, those sectors should be the focus of more effort. Those that had to be broken had to be broken thoroughly; those that had to be established had to be established correctly. Those five points were relayed to the staff of all bureaus, groups and offices, and they became five working principles for the members of the Work Team.

Many of the Work Team members were asked to go to Shanghai at short notice. To prevent any undesirable mishap, at first the Work Team asked its members "to bring along your ears and eyes only, not your mouth." As the campaign unfolded, this rule was later changed: the Work Team had to give its opinion on any major issues that came up during the campaign. Its members were all people of principle and dared to say what they deemed fit. I have not heard that any one of them abused their power.

October 24. Su Zhenhua called from Beijing, saying: "Members of the Work Team are to go to the bureaus, groups and offices as soon as possible to take control, and discuss with the Party committee members of those entities how to carry out the campaign. Persuade people not to hold demonstrations or large gatherings without authorization.

Large gatherings should be organized under the leadership of the Party committee. They should not establish any ties between different organizations. They are not to form factions. Such practices of the Gang of Four must be cast away. Study hard Document No. 16, and put what you have learned from such study into the actual work. People should take part in the campaign in their own units."

October 25. From that day on, the Work Team members entered various bureaus, groups and offices of the Municipal Party Committee and the Municipal Revolutionary Committee, and were warmly welcomed by their staff and local residents. Large slogans were put up in Nanjing Road to hail the entry of the Work Team into those entities. As I was in charge of universities, students, who always stand in the van of political campaigns, included me by name in their big slogans and big-character posters. "You've become a public figure now," someone joked. I quipped back: "A world without heroes makes a nobody famous." The downfall of the Gang of Four propelled people like myself to the front.

I still remember what I saw when we first entered the building of the Culture and Education Group. About a dozen people were waiting for us at the entrance because they had complaints to make. The first complainer I talked to was a man named Zhu Jinduo from the Shanghai Yueju Opera Troupe. He had been arrested on a charge of criticizing the Gang of Four. I heard him out and found that he was totally innocent. Soon he was exonerated. Later on, he was very active in the campaign to expose and repudiate the crimes of the Gang of Four.

Shortly after, the Work Team felt a shortage of manpower, and had to ask various ministries and commissions in Beijing to dispatch more people. Pretty soon, more people came to join us. In early November, more people were sent, either in the name of the Work Team detachment or as liaison to some key enterprises, such as No. 17 National Textile Plant, where Wang Hongwen had worked and controlled,

No. 31 National Textile Plant, where Wang Xiuzhen had worked, and Jiangnan Shipyard, where Huang Tao had worked, to strengthen the leadership over the campaign.

October 26. The Party Central Committee issued a notice of the decision to reorganize the leading body of the Shanghai Municipal Party Committee. The Notice read: "In order to strengthen the leadership of the Shanghai Municipal Party Committee, the Party Central Committee has decided to appoint Su Zhenhua concurrently First Secretary of the Shanghai Municipal Party Committee and Chairman of the Shanghai Municipal Revolutionary Committee; Ni Zhifu concurrently Second Secretary of the Shanghai Municipal Party Committee and First Vice Chairman of the Shanghai Municipal Revolutionary Committee; Peng Chong concurrently Third Secretary of the Shanghai Municipal Party Committee and Second Vice Chairman of the Shanghai Municipal Revolutionary Committee. Zhang Chunqiao, Yao Wenyuan and Wang Hongwen are removed from all their posts, both in and outside the Party in Shanghai." Later Su Zhenhua told us at a meeting that Hua Guofeng had said: "There are not many people in the Political Bureau. Even so, we sent two of them to Shanghai. This shows how much importance the Political Bureau placed on Shanghai. It is also the greatest support to Shanghai." Former leaders of Shanghai, such as Wang Yiping, Han Zheyi, Liang Guobin, Li Gancheng, who had been removed by the Gang of Four, Ma Tianshui, Xu Jingxian and Wang Xiuzhen, were reappointed, one after the other, to high posts in Shanghai.

October 27. Su Zhenhua, Ni Zhifu and Peng Chong chaired a meeting attended by leading members of all bureaus, groups, offices, districts and counties under the Municipal Party Committee and the Revolutionary Committee. They first announced the decision of the Party Central Committee to reshuffle the Party leadership in Shanghai. The audience hailed this news. I could feel that the support was genuine. Then Su made a speech, his first public speech since coming to

Shanghai. He emphasized that the city of Shanghai must not be separated from the Party Central Committee and the rest of the country. We had to differentiate the broad masses of the people of Shanghai from the Gang of Four and its followers, to differentiate Shanghai's militiamen from the handful of plotters of the insurrection. He made public the attempt by Ma, Xu and Wang to stage an insurrection. I was confident that we would make a breakthrough once their conspiracy was exposed, because the majority of the officials and ordinary citizens would see through them and break loose from their control. So those plotters would be isolated. Su's speech well reflected the policies of the Party Central Committee towards Shanghai, yet it was highly tactical. The meeting drew a clear line between ordinary people and the Gang of Four, between militiamen and plotters of the insurrection. This eased the minds of many people. Thus a favorable situation was created, which was very helpful to the efforts to expose, repudiate and investigate the crimes of the Gang of Four and its lackeys.

This meeting made a great stir in society too. Here I'd like to cite two examples. At that meeting, Zhang Chengzong, who had formerly served as Vice Mayor of Shanghai, stood up and criticized Ma Tianshui to his face. Zhang had been the head of the Shanghai underground Communists before the founding of New China and, after its founding, had for a long time been in charge of work concerning non-CPC parties and persons without party affiliation. He said that Ma Tianshui had once ordered some factories to manufacture tens of thousands of handcuffs. He demanded: "Why did you want so many handcuffs? Whom did you want to handcuff? Who asked you to do so?" Those questions had Ma flabbergasted. He was unable to answer, and had not the guts to answer. More questions were fired about the insurrection and activities concerning usurpation of the Party, and the atmosphere was rather tense.

Another example happened in the Culture and Education Group.

When we first entered this Group, we first talked to those who were politically reliable so as to learn more about the situation there. I was introduced to a man called He Ruyi. He was the Deputy Head of the Group and had once worked in the General Office of the Party Central Committee. He had followed Tan Zhenlin to Beijing from East China. Later he returned to Shanghai. Being such a veteran, I thought we could trust him. I had a talk with him hoping to find out whether there were any Gang of Four lackey activities in the Group. I said to him: "Please do help us. We trust you." He volunteered some useful information. At the October 27 meeting, I saw him again. But the next day, about 5 am, Yang Kai, Party Secretary of Shanghai Jiaotong University (later Head of the Culture and Education Group and Vice Mayor of Shanghai), called to tell me that He Ruyi had committed suicide by jumping off a building. I could not believe my ears, and said I had seen him only the previous day. He had even said a few words to me, and I had not detected anything unusual. "Did he leave any last words?" I asked. "I don't know," he replied. I said I would go to his residence right away. I saw the body on the ground, and asked a policeman what had actually happened, whether he had left any testament, or if there were any clues. He told me that there was a piece of paper on the body and written on it were the words "Utterly shameful!" What does that mean? I wondered. I learned later that during the late 1975–early 1976 period, when Deng Xiaoping was once again removed from office, and people were under great political pressure, He Ruyi had knuckled under and written a letter to followers of the Gang of Four, denouncing his daughter's father-in-law, accusing him of making unfavorable comments about Jiang Qing. At the October 27 meeting, seeing the exposure of even a secret like Ma Tianshui's instruction to manufacture handcuffs, he thought he could no longer keep secret the denunciation he had made. Sooner or later, he too would be exposed at a meeting. That would be utterly shameful. That led him to commit suicide. From this example, I must say that the October 27 meeting really shook the city.

October 28. Following the principle of "solving problems, stabilize Shanghai," the Work Team and the new Shanghai Municipal Party Committee began to expose the crimes of the Gang of Four and investigate the network of its followers. But where to start? Where would we be able to make a breakthrough? After much deliberation, Su, Ni and Peng unanimously agreed that we would start by tackling the insurrection plotted by some members of the Standing Committee of the former Shanghai Municipal Party Committee. With this, we could push forward the drive to expose, repudiate and investigate the Gang of Four and its followers. Chaired by Su, Ni and Peng, the meeting was held for days on end in the name of the Standing Committee meeting. Ma Tianshui, Xu Jingxian and Wang Xiuzhen were asked to attend the meeting too. They were required to confess their own errors and expose each other. At the very start of the meeting, Su expressly pointed out: "The conspiracy of the Gang of Four to usurp the Party started in Shanghai. It is difficult to discover all their crimes in a short period of time. Now you must come clean about your involvement in the insurrection first. You may tell us what you did personally for the insurrection or what the others did. I'd suggest that you give a day-by-day account." Despite Su's repeated emphasis on the Party's policies and reasoning, they just beat about the bush, trying hard to cover up. Realizing this wasn't working as expected, the Work Team and the new Shanghai Municipal Party Committee decided to arouse the local residents and militiamen to expose the insurrection plot, as well as sending out the Team members to gather information. Those who were directly involved in the insurrection conspiracy and those who had done wicked things to harm others were detained. In this way, our work began to unfold smoothly, and many facts began to emerge.

October 29. Peng Chong called a forum for members of the Work Team. He said at the meeting: "The timely support of various ministries and commissions has helped ease the strain of manpower of the Work Team. Ma, Xu and Wang did not expect the campaign to move so fast. The present task is to expose them, and the breakthrough will come through exposing the insurrection plot. At the meetings of the Standing Committee, they still try in vain to unify their versions of certain facts, cover up the truth, and evade their responsibility. In their recent articles, they have carefully chosen the word 'riot' instead of 'insurrection.' We have already criticized them for this. Only a few days ago, Xu Jingxian said that it was hard for him to change sides emotionally. This is not an emotional matter at all, but a matter of political stance." Peng also said that from then on, those who attended the Standing Committee meeting but without voting rights would be stopped from attending such meetings.

October 30. The Work Team held a plenary meeting. Su, Ni and Peng were present and Su was the first to speak. He said: "The Party Central Committee has paid great attention to the work in Shanghai, and wants us to do a good job in carrying out the campaign to expose and repudiate the Gang of Four. It has chosen many people from various ministries and commissions, the Beijing Municipal Party Committee and the army to support us. It is an honor to be part of the Work Team, but it is also a hard task. The Gang of Four pushed its own line of work in Shanghai and turned a deaf ear to the Party Central Committee. They meddled with matters in other cities and provinces and disrupted the work of others. The Gang of Four tried in vain to turn Shanghai into its base to promote its counter-revolutionary, revisionist line. We must not overlook their influence, but be prepared for its destructive effect. Now, the Party Central Committee has sent us to Shanghai, and placed a great deal of hope on us. The Shanghai people longed to see the arrival of the Work Team. Now we are here, and we must not let them down. We must devote all our attention and energy to our work, and do a good job in Shanghai. First, act according to the policies of the Party Central Committee. Second, rely on the people. Third, the Party committees at all levels must exercise a unified leadership. You work in entities whose work might not be familiar to you. For most officials and staff, our policy is to rectify past mistakes so as to avoid future ones. First, make correct judgments and then give help. Strictly differentiate those who were directly involved in the conspiracy from those who said or did something wrong due to Gang of Four propaganda." Su encouraged us to work boldly and would take responsibility for us if anything went wrong. Then Ni said he hoped that each one of us would work all out and overcome homesickness. Peng Chong also said: "Things are moving faster in Shanghai than we expected. But there is still a large amount of work to do, and we must continuously work hard to do our job well."

That day, the *People's Daily* published on the front page an article "Encouraging Situation in Shanghai," written by a special columnist. We were all very happy to see our work bearing fruit.

Exposing, Repudiating and Investigating the Crimes of the Gang of Four and Its Followers

The Gang of Four had long harbored the idea of establishing its own military forces. As early as the Second Plenary Session of the Ninth Central Committee of the CPC in 1971, Jiang Qing and Zhang Chunqiao had said to Ma Tianshui, Wang Xiuzhen and Xu Jingxian: "All of us are scholars, not military." Wang Hongwen had also said: "What troubles me most is that we have no control of military forces, and we have no one in the army." So Wang Hongwen had meant all along to transform the militia into a second military force. On May 3, 1975, Mao Zedong criticized the Gang of Four at a Political Bureau meeting. On June 14, Wang Hongwen wrote a letter of self-criticism to Mao Zedong. Afterwards, on the pretext of helping Shanghai and Zhejiang solve certain problems, he went to Shanghai and stayed there for 105 days. One of his major tasks in Shanghai was to inspect the Shanghai Militia and allocate tasks to his followers. On September 18, he confided in those in the Shanghai Militia Command, stressing: "The militia is most important. You must be prepared for battles in the future. Be on high alert. The militiamen must never listen to others, but obey the instructions of the Command. When we are struck at, we'll see if we can take it." On September 20, 1976, a fortnight before the down-fall of the Gang of Four, Xu Jingxian went to see Zhang Chunqiao in Beijing. Zhang made a note to ask Xu to run the Shanghai Militia well. Later investigation showed that Shanghai had directed heavy financial and material input into the building of the Shanghai Militia. According to the statistics issued by the Financial Bureau of Shanghai, between 1974 and September 1975, the Gang of Four and its followers had manufactured or bought 48,462 rifles, ten command vehicles, ten sets of radar instruments, and over 400,000 parts and components for rifles and machine-guns from Shanghai, Hunan and Anhui. They planned to equip 30 infantry regiments, ten antiaircraft artillery divisions, three ground gun divisions, one tank division, and one motorcycle regiment with altogether 108 rockets (130mm) and 782 antiaircraft guns. On September 28, Zhang Chunqiao sent his secretary to Shanghai and relayed this instruction: "Keep a watch on the tendency of the class struggle. Be vigilant on the one side; enhance confidence on the other. We must see that bourgeoisie is still powerful. The critical issue is who is in command now. Shanghai has not truly experienced any severe test. There will be big test for Shanghai. Be prepared for battles." Those instruc-tions of Wang and Zhang served as political mobilization and mental preparation for the insurrection by the lackeys of the Gang of Four in Shanghai.

The October 8 meeting chaired by Xu Jingxian had decided that Shi Shangying and Zhang Jingbiao, two heads of the Shanghai Militia, were to draw up on that night two plans for the insurrection with the codes "Han—No. 1" and "Han—No. 2" ("Han" meant defending the so-called "proletarian headquarters"). Han—No. 1 covered deployment of forces to control leading bodies, newspapers, radio centers, airport, major bridges, docks, communication hubs, etc. Han—No. 2 covered the establishment of three control areas from the downtown area to the Shanghai suburbs with the aim of defending the city against attacks from Jiangsu and Zhejiang. The two plans covered the following ten aspects:

(1) "The whole city shall mobilize 33,000 armed militiamen, 85 big guns and rocket launchers, 78 machine-guns, 27,000 rifles and tommy guns and 2.96 million bullets.

(2) The militiamen shall be on duty day and night. They should be formed in groups and equipped with automobiles and weapons.

(3) Set up a sub-command in the Jiangnan Shipyards, a backup sub-command in China Textile Machinery Plant; militiamen to man the sub-commands must be in place before 11 am on October 9.

(4) The Militia Command and the mobile militia divisions should also set up sub-commands.

(5) Set up a command network and two telecommunications networks which should be interconnected at 6 pm on October 9. (Later the two telecommunications networks received a total of 75 telegrams and stopped operations on October 15.)

(6) To facilitate back-up troops and telecommunications, make ready 125 automobiles, 100 motorcycles and some bicycles.

(7) Set up six control points and one control area at Liuhe, Anting and Gelong in the border areas between Shanghai, Zhejiang and Jiangsu; in the other two control areas between the first control area and the downtown, set up 17 control points in the central control area and 16 in the inner control area; each district and county is required to establish a reserve task force and assign tasks.

(8) Wusongkou has dispatched two or three ships to reinforce sea patrols; get a few motor-powered fishing boats ready for emergency, get control of all ferries along the Huangpu River, waterways and aqueducts across the river. They may be closed if necessary.

(9) Plans of key points for support, measures against paratroops, storage of ammunition and repair of weapons.

(10) Create passwords and slogans."

As the insurrection conspiracy was doomed, all those measures, apart from setting up command radio stations and assembling militiamen, fell flat. The reasons for this result are, in my view, as follows:

One: the decision of the Political Bureau to detain the four members of the Gang won the strong support of the people, therefore, politically, the Party Central Committee had an absolute advantage over the Gang of Four. The Gang of Four's evil doings had brought great harm to the state and the people. It was the people's wish to have them fettered and punished. The desperate struggle for an insurrection plotted by its lackeys went against the tide and was doomed to fail.

Two: the Political Bureau's summoning of Xu Jingxian and Wang Xiuzhen to Beijing on October 9. This jeopardized the insurrection plot as it left no ringleader in Shanghai. The three other members of the Standing Committee, realizing their doomed fate, delayed the insurrection on the pretext of waiting for the return of Ma Tianshui to make the decision. This made the situation worse for them.

Three: the Work Team led by Su, Ni and Peng arrived in Shanghai at the right time, quickly took control of Shanghai, relayed the policies of the Party Central Committee and Mao Zedong's criticism of Gang of Four to the broad masses of the people of Shanghai, which landed the followers of the Gang of Four into a storm of anger. Anything they tried was destined for defeat.

Four: the policies and strategies of the Work Team and the new Shanghai Municipal Party Committee in dealing with insurrection were appropriate. The truth about the insurrection was quickly discovered and the pressure was taken off most of those who had been cheated by the followers of the Gang of Four and led to take part in the insurrection plot. The situation in Shanghai grew stable.

Meanwhile, all the Party and government agencies, all districts and counties stirred the people to further expose the crimes of the Gang of Four and its followers. Some 5,400 people were under investigation, of whom 1,683 were arrested, detained or suspended from work; of these, 458 people who had used violence to harm others were dealt with and punished. More than 300 major cases were investigated, of which 12 directly related to usurping the Party. By the end of 1977, all those cases had been carefully handled and wound up. Of all those cases, 98 cases were included in the three batches of evidence material relating to the crimes of the Gang of Four compiled by the Party Central Committee; 174 were presented in evidence to the Special Court trying the two anti-Party cliques headed by Lin Biao and the Gang of Four. Later, at the Municipal Standing Committee meeting, Yan Youmin passed on the words of Peng Zhen: "The struggles against the Gang of Four and its followers in Shanghai were well done. Evidence materials provided by Shanghai and quoted at the Special Court accounted for one third of the total evidence." Peng Zhen also said that without the evidence from Shanghai, it would have been impossible to conduct the trial of the Gang of Four.

A leader of the General Office of the Special Court in charge of the two cases said at a meeting on July 13, 1981: "The political campaign of exposing, repudiating and investigating the crimes of the Gang of Four in various places can be classified into three types. One type was where the campaign was smooth and healthy and the Party policies well implemented. Not many people were punished, and their problems were not serious, so few people made complaints later. The policies were observed and the reasons for punishment were convincing. Shanghai belongs to this type." I think his assertion was objective. He cited only Shanghai as an example, not anywhere else. As a member of the Work Team, I truly felt that we had faithfully followed the provisions of Document No. 16, adhered to the principle of winning over the majority of the people, strictly differentiated the handful of evil doers from the hoodwinked majority. We took great care to keep down the number of people for punishment. In the sector of culture, education and sports, which was in my charge, there was a basketball player who had beaten up more than 200 people during the "Cultural Revolution." Once when he was exhausted, he had forced the people in detention to knock each other about. People were most angry about him, and he could have been punished severely. But he had only been 16 at that time. In consideration of factors such as his age, and being egged on by the followers of the Gang of Four, he was sentenced to only three years' imprisonment.

During the campaign, we convened all kinds of Gang of Four denunciation meetings. During the more than one year period from the arrival of the Work Team till the end of 1977, we held four municipal meetings including one in the main, 10,000-capacity conference hall, which was broadcast live. Over 230,000 branch committee members under the Shanghai Municipal Party Committee attended meetings in their own units. Over 20 meetings of more than 10,000 people denouncing the Gang of Four were held by various sectors. Those meetings were large in scale and profound in criticism. The indignation of the people present at the meetings was unprecedented. It was most beneficial to eradicating the influence of the Gang of Four, helping change people's minds. I recall such a meeting held by the Culture and Education Sector in the cinema of the Shanghai Exhibition Hall, where Xu Jingxian was standing on stage listening to people's criticisms. There were four people sitting on the platform. Ba Jin, the renowned writer, sat beside me and said: "When the 'Cultural Revolution' was at its height 10 years ago, probably in November too, Xu Jingxian chaired a 10,000-people meeting in Culture Square, denounced and disgraced Chen Pixian (then Party Secretary of the Municipal Committee) and Cao Diqiu (then Mayor of Shanghai), and a few people including myself were also taken to the platform to be disgraced. Xu never dreamed that he too would be standing on the same stage to be criticized 10 years on. Heaven certainly has eyes. This is perhaps what is called retribution." I said: "Our forefathers said that 'he who perpetrates many injustices is doomed to destruction.' These people have done too many wicked things."

Rectifying the Leading Bodies and Implementing the Party's Policies

While engaged in the political campaign, we did our utmost to appraise those working in the leading bodies. Only a few months later after we entered Shanghai, perhaps at the end of 1976, the Work Team began to assess all 103 leading bodies of the bureaus, groups and offices under the Municipal Party Committee and the Revolutionary Committee, districts and counties of Shanghai. Those leading bodies were divided into three categories. The first category comprised the 31 leading bodies that were basically sound, accounting for 30 percent of the total. Members of such leading bodies were adamant in the struggle against the Gang of Four and won the trust of the people. They were good at both production and making revolution. The second category contained mediocre ones, 44 in number, accounting for 43 percent of the total. The major problems with such leading bodies were that some of their members had made mistakes, though not serious ones, or that they were rather weak. They lacked initiative, or had some other difficulties. For such leading bodies, Su Zhenhua stressed that assistance should be given to them, to help them stand up in the campaign. They should be promoted gradually into the first category. The third category comprised those with serious problems. There were 28 of them, representing 27 percent of the total. Such leading bodies, which had been controlled by the Gang of Four for a long time, were rotten and useless and should be reorganized. In the process of reorganization, Su, Ni and Peng decided to invite former leading members of those leading bodies back to the responsible positions. "They were persecuted and expelled from those leading bodies during the 'Cultural Revolution.' Let them come out to work first and get familiar with the working environment and the Party's policies. When time comes, appoint them to suitable posts." In the period when the Gang of Four was in power in Shanghai, there were 1,170 officials at or above district (county) level, of whom 478 were on the investigation list during the campaign against the Gang of Four, accounting for 41 percent; 249 of these officials were removed from their posts. Sixty percent of the leading bodies underwent reorganization, and the leader was changed in 80 percent of these. It was no easy job, and the members of the Work Team put in a great deal of effort.

During the "Cultural Revolution," aiming to usurp the Party leadership, the Gang of Four took every opportunity possible to persecute high officials, most of them veteran revolutionaries and intellectuals. In Shanghai alone, 106,264 veteran officials were persecuted. After more than a year of hard work, the Work Team re-examined 91,917 cases, accounting for 86.5 percent of the total number of veteran revolutionaries subject to re-examination, and re-examined and exonerated 1,400 senior intellectuals, accounting for 96.5 percent of the total number of intellectuals subject to re-examination. Within just a short time, so many veterans and intellectuals had their names cleared. The workload for this activity alone was huge. I remember, in those days, we could only snatch a few hours' sleep every day, since we went to bed in the early hours—at one or two o'clock—and had to get up at seven. Our work was intense but fruitful. However, there were still a few people who were not exonerated promptly. This is because they were said to have committed some "historical mistakes" before the founding of New China. Since the Party Central Committee of the earlier days had made conclusions about certain historical events in which many were involved and such events had not yet been reviewed, we could do nothing about it. Later such historical events were re-examined, the earlier conclusions reversed and those veteran revolutionaries hence exonerated. This has to be viewed in historical context. As for ordinary intellectuals, the Party's policies were properly implemented.

Shanghai's culture and arts sector encompassed publishing, film, drama, music, and fine art industries. They were hugely influential across China, and were known as "half of the country." As I was in charge of this sector, I got to know many specialists and performers. When they had a problem, they would often come to me for help. We were on very good terms. I remember, one night, around one in the morning, my secretary told me I was wanted on the phone. "Who is it? This is quite late," I asked. "He's from the Shanghai Peking Opera Troupe." I recognized the voice. It was Zhang Xuejin, a performer who excelled in playing old man roles. He was agitated and talked for a long time about a conflict with his wife. In a case such as this, it was difficult for me to put in a word for him. So I just tried to calm him down. "It's pretty late today. Shall we find another time to talk over the matter?" He agreed. Just think, if we were not on good terms, would a man call you at midnight to talk about his personal affairs? I often said to myself: "People like me in the economic sector should make friends in world of literature and arts. Their lives are rich and colorful." Unfortunately, I had no such chances later. Here are a few examples of such friendships.

The first example concerns Yuan Xuefen, a famous Yueju Opera actress. The day after my arrival at the office of the Municipal Culture and Education Group, Yuan Xuefen sent me a letter via a friend of hers. It was a large envelope bearing the words "To Comrade Chen Jinhua." I broke the seal and saw another envelope on which were the words "To Comrade Peng Chong, c/o Comrade Chen Jinhua." So I complied.

When Peng opened the letter, there was yet another envelope addressed "To Su Zhenhua, c/o Peng Chong." Peng passed the letter to Su at a meeting. Su opened it, saying: "Letters within letters, what's the secret inside?" The letter read that before the "Cultural Revolution", Premier Zhou Enlai had written her over 20 letters, which she had cherished dearly. But they had been taken away when her home was raided by Red Guards. She requested the Work Team to recover those letters for her. She was so cautious. This shows that celebrities in the world of literature and arts still suffered from fear of the "Cultural Revolution."

The second example concerns the exoneration of Zhao Dan, a famous movie star. One Sunday afternoon, perhaps around five, I was on my way home, carrying some documents with me, since my office was very close to my residence. This had two entrances—the main entrance and the door into my kitchen. As I approached my residence, I saw Yang Yanjin, a young film director, and a stranger standing at the kitchen door. The stranger seemed familiar, but I could not figure out who he was. At that time, my daughter Chen Yue had just started middle school. She nudged me, saying: "Dad, that's Zhao Dan!" Now I recognized him, and I invited them in and asked them to sit down. Zhao said to me: "Vice Mayor (I was appointed Vice Mayor of Shanghai at that time), I'm sorry to disturb you at this hour. It's time you ought to be resting. But..." "It's all right," said I. "Is there anything I can do for you?" "It concerns myself. I'd like to talk to you about my case and would like to know when the policies of the Party might shine on me." "Of course. But I'm afraid we've got to find another time, because I have had an appointment tonight. What do you say?" "Sure," he said, "any time. I leave the decision to you." We agreed to meet the following Sunday. That day, he came together with his wife Huang Zongying and recounted his bitter experiences during the "Cultural Revolution." He had been publicly criticized, disgraced and even beaten up in the film studios and in the May 7th Cadres School. At first, he kept his emotions under control. But after a while he stood up while speaking, getting more and more worked up. When it came to the sad part, he could no longer hold back his tears. His wife tugged his sleeve and said: "Please contain yourself. Didn't we agree not to be emotional? How can Mayor Chen listen to you if you speak like this?" I said: "Never mind, never mind. This bitterness has been pent up for so many years. It's understandable. If he doesn't come to the Municipal Party Committee to pour it all out, where else can he go?" On hearing this, Zhao Dan became even more emotional. He sobbed bitterly, just like a child. He said: "I have not heard such words for many years." Once at a meeting, he had been criticized, which made him very upset. Chen Yi, Mayor of Shanghai at that time, had consoled him like I was doing now. Zhao's main point was get himself exonerated. Before the founding of New China, he had been thrown into prison by the warlord Sheng Shicai in Xinjiang. He had later been suspected of working for Sheng, but this had all been cleared up later. During the "Cultural Revolution," he had groundlessly been called a revisionist. Finally, I said: "Don't worry. I'll see to it. If I have any questions, I'll come to you. If you have any questions, you come to me. I promise I'll look into your case as soon as possible." The following day, I sent for Dai Xingming, Party Secretary of the Film Bureau and talked to him about Zhao Dan's case. I said: "Zhao Dan came to see me. He is a man of high reputation. Please look into his case as soon as possible. Clearing his name will have big repercussions." Dai agreed, saying: "We'll act right away." Soon the cases of renowned figures, group after group, were put on the agenda of the Municipal Party Committee. When it came to Zhao Dan, I said at the meeting: "Zhao Dan has talked to me. I don't think the so-called 'crimes' of his are problems at all." The meeting discussed his case and agreed that Zhao was to be exonerated. It took us about 10 to 15 days to solve Zhao's case, which was not too long.

The third example concerned Li Yuru, a famous, talented Peking

Opera actress. She was able to play the role of young or middle-aged women and also warriors in the styles of Mei Lanfang and Cheng Yan-qiu (established Peking Opera actors playing female roles). Premier Zhou thought highly of her, and once gave her as a gift a copy of the film *Tears at Barren Hill* in which Cheng Yanqiu played the heroine and asked her to learn from the film. Li also revered the Premier. During the "Cultural Revolution," the Gang of Four left no stone unturned in their search for "mistakes" by Premier Zhou in a bid to topple him, and because of Li's friendship with the Premier, she had been detained and persecuted by the Gang of Four. She was deprived of the right to perform and not even allowed to mount the stage. Later she came to me and told me all her grievances. I said: "I'll talk to them and try to solve your problem as soon as possible." Not knowing much about her case, I talked to Li Taichen, the Party Secretary of the Cultural Bureau. "Li Yuru came to see me the other day. Would it be possible to look into and solve her case as soon as possible? Let her go on stage." Li replied cautiously: "Why not have a look at her files first?" In her files were her own confessions and records of interrogations. There were also some reports against her filed by others. I just leafed through them, without reading them thoroughly. I passed them over to the member of the Work Team who liaised with the Cultural Bureau and asked him to have a good look at them. Once he had read them, I asked: "Is there any evidence of her being against the Party, socialism, and the revolution?" "No," he replied, "Most of the stuff is remarks about Jiang Qing." "Talking about Jiang Qing? That's not a crime. Besides, those so-called confessions were the results of torture. They are not convincing." There was not a single piece of evidence to prove she was anti-Party, anti-socialism or anti-revolution. I then said to Li Taichen: "I asked the members of the Work Team to review her case and found no evidence of anti-Party, anti-socialism or anti-revolution activities. She did talk about Jiang Qing. She said that Jiang Qing was a laywoman of

Peking Opera, and the model revolutionary operas promoted by Jiang were not of high quality. There was nothing wrong about saying these things. Have her exonerated immediately and let her resume her acting life." Very soon, Li Yuru was thus exonerated. Many years later, perhaps during the Chinese New Year of 1985 or 1986, when I was already back in Beijing and was chairman of the executive council of the Capital Entrepreneurs Club, the Club sponsored a song and dance performance in the Banquet Hall of the Beijing Hotel and invited many celebrities to the show. As I was about to leave the Hall at the end, I came across Li Yuru, who was accompanying her husband Cao Yu, the famous playwright. It had been years since I saw her last. At the sight of me, she was excited and cried out: "Mayor Chen! It's so nice to see you here." "Same here!" said I. "How did you know we'd sponsored this show?" "We were at a party in the French Embassy and heard you would be present at the show tonight. So we came here right away to find you." Then she turned to Cao Yu and said: "This is Mayor Chen I've often mentioned to you. It was he who got my name cleared." I felt embarrassed and said at once: "Don't mention it. You'd suffered for a long time. We should have done it long ago." Cao Yu said: "Thank you very much! Yuru has often talked to me about you. She says you are a really good man." "You're welcome. Please don't mention it." I often think that Chinese intellectuals and celebrities are really generous and kind-hearted. They had endured persecution and suffering for so long, and had every right to be exonerated. When you did something for them, they felt grateful to you and thought about you for years. Where else in the world can you find such celebrities? Li Yuru was one of them. Since that encounter, I have not met her again.

The fourth example concerned the films *Legend at Mt. Tianyun* and *Love at Mt. Lushan*. It happened after the Work Team had left Shanghai, but it was through being a member of the Team that I had got to know these film people. There was a huge dispute over the film *Legend at Mt. Tianyun*.

Some people said that the film's agenda was to disgrace the CPC and to reverse the verdict on "Rightists" (many intellectuals and educated people were wrongly labeled as Rightists and persecuted in 1957-1958). At the time of the controversy, I was serving as Deputy Secretary of the Shanghai Municipal Party Committee, Executive Vice Mayor and concurrently Director-general of the Municipal Planning Committee. When I delivered a report on the national economic plan at the Municipal People's Congress, I deliberately inserted a few words in praise of the *Legend at Mt. Tianyun*. Later the film director, Xie Jin, told me: "What you said has given me great support!" As a matter of fact, I didn't think too much of the film, but believed it did not deserve the criticisms aimed at it. On the contrary, there were many things in it that Communists needed to ponder. When the hero, a "Rightist," met his persecutor the Party Secretary of the prefecture, at a bridge, he said: "Surely you know that ordinary people also want a decent life since you yourself are seeking a decent life." I don't remember the exact words, but what he said left an indelible impression on me. It was the simple truth, plain and clear. I remember when my draft report was being discussed at the Municipal Party Committee, not one objection was raised to my affirmation of the film. The draft was accepted unanimously. I was responsible for what I said. If the film had been criticized, I would have been blamed as well.

Another film was *Love at Mt. Lushan*, also made by Shanghai Film Studios. It had been highly acclaimed by audiences. Zhang Junxiang, the director, said to me: "*Love at Mt. Lushan* has made a breakthrough. It broke the fetter of love stories being banned during the 'Cultural Revolution'." He also praised the acting skill of Zhang Yu, who had played the heroine. A leading member of the Shanghai Municipal Party Committee even said in public that she should have a pay raise awarded because of her excellent performance. If I remember correctly, her salary at that time was no more than 60-70 yuan a month. A one grade higher salary would be eight to ten *yuan*. But even a small amount like that did not materialize fast. Why not? The reason was that there was no rule about higher salaries for good performance. There was no budget for it. But it did not look right that a leading member of the Municipal Party Committee was unable to deliver on his promise. Later this leading comrade came to me and asked me to find a way out. Since I was concurrently head of the Municipal Labor and Salary Commission under the Municipal Party Committee, pay increases were part of my job. I sent for the Director-general of the Labor Bureau Yu Yongshi and asked him to help me out. After pondering for quite some time, we finally came up with an idea. According to one state document, a director of an enterprise had the right to increase the salary of three percent of his staff. The Shanghai Film Studios could be regarded as an enterprise. So we telephoned Xu Sangchu, Director of the Film Studios. In this way, Zhang Yu got a pay raise. Such a thing would be unimaginable today.

The fifth example concerned the problem of accommodation for the Performers Troupe. One day, Zhang Ruifang and some of her colleagues burst into my office. Zhang was a famous film star and I knew her quite well. And she liked to talk to me. This time, she came about accommodation for her troupe. At that time, famous actors and actresses such as Zhao Dan, Bai Yang and Wang Danfeng all belonged to the Performers Troupe under the Shanghai Film Bureau. Before the "Cultural Revolution," the Troupe had had a villa in which they rehearsed. With the advent of the "Cultural Revolution," they had been driven out of that villa and were forced to rehearse in a makeshift workshop and a few sheds, which were too small for over 100 performers to rehearse. They had found an ideal villa belonging to the Municipal Instrument Bureau and had asked whether the Troupe could use it. They had talked to the Bureau several times but to no avail. So they had come to me. Hearing this, I called the head of the Instrument Bureau who told me that Zhang Ruifang and others had talked to him several times, but he could not give consent since the Bureau needed it for its own use. I discussed with him over the phone to find a good solution. At that time, the Bureau was negotiating with Foxboro of the USA to establish an instrument joint venture (later President Reagan visited this joint venture enterprise when he visited Shanghai). I said: "If you give the villa to the Performers Troupe, I'll grant you more funds to construct another building when I examine the joint venture project." He agreed at once. When I told Zhang Ruifang, Niu Ben and the other performers, they were overjoyed.

The sixth example concerned implementing the policy concerning compensation to former capitalists. During the "Cultural Revolution," a stop was put on interest payments to capitalists for their assets sold to the state. After the "Cultural Revolution," in the period of "implementing policies," the Work Team and the new Shanghai Municipal Party Committee decided to compensate them. In those days, capitalists were concentrated in Shanghai. Calculations showed that the compensation would be as high as three billion *yuan*. This was no small figure. After deliberation, the Municipal Party Committee decided to file a report to the Party Central Committee, stating that all the compensation should be paid. The key compensation recipient in Shanghai was Rong Yiren, and he thought highly of the Municipal Party Committee's decision. In order to widen the impact of government compensation to capitalists both in and outside China, Rong Yiren was the first to come to Shanghai to obtain the compensation. He came with his wife Yang Jianqing. I don't remember the precise amount of compensation: it was a large sum, anyway. As soon as he arrived in Shanghai, I was informed. Before they returned to Beijing after receiving the money, I invited the Rongs to a dinner at the Jinjiang Hotel. Peng Chong was invited too. Rong and I had known each other for years. When he was appointed Vice Minister of Textile Industry in 1958, I was Director of the Policy Study Office of that ministry. Whenever he had something to check, draft or improve, he would often come to me. At the banquet, I told him about an event in the past, which he knew about in part but not the whole story. After August 18, 1966, when Chairman Mao received Red Guards from outside Beijing, the Red Guards movement in Beijing surged like a tidal wave. They broke into the homes of many renowned figures, looting everything possible, ever more violently, on an ever greater scale. Rong Yiren's residence then was located in North Taipingzhuang and his daughter was a student of the Middle School attached to Beijing Normal University. Many of her schoolmates knew where she lived. On August 20, a group of Red Guards swarmed into Rong Yiren's residence. They were all girl students in fact. Among them were also persons of unknown identity. They raised havoc in the Rong's residence and publicly disgraced the couple. They even used Rong's home movie camera to record it all and said they would send the film to his relatives abroad. Knowing the adverse effects it would cause, Rong gave them false addresses for his relatives. His wife Yang Jianqing was beaten and injured. But nobody in the Ministry knew anything about it. August 20 happened to be payday and when delivering Rong's salary, his driver Zheng Yaochen saw what had happened and reported it to the Ministry. At that time, I was the Director of the Cultural Revolutionary Committee of the Ministry, and one of my duties was to see to such things. I reported the tragedy to Qian Zhiguang, the Secretary of the Party Leading Group of the Ministry. He said: "Write a report immediately to Premier Zhou, and deliver it to the General Office of the Premier as an extra express letter." I prepared the report and had it sent to Premier Zhou, and also called the General Office of Li Fuchun. At that time, Li Fuchun was in charge of the political movement in the sector of ministries of industries and communications. He suggested we send the Rongs to hospital for their protection. One of our Vice Ministers, Zhang Qinqiu, happened to be married to Su Jingguan, a Vice Minister of Public Health. She was very familiar with Beijing Hospital and called the president of the hospital. The president said: "Big Sister, it's impossible. All our floors are full of Red Guards, and they've held several meetings to criticize and disgrace my patients. The Rongs can't escape it if they come here." Then we had to turn to the General Office of Premier Zhou for help, but there was no answer. A little after 1 am, Zhou Rongxin, Secretary-general of the State Council, called Qian Zhiguang and asked him to go to see Premier Zhou right away in the Great Hall of the People. Qian had already gone to bed, having taken sleeping pills. Even so, he got up and set off. When he arrived, Premier Zhou asked what had actually happened to the Rongs. Qian gave a brief account of how the Red Guards had raided their residence and beaten them up. "Why didn't you report at once?" "We did write and send out a report." "What time is this? Writing a report takes a long time. You should have telephoned. For the time being, there are only two persons the State Council can protect—Soong Ching-ling and Guo Moruo. As for others, you've got to handle it yourself. Rong Yiren must be well protected. He is the representative of Chinese national bourgeoisie and has great influence both in and outside China. It is imperative to protect him." That was the instruction. An hour later, Qian Zhiguang returned to the office and discussed with us how to carry out Premier Zhou's instruction. "We've got to find a way, as Premier Zhou instructed, to protect Rong Yiren well," said Qian. "We must ensure nothing happens to the Rongs again." At that time, there was a tactic of "Red Guards vs. Red Guards," said to have been invented by the East China Party Committee in Shanghai. This entailed using Red Guards of an entity in order to deal with Red Guards from outside that entity or from outside Beijing. So, we sent for the chief of the Red Guards of the Ministry and persuaded him to take a dozen Red Guards to the residence of Rong Yiren. When they got there, they saw some girl Red Guards lying about in the sitting room. They said to the girls: "We are Red Guards of the Ministry of Textile Industry. Rong Yiren is a Vice

Minister of the Ministry, a bourgeoisie big shot. We'll hold meetings to criticize him and demand that he confesses his crimes. Please hand him over to us and let us deal with him." At first, the girl Red Guards were reluctant, but being young and inexperienced and they were easily persuaded and finally said: "All right. But we have conditions. He must honestly confess his crimes. Make him do manual labor, sweep the compound and clean the place. He is allowed to drink tap water, eat steamed corn buns and pickles only. No comforts for him any more!" The Red Guards of the Ministry agreed with all their conditions. Then the girl Red Guards left. As soon as they left, Rong Yiren asked that his wife should be taken to hospital as soon as possible. But it turned out that no hospital would even admit her, let alone treat her. The chief of the Red Guards of the Ministry was very clever. They sent her to Jishuitan Hospital, saying that this woman was an important witness and would have to give verbal testimony when recovered, and they would not let her die. They asked the doctors to do all in their power to save her life. At this, the doctors treated her immediately. In this way, Yang Jianqing was saved. The next day, the Red Guards of the Ministry asked the daughter, a doctor too, of Hu Ziying, Vice Minister of Commerce, a renowned personage, who also lived in the same compound, to prescribe and purchase medicine for Yang Jianqing.

I recounted how Premier Zhou had been concerned for them and how the Ministry had taken measures to protect them. On hearing all this, Rong was deeply moved. He stood up and toasted me to express his gratitude. I said: "It's not me you should thank. It was Premier Zhou who was behind it all." "I know all about the treatment measures, but I hadn't the faintest idea about how those treatments were provided and how it was possible in those days. Now I know it all, thanks to your account. All of my family are most grateful to Premier Zhou. Without his instruction to you to take measures to protect me, I would not be alive today." He was very emotional that day.

As early as March 1948, Mao Zedong said: "Policy and tactics are the life of the Party; leading comrades at all levels must give them full attention and must never on any account neglect them." China's history of revolution and construction has proved that a good policy that is well implemented is bound to win over people's hearts, bring together forces and accomplish things well. By the same token, an erroneous policy, or a good policy poorly implemented, or one that goes off-course in implementation, is bound to lose people's trust and support, which would lead to failure. The examples I have cited above do not mean how capable I am. They came about thanks to the good policies of the Party Central Committee, which have been carried out faithfully. Without them, nobody, no mater how talented, can achieve good fruits. If a good policy is implemented for one person, the results will be enjoyed, not by that person alone but will spread and set off a chain reaction. It will attract more people, bring together more forces and have better effects. Many people of today, young officials in particular, take less stock of policies and have little understanding of their importance. People of our generation learned a great deal from policy education. When one wrote an appraisal of a person's work, he had to quote policies first. The reason I'm saying this is that I would like to state why the Party's policies are "the life of the Party," why people "must never on any account neglect them." Chairman Mao compared policies with the life of the Party. Is there any theory more important and profound than that?

Making Revolution, Promoting Production, Work and Combat Readiness

While carrying out the political campaign to expose, repudiate and investigate crimes of the Gang of Four and their followers, reshuffling members of the leading bodies at all levels, and implementing the Party's policies concerning officials and intellectuals, we also paid great attention to promoting production, work, and combat readiness. "Making revolution, promoting production, work and combat readiness" is a historical slogan, representing the overall requirement of that age. It was laid down in Document No. 16 of the CPC. Before the Work Team set off for Shanghai, the Political Bureau members expressly pointed out: "Be careful not to affect production. Shanghai is the economic center of China, our largest industrial city. Its products, means of production and consumer demand serve the whole country. It is of vital importance for the national economy and the life of the people. The suspension of such supplies would immediately affect not just Shanghai itself, but the whole nation." Xu Liangtu, a member of the Work Team, who used to be engaged in goods supply coordination in the State Planning Commission, did a good job in planning and arranging the supply to Shanghai of grain, fuel and raw materials from the rest of the country. Members of the Work Team came from various ministries and commissions, and in case of any need, they would call the relevant ministries and commissions for help. Generally speaking, all our requirements were satisfied. So in the period when the Work Team worked in Shanghai, neither production nor the life of the people were affected. I remember that at one meeting held jointly by the Work Team and the new Shanghai Municipal Party Committee, Peng Chong repeatedly stressed that we should regularly review for the presence of any instability factors. The most important issue was the supply of grain and coal. Without coal, industries would collapse. Without grain, people would go hungry. So it was imperative to review from time to time the amount of grain and coal remaining in Shanghai, how long they would last and how long it would take to transport in grain and coal from outside. Relevant information should be publicly released at relevant meetings. In case of emergency, we were to raise the issue as soon as possible, allowing enough time for transport, to avoid interruption of supplies.

Apart from production, the Work Team also appointed dedicated people to be responsible for assisting capital construction and key projects. Shanghai Petroleum & Chemical Plant was Shanghai's key project, as well as one of the national key projects. However, because of interference and disruption by the Gang of Four, there were many quality problems. The ethylene facility could not be used. The auxiliary acrylic fiber factory, the largest support project using domestic technology, could not be put in place. Product quality was not up to standard and its goods inventory kept on growing. The Work Team sent Li Zhengguang, Vice Minister of Textile Industry, to lead a small group to the plant. They worked in the workshops, did a lot of investigation, strengthened management and labor discipline, and improved technologies. Their work was thorough and detailed. Only a few months later, production began to get back on the right track and management was standardized. Shanghai Petroleum & Chemical Plant was later cited as a role model in the importation of foreign equipment and technology specified in the "Four-three Plan."

Shanghai's economic activities were put on the right track, and the materials needed by Shanghai streamed in without interruption from all parts of the country. Goods from Shanghai were transported to wherever they were needed in other parts of the country. The followers of the Gang of Four had created panic buying of towels and matches in the hope of distracting people's attention from the struggle against the Gang of Four. The Work Team quickly transferred such goods from Jiangsu and Zhejiang; adequate supplies made that scheme fall flat and the market soon became normal. We spent our first Chinese New Year in Shanghai in early 1977. Supplies on the market had never been so good in years. Li Xiannian's nurse was a native of Shanghai. That year, she returned home for the New Year. When Li asked her about the market in Shanghai, she told him that that year was the best of many years. Li asked her what men in the street were saying about the situation in Shanghai. She replied that they were all very happy, apart from the scarcity of large yellow croaker. Shanghai people had the custom of eating large yellow croaker on the New Year, but because of over fishing the output of this species had dropped remarkably. That was why supplies were inadequate.

Through concerted effort, by the end of 1977, the overall economic situation in Shanghai had recovered. Its gross domestic product was 9.5 percent higher than in 1976, breaking records since the advent of the "Cultural Revolution." The major indicators are listed in Table 3.

Table 3 Shanghai's major economic indicators in 1977

Name	Unit	1977	Growth over 1976 (%)
GDP	1 billion *yuan*	23.036	9.5
Total foreign trade volume	US$ 1 billion	2.321	10.4
Revenue	1 billion *yuan*	15.991	10.7

Output of major industrial products			
Steel	1,000 tons	4,090.4	9.4
Finished steel products	1,000 tons	3,037.9	8.2
Cloth	1 billion meters	1.404	3.6
Chemical fiber	1,000 tons	69.5	75.5
Watches	1,000	5,100.7	23.5
Bicycles	1,000	2,812.7	13.1
Sewing-machines	1,000	1,641.8	9.9

Before May Day 1977, under the leadership of the new Shanghai Municipal Party Committee, the Work Team had reorganized the leading bodies, wrested back the power of the Party and the government from the followers of the Gang of Four, smoothly carried out the campaign to expose, repudiate and investigate crimes of the Gang of Four and its remnants, and basically accomplished the mission of "solving problems and stabilizing Shanghai." Shanghai got back on its normal track. On the evening of April 14, the Work Team convened a meeting. Ni Zhifu, Peng Chong and Lin Hujia announced that members of the Work Team might withdraw from the groups, offices and bureaus of the Municipal Party Committee and the Revolutionary Committee where the new leading body had been formed and the political campaign was going on smoothly. The day before May Day, most of the members of the Work Team left Shanghai and returned to their respective units. Before long, Lin Hujia was transferred to Tianjin, Yan Youmin to Anhui Province and Mao Lianjue to Beijing. Finally the only remaining members of the Work Team left in Shanghai were Zhao Xingzhi (sent by the Ministry of Foreign Affairs to be in charge of foreign affairs, later appointed Secretary of the Shanghai Municipal Party Committee, Vice Mayor of Shanghai) and myself, as well as Zhao Zhenqing from the Organization Department of the Central Committee of the

CPC (later Deputy Head of the Organization Department).

We worked at full stretch for a period of 200 days—October 9, 1976 when the Work Team entered Shanghai to May Day, 1977 when most members of the Work Team withdrew from the city. Every morning, we got up at six or seven and went to bed after midnight. Full of energy, we worked day and night for 200 days on the run—an unforgettable memory. It was also the 200-day historical period in which we routed out the followers of the Gang of Four in Shanghai. Why were we so united, so devoted to our work? The reason is that we all hated the evil doings of the Gang of Four and were exultant at their downfall and the end of the "Cultural Revolution." We yearned to put right what was wrong and burned with desire to make up for lost time.

On March 18, 2004, I invited Xie Hongsheng, Lu Wanzhang, Wang Jinguang, Xu Zheng, Zheng Dingquan, Zhou Pengnian, Ling Jinliang, all members of the Work Team, to a forum. Xie Hongsheng had been a Red Army man in the war days; all the others were veteran revolutionaries too. Our reminiscences showed that we all shared the following points for our success.

One: earnestly and steadily implementing policies. Document No. 16 and Su Zhenhua both stressed that we must take care to win over the majority, strictly differentiating those directly involved in the conspiracy to usurp the Party from those who were hoodwinked and therefore made mistakes. The members of the Work Team stuck to the Party's policies and did their utmost to avoid widening the punishment net. After the political campaign, there had been no aftermath. Wang Jinguang gave an example. At the end of 1976, the faction that had protected Su Zhenhua in the Navy headquarters during the "Cultural Revolution" sent a few people to Shanghai, hoping to seize a few men who had denounced and disgraced Su in public and were now working in the Shanghai Music Conservatory and take them to Beijing for retaliation. After discussion, the Work Team members decided to prevent them from doing so, rather than consenting so as to ingratiate themselves with Su. Indeed the members persuaded them to go back by reasoning based on policies, and categorically turned down their request to take people away. Su learned about this later and agreed with the decision made by the members concerned, saying that it was absolutely right to refuse the Navy headquarters people to detain other people at will.

Two: trusting and relying on the people. All those present at the forum said that the working class and the local residents of Shanghai were really nice and kind-hearted people. Though many of them had been persecuted, detained, beaten up or even injured during the "Cultural Revolution," after the fall of the Gang of Four, they had not punished those opponents in retaliation for harm or injury done to them. They said that they regarded the downfall of the Gang of Four as the "second liberation." They devoted themselves to production and work. Xu Zheng told us that once she had led a few colleagues to Shanghai Chemical Fiber Plant. The moment they entered, they were mobbed by almost a thousand workers and could not move. So she said at the top of her voice: "You all want the Work Team to enter the plant. Now we are here. How can we work if you keep us here?" A few simple words dispersed the crowd at once. Actually there were a few would-be troublemakers, but seeing they had nothing to gain, they had to leave, crest-fallen. Xu Zheng still remembered the scene many years later. "The workers were really nice to us," she said.

Three: carrying out all kinds of work under the unified leadership of the Party. The members of the Work Team did not replace others doing administrative work; we did not allow the practice of "kicking aside the Party committee to make revolution" that had prevailed during the "Cultural Revolution." If a Party committee was incapable, we gave help; if it needed to be reformed, it was simply reformed; if the head of the Party committee needed to be removed, he was simply removed by following the appropriate procedure. It was precisely because we stuck to this principle that we ensured normal order for all entities. All work in an entity was carried out in an orderly manner under the unified leadership of the Party committee.

At the forum, we all recalled those unforgettable days with deep feeling. The guiding principle of the Party Central Committee was to solve problems and stabilize Shanghai. That was in the mind of each member of the Work Team. Lu Wanzhang said: "All we did was to observe the Party policies, rely on the masses, liberate the good people, throw out the bad apples." The overall situation of Shanghai was formed by the actual work of each entity. Once we had done a good job in a place assigned by the Work Team, we had made our contribution to ensuring that Shanghai would pass smoothly into a new historical age.

Chapter III

New China's Third Round Large-scale Importation of Complete Sets of Technology and Equipment and the Construction of Shanghai Baoshan Iron and Steel Company

- The Macro-economic Situation and Implementation of the Plan
- Background to the Decision, the Construction Process and Demonstration Effect of Shanghai Baoshan Steel
- The Great Success and Lessons of the Importation

The third round large-scale importation of complete sets of technology and equipment represented another major and concentrated effort by the Chinese Government to bring in complete sets of equipment after the "Four-three Plan" implemented in the first half of the 1970s. Subsequently China started to implement the reform and the opening-up policy, signaling the end of this kind of importation, which had been characterized by centralized decision-making by the Party Central Committee, unified planning and examination by the State Planning Commission and the importation of whole sets of equipment undertaken by the various Chinese ministries. Instead, the importations were done individually, by sole ownership, joint venture or cooperative production importers.

Between November 1976 and February 1983, I held a succession of posts— member of the Standing Committee of the Shanghai Municipal Party Committee, Deputy Director of Shanghai Revolutionary Committee, Deputy Secretary of Shanghai Municipal Party Committee and Standing Vice Mayor of Shanghai. I also acted as Secretary of the Party committee and Political Commissar of the headquarters for the construction of Shanghai Baoshan Iron and Steel Company and headed the leading group of Phase 2 construction of Shanghai Petroleum & Chemical Plant. In March 1983, I was assigned to Beijing to be in charge of building the China National Petrochemical Company and was made its General Manager in July that year. In October 1990, I was reassigned to become Director of the State Commission for Restructuring the Economy (SCRE). The period when I was working first in Shanghai and then in the China National Petrochemical Company coincided with the time that contracts were being carried out for the 22 major projects under the third large-scale importation. I was involved in leading the installation and management of nine of these projects, namely: the Shanghai Baoshan Iron and Steel Company, Phase

2 of Shanghai Petroleum & Chemical Plant; four 300,000-ton ethylene facilities for Daqing, Qilu, Yangzi and Shanghai respectively; three chemical fertilizer facilities for Zhenhai, Yinchuan and Urumqi respectively, with yearly production capacities of 300,000-ton synthetic ammonia and 520,000-ton urea each.

The third round large-scale importation of complete sets of equipment enriched, promoted and raised the level of China's opening-up to the world and her domestic reforms. It accelerated China's industrial modernization, establishing a new pattern for intensifying the progress of heavy chemical industry and thereafter moved this basic industry of China onto a new level.

The Macro-economic Situation and Implementation of the Plan

During the ten-year turmoil of the "Cultural Revolution," ultra-leftism and anarchism were rampant and the Gang of Four caused serious disruption and sabotage to China's economic work. By 1976, the year that the Gang of Four was finally crushed, the entire national economy was on the verge of total collapse. The combined output of China's industry and agriculture had grown by only 1.7 percent from the previous year, that of agriculture falling by 0.4 percent and industrial output rising by only 2.4 percent, not to mention the serious shortage of market commodities. When the Gang of Four was overthrown at one swoop in October 1976 and the "Cultural Revolution" was over, the entire Chinese nation felt the keen pain of the wasted years and the heavy losses in all areas. People were eager to make up for lost time and speed up the modernization of the nation. Hence the guiding ideology for all China at the time failed to start from the actual difficult situation after the "Cultural Revolution," but rushed into putting things right fast, carried away by the mood of going all out as soon as possible. In December 1976, China's State Council held the Second National Conference of Learning from Dazhai[3] and made the decision to develop at least one third of all counties on the Dazhai model and to achieve basic agricultural mechanization in the whole country by the year 1980.

By 1977, China's economic situation was improving and each major target quota in the national economy was going well. The GNP grew by 7.6 percent compared with 1976 and outputs for 52 of the 80 main industrial products surpassed their highest-ever recorded levels. In its "Report on the Industrial Production in the First Six Months of 1977" to all government departments and regions, the State Council announced that the economic recovery of the first six months of 1977 symbolized "a new leap forward situation emerging in our national economy." It was precisely because of this over-optimistic assessment that all government departments and regions started vying with each other to draw up their own "New Leap Forward" plans. On October 29, 1977, reporting to the Political Bureau on its long-term coal production development plan, the Ministry of Coal Industry claimed that they would "manage to reach unprecedented speed" to achieve the production of two billion tons of coal by the end of the 20th century. The Ministry of Metallurgical Industry reported to the Central Party Political Bureau on November 9, 1977, that their long-term plan for iron and steel manufacture was to build more than 20 steel bases as large as Anshan Steel. The Political Bureau forwarded the "Summarized Points of the National Economic Plan" by the SPC on February 5, 1978. The summarized points proposed the development of 10 big oil-gas fields, and the building of 10 large iron and steel bases, nine large non-ferrous metal bases, 10 large chemical fiber plants, 10 large petrochemical works and others, in addition to the construction of 14 large heavy industry

---

3. Dazhai, a village located in Xiyang County of north China's Shanxi Province, became famous throughout China in the early 1960s after its villagers created high-yield terraced farmland out of barren hillsides and won praises from late Chairman Mao Zedong. It was held up as a fine example in China's agricultural sector for more than 10 years.

bases across the country on the basis of integrating existing enterprises. The SPC summary stated that China would achieve overall modernization and move her economy to the front ranks of the world by the year 2000.

In order to realize these grand "leap forward" goals in economic construction, the central Party and national leaders of the day took the view that it would not be enough to rely on Chinese strength only, but that the nation would need overseas funding to buy advanced equipment from foreign manufacturers on a massive scale. Authorized by the Party Central Committee in February 1978, the SPC formulated a plan for the State Council in which it proposed the importation of 68 or 69 complete sets of equipment over the following eight years. The first batch of 45 would be completed in 1978 at US$ six billion. The second batch of 23 or 24 lines at US$ eight billion was set to complete in 1979 and 1980. In total, the two batches of imported facilities together with their supplementary parts, main machines and patent payments would cost US$ 18 billion of our foreign exchange. Taking into account the domestic cost of installations and construction, the total investment required 130 billion *yuan*. The complete sets of equipment to be brought in under the importation plan would be proposed by ministries and departments including those of coal, electrical power, petroleum, metallurgy, chemical industry, light industry, textile industry, the No. 1 Ministry of Machinery Industry, building materials, transportation, railways, defense, geology, construction, post and telecommunications, farming and forestry, water conservation and the Chinese Academy of Science.

According to its 1978 files, the China National Technology Import and Export Co. responsible for the actual importation work made 45 purchase agreements for complete sets of equipment in 1978, fulfilling the first batch of the quota set by the SPC. However, the total cost of the purchases amounted to US$ 8.559 billion, exceeding the original estimate of US$ six billion. Besides, another batch of smaller production lines, machines and technical programs were also purchased at a cost of US$ four billion. About 80 percent of the total cost, about US$ six billion, of the purchase agreements signed in 1978 went on the importation of large-scale facilities. Known later as the "22 large projects," they comprised: three 300,000-ton ethylene facilities for Shanghai Baoshan Iron and Steel Company and Daqing Petroleum and Chemical Plant and Qilu Petroleum and Chemical Plant respectively; two 300,000-ton ethylene facilities for Nanjing; one 110,000-ton essential ethylene facility for Jilin Chemical Industry Co. (a postponed project from 1972's "Four-three Plan"); three 300,000-ton synthetic ammonia and 520,000-ton urea facilities for Zhejiang Zhenhai Refinery, Xinjiang Urumqi Refinery and Ningxia Yinchuan Petroleum and Chemical Plant respectively; one 300,000-ton synthetic ammonia facility using coal as the raw material for Shanxi Chemical Fertilizer Plant; a hundred sets of coal mining equipment; copper mining plant for Dexing; the Guizhou Aluminum Plant; the Chemical Fiber Phase Two for Shanghai Petroleum & Chemical Plant; the Yizheng Chemical Fiber Plant; the Pingdingshan Tire Cord Plant; the Shandong Synthetic Leather Factory; the Lanzhou Synthetic Leather Factory; the Yunnan Sodium Phosphate Project; the Huolinhe Coal Mine; the Kailuan Coal Mine; the Shaanxi Xianyang Color Television Tube Production Line.

The Third Plenary Session of the 11th Central Committee of the Party was held in Beijing during December 18-22, 1978. The conference decided to shift the Party's focus to the modern construction of socialism from 1979 on. The resolution stated that as a result of the long years of sabotage by Lin Biao and the Gang of Four, serious imbalances in the national economy were waiting to be put right. Chaotic phenomena in the fields of production, construction, circulation and distribution had to be eliminated completely. The raft of problems that had accumulated gradually over the years in our cities and countryside had to be resolved in the coming few years. As regards the "Leap Forward" situation emerging in the economic field, the conference emphasized overall balance had to be maintained and basic construction carried out in a positive but cautious and orderly manner. The conference discussed issues of economic planning and how to increase agricultural output in 1979 and 1980, and made significant decisions as regards how to implement the economic reform and opening-up policy. The conference pointed out that China must, first and foremost, rely on her own efforts before going in for economic cooperation with other countries based on the principle of equality and mutual benefit. China must strive to use the world's vanguard technologies and equipment and strengthen the scientific research and education required by the modernization.

At a Political Bureau meeting discussing the national plan for 1979 on March 21, 1979, Chen Yun referred to four viewpoints: "1) We must be realistic in carrying out the four modernizations. 2) Balanced development is the fastest development. It has been proven that emphasis solely on steel cannot be sustained long term. The development won't last if we rely solely on foreign loans rather than stick to balanced development. 3) Let's adjust our situation over three years. Our national economy is out of balance now, much more seriously even than in 1961-1962. 4) It will be OK if we can take steel output up to 80 million tons by 2000; the focus must be on the quality and variety of steel products, rather than quantity." Deng Xiaoping pointed out: "Our central task currently is adjustment. First and foremost we must be resolute. It will not do to try to take care of everything everywhere. In the past we used to set our targets on grain and steel production, but now it is time to absorb those lessons. The industrial level of a nation cannot be determined by steel only. We should reduce our target quota for steel production in order to do other things too." As a result, the meeting decided to adjust the national economy over three years, and the Central Work Conference made the further decision to adopt the measure of "adjustment, reform, reorganization and enhancement" in the national economic work in April 1979.

The 22 large importation projects signed up in 1978 became the key objects for economic adjustment in 1979. At the time when these agreements were being negotiated and signed with foreign manufacturers in 1978, China had been over-eager to bring in as much advanced equipment as possible and this penchant had led to overwhelming purchases far in excess of what we could then afford. In 1977, when the decision was made to import large-scale and complete facilities from overseas, China's entire financial revenue was but 87.4 billion *yuan*. Our total export earning was a mere US$ 7.6 billion and our total investment in capital construction was only 38.2 billion *yuan*. Set against the US$ 18 billion of foreign exchange planned for the importation and the 130 billion *yuan* needed for installing them, the disparity was simply too great. It was just not realistic to hope to borrow money from overseas either, given the inadequacy of our domestic budget. Neither China's commodity resources for exported goods nor our foreign exchange could rocket immediately. China did not have the ability to repay the debt in a limited time. As time went on, the difficulty of importing the 22 complete sets of equipment became increasingly obvious. One policy fault after another showed up in various aspects and the Chinese Government was forced to make essential adjustments. Some projects were reduced in scale; contracts were partially cancelled in others. Some were postponed; in others, negotiations in progress stopped. There were four categories of adjustment pertaining to the 22 projects, as outlined below.

Category One: those projects whose importation agreements were completed and implementation already underway in 1978. There were nine such projects basically unaffected by the 1979 adjustment. For example, the 100 coal mining lines had all their equipment shipped in July 1980 and were installed and commissioned gradually. The Shaanxi Xianyang color television tube line (annual output of 640,000 14-inch tubes and 320,000 22-inch tubes) started formal production as scheduled in 1982. The electrolytic aluminum production line (annual capacity 80,000 tons) for Guizhou Aluminum Plant was installed and put into production in 1982, basically on schedule. The Yunnan Sodium Phosphate Project was completed in 1984, after a postponement due to adjustment of the factory site. Also belonging in this category were the synthetic leather facility for Shandong Synthetic Leather Factory (annual output 3,000,000 sq. m.) and the big chemical fertilizer facility for Zhenhai Refinery (annual output 300,000 tons of synthetic ammonia and 520,000 tons of urea).

Category Two: those for which agreements were basically signed in 1978 but had their installation postponed because of the economic adjustment. The installation and operation of the big chemical fertilizer line for the Urumqi Refinery (using heavy oil as raw material and with an annual capacity of 300,000 tons of synthetic ammonia and 520,000 tons of urea) was delayed until 1986; for the big chemical fertilizer project for the Yinchuan Chemical Plant, it was 1992. The Shanxi Chemical Fertilizer Plant using coal as raw material and with annual capacity of 300,000 tons of synthetic ammonia and 900,000 tons of nitric phosphate was postponed to 1988, when it was finally completed and put into operation.

Category Three: those projects whose importation agreements were only partially signed in 1978 but for which the remaining agreement signing and basic construction were postponed due to the economic adjustment. Some had their importation plan modified. In all, there were nine projects in this category and they constituted the main body of the 22 importation projects. How they were adjusted is described below:

Shanghai Baoshan Iron and Steel Company was the largest of the 22 importation projects. The total investment planned for Phase 1 and Phase 2 of construction of Baoshan Steel was set at 30.17 billion *yuan* including foreign exchange of US$ 4.78 billion. The two phases were originally planned for completion in 1982 and 1984 respectively, but because of the "stop and pause" adjustment plan, their completions were delayed until 1985 and 1991 respectively. Furthermore, a significant revision was made to the execution mode of Phase 2. Rather than importing the entire facility, the method of importation was changed to purchasing the manufacturing techniques for the main equipment or co-producing the equipment with foreign producers on condition that its technical level must not be inferior to that of Phase 1. This change to the importation method met the requirement for "China to have a basic foothold in the design and manufacture."

Six importation projects consisting of four 300,000-ton ethylene facilities and ancillary plant (one at Daqing Petroleum and Chemical Plant, one at Qilu Petroleum and Chemical Plant and two for siting in Nanjing), Phase 2 of Shanghai Petroleum & Chemical Plant (200,000-ton polyester) and the synthetic fiber facility (530,000-ton polyester and ancillary plant for Yizheng Chemical Fiber Plant were originally scheduled to complete in 1981 and 1982. Due to the economic adjustment, all six projects were listed either as stopped or delayed, with the exception of the polyester line at Shanghai Petroleum & Chemical Plant. Of these, the final destination of the two 300,000-ton ethylene facilities initially placed at Nanjing could not be determined and all sides were fighting to get them. It was only after the China National Petrochemical Company was founded and Kang Shi'en, Li Renjun and I reported to the main State Council leader on the issue, that the decision was made to give one set of facilities to the Shanghai Petroleum & Chemical Plant, the other remaining in Nanjing for the newly established Yangtze Petroleum & Chemical Company. Besides this, the original plan of importing a polyester short fiber drawing facility for Yizheng Chemical Fiber Plant was altered to importing the main equipment and manufacturing techniques only. The rest was to be made in China.

The large Huolinhe Open-cut Coal Mine had been designed with whole set of imported equipment for annual output of 20 million tons, at an estimated cost of US$ 550 million. Only a preliminary agreement for the foreign vendor's technical service and the purchase of a small-scale peeling line had been signed in 1978. After 1979, the construction plan underwent a radical revision, in which annual output was reduced to seven million tons. The original plan for importing the complete production facility was also cancelled. Instead, its main equipment line would be made in China once the relevant mechanical organization had imported the machine manufacturing technology and become capable of doing the work. As a result, the first and second phases of the Huolinhe Coal Mine were completed in 1984 and 1992 respectively. Kailuan Coal Mine had been authorized to import three four-million-ton coal washing facilities for Fangezhuang, Qianjiaying and another of its coal washing plants in 1978. Even if a part of the agreement had been signed in the same year, the importation and installation of all the facilities were postponed until 1989 except the one destined for Fangezhuang.

Dexing Copper Base in Jiangxi Province was a large comprehensive project, designed to reach annual production of 200,000 tons of copper within five years. The importation agreement to provide a complete line of copper smelting equipment at Guixi Smelting Plant and technical service was signed in 1978, providing for production of 90,000 tons of blister copper a year and ore extraction of 173,000 tons a day. In the adjustment, the original scale was reduced and work on the importation slowed down so the project was not completed until 1985.

Category four: this consisted of one project cancelled in toto—the Lanzhou Synthetic Leather Plant—since the conditions were unsuitable for the designed project.

Background to the Decision, the Construction Process and Demonstration Effect of Shanghai Baoshan Steel

Shanghai Baoshan Steel, one of the 22 complete facilities planned for importation at the time, was the largest industrial project China had ever imported. The dramatic ups and downs during the process of its importation and installation stirred both international attention and fierce controversy within China. It was also the project that commanded the greatest attention and energy on the part of the central leadership. Yao Yilin told me on more than one occasion that Baoshan Steel touched the heart of the whole nation. After Baoshan Steel was founded, it eclipsed all others in terms of scale, enormous investment, advanced technologies, high product quality and variety, and management science. Its scientific and modern concept of enterprise management conforms to the requirements of the market economy. All this has created a widespread and profound demonstration effect on the iron and steel enterprises and even the entire panorama of modern industries in China.

(1) Background of the decision to build Baoshan Steel

By the end of the 1970s, the guiding ideology of going all out to achieve quick success was dominating China's economic work and stimulating all government departments and regions. People were vying with each other to obtain complete sets of equipment so as to intensify the development of their departments or regions. The decision to construct Baoshan Steel was made in the same general context. The shortage of pig iron supply had long handicapped the iron and steel industry in Shanghai, which was why the SPC, the Metallurgy Ministry and Shanghai City were eager to solve this major problem by bringing in complete sets of facilities from abroad. This was the specific context in which the decision to build the Baoshan Steel Base was made.

Well known for its high quality and large product variety, the Shanghai iron and steel industry was an important base for supplying China with steel materials. However, due to the shortage of pig iron, Shanghai could not play its role to the full. For example, in 1976, Shanghai produced 3.76 million tons of steel products that consumed 3.08 million tons of pig iron. However, Shanghai itself could provide only 917,000 tons of pig iron, less than a third of what it consumed for its steel production. The other two thirds, or 2.16 million tons, of pig iron were taken from other iron and steel complexes such as Anshan Steel, Benxi Steel, Ma'anshan Steel and Wuhan Iron and Steel Works. Diverting pig iron from these steel bases meant reducing both their steel production and their profits. So the task of sourcing pig iron was very difficult and it became increasingly so, not to mention the cost of transporting the pig iron to Shanghai and the large amount of coke used to melt these iron materials. It was a real economic waste. Hence, the SPC and the Metallurgy Ministry were trying hard to find a solution to the iron supply problem for Shanghai steel industry. After the Work Team sent by the CPC Central Committee arrived in Shanghai, Lin Hujia took charge of Shanghai's economic work; the effort to get the needed pig iron for Shanghai caused him many difficulties. At Lin's request, the SPC and the Metallurgy Ministry sent a planning group to Shanghai in April 1977 to investigate the case and try to find a solution.

In June 1977, in response to the group's investigation report and suggestions, the Metallurgy Ministry decided to build two 2,500-cubic-meter blast furnaces in Shanghai to help relieve the urgent need for pig iron.

In September 1977, Ye Zhiqiang, Vice Minister of the Metallurgy Ministry, led a delegation of the Chinese Metal Academic Society (including members from the SPC) to visit Japan for the purpose of inspecting Japan's iron and steel industry. There the delegation visited in total 12 iron and steel complexes, focusing its attention on those steel plants belonging to Nippon Steel Corp. (hereafter abbreviated to "Nippon Steel"). On its return, the delegation wrote an inspection report to the State Council describing the development of the iron and steel industry they had studied in Japan. The report said that Japan's steel output had been 22 million tons in 1960 but had soared to 119 million tons in 1973, growing by a factor of 2.5 in 13 years. Around the same time, in 1960, China had made 18.66 million tons of steel, not too far removed from Japan's output. However, in 1973, China's annual steel output still lingered at 25.22 million tons, not even a fifth of Japan's steel output 13 years later. While Japan had more than quadrupled its steel output in 13 years, Chinese output had grown by only 35 percent, or a mere 6.56 million tons, in all that time. The stark contrast showed up the great distance between the steel industries of the two countries. The delegation's report pointed out that Japan's main measure was to import ore, coal and petroleum, buy and absorb new technologies and equipment from around the world to achieve the up-scaling of its steel-making equipment, continuous manufacturing and automation of its steel and iron industry. At the same time, by paying particular attention to the training of steel technicians and workers, Japan achieved labor productivity 10 times that of China for only half of the energy consumption. Therefore, Japan's superb product quality and low cost not only strengthened her competitiveness vis-à-vis the iron and steel enterprises of Europe and the USA, but they also helped enhance other industries such as machinery, shipbuilding and automobile manufacturing. The delegation's report also claimed that since the petroleum crisis in 1973, a worldwide economic depression had appeared. All the major steel enterprises in Japan were unable to operate at full capacity, were eager to find a way out and wanted to export their technologies and equipment. The report, therefore, suggested that China should grasp this opportunity to bring in certain new essential technologies and equipment to help boost our national iron and steel industry. Before the delegation left for home, Nippon Steel gave them a set of films and slides showing the production and construction of its Kimitsu and Oita Steel Works. The State Council leaders read the delegation's report and watched the visual materials, feeling that Japan's experience was worth our learning. Later I managed to borrow these films and slides for Shanghai and show them to Shanghai Party and government officials. The Chinese delegation's Japan visit had a direct influence on the decision-making of constructing the Baoshan Steel Base. In October 1978, Deng Xiaoping visited Japan and he too went to see the Kimitsu Steel Works under Nippon Steel. There he told Yoshihiro Inayama, President of Nippon Steel and Saito Eishiro, the General Manager accompanying him on his visit to Kimitsu Steel Works: "Build a steel plant for us just like this one."

Shanghai badly needed pig iron for its steel production and was particularly eager to build a big iron smelter. When the nation was considering importing complete sets of equipment and technologies, Shanghai Municipal Party Committee saw this as a rare opportunity and was determined to get one for Shanghai. Su Zhenhua, Ni Zhifu, Peng Chong, Lin Hujia and I all went to talk to the central leaders, expressing our strong wish for an imported facility. We won strong support from the SPC, the State Economic Commission, the State Construction Commission and the Metallurgy Ministry. At the time, quite a number of provinces and cities were fighting to get some of these large projects.

The State Council sent a special work team to inspect the situation and, after thorough and comprehensive investigation and balancing, decided to install the first imported project in Shanghai. The facts were later to prove this a sound decision. Shanghai had many advantages over other places for the building of a large-scale, integrated iron and steel complex. First, Shanghai had good market conditions. It could provide matching trades of mechanical and electrical engineering, shipbuilding and automobile manufacturing in Shanghai itself, eastern China and particularly Zhejiang and Jiangsu provinces. These close-at-hand supplies could greatly reduce the costs of transportation and consumption, making it conducive to enlarging the social and economic benefits. Second, Shanghai had good transportation conditions. A large-scale integrated steel complex with an annual output of several million tons would require tremendous freight volumes. The ratio of its output to crude fuel consumption was 1: 3.4. Shipping by water would keep transportation costs to a minimum. Building the steel complex on the Yangtze River Delta in Shanghai would be right on a major river and by the sea, making both internal and overseas water-borne transportation extremely convenient and economical. Thirdly, one important factor I particularly emphasized was that a world-class large steel enterprise of the late 1970s such as Baoshan Steel must have a roughly matching social environment in order to help it operate normally. Otherwise, it would be hard for the steel complex to achieve its target of speedy introduction, assimilation and innovation and it might even fail to reach its design capacity for ages. Being the largest industrial city in China, Shanghai possessed comparatively more comprehensive and satisfactory conditions in terms of material and technical foundations, personnel, management and knowledge base. Shanghai should be able to undertake such a heavy responsibility. In May 1979, Chen Yun went to inspect the site for Baoshan Steel. He expressed a special concern for the human quality of Baoshan's people and inquired carefully about the project's auxiliary elements. I told him we had also been pretty worried about this subject. We knew that the 1,700 mm sheet rolling mills imported for Wuhan Iron and Steel Works had not met its design level after starting operation. It wasn't that the rolling mills were not good enough but that the quantity and quality of Wuhan Iron and Steel Works' steel billets did not match the requirements of the new rolling mills. With this, plus problems in external conditions of electrical supply and other aspects, the advanced equipment imported from overseas had finally failed to play its expected role to the full. Chen Yun then asked about the 10,000-ton hydraulic compressor at Shanghai. I said it faced the same challenge of getting the matching auxiliary elements. It had been a great event when Shanghai relied on its own strength to build the 12,000-ton hydraulic compressor. However, precisely because Shanghai had not tackled the issue of getting corresponding auxiliary elements, the compressor could operate only at 20 percent capacity and had failed to play its anticipated role for a long time. For such a large project as Baoshan Steel, we had spent so much money on the main part already, and we must do a good job in getting the right auxiliary elements for it so we could display its superiority and recover our investment in full. Chen Yun agreed with me. In fact, it was not just the case with Baoshan Steel, but location selection for all other large imported projects must also take into account supporting conditions.

Comrade Bo Yibo visited Shanghai in March 1981, his first visit to Shanghai since the downfall of the Gang of Four. I accompanied him during his visit and he was very pleased after his inspection of the Shanghai Petroleum & Chemical Plant at Jinshan. The plant was one of the projects erected during the early 1970s as part of New China's second round of large-scale importation of complete sets of equipment. Although constructed during the "Cultural Revolution," it was designed for annual output of 115,000 tons of ethylene, related plastics and chemical fiber and had operated smoothly since construction. Bo

Yibo was very satisfied about its work, feeling that its construction, production and management had all been done well. He asked me: "Jin-hua, several other projects were imported together with the facilities at Shanghai Petroleum & Chemical Plant at the time. Why did the other projects fail to operate smoothly or meet their design targets for a long time?" I replied: "Apart from the varying degrees of interference and sabotage by the Gang of Four and their followers around the country, a very important reason was that in many places the ancillary elements did not meet the requirements of production. Those projects reflected the highest level technologies of the early 1970s and they required basically matching conditions to accommodate their smooth operations. These conditions included supply of raw materials, supplementary materials, equipment, spare parts, machine maintenance, technical service and all kinds of professionals and managers, as well as suitable markets and social services. All these conditions must be in place and combine to create an overall fine environment to guarantee the smooth construction and production of these projects. Should any of the conditions fail to meet those requirements, a project would be delayed or fail to operate smoothly. In the chemical fiber projects in which I myself was involved, the combined conditions of Liaoning, Tianjin and Sichuan were all unsatisfactory so the projects in these places were all prolonged. Shanghai, on the other hand, was dramatically different. Being the most important industrial city of China, Shanghai enjoyed an advantageous location by a major river and the sea and a good market environment. These favorable factors could play positive roles in the smooth completion of Shanghai Petroleum & Chemical Plant. At the same time, the technical and service level of tens of hundreds of Shanghai enterprises were improved through their assisting the construction and the production of the most advanced petrochemical plant at the time. They learned to do things they had not previously known and improved in areas where they had previously failed. So a fine interaction mechanism was formed through the coordination. Though it did not have to come from Shanghai to be successful, if other places failed to do a good job, made things expensive, failed to provide satisfactory service or fulfill a task on time, buyers would certainly feel dissatisfied and unwilling to use products made in those other places." Bo Yibo agreed with my comment and felt what I said made sense.

In late November 1977, the SPC, the Metallurgy Ministry and the Ministry of Foreign Trade jointly composed the "Report on Introducing New Technology and Equipment and Accelerating Iron and Steel Development" to the State Council, proposing a "rush to build the Shanghai Iron Works," "plan to import two 4,000-cubic-meter blast furnaces," "import Australian ore until we can find domestic ore" and "plan to build the first blast furnace by 1980." The report was approved by the State Council with the instruction to "focus primarily on our exports and try to save foreign exchange having regard to our payment capability." On November 29 the same year, Li Xiannian received Yoshihiro Inayama, Chairman of the Japan-China Medium- and Long-term Trade Promotion Committee and President of Nippon Steel, and they discussed the cooperative construction of a large-scale steel plant. Yoshihiro Inayama responded positively to the idea. Taking this meeting as a turning point and authorized by the State Council, the Metallurgy Ministry invited a technical advisory group from Nippon Steel, to Beijing to discuss the technical issues of location, scale, products, crude fuel source and other aspects of the new plant. The Japanese advisory group headed by executive director of Nippon Steel, Ogaki Makoto, arrived in China on December 13, 1977. They spent nearly a month visiting many factories in China and finally handed over two reports: "New Technical Data of Building an Integrated Steel Plant" and "Project Plan Concerning the Site Inspection."

Following the suggestions in the Nippon Steel advisory group reports, the SPC and the Metallurgy Ministry sent a planning team to

Shanghai from mid-December 1977 to mid-January 1978 to discuss with Shanghai about building the steel plant. Gu Ming and Jin Xiying from the SPC, Xie Beiyi from the State Construction Commission, Tang Ke and Liu Xuexin from the Metallurgy Ministry, Zhou Jian'nan from No. 1 Ministry of Machinery Industry and Cui Qun from the Ministry of Foreign Trade were in the team. On January 6, 1978, the Shanghai Municipal Party Committee heard the team's formal report in the small assembly hall in the Jinjiang Hotel. Su Zhenhua, Ni Zhifu, Peng Chong, Lin Hujia, Yan Youmin, Han Zheyi and I all attended the report meeting. Liu Xuexin, Vice Minister of the Metallurgy Ministry, was the main speaker. He recommended building the large steel plant in Shanghai, talking about issues such as the new plant's location, scale and composition, its shipping route along the Yangtze River and the trans-shipment site at Lühua Hill. After hearing the reports by the team members, Su Zhenhua and other Shanghai leaders immediately expressed their support for the team's construction plan. The plan outlined mainly the construction of two 4,000-cubic-meter blast furnaces and three 300-ton converters in the new plant, setting its annual output at 6.5 million tons of pig iron, 6.71 million tons of steel and 6.04 million tons of billets. The new plant would supply 2.32 million tons of billets, 3.2 million tons of hot-rolled steel plates and 480,000 tons of seamless steel pipes to Shanghai iron and steel plants. On January 7-8, a total of 108 attendees, including Lin Hujia, Han Zheyi, Gu Ming, Tang Ke, myself and the planning team, inspected the Yangtze River route, Lühua Hill wharf and Beilun at Zhenhai in a guided-missile destroyer specifically sent by Su Zhenhua. Before long, based upon the planning team's report and with the Metallurgy Ministry taking the lead, the SPC, the State Economic Commission, the State Construction Commission, the Metallurgy Ministry and Shanghai City submitted a joint report to the Central Party Committee and the State Council asking to construct the Shanghai Steel General Plant. This was the report generally known as the "Report by three state commissions, one ministry and one city."

After the initial plan for the new steel plant was basically confirmed, I led a delegation to Japan on January 25, 1978, as Vice Director of the Chinese Metal Academic Society. Our delegation had 21 members including Li Dongye as consultant and Lu Jihua and Xu Yan as deputy heads of the delegation. At our first meeting with Yoshihiro Inayama, President of Nippon Steel, at its headquarters, he emphasized to me several times that the iron and steel industry played a central role in a nation's industrialization. If a country's basic material industry lagged behind, it would definitely affect that country's industrialization and modernization. He also stressed that China was a large country with an underdeveloped agriculture. To modernize her agriculture, China must first of all have a developed iron and steel industry. He repeatedly advocated the importance of putting the iron and steel industry in a dominant position in our national blueprint for industrialization. I told him we shared his opinion on the issue. Mao Zedong had a famous saying: "One crucial issue is the grain and the other is the steel. Whoever has a grip on these two things, nothing can stop them." We did follow this guideline in the past. Mr. Inayama commented approvingly: "Well-said, well-said!" While in Japan, we also visited Oita Steel Works, Kimitsu Steel Works and an equipment manufacturing plant in Yawata. These inspections truly opened our eyes. We were deeply impressed with the efficiency, scale, high standard and degree of automation in those large Japanese plants. I still remember today when we visited the hot rolling workshop in Oita Steel Works. There we bumped into an American metallurgy delegation including one American expert so obviously deeply stirred that he wanted to vent his feelings and engaged us in conversation: "The Japanese are incredible!   Everything we wanted but have so far failed to do—they've done it all!" In fact, we were every bit as deeply impressed as he and his colleagues. It was impossible not to feel shaken when seeing the reality there. When our delegation sat down and discussed what we should say when exchanging ideas with our Nippon Steel hosts before the conclusion of our visit, some of our experts suggested that Nippon Steel's technologies truly covered every vanguard field in the world at the time. Nevertheless, they seemed to have not yet adopted a number of the new techniques in the world such as the bell-less, coke dry quenching and smoke heat recycling. Our experts had read about these new techniques in science journals but had not yet seen the real inventions. Hence, at the wind-up meeting with our host, I raised the topic and expressed our hope that Nippon Steel could provide us with information about these new techniques. They replied that they did not currently have them either, and that they would have to buy them elsewhere if we really wanted to order them, so they could not sell us these yet. When we repeatedly pressed the point, Nippon Steel finally promised to work toward getting them to us, but they never confirmed this promise subsequently.

Yoshihiro Inayama, President of Nippon Steel played a vital role in the Sino-Japanese cooperative construction of Baoshan Steel. Enjoying very high prestige in the Japanese financial world and pushing for friendly relations between China and Japan, Mr. Inayama had been engaged in Sino-Japanese trade activities for a long time, signing a Japan-China iron and steel agreement as long ago as February 1958. But his insistence upon the two nations' friendly cooperation in constructing Baoshan Steel meant he faced huge pressure from both sides. During the "Cultural Revolution" period, Nippon Steel had cooperated with China to build a 1,700 mm continuous sheet rolling mill at Wuhan Iron and Steel Works. Wuhan was experiencing most fierce factional fighting at the time, which seriously interfered with the construction. Mr. Inayama and others at Nippon Steel had vivid memories of the destruction wrought by the "Cultural Revolution" and worried whether Baoshan Steel would run into a similar situation again. By the end of 1978, influenced by Beijing's Xidan Wall activity, many big-character posters were put up at Huaihai Road in Shanghai too. The Japanese side was concerned whether the Baoshan Steel commencement ceremony could be held on schedule. In the event, the ceremony took place punctually at Baoshan after the Third Plenary Session of the 11th Central Committee of the CPC. Mr. Inayama came to China to attend the ceremony and I greeted him at the airport. It was obvious that he was deeply affected by what had happened with the 1,700 mm continuous sheet rolling mill in Wuhan. He asked me gloomily if the same thing might happen again. I told him it should not. The Third Plenary Session of the 11th Central Committee of the CPC had decided to focus our work on economic construction and another cultural revolution would not occur. To ensure the smooth construction of Baoshan Steel, the State Council had decided to assign Han Guang, Director of the State Construction Commission, as its representative coordinating the various sides involved in the construction. Hence, I assured him, Baoshan Steel should not go through big ups and downs. Inayama just listened and nodded; I could see he was still worried. But Baoshan Steel did run into trouble before long. The Baoshan Steel project plan had to undergo adjustment and this affected Nippon Steel too. Old conflicts in Nippon Steel itself were stirred up by the issue too. (Nippon Steel Corp. was formed after World War II by merging the Yawata and Fuji steel works. Although the merger had taken place a long time before, the old conflicts between former employees of the two steel works never really disappeared. As soon as there was a problem, the old scab of controversy between the two sections would be picked at and the two sides would seize the chance to create trouble and even attack each other.) Nippon Steel held a management meeting and Ogaki Makoto was accused at the meeting. Even Mr. Inayama was affected. Despite all the troubles, Mr. Inayama bravely insisted that China would keep her promise and China's adjustment to the Baoshan Steel project was made satisfactorily. He wrote explicitly in his autobiography: "In my opinion, China's arrangement was extremely well done." He also mentioned two foreign celebrities whom he greatly admired: one was China's Premier Zhou Enlai and the other was Cuba's President Castro.

Our visit to Japan over, we flew back to Shanghai where Lin Hujia came to meet me at the airport, informing me that I had to go to Beijing the next day to attend a discussion meeting on the subject of Baoshan Steel sponsored by the State Council. The State Council meeting was chaired by Vice Premier Li Xiannian and vice premiers Yu Qiuli, Gu Mu, Fang Yi, Kang Shi'en, with quite a number of attendees. The discussion focused on the Baoshan Steel project report compiled by the SPC, the State Economic Commission, the State Construction Commission, the Metallurgy Ministry and Shanghai City. The meeting was held in three half-days. Some relevant departments raised several questions at the meeting but no one opposed the construction of Baoshan Steel itself. Finally the meeting passed the "Report by three state commissions, one ministry and one city" in principle. Later comment that Baoshan Steel was started hastily without undergoing careful scrutiny by the State Council was not true. At the meeting Lin Hujia told Li Xiannian that I had just returned from Japan and perhaps I should say something on my impressions of the Japanese iron and steel industry. So I made two points on the spot. One was that the Baoshan Steel project affected Japan widely, had aroused great attention on all sides and would exert a great influence on friendship and economic cooperation between the two countries. Doko Toshio, Chairman of the Japan Federation of Economic Organizations at the time estimated that if Japan helped China to build a large steel complex like Baoshan Steel, it would help stimulate Japan's own iron and steel industry, mechanical manufacturing and other related fields and could raise the Japanese GNP by two percent. (His remark was based on what I heard from our interpreter while in Japan, not what I had read in his original text.) Li

Xiannian paid special attention to this message. Next, I stressed the ancillary facilities for Baoshan Steel. Completing the construction process did not mean that Baoshan Steel would start production smoothly, or that it would achieve the design output target. The new Baoshan Steel must get synchronized support from all the ancillary elements. From Shandong's Xinglongzhuang Coal Mine to the refractory material plant, from electric power supply to water works, all these coordinating units must play their responsive roles without problems. In the event of delay by any work unit, there would be a big problem for the operation of Baoshan Steel. The principal production line imported from Japan was of the top standard in the world and its auxiliary needs were huge. With regards to systems engineering, the support elements must be worked on early since delay would affect the completion of Baoshan Steel construction, operation and payback on investment. The supporting parts that had to be built together with the principal facility included raw material supplies, supplementary materials, fire-proofing materials, coal, electricity, water and steam as well as wharfs, railroads, motorway, and post and telecommunications facilities. If any of these failed to operate smoothly, Baoshan Steel could not start official production or would have to reduce output and its economic performance would be poor. Li Xiannian listened to what I said and approved my opinion readily. He commented that our main problem was paying too much attention to the main production facility but often neglecting the supporting parts. Unbalanced, unsynchronized work often had implications for the operation of the entire project whenever a small problem arose.

(2) Rush to build, adjustment, return to zero, restoration and expansion

Initially, the construction of Baoshan Steel was under the joint leadership of the Metallurgy Ministry and of Shanghai City, the latter being the primary promoter. On Shanghai's part, we relied mainly on the

Shanghai Metallurgy Bureau and Shanghai No. 1, 3 and 5 Steel Works to organize the manpower and assign cadres to the construction of the steel plant; when building the support factories, we learned from previous experience in the construction of Shanghai Petroleum & Chemical Plant to sub-let tasks to corresponding bureaus in Shanghai. In order to quickly assemble the necessary human talents for the construction and to strengthen its leadership, Zhao Zhenqing, who was heading the Shanghai Organization Department and also a member of the Shanghai Party Standing Committee, volunteered at a meeting of the Standing Committee of the Shanghai Party Committee to lead the task of assembling human talents. He started work right after the meeting, borrowing office space from the Shanghai General Labor Union and calling the human resource director of each bureau concerned to draw up a list of names. When approving the candidates for Baoshan Steel construction, his office sent notices to transfer the chosen people, asking them to report to the construction site by the stated deadline and start the busy preparatory work immediately. As the project was not yet officially listed in the national plan at the time, the finance for its construction was not yet in place. So Shanghai City first put in tens of millions of *yuan* to start the demolition and relocation process, and build a batch of permanent buildings to replace the temporary large structures. Not only did we save a great deal in land usage and financial investment, but we also established a successful model for all subsequent construction of state-level and large-scale projects.

After the Party Central Committee authorized the construction of Baoshan Steel, the Shanghai Municipal Party Committee convened a mobilizing rally on March 30, 1978, at the then Leifeng Middle School. The rally was attended by all government departments, committees, districts, counties and bureaus of Shanghai at the construction site. Presiding over the rally, Peng Chong conveyed the instructions from the Party Central Committee and mobilized all trades and branches in

Shanghai to give the green light to the construction of Baoshan Steel. He asked everyone to provide full support to Baoshan in human, physical, financial and other resources and to contribute whatever would be needed. He also emphasized the great significance of the Baoshan Steel project for the future of Shanghai industry and the several eastern Chinese provinces in terms of their machine production, steel and iron manufacturing and transportation. I also spoke at the rally, telling people: "We have a gold hill (Jinshan—the location of Shanghai Petroleum & Chemical Plant) in the south of Shanghai and a treasure hill (Baoshan Steel) in the north. The two treasure hills will create and accumulate wealth for Shanghai's 'Four Modernizations' and turn into real hills of gold and treasure." This mobilizing rally displayed the strong leadership of the Shanghai Municipal Party Committee and the superiority of industrial Shanghai in centralizing all its efforts to coordinate this large construction project. After the rally, all the builders' troops went quickly to their posts and the early stage of the construction went full steam ahead. Right after the mobilizing rally, members of the Standing Committee of the Shanghai Municipal Party Committee met overnight to discuss the issue of land expropriation and decided to "draft 10,000 mu (a unit of measurement equal to 1/15 of a hectare) [=667 hectares] in a single authorization and to use the approved land piece by piece" and to "base the speed of appropriation and relocation on the actual progress of construction." The meeting also decided to build Yuepu and Shengqiao, two new residential villages for those peasants affected by the land draft. After the two new villages were built, all the Shanghai Party and government leaders went to inspect them and felt rather satisfied. During the first stage of intense construction, dedicated work on the project was put in by all Shanghai government branches such as the Metallurgical Bureau, Municipal Construction Committee, Constructive Execution Bureau, Urban Construction Bureau, Planning Bureau, No. 3 Navigation Bureau, Commodity Bureau and East China Electric-

ity Administrative Bureau as well as the Municipal Planning Committee, Economic Committee, Finance Bureau, No. 2 Commerce Bureau,
Construction Bank, Yangpu District Party Committee and Baoshan
County Party Committee. They gave their full support to the building
of Baoshan Steel, acting energetically and promptly upon the mobilization and deployment of the Shanghai Municipal Party Committee. The
entire construction progressed speedily. Our work during this period
demonstrated how right a decision it was to locate a mega-project such
as Baoshan Steel in Shanghai.

Clause 4 in the general agreement of building Baoshan Steel between
China's Metallurgy Ministry and Nippon Steel stipulated that the No.
1 blast furnace would be completed and start operation in 1980. Before
the actual construction of the furnace started in 1978, the Metallurgy
Ministry changed the deadline to the end of 1981 and the furnace's full
operation to early 1982. This meant that only three years were allowed
for completion of the furnace facility with everything included. The
time was extremely limited. For this reason the Baoshan Steel construction headquarters claimed they must "rush to build" and demanded that
every section of the constructors should work flat out against the clock.

After the mobilizing rally convened by the Shanghai Municipal Party Committee, large squads of all sections marched onto the worksite,
establishing work and living quarters and building command centers.
All this took only three months. A project director who had worked
on many large-scale projects in the past commented on the record-
setting efficiency of the preparatory work for Baoshan Steel, which was
faster than any other project he had ever been involved in. That was the
advantage of Shanghai. Once mobilized, everyone will act. The Metallurgy Ministry assembled the best talents from around the country into
the construction of Baoshan Steel. The design institutes for Baoshan
Steel included Chongqing Steel and Iron Design Institute, Wuhan Steel
and Iron Design Institute, Anshan Coke and Fire-resistance Design In-

stitute, Beijing Steel and Iron Design Institute, Changsha Mine Design Institute, Design Institute of No. 3 Navigation Bureau under the Ministry of Communications, Shanghai Electric Power Design Institute, Shanghai Metallurgy Design Institute as well as the Wuhan Exploration Institute. The main building companies included the No. 5 Metallurgy Construction Company under the Metallurgy Ministry, (No. 5 Metallurgy for short), Nos. 13, 19 and 20 metallurgy construction companies, crews 0029 and 0039 of the Construction Engineering Corps, Shanghai Construction Bureau, Shanghai Bureau of Public Works, No. 3 Navigation Bureau of the Ministry of Communications, East China Electrical Power Office and Shanghai Railroad Bureau. The total number participating in the construction of Baoshan Steel reached 64,000 at its peak. One can imagine the difficulties of so many people gathered in an outer suburban area of less than 20 square kilometers without roads or houses at the time. The old village wells quickly dried up with so many people drinking from them. So every day we sent out water tankers to ship drinking water from city to the worksite. With no water resource around the living quarters, in the hot and humid climate of southern China, the workers had to bathe in a nearby river. However, as most of the builders were from the north and not good at swimming, drowning was a frequent occurrence. The temporary workers' dormitories were built in former rice paddies so the ground was painfully wet. The roofs were made of two reed mats plus a piece of roofing felt. The summer sun baked them quickly and any storm would make them leak badly. Living conditions for the construction workers were extremely harsh. Despite all these hardships, however, the Baoshan Steel builders maintained their high spirit. Nobody grumbled at the hardships but proclaimed how proud and honored they felt to be building China's Number One project. Fatigue and the harsh environment were just nothing.

In September 1978, the Metallurgy Ministry sent its Vice Minister Ye Zhiqiang to Shanghai to supervise the construction of Baoshan Steel.

After investigating the situation for a while, he asked to change the existing project leadership structure, namely to change from the former joint leadership of Metallurgy Ministry and Shanghai City with the latter having the final say to the main and direct leadership of the Metallurgy Ministry. I was attending a national planning meeting in Beijing at the time and the Shanghai Municipal Party Committee agreed with Ye's suggestion after a collective discussion. Peng Chong phoned me for my opinion. I said I had no problem with the change since I knew that the support elements of Baoshan Steel would be enormous, involving organizing the raw material mine and supplementary material mine projects, spare part supplies, and steel and iron technical expertise. Moreover, the deadline set for the construction was very tight and a great number of professional designers and builders were required. Furthermore, building teams from Shanghai accounted for just a small percentage of the squad. The majority of the builders of Baoshan Steel came from the several construction companies under the Metallurgy Ministry and Nos. 2 and 3 crews from the Construction Engineering Corps of the People's Liberation Army (PLA). Later Su Zhenhua came back to ask once more what I felt. I said I had consented because such a change was appropriate. Today when I look back and summarize the experience of those days, I still think that the timely change to the leadership structure was correct, but that some issues could have been better resolved. The main problem area was in personnel changes and relationships. The leading cadres sent to the Baoshan site by Shanghai were veterans in the field, with a wealth of experience in metallurgy, who had made great contributions to the development of Shanghai's iron and steel industry. Most valuable was their high enthusiasm for Baoshan Steel and dedication to its construction. They had done a great deal of work at the preparatory stage, with significant results. However, some comrades in the Metallurgy Ministry did not fully appreciate the strengths of the Shanghai cadres, failing to realize that they were not at Baoshan Steel for themselves but represented Shanghai's metal-lurgy sector and the ranks of technical personnel as a whole. They had brought with them the deep affection for Baoshan Steel felt by Shang-hai's people. Their transfer back from the project headquarters, one after the other, not only dampened the enthusiasm of the Shanghai cad-res, but also stirred concern and general discontent among the Shanghai city departments and cadres. Out of respect for the direction of the Metallurgy Ministry leader, the Shanghai Municipal Party Committee did not reject the decision to send the Shanghai cadres away from the Baoshan Steel construction headquarters, but these comrades were un-happy about their reassignment and their loud complaints reached the Shanghai Municipal Party Committee. The Shanghai leadership asked me to tackle the problem and persuade these comrades to consider the interests of the whole. So, I called them for a meeting and talked to some of them individually. At a conference of the construction head-quarters, I also praised the contributions they had all made to the con-struction of Baoshan Steel. These comrades behaved extremely well, saying nothing negative about Baoshan Steel, but continuing to defend, care about and support Baoshan Steel over the following years when it was mired in one difficulty after another and criticized by many. These Shanghai cadres showed their broad mind in getting their nation mod-ernized and held an unswerving passion for "Baosteel." I have always had high respect for these comrades and felt sorry they were unable to continue their work at Baoshan Steel.

After the Baoshan Steel project was placed under the direct lead-ership of the Metallurgy Ministry, I commented that the change was intended to mobilize strength of the metallurgy sector from across all China and would not prevent Shanghai making its contribution to the construction. It was the goal of one and all to build an outstanding Baoshan Steel base and we must not repeat the Panzhihua Steel experi-ence at Baoshan. Panzhihua Steel had been built in a remote mountain location behind ancient forests and this isolated environment had led to the "hegemony of a certain person in this enclave." But there was a big difference between Panzhihua and Shanghai. Being the economic center of the nation and an open, international metropolis, Shanghai was rich in talent and experienced professionals. Working with Shanghai, one must respect and give full play to local enthusiasm and rely on Shanghai's cadres, experts, technicians and intellectuals. The success of the Shanghai Petroleum & Chemical Plant and the veteran experience of the Baoshan Steel Advisory Commission verified this fact. The Advisory Commission was formed at the suggestion of Ye Zhiqiang with the approval of the Shanghai Municipal Party Committee. It was a beautiful job. I believe that not only the Commission made an important contribution to Baoshan Steel but that its respect for knowledge and talent had universal influence for the whole country in exploiting China's strengths to the full.

During the "rush to build" period, it happened that a foundation pile became displaced causing some to spread the rumor that the entire Baoshan Steel might slip into the Yangtze. However, construction remained unaffected and it progressed quite well. Later, the damage caused by the "Cultural Revolution" and the Gang of Four became increasingly obvious and more problems in the national economy came to light, particularly in the fields of finance, foreign exchange and supply of important commodities. Then society started to question the large projects China had decided to import in 1978; Baoshan Steel was a particularly obvious target of this wave of criticism. Given this situation, Chen Yun came to Shanghai to look into the Baoshan Steel issue on May 30, 1979. First he met with experts from the Nos. 1, 3 and 5 construction teams under the Shanghai Metallurgical Bureau. His office director Wang Yuqing and I were also present. Then, he talked to Yan Youmin, Han Zheyi and myself from the Shanghai Municipal Party Committee (Chen Guodong, Hu Lijiao and Wang Daohan were occupied elsewhere and could not be present). After hearing from every side, Chen concluded that the launch of the Baoshan Steel project had indeed been somewhat over-hasty, without sufficient consideration and comparison. There were surely some problems in our work. Nevertheless, Chen Yun also stressed that the steel products made by Baoshan Steel were badly needed by China and that the project was vitally important to us. He added that he had sent somebody to inspect the Baoshan Steel worksite already and was pleased to learn that the progress and quality of its construction was good. Now that there were some arguments about the project, he was asking those concerned with the project in Beijing, including the former leaders and steel industry experts, to look into the Baoshan Steel issue. Chen Yun encouraged the Shanghai Municipal Party Committee members and other Shanghai comrades, saying that the Party Central Committee had made up its mind to build Baoshan Steel and would stick with it to the end without any wavering. "Now that we have signed the import agreement for Baoshan Steel, it has the attention of everyone inside and outside the Party, around the country and across the world. We can only succeed: failure is not an option." He asked if the construction schedule could be prolonged a little. "Why bind ourselves so tight? Let's stretch the schedule and move at a steadier pace. It would be faster to move carefully rather than stop midway." He also told me repeatedly that we must be realistic. "Starting from when the Japanese invaders began building Anshan Iron and Steel Works in northeast China, they took 60 years to be able to produce six million tons of steel. Is it really possible for Baoshan Steel to make six million tons within six years?"

Although Chen Yun stressed that there should be no wavering and that everyone must put their best into building Baoshan Steel, certain people in Shanghai, mainly individual city leaders, still took a contrary stand. They used "populace discussions" and jeered openly at Shanghai city meetings on the issue that "the burden of the two hills (Jinshan and

Baoshan) make us gasp for air" and that "the government owes a huge debt for building housing for locals but goes pouring so much money into a big project like this!" I contended that building Baoshan Steel was a decision taken by the Party Central Committee, so we the local Party leadership could only implement that decision—not sing a different, anti-project tune. More importantly, Baoshan Steel meant a great deal for our national economic construction, and profited none other but the Shanghai region above all. Even if Shanghai sent only a few thousand (mostly withdrawn after 1982) of the 60,000 plus builders of Baoshan Steel, the project still brought tremendous benefits to the city. Baoshan Steel spent nearly 100 million US dollars to import large construction machinery, of which the equipment worth of almost 10 million US dollars was given to Shanghai. Baoshan Steel had invested great sums in the construction, expansion and renovation of auxiliary plants, roads, bridges, railroad, wharfs, postal and telecommunication facilities and residential quarters. Some of these had for years been an unrealizable dream for Shanghai. The construction of Baoshan Steel was effectively helping, leading and promoting Shanghai's economic and municipal construction. Why did some of our comrades keep ignoring such a great change! Young and bold at the time, and helped by the opportunity of conveying Chen Yun's words at an expanded meeting of the Standing Committee of the Shanghai Municipal Party Committee I criticized the negative thinking. After discussing Chen Yun's direction, the Shanghai Municipal Party Committee decided to follow Chen Yun's instruction and continue to give full support to the construction of Baoshan Steel under the leadership of the Metallurgy Ministry.

Chen Yun returned to Beijing and called three meetings of the Financial and Economic Committee under the State Council to discuss the Baoshan Steel issue. At the last meeting on June 16, he made an important speech, to the effect that Baoshan Steel was a huge project of great significance to the entire country and to the city of Shanghai. It was a critical project of over-arching significance on which an enormous investment of over 20 billion *yuan* had already been spent. It was true that the Baoshan Steel project had been launched too hastily and that state leaders should have solicited opinion more widely and taken more time to consider the pros and cons. However, the Baoshan Steel project was already underway, some 50,000 builders were currently working on site, the project was making good headway and progress was promising. In order to compensate for and to correct past problems, various aspects of Baoshan Steel needed greater consideration. Then, he gave eight important directions: "1) I agree with Comrade Li Xiannian that the construction of Baoshan Steel must be completed. It was wrong to hesitate about it, though its scale may be reduced or enlarged during construction. 2) Make sure not to miss out any program in the project. It is always better to cover every angle than discovering something missing and trying to compensate later. The external supporting links such as supply of coal, electric power, shipping and wharfage must be thoroughly considered. 3) Buy equipment as well as their technologies and patents. 4) We must train our own technicians ahead of time. A big industrial complex like Baoshan Steel possesses top technologies and requires high standards in every regard. Qualified technicians must be made ready ahead of time so that we master the advanced technologies to ensure the quality of our production. Once these advanced technologies are mastered, they can be applied in our other steel works such as Anshan Steel and Wuhan Iron and Steel Works. For example, the proportion of ash in the coke must not surpass 8.5 percent and sulfur in the hard powdered ore must not exceed 0.6 percent. These issues must be resolved ahead of time. 5) Place the construction of Baoshan Steel directly under the leadership of the State Construction Commission. The No.1 person in charge is Gu Mu. The No. 2 person in charge is Han Guang, plus Ye Zhiqiang from the Metallurgy Ministry and Shanghai's Chen Jinhua. They must hand in a written pledge to fulfill the task, willing to 'give up their life' if they fail. 6) Formulate strict—even harsh—rules for the construction of Baoshan Steel. The builders are allowed only to succeed; failure is not an option. Baoshan Steel is the first huge project in China's striving to realize the four modernizations; as such, it must set a good example. 7) The Metallurgy Ministry is responsible for motivating all other departments participating in the Baoshan Steel project, including machinery, coal, railroads and electric power. In particular, it must help strengthen the machine manufacturing capability of the No. 1 Ministry of Machinery Industry. The Metallurgy Ministry should possess such an overall perspective. On the other hand, all these departments must work together in concert to build Baoshan Steel well. 8) The Metallurgy Ministry must organize all its cadres and invite all metallurgical experts to study the Baoshan Steel task. The foreign experts hired by China on long-term contracts for Baoshan Steel represent only a small percentage. The actual management of post-installation Baoshan Steel will rely on our own experts and workers. The purpose of the study by the cadres and experts was to find how to make Baoshan Steel perform well. We must accept their helpful suggestions and listen to different opinions."

Everyone attending the meeting of the Finance and Economic Committee of the State Council applauded Chen Yun's speech. As directed by Chen Yun and Li Xiannian, after the meeting we wrote an official report to the Central Party Committee, which was quickly approved by the central leadership.

The Baoshan Steel project headquarters conveyed and earnestly discussed Chen Yun's directions, particularly his request on strict rules, and formulated concrete measures. I made five points about how to carry out Chen's directions.

Because discussion of Chen Yun's guidance on Baoshan Steel was confined to our constructors and public awareness of his words was both inadequate and inaccurate, the public continued to question the project. At the Third Session of the Fifth Plenary Conference of the NPC held on September 4, 1980, five delegations from Beijing, Tianjin, Shanghai and other regions challenged the Metallurgy Ministry four times with a total of 60 questions about Baoshan Steel. The questions mainly concerned the decision-making, scale, construction progress and site selection of Baoshan Steel. As the plant was built on a layer of soft ground and representatives had heard talk about a pile foundation being displaced and the new plant nearly slipping into the Yangtze, they asked whether these stories were true. Also, what about environmental protection? Would foreigners control the raw ore for China's future production? And what about the investment? Would Baoshan Steel become a bottomless pit? As for social and economic returns, could Baoshan Steel project recoup its investment in 13 years as Tang Ke had promised? The Metallurgy Minister Tang Ke, vice ministers Ye Zhiqiang, Li Feiping and Zhou Chuandian and others answered these questions sincerely and provided detailed data. However, the representatives remained dissatisfied and indicated they would continue to pay close attention to the construction of Baoshan Steel. Not being a representative of the congress, I did not attend the conference. The secretary general of the Shanghai delegation, Zhang Shizhu told me later that a Shanghai representative had fiercely criticized the Baoshan Steel project and requested "an investigation into the responsibility of the Shanghai Municipal Party Committee for the mistakes in building Baoshan Steel, the chief criminals being Lin Hujia and Chen Jinhua." Han Zheyi, Deputy Secretary of the Shanghai Municipal Party Committee and member of the Shanghai delegation, knew this angry economist well and tried to calm him down: "Don't be so emotional. Don't be so emotional. Calm down." This representative retorted: "Why shouldn't I be emotional? Baoshan Steel will cost us 20 billion. Divided between one billion Chinese, each person will have to pay 20 *yuan*. Doesn't this 20 *yuan* buy me the right to speak out?" Hearing about this, I smiled and said: "He has elevated my status. The title of 'chief criminal' is flattering. The Baoshan Steel project was authorized by Deng Xiaoping and I am only executing the work. How could I be a chief criminal?" Nevertheless, I have to admit that I did play an active role in the project. I have thrashed the Baoshan Steel issue back and forth in my mind. It is true that when China made the decision to build Baoshan Steel I had not much idea about China's macro-economic situation nor the serious consequences of the damage done by the Gang of Four. Indeed, the project had been started too hastily. The "rush to build" slogan was inappropriate and the proposal of completing the entire Baoshan Steel project in three years was unrealistic. Chen Yun had pointed out the same problem to me when he inspected the Baoshan Steel site and had compared Anshan Steel with Baoshan Steel when questioning the unrealistic completion target at Baoshan. I could understand his caution at the time. I had been in charge of other large projects before Baoshan Steel and I was aware of the incredible complexities of building a big steel base. I agreed with the criticism. From a macro-economic perspective, the Baoshan Steel project was too heavy for the country to bear in those years. The construction itself was started too eagerly and hurriedly. In any event, it was not right to launch such a huge construction without a thorough examination. I regret to say that, had we only been able to conduct more investigations before starting construction, keeping a calmer and more scientific mind and working more carefully, the early stages of Baoshan Steel's construction could have been more efficiently carried out.

The *People's Daily* reported the representatives' questioning of Minister Tang Ke, vice ministers Ye Zhiqiang and others of the Metallurgy Ministry at the NPC. The news aroused wide attention inside and outside China. Nippon Steel did not know what was happening and became particularly anxious. Afraid they might run into the same trouble as with the 1,700 mm continuous sheet rolling mill at Wuhan Iron and Steel Works, they asked the Chinese Embassy in Tokyo about it. Receiving no information from the Chinese Government, the embassy was unable to provide any explanation to relieve their concern. Nor could Nippon Steel get any answers from Beijing. At their wits' end, the company sent Mr. Suzuki, Vice President of Asahi Trading Co. Ltd. to Shanghai. Mr. Suzuki told the Foreign Affairs Office of Shanghai that Mr. Inayama and Mr. Saito had asked him to talk to me even if only for five minutes. As Suzuki and I knew each other through our work in the past, I could not refuse his request so I met him. He told me that Nippon Steel had seen the *People's Daily* report about the representative questioning and was deeply concerned about the Baoshan Steel project, and that Mr. Ianyama and Mr. Saito had sent him to Shanghai in an attempt to find what was going on as regards the questioning at the NPC. Would the Baoshan Steel project be stopped? Would Minister Tang Ke step down? Would the Shanghai people question Mayor Chen too? Frankly, I was uncertain what might happen at the time. I could only talk positively in general terms and said the questioning at the NPC was a good phenomenon of the democratization of China's political life and that we should be pleased about what was happening. People were questioning the Baoshan Steel project at the highest organ of state power—the National People's Congress—and demanding answers from our Metallurgy Ministry. "It shows how greatly we care about Baoshan Steel in China. It is a good thing! Our government department responsible for Baoshan Steel is obliged to answer representatives' questions. Don't you have similar situations in your parliament? The construction of the Shinkansen railway and Narita airport were also debated in your parliament for a long time. I don't know whether the Baoshan Steel project might be stopped and I have no idea whether Tang Ke might step down. But China is now in the process of abolishing the lifelong official system and the redeployment of state ministers is normal procedure. I won't necessarily be the Vice Mayor of Shanghai forever. The lifelong official system will be cancelled but our government policy will be consistent and stable. It won't be interrupted just because of changes of leadership tenure. Baoshan Steel is the first large project signed after China and Japan made the long-term trade agreement. Our government will keep to its word and fulfill the contract we have signed. Please tell Mr. Inayama not to worry as we will surely continue our cooperation and do a good job for a cause as beneficial as Baoshan Steel to the friendship of generations of Chinese and Japanese." After the meeting, I asked the Shanghai Foreign Affairs Office to print the notes of our conversation and sent it to Gu Mu and other central Chinese leaders to keep them informed about the situation overseas. When I recall the event now, I believe this is all I could have said at that time and the Japanese side did not have much to say either. To be frank, when there was any change to decisions at the high national level, local officials did not know the details and had a hard time carrying out their routine tasks. Our generation experienced the "Cultural Revolution" and so remain acutely conscious of it.

In November 1980, the State Council held a meeting for all provincial governors and mayors as well as a national planning meeting in Beijing. The two meetings discussed China's economic situation and decided to halt the construction of "Baoshan Steel." After the meetings but before the Baoshan Steel constructors had been notified of the decision by the State Council and the Metallurgy Ministry, some of the attendees returned to their own provinces and conveyed the gist of the meeting to local cadres. They were told that Baoshan Steel would be discontinued and that the builders their provinces had dispatched to Baoshan should be recalled. Hence, the news spread, causing a tide of confusion and disturbance among the Baoshan builders. Soon the State Council announced the decision officially, but without giving a detailed explanation. The notice stated mainly that "Phase 1 will be stopped and the negotiations for Phase 2 will be canceled and the two sheets (i.e. hot and the cold rolling steel sheets) returned to the vendors." The notice also asked to keep losses to a minimum or even zero. What could we do faced with such a situation? Without a clear solution, we could only meet behind closed doors every day, taking no notes but opening up our minds to one another. We tried to convince ourselves before calming our staff to obey the overall situation. In our discussions, we felt that the State Council was firm about the "two sheets to be returned" but displayed a certain ambiguity, a sort of hesitation, in requesting the "stop of Phase 1." Provided we kept the construction site intact, we might be able to win a restart of the project once the national finances improved. Based on this understanding, we did not follow the notice instructing us to build new warehouses to store the equipment after the project cancellation. Instead, we designed the plan of "on-site preservation" and "moving maintenance" to continue factory construction according to the original plan to store the installed equipment *in situ*. Practice later proved that our plan was successful. It not only saved a great deal of money, but also ensured that the building of Baoshan Steel did not really cease during the "slow down and stop" period. The progress of its construction was not seriously affected.

On the evening of December 23, 1980, the State Council leader held a meeting with the Central Finance and Economic Leading Group to discuss the Baoshan Steel project. The meeting was attended by Wan Li, Yao Yilin, Gu Mu, the leaders from the SPC and the State Construction Commission, several leading officials of the Metallurgy Ministry and Shanghai leaders Chen Guodong, Hu Lijiao and myself. The meeting made the decision to "adjust, return and properly terminate" the Baoshan Steel project. At the time, the pressure to discontinue Baoshan Steel was quite high. Those from the SPC and the Metallurgy Ministry responsible for Baoshan Steel all hung their heads and remained silent as though they had done something wrong and were now awaiting punishment. Coming from the local level, I insisted on explaining the real situation at Baoshan Steel. I told them that imported equipment and materials kept arriving in a steady flow and that 60,000 constructors were hard at work on the site too and that to discontinue the project at this stage would cause enormous waste. Holding the photo of the blast furnace construction site I had given him to show all at the meeting, Gu Mu told the attendees that the losses would be huge if the project were simply killed off at this advanced stage of installation. The meeting attendees were divided on the issue. Chen Guodong tried to appease the arguers with the suggestion that further analysis of the project be made. The meeting accepted his suggestion to postpone the decision. Afterwards, I caught up with Wan Li in the corridor and told him that if we cut the project, we would still have to pay all the bills for the equipment shipped in from overseas, pay the interest on all the loans required by the agreement and pay the wages of the tens of thousands of Baoshan Steel builders. None of this expenditure could be avoided. However, provided we could continue the project, just dozens of million *yuan* more to buy bricks and sand would be enough for the year's construction plan and the project could go on. Having headed large-scale projects himself, Wan Li was familiar with capital construction and after hearing me out agreed that we could give more consideration to the issue if what I said was true.

That night I slept at the Beijing Office of the Shanghai government. I tossed and turned, unable to sleep and remembered Chen Yun's words to me when he visited Shanghai, that if there were any difficulties, I could seek his help. I thought it was time to do so and early next morning phoned Wang Yuqing, the director of Chen Yun's office, telling him about the argument at the meeting the previous night. I asked him to tell Chen Yun what I had said and wondered whether I could talk to him. Wang said that Chen Yun no longer headed the Central Finance and Economic Leading Group, so it was not appropriate for Chen Yun to intervene in the issue any more. I said that if he could just convey what I said to Chen Yun and let me talk to him, I would not return to Shanghai on the 10 am flight. But I waited until after 10 am and got no phone call. So I flew back to Shanghai, mulling over the matter on the return journey. I had always thought it senseless to spend thousands of millions of dollars on importing millions of tons of steel products from overseas and letting others make all the money. Once Baoshan Steel was operational, it could manufacture over four million tons of fine steel sheet and pipe per annum. Baoshan Steel products could replace the imports and save us valuable foreign exchange, not to mention that we could use the most advanced equipment and management to promote China's metallurgical industry and the modernization of our entire industry. What a wonderful prospect! Seeing that this great technical project might be abandoned, I simply could not resign myself to such an outcome. I recalled the time when I visited Japan and they said to us: "You people buy eggs for meals every day without complaining, but as soon as you want to buy a hen to lay eggs for your meals, all kinds of complaints arise." Could one deny the truth of this comment by the Japanese? Could one really refute their reasoning? Having considered the issue over and over, I determined that since I was closely involved in the actual construction, I had a responsibility to report the situation to the decision-makers, to voice my personal opinion to the top level. Therefore, I decided to write a letter to the central leaders.

Back in Shanghai, I talked with the vice commanders of the Baoshan Steel Construction Headquarters (Ma Chengde, Huang Jinfa, Fang Ruyu, Han Qingquan) to further clarify my understanding of the situation, and then sat down to write a letter to the State Council. Of the current situation of Baoshan Steel I wrote that: 1) construction had already reached its peak and that 20 of the 23 sub-projects for the No. 1 blast furnace were already underway. 2) Of the 360,000 tons of equipment purchased from overseas for the No. 1 blast furnace, 168,000 tons had already been shipped in. The next year would see the shipment of another 175,000 tons, reaching 343,000 tons by the end of 1981, representing 95 percent of the total. 3) Of the 250,000 tons of materials imported for the No. 1 blast furnace, 120,000 tons were already in and another 100,000 tons would be shipped in by 1981. 4) At the time of writing, there were 70,000 workers on site including over 60,000 builders and 13,000 steel workers. We would need only wages for these builders plus a small quantity of building materials from domestic suppliers to enable the construction of Baoshan Steel to continue, whereas canceling the project would cause a huge loss. So I suggested: "Just add ten million or so *yuan* to what the state would have to pay for halting the construction of Baoshan Steel. It will keep the project alive, albeit just ticking over. It will not only help stabilize the builders' morale, but will also benefit our future constructions and even mitigate the consequences in China and internationally." After dispatching the letter, I distributed copies to the other leading members of the Shanghai Municipal Party Committee, telling them I was sole author of the letter and would be responsible for anything improperly said in the letter. Later I heard that Li Xiannian had mentioned my letter on several occasions, saying that amid all the cries against Baoshan Steel, only one person had voiced a different opinion, that person being me. The truth is that many others shared this opinion at the time, but did not say so out loud for various different reasons. For example, Ma Chengde also wrote to the Party Central Committee against halting the construction of Baoshan Steel.

In late January 1981, a group of experts and leaders from the government departments concerned led by Jin Xiying from the SPC, Li Jingzhao from the State Construction Commission, Ma Hong from the Chinese Academy of Social Sciences and others arrived at the Baoshan Steel site. They held a forum on the Baoshan Steel issue, at which the attendees opened up their minds and poured out their feelings. Voicing their strong opposition to the top-level decision to stop the Baoshan

Steel project, those of the Baoshan Steel Advisory Commission argued: "We must not view Baoshan Steel just in terms of Baoshan Steel itself, but should examine it from a wider perspective." "Do not discuss Baoshan Steel from square one, but from where it stands today." "We must not only look at Baoshan Steel on the basis of money, but examine it on the basis of tomorrow." They proposed to "keep Baoshan Steel alive while slowing the rate of construction." Some committee members even requested that their suggestions be documented in the historical record so posterity would know what really happened. A professor on the advisory commission even announced his willingness to "become a street peddler to raise money for the project" should Baoshan Steel have to be cancelled for lack of funds. These comrades showed their utter loyalty to "Baoshan Steel;" they would not profit personally from the project once the base started production. They spoke from conviction that Baoshan Steel would truly benefit the process of China's modernization. The experts from Beijing brought my letter to the State Council along to the forum with comments made by the State Council leader. Since the forum organizers were trying not to influence the others' opinions, they did not print and circulate my letter, nor did I speak at the forum. It was only after the organizers had reported to the State Council what had been said at the forum that my letter was officially copied and distributed to everyone.

Before the forum was over, members of the Shanghai Municipal Party Committee met and listened to the report about the opinions of the forum. Chen Guodong presided over the meeting, which was attended by all standing committee members of the Party committee. The committee approved the positive plan made by the Director of the Shanghai Planning Committee Ma Yixing on behalf of the Planning Committee, Economic Committee, the Construction Committee and other departments of Shanghai government. The plan proposed to continue the construction of the power plant and the coke oven of

Assembly line of the Shaanxi Color Television Tube Factory

Kang Shi'en (fifth right, front row), accompanied by Chen Jinhua (third right, front row), attended the commissioning ceremony for the Phase 1 construction of the 300,000-ton ethylene facility at the Daqing Petroleum and Chemical Plant and inspected the plant in August 1986.

Premier Zhou Enlai talking with Yoshihiro Inayama

China and Japan signed a general agreement on the former buying complete
sets of equipment for Baoshan Steel in Shanghai in December 1978. Chen
Jinhua is third right, front row.

The first foundation pile for the Baoshan Steel in December 1978

Chen Yun (center) discussed the construction of Baoshan Steel with Chen Jinhua (right) in May 1979.

Gu Mu (second left, front row) on an inspection tour of Baoshan Steel in 1982

Chen Jinhua (sixth right, front row) accompanied Japanese Prime Minister Zenko Suzuki (seventh right, front row) on a visit to the wharf of Baoshan Steel in September 1982.

Deng Xiaoping (second left, front row) inspecting Baoshan Steel in February 1984

Phase 2 of the Baoshan Steel Project under construction

Chen Jinhua (first right) accompanied President Fidel Castro (first left) of Cuba on a visit to Baoshan Steel in 1995.

Chen Jinhua (center) on an inspection tour of the Zhenhai Petrochemical Factory in August 1992

The refinery of Shanghai
Gaoqiao Petrochemical
Company

Chen Jinhua (center) with
Li Ruihuan (right) and
Kang Shi'en (left)

Conference for the founding of Sinopec, July 1983. The left photo shows Chen Jinhua giving a speech at the conference; the right one is a view of the conference.

李人俊、陈锦华同志、

　　十二月三日来信收到，看了非常高兴！

　　石化总公司成立以来，生产、建设、科研、改革、经济效益等各方面，都取得了很大成绩，可喜可贺！这是在中央正确方针指引下，经过同志们的艰苦努力而取得的，当然也同过去打下的基础分不开的。

　　石化工业形势这么好，我觉

Letter of congratulations from Li Xiannian to the forums of plant managers of Sinopec

Chen Jinhua (right) and Li Peng (center) at the commencement ceremony for the construction of the 300,000-ton ethylene facility in the Shanghai Petroleum & Chemical Plant

Li Xiannian (seventh right, front row) meeting with foreign experts who were involved in the construction of 300,000-ton ethylene facilities at China National Petrochemical Company in September 1987 (Chen Jinhua, ninth right, front row)

The report in the *People's Daily* about Sinopec going public on the Hong Kong, New York and London stock markets

Chen Jinhua (right) meeting with the President of BASF, a leading multinational company as well as the largest chemical enterprise in Germany

Chen Jinhua (third left) inspecting Jiujiang Refinery in May 1996

Chen Jinhua (first right) and Yu Qiuli (second left) at Yanshan Petrochemical Company

Chen Jinhua (fifth left, front row) with the new Sinopec management in March 2003 (Sheng Huaren, sixth left, Li Yizhong, fourth left and Chen Tonghai, third right)

Baoshan Steel. Once Baoshan Steel started production, Shanghai would buy its products and Baoshan Steel could keep the income to itself. By "nurturing itself through its own work," Baoshan Steel could grow healthily. Also, by halting the other parts of the construction, Baoshan Steel could concentrate all its strength on maintaining the equipment already in place. In particular, precision equipment such as the computers and electric appliances on site must be kept carefully without being damaged.

On February 10, 1981, the State Council held a meeting on the Baoshan Steel issue to hear the outcome of the forum. Ma Chengde, Vice Commander of the Baoshan Steel Construction Headquarters and Vice Minister of the Metallurgy Ministry, spoke at the meeting: "Stopping the construction of Baoshan Steel will cost us 1.5 billion *yuan*. However, for a cost of 2.5 billion *yuan*, we would be able to continue the project." Hearing his words, the State Council leader asked him: "Do you mean that by putting in just one billion *yuan* more, we can revive the over 10 billion already spent on 'Baoshan Steel?' But that for the sake of trying to save one billion *yuan*, the 10 billion already invested will be thrown away?" Ma Chengde replied: "Yes, that is what I mean."

In July 1981, the State Council leader visited Shanghai. Right after stepping off the train he told the official from Shanghai Security Department that he would first go to see Baoshan Steel and then meet with Chen Guodong, Hu Lijiao, Wang Daohan and others from Shanghai two days later. Having been tipped off on the phone by our security official, I suggested to Wang Daohan to let me accompany the leader on his tour so I might help him promptly with whatever he needed to know. Wang Daohan agreed to my suggestion. When I arrived at the guesthouse he was staying, he was in the middle of breakfast and asked me: "How come you are here? Didn't I say we would meet in two days' time?" I replied that the rest of us were following his direction not to come to see him, but I was there simply to see if there was anything he might need. I ended up accompanying him on his visit to Baoshan Steel and then inspecting Jinshan. After that we visited the Shanghai Light Bulb Factory, Shanghai Toothpaste Factory and Shanghai Refinery. Seeing the Baoshan Steel worksite and listening to the builders' report he commented at once that "since the construction of Baoshan Steel is at such an advanced stage, we'd better keep on with doing the job well. Now we must try to keep the worksite as intact as possible." On his return to Beijing, he wrote on Han Guang's report on August 1, "There must be no hesitation about continuing Phase 1 construction of Baoshan Steel. The SPC must settle the issue as soon as possible." Before August 1, three vice premiers—Yao Yilin, Gu Mu, and Bo Yibo— also visited Baoshan Steel in succession and gave full affirmation to the construction work, providing support in various degrees to the plan designed by the Baoshan Steel Construction Headquarters. On August 7, the Metallurgy Ministry also handed down the written direction from the SPC and the State Construction Commission, announcing the change that Baoshan Steel would henceforth be an ongoing project. Following the direction's request to complete the Phase 1 of Baoshan Steel construction by 1985, the Baoshan Steel Construction Headquarters drew up the plan for its capital construction for the Sixth Five-year Plan period (1981-1985).

Just six months elapsed between the announcement of the central authorities' decision to "adjust, return and properly terminate" the Baoshan Steel project and the point when the country decided to restore the construction of Baoshan Steel. However, the turbulence stirred up by the changes was by no means minor. At a standing committee meeting of the Shanghai Municipal Party Committee one afternoon, a deputy secretary of the committee and Vice Mayor in charge of the science and technology section said he had been told by the Shanghai Science Committee that a cadre at the State Science Committee had said that Fang Yi, the Vice Premier in charge of science and technology at national level had told a State Council meeting that Shanghai peasants were pilfering things from the Baoshan Steel worksite. I happened to have been at the site that morning, just returning at noon. I pointed out that the worksite was extremely trouble-free, and that no such thing as pilfering ever occurred there. Lu Zhaoqi, the Vice Commander of Baoshan Steel Construction Headquarters, who had participated in the construction of Anshan Steel, Wuhan Steel and Panzhihua Steel wrote in a memoir years later that "Not one piece of nearly 400,000 tons of equipment and 200,000 tons of materials was ever lost, damaged or rendered ineffective. The cost of the maintenance work—which was a complete success—was kept at the lowest margin. Not only was this maintenance work the first in China with such a wonderful record, it was also a rare occurrence in the world." Now when we recollect these events, such outstanding work was indeed a great achievement.

Deng Xiaoping once asked me to my face whether there was any truth in reports that the Japanese had sold us old equipment. I answered him right away that this referred to the several dozens of diesel pile hammers imported from Japan. When the Shanghai Commodity Inspection Bureau inspected the shipment, a number of the hammers were found to have surface scratches when the inspectors tried to pull out the pistons. Someone from the Shanghai Measurement Bureau was on the scene and he spread the word back to office that the scratched hammers were old ones that had been used in Iran. Hence, the story was blown up into a big problem that Japanese had sold us second-hand products. I had called a meeting to look into the rumor, at which the Shanghai Measurement Bureau people admitted that their bulletin message was inaccurate and exaggerated by some subjective "analyses" and "possibly" syntax too. In fact the type of pile hammer imported for Baoshan Steel was not in existence when Iran built its sports stadium! Hearing my explanation, Comrade Deng Xiaoping said with relief: "You and others should step up and tell the true story." I said that we would try our best but bewildering stories popped up every now and then. We were really no match for the rumormongers!

I believe there were two things during this period that we did pretty well and which deserve recording in the company history of Baoshan Steel. One was that all the leading members of Baoshan Steel Construction Headquarters were united as one from start to last. While actively trying our best to let the senior leadership know the real situation on site, we also did our utmost to search for feasible solutions to problems and provide suggestions. While doing a good job on site for taking delivery of, transporting and storing the new equipment and parts, we also tried everything to calm and stabilize the mood of the builders. Besides carrying out the Party Central Committee's directions, we stuck to our posts throughout, refusing to wilt under the pressure. The Baoshan Steel construction leading group was a dedicated group. The second-level leading groups were equally great. They united as one and worked with their combined strength. The other factor was the leading members on site from the Metallurgy Ministry. While the construction of Baoshan Steel was a roller coaster ride, lurching dramatically from hasty launch to stop, then resumption and continuation, the Metallurgy Ministry's leaders stationed at the Baoshan Steel site, resolutely supported by their office, worked on and kept the construction flowing. They braved one new problem after another and protected the building of Baoshan Steel from any major fluctuation or damage. They were really extraordinary. Six or seven vice ministers of the Metallurgy Ministry in succession lived on the spot directing the construction. The first was Ye Zhiqiang. The second was Ma Chengde and the third Li Feiping, the latter two now deceased. As for myself, I was there during all their tours of duty. I was then the Deputy Secretary of Shanghai Municipal Party Committee and the Standing Vice Mayor of Shanghai City. Besides being Director of the Municipal Planning Committee at the time, I also held the posts of Director of the Working Committee under the Shanghai Municipal Party Committee, Party Secretary and Political Commissar of Baoshan Steel Construction Headquarters, and the Group Leader of Phase 2 of the Shanghai Petroleum & Chemical Plant. I was busy all day long. But no matter how busy I was, if Baoshan Steel Construction Headquarters needed me, I was on call all the time. I would go to the Baoshan Steel site at least once a fortnight. Even if extremely occupied by other tasks, I would go to the site on Sundays or on weekday evenings. Ma Chengde lived on the site to look after the construction on behalf of the Metallurgy Ministry. Being a conscientious and self-disciplined leader, he never complained how difficult the task got sometimes but persisted in working on the frontline despite poor health. He was such a valuable leader; I respected him all along and always cooperated with him well in our work. Han Qingquan was another good leader who never complained or gave up in the face of hardship. He did a fine job of calming the builders sent by the Metallurgy Ministry and of maintaining a smooth relationship with Shanghai locals. Before the building of Baoshan Steel, I had known hardly anyone in the Metallurgy Ministry. Our cooperation on the Baoshan Steel project really made us friends and I learned so much from them.

I would emphasize here that the successful construction of Baoshan Steel came from the superiority of our socialist system, the leadership of our Party and government and the massive cooperation of all sides. When society did not know the actual situation of Baoshan Steel's construction and was vociferously challenging the project, the Central Party leaders gave an instruction to universities to send student representatives to the Baoshan Steel site to learn about it at first-hand, on the spot. This achieved solid results. Representing the State Council, first Han Guang and then Li Dongye coordinated all aspects of work on the construction, promptly and effectively helping to solve all kinds of difficult issues related to the construction. Furthermore, the Metallurgy Ministry mobilized all its human, material and financial muscle to help the Baoshan Steel project. Shanghai City was also trying in every way to support the construction. When I accompanied President Castro on his visit to Baoshan Steel in 1995, Comrade Huang Ju was telling Castro what I had done for Baoshan Steel. I picked up the topic and said I had worked only on the first phase and that the glory Baoshan Steel achieved came after I had left. Indicating Huang Ju, Li Ming and Xie Qihua, I told President Castro that they had done most of the work, better and more than I had done. Due to her successful job in reorganizing and merging enterprises, Xie Qihua was several times selected as one of the Global 50 Most Powerful Women in Business by *Fortune* magazine.

The construction of Baoshan Steel trudged a winding and bumpy road passing from "rush to build" stage, to "adjustment," "return to zero" and "restoration," and surmounting one difficulty after another. Nevertheless, its eventual completion proved the truth of Deng Xiaoping's words: "History will prove that the decision to build Baoshan Steel was correct." From completion, going on stream, and ranking among the Global 500 Companies, Baoshan Steel has sent a clear message to the world that the Chinese people have the spirit and the capability to construct and manage a world-class industrial complex. The success of Baoshan Steel was made possible by the leadership of the Party Central Committee and the State Council, the all-around support and participation of Shanghai City, the Metallurgy Ministry and other government departments, and the hard work of the hundreds of organizations involved. The most significant part of all, I feel, was the strong leadership and support of Comrade Deng Xiaoping. At the most difficult moment, when conflicting opinions filled the country and many were pointing the finger at Baoshan Steel, Deng Xiaoping, empowered by his lofty prestige in the nation and the Party and by his keen vision of China's modernization mission, made his important and timely speech about Baoshan Steel. It had a most decisive influence on the whole question. On the morning of July 21, 1979, Deng Xiaoping received the members of the Standing Committee of the Shanghai Municipal Party Committee and pointed out that "Shanghai Municipal Party Committee should continue to take care of Baoshan Steel: First, just do it. Second, do it well." "There are a lot of comments about Baoshan Steel inside and outside China. We do not regret our decision but the main issue is to do a good job." At the time, we on-the-spot leaders of the construction of Baoshan Steel were pressured by a huge burden. When the Baoshan Steel project was first launched, the "rush to build" slogan could be heard everywhere and we got the green light on every side. Later, when the project underwent adjustment and was almost killed off, we were subject to all sorts of blame and red lights flashed everywhere. People jeered at us: "What are you busy with? Why don't you clear off fast?" From riches to rags, the contrast was too stark and we found it hard to keep any peace of mind. Deng Xiaoping's warm encouragement gave us much comfort. After hearing me transmit Deng Xiaoping's speech, the comrades in the Baoshan Steel Construction Headquarters unanimously voiced their gratitude, feeling they must complete the task well to show their gratitude to Comrade Xiaoping for his understanding and support. They would not disappoint him.

(3) China's first competitive business to enter the Global 500

Baoshan Steel's growth and expansion resulted directly from China's reform and opening-up policy. The two complemented each other, to say the least. The original construction plan for Baoshan Steel was not divided into two phases. It was only when the project was revised and adjusted that the two-phase construction was set up, the aim being to scale down the Baoshan Steel investment and construction. In line with the revised plan approved by the state, Baoshan Steel Phase 1 became operational on schedule in September 1985. Before then, in February 1984, when the Baoshan Steel Construction Headquarters was designing Phase 2 of the construction, Deng Xiaoping came to Baoshan to inspect the construction once more. Having seen the work on Phase 1 and listened to our report, he said right there and then that Phase 2 should not only be implemented, but should be started sooner than actually planned. Back in Beijing, responding to a question whether Baoshan Steel Phase 2 should be launched ahead of time, Deng Xiaoping announced openly that Phase 2 had been set to start during the Seventh Five-year Plan period (1986-1990). "At present we have to import 10 million tons of steel every year and every ton costs us US$ 300. If we had Baoshan Steel Phase 2, we could reduce China's steel imports by three million tons a year. After all, Baoshan Steel should find a way to start Phase 2 earlier, even if we have to get loans and pay interest. Overall it will work to our benefit to make our own steel." Under the direct instructions of Deng Xiaoping, Chen Yun and Li Xiannian, one Phase 2 sub-project after another was speedily launched, including a key element, the installation of No. 2 blast furnace, which was started on July 1, 1987. The original plan for Baoshan Steel had been to build two 4,063-cubic-meter blast furnaces, but this had been later revised to just a single blast furnace. Mr. Inayama warned myself and Peng Chong that it was too risky for such a large complex as Baoshan Steel to have only one furnace. Should something go wrong with the only furnace, the supply of pig iron would stop, affecting all production. It made everyone nervous. Therefore, when I heard that the installation of No. 2 blast furnace had started, I was really happy even though I had already left Baoshan Steel by that time. As a Baoshan Steel veteran, the news was a great weight off our minds. Phase 2 of Baoshan Steel was completed in June 1991. Soon the 28 sub-projects of Phase 3 were launched one after another, and all were installed and operational by the end of 2000. Achieving annual steel output of 10 million tons, Baoshan Steel made reality of what Jiang Zemin had proposed in his report at the 14th CPC Congress: "China will achieve the goal of building major iron and steel enterprises with output of ten million tons by the end of the 20th century."

With the completion of Phase 3, Baoshan Steel possessed no less than three 4,000-cubic-meter blast furnaces, three 300-ton and two 250-ton top and bottom combined blowing converters, one 150-ton dual shell direct-current electric arc furnace, two 1,900 mm twin-strand slab continuous casters, one six strands round billet continuous caster, two 1,450 mm slab continuous casters, one 1,300 mm blooming mill and one 1,300 mm square billet continuous caster. On top of this, it had one 2,050 mm straight tandem mill, one 2,030 mm cold rolling mill, one 140 mm caliber tube tandem mill, one 2,050 mm strip hot rolling mill, one 1,580 mm strip hot rolling mill, one 2,030 mm strip cold rolling mill, one 1,420 mm strip cold rolling mill and one 1,550 mm strip cold rolling mill, plus the support facilities including wharfage, shipping, electric power, water supply and drainage, and environmental protection. Empowered by these equipment and facilities, Baoshan Steel was able to manufacture oil pipes for oil fields, automobile steel plate, color-coated steel sheet needed in household appliances, cold and hot rolled thin sheet of various kinds, general color-coated steel sheet as well as various types of steel for construction. The appearance of Baoshan Steel changed the sorry situation of China's long-standing reliance on foreign imports for her industries of petroleum and petrochemical engineering, auto making and shipbuilding, household appliances, machine building and others. The birth of Baoshan Steel effectively promoted the market competitiveness of Chinese products in the world.

To adapt to the needs of strong, fast growth and with the support of the State Council and Shanghai City, Baoshan Steel absorbed Shanghai Metallurgy Holding Corporation and Shanghai Meishan Steel Co. Ltd. to form the Baoshan Steel Group on November 17, 1998. At the same time, the strengthened Baoshan Steel reorganized and reformed its new constituents. After the reorganization, Baoshan Steel went public on the Shanghai Stock Market on December 12, 2000. Helped by its advantageous ore import facility at Beilun Port, Baoshan Steel built a stainless steel plant, a joint venture with Japanese Nisshen Corporation and Ningbo City. It joined hands successively with China's three big automobile makers—First Automobile Corporation, Shanghai Automobile Corporation and Dongfeng Automobile Corporation—to develop and consolidate the sales network for automobile steel plate. Baoshan Steel signed a users' agreement with China Petrochemical Group. Forming a partnership with a private cold-rolling mill in Guangdong, Baoshan Steel helped the Guangdong enterprise to operate Baoshan Steel-style management, procedures, quality control and production line. Then it allowed the Guangdong mill to sell its products through the Baoshan Steel sales network in southern China. Through multiple forms of scientific and technical cooperation and alignment with domestic and foreign enterprises, Baoshan Steel accelerated its march into the international market. By implementing a policy of world operation, Baoshan Steel set up a global sales network with nearly 20 domestic and foreign trading corporations. By the end of 2003, it cooperated with Nippon Steel Corp. and Arcelor, the world's two largest iron and steel companies, to manufacture top-class automobile steel plate. In early 2004, Baoshan Steel went into a billion dollar plus joint venture with the River Valley Mining Corporation (CVRD), the largest mining company in Brazil, to build a large steel plant in Brazil.

In February 2004, the editor-in-chief of the Chinese edition of US *Fortune* magazine visited Baoshan Steel to discuss the possibility of selecting Baoshan Steel as one of the Global 500 Companies. In 2003, the annual sales of Baoshan Steel reached 115.03 billion *yuan* or US$ 13.87 billion at the prevailing exchange rate. Since the 500th enterprise in *Fortune's* Global 500 Companies published in 2002 had sales of US$ 10.25 billion, Baoshan Steel's annual sales of US$ 13.87 billion put it among the top 400 companies already, so it was fully qualified to be selected. So, in May 2004, Baoshan Steel made a formal ranking application to *Fortune* magazine. With annual sales amounting to US$ 14.548 billion for the year 2003, Baoshan Steel was elected No. 372 among the 500 strongest companies in the world as revealed in the 2004 July issue of the *Fortune* magazine. It became the first Chinese competitive enterprise to enter the Global 500 Companies. The great significance of this landmark event has influenced and led more Chinese enterprises and corporations to grow strong and large before they too stride confidently onto the international stage.

(4) Baoshan Steel's demonstration effect on China's iron and steel industry

In 1995, I accompanied President Castro of Cuba on his visit to Baoshan Steel. He enjoyed the visit greatly and was full of praise for what he had seen there, saying that he had visited more than 60 countries, but had never seen such an attractive factory. He commented that it was the pride of China and the pride of socialism. The attractiveness of Baoshan Steel was certainly not just its appearance. It is commendable in many aspects, particularly for its role model and motivating effect on the iron and steel industry throughout China. After the Metallurgy Ministry delegation visited Japan in 1977, they explicitly proposed learning from Japanese experience, speeding up the development of China's iron and steel industry and following a new path in aspects such as ore importation, deep water wharf construction, having large-scale equipment and computed-aided management. China should follow a new path rather than the old. People had heard or read about these new ways, but no one seemed to know how to start. It was impractical for everyone to go to Japan to find out. Hence, once Baoshan Steel was erected it provided a vivid and actual example, demonstrating how to enter the advanced realms in a concrete and systematic manner. Open-minded since day one, Baoshan Steel has always had a warm welcome for visitors, for inspections or those coming to learn. Baoshan Steel satisfies all requests, answering questions, distributing materials or holding training sessions. With 900-plus achievements to offer other Chinese enterprises in metallurgy, machinery, electronics, etc., Baoshan Steel has absorbed and adapted technologies brought in from overseas, then shared the results with them whole-heartedly. In this sense, Baoshan Steel has become a bridge, a platform and training ground for other Chinese enterprises to learn the advanced technologies of the world. The successful experience of the international iron and steel industry is absorbed and filtered through Baoshan Steel. Then, having been tested and adapted, they are converted into a vigorous package of development mode, operation concept, management ideas and operation mechanism, all rich in Chinese characteristics, before being disseminated to the great mass of China's enterprises, particularly those in iron and steel. All iron and steel enterprises, particularly the large-scale steel complexes, follow the Baoshan Steel model, according to their particular conditions. Baoshan Steel has taught how to utilize domestic and overseas resources and markets. Baoshan Steel initiated the importing of iron ore from Brazil, Australia and India, and also the construction of large 200,000-tonnage and even 400,000-tonnage deepwater wharfs by exploiting the qualities of our harbors. The practice of building and up-sizing big sets of equipment also came from Baoshan Steel. Large blast furnaces in China used to be 200, 300, 600 or 1,000 cubic meters in volume. But Japan's large blast furnaces are at least 4,000 cubic meters, the largest being 5,000 cubic meters. Therefore the 4,063-cubic-meter blast furnace built at Baoshan Steel has a most dramatic demonstration effect for enterprises in China. Having Baoshan Steel makes a huge difference, as would not having it. Because of the good example set by Baoshan Steel, the Chinese iron and steel industry can learn from advanced models and discover how to step up their own pace. In less than two short decades, China's steel output rose from fifth in the world in 1978 to first in 1996. Baoshan Steel has been of tremendous benefit to all the other related industries in China too, including coal, electric power, transportation and electrical technology. Baoshan Steel's lead and demonstration roles have also promoted and expanded China's automobile, shipbuilding, household appliance and equipment manufacturing markets, as well as real estate development. Take equipment manufacturing for example. In the first phase of Baoshan Steel, Chinese-made products accounted for 12 percent of the production equipment. Boosted by cooperative design and production in Phase 2, the Chinese-made proportion reached 43.5 percent in the more technically demanding domains of cold and hot rolling and continuous casting; in the less demanding areas of blast furnace, agglutination and coke plant the proportion was 86 percent. When Phase 3 was completed, the share of domestically produced equipment rose even more significantly. I think the following four aspects best summarize the demonstration effect of Baoshan Steel.

One, development mode. Developing its iron and steel industry, China tried different development patterns. By following the Soviet Union during the First Five-year Plan, China experienced a slow growth pattern. Launching a mass movement of making steel with "small home-made furnaces" and "small foreign furnaces" in 1958, China adopted a different pattern but it ended in failure. In the 1960s, China reorganized the national economy and implemented "The Measures of Anshan Steel," but our iron and steel industry remained sluggish and backward. Finally, China chose to reform and open up to the outside world, bringing in advanced technologies, equipment and management skills from Japan, assimilating and adapting them in the giant laboratory that was Baoshan Steel. Only then did China find the right pattern to speed up development; henceforth, the steel and iron industry entered a new era of development by leaps and bounds.

Two, a fine scientific development perspective. Persisting in the goal of comprehensive and sustainable development in all three phases, Baoshan Steel nurtures the humanist concept of building harmonious relations between the economy and society, man and nature, resources and environment, the material and the spiritual. Baoshan Steel utilizes resources efficiently, working relentlessly to reduce consumption and trying everything to protect the eco-environment. Eager to repay the public and society, Baoshan Steel practices charitable sponsorship, injecting tens of millions of *yuan* into the Baoshan Steel Art Prize and the Baoshan Steel Education Prize. A large number of writers and artists, outstanding teachers and students have been awarded substantial prizes. Under the "Hope Project," Baoshan Steel has built a dozen primary schools along the route of the Red Army's Long March. In Tibet, high on the snow plateau, it has also provided active support to building the economy.

Here, I must give particular praise to Baoshan Steel's environmental protection effort. When the project was originally started, the builders of Baoshan Steel set the "001 target," namely keeping coal gas emissions from both its blast and coke furnaces at zero and recycling 100 percent of coal gas emissions from its converters. Since Baoshan Steel went into production, in its steel making it has maintained a negative energy-consumption level since 1991, i.e. Baoshan Steel has succeeded in maintaining energy recycling higher than its energy consumption for steel production. It recycles 96.82 percent of its water in circulation. All the figures meet the ideal targets of a recycling economy currently recommended in international society. In 1984, when I was already assigned to work in Beijing, some of my former colleagues at Baoshan Steel came to visit me in the capital. They mentioned that the Shanghai deputies to the NPC were doubtful about Baoshan Steel's environmental protection and were seething with worry. In particular, Yuan Xuefen, a famous Yueju Opera actress, was the hardest to convince. By coincidence, the National People's Congress was holding a standing committee meeting at the time and "Big Sister Yuan," as a member of that committee, was in Beijing to attend the meeting. She visited me at my home during a recess (I lived nearby at Muxidi in Beijing at the time) and I took the opportunity of discussing Baoshan Steel environmental issues with her. She said that "a dozen yellow dragons" were already choking Shanghai and its citizens were really upset about having to put up with new dragons. The "yellow dragons" referred to the dozen big chimneys of Shanghai No. 1, 3 and 5 Steelworks that continuously belched out dusty yellow smoke into Shanghai sky. These chimneys had no devices for dust removal and cleaning, which was why locals nicknamed them "yellow dragons." I assured her that Baoshan Steel would definitely not create any more "yellow dragons," since it had been built strictly according to the Kimitsu Steelworks environmental protection standards. I had visited that Japanese plant myself and seen that the plumes emerging from its chimneys were all clear. I added that Deng Xiaoping visited Kimitsu too, that he too had praised it and asked Nippon Steel Corp. to build our Baoshan Steel in an identical manner. I urged her not to raise the "yellow dragon" issue at the People's Congress meeting, which would put unnecessary pressure on the Baoshan builders. Based on what I had said and on her confidence in my trustworthiness, she promised to stop voicing her doubts on official occasions. I later learned from the Baoshan comrades that she went to visit Baoshan Steel once it was in production. Greatly satisfied, she commended that Baoshan Steel was indeed clean and garden-like. When approving the work plan of Baoshan Steel, the SPC had explicitly demanded that the new steel complex be an environmentally clean plant meeting the highest international standards and become a model for all domestic iron and steel works. Following this requirement, Baoshan Steel's investment in environmental protection accounted for 5.3 percent of the total expenditure for Phase 1 and 3.3 percent of that for Phase 2. Baoshan Steel has not only fully met the state's demand for environmental protection, but has even exceeded expectations in certain respects. Baoshan Steel was the first enterprise in China's metallurgy sector to pass the ISO-14001 Environmental Standard. The afforested area of its factory district represents

42.71 percent of the total area and its carbon dioxide, nitrogen oxide and carbon monoxide emission figures are all better than the national first class environmental standard for scenic spots. All this profoundly impresses visitors to Baoshan Steel. I have been to many famous factories in China and overseas, but, from what ever angle one judges, Baoshan Steel's environmental protection ranks among the best, if not the very best. I have visited Voestalpine AG in Austria, but I have the impression that the environmental protection of this most famous European steelworks lags far behind when compared with Baoshan Steel.

Three, learning aptitude and striving for innovation. Handling a large complex imported *in toto* from abroad, the people of Baoshan Steel never rested on its laurels as a world-leading enterprise, but followed Deng Xiaoping's direction firmly to be "good at learning and better at innovation." Starting from a high point of possessing the newest technologies introduced from overseas, the people of Baoshan Steel formulated scientific and technical guidelines of introduction, assimilation, development and renewal, as well as medium-term, long-term and annual plans for its strategic tasks. Strengthened by cooperation from all sides of society, the enthusiasm of everyone in Baoshan Steel was put fully to use in the creation and setting up of advanced systems and methods in all aspects, including engineering construction, manufacturing technology, enterprise management and political work. Thanks to their hard work, the people of Baoshan Steel have made as many as 739 scientific and technical innovations and created 104 new products. Baoshan Steel attributed 65.28 percent of its output increase to technical progress back in the early 1990s. Sharing many of its inventions with other enterprises, Baoshan Steel has never tried to blank off others or keep them in dark. This open attitude is popular with and praised by large numbers of enterprises in China.

Four, a clear understanding of the choicest products. Baoshan Steel is very aware that the crucial issue is no longer how many tons of iron and steel China can make, but how good the quality of their products and how many varieties China can achieve. What China needs most, both now and in the future, is the choicest products with high added value. In the future market for steel products, enterprises will have no status or competitiveness if they cannot manufacture prime products. Baoshan Steel realize that they must make full use of their superior facilities and technical talents to work hard to explore, manufacture and supply top of the range products, putting into practice their understanding of competitive products. Under the unified planning of state and city, and centered on the Baoshan Steel Corporation, the people of Baoshan Steel are now striving to forge a top-class base of the choicest steel products in the world.

The demonstration effect of Baoshan Steel on Chinese industries, particularly on large enterprises and businesses, is multi-faceted. The reason I emphasize the aspects of which Baoshan Steel provides an outstanding example—development pattern, scientific view of development, combining learning with innovation, and understanding of choicest products—is that these features have universal significance for the development of Chinese enterprises into the 21st century. The comprehensive, coordinated and sustainable concept of scientific development, formulated at the Third Plenary Session of the 16th Party Central Committee, is a highly strategic concept about world trends in the 21st century, the guideline for Chinese enterprises to face and compete with international challenges. Baoshan Steel has succeeded by following this guideline, starting from scratch, growing stronger and expanding larger over two short decades. The trail blazed by Baoshan Steel should be an example for all Chinese enterprises. Baoshan Steel's comprehensive competitiveness was ranked No. 2 in the world in 2003 by WSD, the most authoritative steel journal. The US magazine *Fortune* (Chinese edition) noted, in its evaluation of Chinese stock market listed companies, that Baoshan Steel's comprehensive competitiveness was of world-leading class. Appraising Baoshan Steel as possessing stable future prospects, Standard & Poor raised Baoshan Steel's credit status to BBB in 2003.

(5) China has fulfilled its dream of becoming a strong iron and steel producing country

The invention and use of iron was a particularly significant landmark in the history of human civilization. Friedrich Engels called the Iron Age a heroic time for all civilized peoples, describing iron as "the most significant and the last of all raw materials playing revolutionary roles in the past." The Chinese emotional attitude to iron and steel is deep-rooted and long-standing; iron smelting occurred in China way back in the late Spring and Autumn Period (sixth century BC) and steel making appeared four centuries later. Having been a world leader in iron and steel casting for a long time, China fell behind in later centuries after repeated defeats and invasions by imperial powers possessing modern steel-making technology. In the latter 1800s, those Chinese with lofty ideals were relentlessly scouring West and East for ways to enrich and strengthen China. Their pursuits were all led by the dream to acquire the "sturdy ships and powerful guns." The prerequisite for making modern ships and artillery was iron and steel. The first Chinese to make mechanical iron casting a reality in modern times was Zhang Zhidong, who founded the Hanyang Ironworks to smelt iron with machines in Hanyang, Hubei Province. The TV drama *Becoming a Republic* has a vivid depiction of this event but the show portrays Zhang Zhidong as a leading figure in the "Pure Talk School," seeming only to discuss ideals but failing to act, thereby often becoming a laughing stock when advocating westernization for China. The portrayal is clearly neither fair nor truthful. In fact, dating from his appointment as provincial governor of Shaanxi in 1881, a change occurred in Zhang Zhidong's political stance and he began to work energetically for China's westernization. In particular, during the 18 years following his transfer in 1889 to govern a region covering Hubei, Hunan, Guangdong and Guangxi provinces, Zhang was more active in arranging the importation of machines from various foreign countries and founding such modern enterprises as railroads, marine transportation, textile, artillery and telecommunications. Succeeding Li Hongzhang as leader of the "Westernization School," Zhang steered the helm of China's westernization movement for two decades. According to historical records, Hanyang Steelworks made a cumulative total of 500,000 tons of steel during its lifetime, responsible for 75 percent of China's total steel production at the time. The impressive quantity and share indicate the significant influence upon the iron and steel industry of China of Zhang Zhidong and his Hanyang Steelworks.

Despite the appearance of such outstanding far-sighted and idealistic figures as Zhang Zhidong who worked hard to introduce a modern iron and steel industry into the country, it was extremely hard to develop the iron and steel domain in Old China, assaulted and oppressed, as it then was, by imperialist powers and burdened with its own backward political system and rampant corruption. In 1949, the steel output of all China was a mere 158,000 tons. It was only after the founding of the People's Republic that China's iron and steel industry was upgraded to an unprecedented level. In December 1949, hardly before the smoke of warfare had dispersed, the first national industrial conference to be held discussed the issue of steel and iron production by the Heavy Industry Ministry. In February 1956, having heard the meeting report from the Heavy Industry Ministry, Mao Zedong made the explicit proposal that steel output should double every five years. At the preparatory meeting for the Eighth National Congress of the CPC, Mao Zedong said that its lack of a steel industry was the reason that international society had looked down on Old China. He demanded that China must work hard to surpass the USA over the next 50-60 years. If the country failed to achieve this goal, he said: "China's world citizenship would be revoked." On November 18, 1957, Mao Zedong spoke at the communist and workers parties' conference in Moscow, announcing that China would catch up with Britain in output of steel and other essential industrial products within 15 years. Mao Zedong said: "Comrade Khrushchev told us that the Soviet Union would overtake the USA in 15 years. I will say here that we too can catch up or even overtake Britain within 15 years. The reason I say so is that I have twice talked to Comrade Pollitt and Comrade Goland. I asked them about their country and they mentioned that Britain's annual steel output now stands at 20 million tons and may climb to 30 million in 15 years. As for China's steel production, we could produce 40 million tons within 15 years. Isn't it right that China will catch up or even surpass Britain?" In his speech at the Eighth National Congress of All-China Federation of Trade Unions in February 1958, Liu Shaoqi announced formally that China's national target was to catch up and surpass Britain in output of steel and other essential industrial products in about 15 years. In Bo Yibo's report on national economic planning at the Fifth Session of the First National People's Congress on February 3, 1958, he also announced that China's annual steel production for 1958 would be 6.248 million tons, a 17 percent rise over the 1957 figure. This target was based on the goal of catching up and surpassing Britain within 15 years.

I consulted Volume Seven of *Mao Zedong Manuscripts since the Foundation of New China*, including Mao Zedong's 1958 writings and the final volume of Bo Yibo's *My Recollections of Certain Major Policy-makings and Events*. According to these books, in Mao's reports, speeches, written comments and letters, he referred 28 times to catching up and surpassing Britain within 15 years, though by my estimate the actual number is more than 28. It was unique in the history of New China for Mao Zedong to pay such full attention to one industrial sector and one major product in a single year. Had it not been for its great strategic importance and his special eagerness to banish poverty and backwardness from China, Mao would not have behaved that way. Certainly, due to the limitations of history, Mao Zedong was not familiar with the sector, nor did he have a good understanding of the objective laws of steel production. Using his familiar method of launching revolutionary mass movement, he tried his best to speed up China's steel production. He mobilized 60 million people—90 million at the peak—to swarm into the mountains and have the masses smelt steel in "small home-made furnaces" and "small western furnaces." Also, in the name of the Party Central Committee, Mao Zedong issued a series of directions: these included "launching a grand iron and steel making movement by the whole Party and the whole nation under the command of Party secretaries," "taking steel as the key" and "the marshals of iron and steel will set about his task." After the Beidaihe Meeting in August 1958, the secretariat of the Party Central Committee convened four telephone conferences to organize the task of doubling steel output. The *People's Daily* published an editorial asking all walks of life to "stop and give way to steel." However, all these efforts ultimately failed to produce the anticipated result. In 1958 national steel output reached 10.73 million tons, of which only eight million came up to the mark. It should be concluded that the mass movement of making steel was a dismal failure. The catchphrase of "catching up with Britain in steel within 15 years" was no longer mentioned in the years that followed.

Even so, Mao Zedong did not admit that the mass-movement steel-making effort by the whole nation had been a mistake, nor that the loss had outweighed the gains. He viewed the issue from a different, deeper level. I once chatted with Zhou Gucheng about his association with Mao when we both attended the Shanghai People's Congress meeting in 1980. Zhou Gucheng said Chairman Mao had a dominating personal charisma that would create a deep impression on anyone he talked with. It was a special demeanor that average guys could not imagine. Chairman Mao used to remark that one must take the high ground with irresistible force when writing articles or making speeches.

This may well describe Mao's personality. During the mass movement in 1958, when steel was being made everywhere, even in people's backyards, many voiced their worries, criticizing its wastefulness and that the losses outweighed the gains. Once, Chairman Mao was chatting with Zhou Gucheng and the subject of the "Great Leap Forward" and the mass steel-making movement came up. Zhou, who had not agreed with the action, tactfully cited others to criticize the wastefulness of backyard steel making. As soon as the words were out of Zhou's mouth, Mao looked unhappy, saying: "The mass movement of making steel was not just steel making; the movement also shaped people and their thinking!" Making steel was itself a physical act that one could see, touch and trace, but once elevated to the level of shaping people and their minds, it became an abstract matter, so Zhou Gucheng could only shut up and look convinced. Reflecting on this anecdote that Zhou Gucheng told me years ago, I always feel the story displays a deep complex about steel making on the part of Mao Zedong, illustrating the keen aspirations for steel by the Chinese people. Mao Zedong's chief nurse Wu Xujun recalled that after Chairman Mao became seriously ill in 1972, he never recovered. Once the Chairman wanted to sleep but could not lie down because he felt he would suffocate. Wu Xujun wept in sadness, seeing Chairman Mao suffering so, but he said to her: "Don't worry. I won't die yet. Are you worried I'm going to die? If I do die and see Marx, he'll say I'm too eager to report to him and will send me back saying China has so little steel and grain you can't leave it behind yet." Even when he was terminally ill, Mao still thought about steel. It shows the depth of his iron and steel fixation, and the same ambitions for grain and steel production remained with him unchanged throughout his life. His steel obsession educated and influenced one generation of Chinese leaders and administrators after another, and become a powerful spiritual resource for them to build China into a strong nation with a modern steel industry. Actually, apropos of Chairman Mao's 1957 aspiration to catch up and surpass Britain in 15 years, with the help of economic adjustment and various other measures, China did produce 23.38 million tons in 1972, even if the output fell short of the target set by Mao of making 40 million tons of steel a year by 1972. By a margin of over one million tons we exceeded Britain's output of 22.32 million tons, demonstrating that, provided China follows scientific procedure, the slogan of "catching up with Britain in 15 years" was a sound and perfectly achievable target.

Over 40 years have gone by and our experience proves the truth of the old Chinese saying "Time changes everything dramatically." The new generation of Chinese leaders and officials at various government levels has matured, nurtured by the spirit of the old generation of revolutionaries led by Mao Zedong. Choosing not to follow the old path and getting smarter than their predecessors, they understand the laws of science and know how to apply them. Hence they are doing better. From 1996 on, China was the world's largest steel maker for eight years in succession. In 2003, China's steel output accounted for 23.1 percent of world total volume. In world steel industry history, getting from annual production of one million tons to 100 million tons took 73 years for the USA, 71 for the Soviet Union and 49 for Japan; but China took only 45 years. After USA and Japan reached annual steel output of 100 million tons, steel manufacture in both countries stood still and even fell. By contrast, China kept climbing from that landmark point until it broke the 200 million tons record. From a total 101.2 million tons in 1996 to reach 222.34 million tons in 2003 took China only seven years. The first and the only country to produce 200 million tons of steel per annum, China has created a miracle in world steel making history. I am sure that if Mao Zedong could see what is happening today, he would be "shedding tears like a summer downpour."

Of course, China is not yet a powerful steel making country despite being the world's largest producer in terms of output quantity. Nor do we yet have the world's most advanced steel making industry. We must have a sober appreciation of the big gap that exists between China's steel production and that of the advanced countries in such major economic and technical aspects as variety, quality, material and energy consumption, labor productivity, and, in particular, our enterprises' research and innovation capability. China imported 37.17 million tons of steel products in 2003, 90 percent of which was high added value steel plate, and the volume of these imported products represented between 35 and 70 percent of our domestic market. Besides, the degree of concentration in our steel industry is not ideal, meaning that the quality of our steel products does not match up to our output quantity, the world's highest. Only eight of China's 280 steel enterprises have capability in excess of five million tons per annum. Of the world's top 30 steel enterprises, only four are from China—Baoshan Steel, Anshan Steel, Beijing Steel and Wuhan Steel. Most of our steel plants are still medium and small scale, as yet incapable of high quality production. Furthermore, they are often burdened by over-manning, serious energy consumption, low quality products and weak international competitiveness. The most advanced steel enterprises now measure their labor productivity in tons per capita (i.e. number of tons of steel made per year per worker) at around 2,000; but the average figure in China's steel enterprises is less than 100 tons per capita. Faced with such a challenging situation, our steel industry has a long and rocky road ahead. China must strive to catch up and become not only a great nation of steel production in the world, but also try to become a world power in steel.

The Great Success and Lessons of the Importation

In terms of technology levels, the per capita productivity and the quality and variety of products, the third large-scale introduction of complete facilities moved our importation work on from the previous "Four-three Plan" into a new stage, filling in certain major vacant areas in our industrial production, and rearing a batch of giant manufacturing complexes. The third importation also enriched China's opening-up policy and moved our cooperation with international enterprises up to a higher level.

In broad terms, the implementation of China's opening-up over the last 20-plus years has had two dimensions—"inviting in" and "going out,"—with the former playing the predominant role. "Inviting in" took the forms of direct foreign investment, building special economic zones and development areas, "three ship-ins and one compensation" (the shipping in of raw materials, parts and samples for processing, and compensatory trade), and import-export trading. Of these (often interconnected) forms of "inviting in," the "three ship-ins and one compensation" was practiced earlier and more widely than others. In the 20 or more years since Guangdong brought in the first contract for raw material processing in 1978, the practice has brought China an output value that has risen from US$ 235 million at the start to US$ 241.9 billion in

2003. Exhibiting thousand-fold growth and being a significant form of China's processing trade, it has made an eternal contribution to the performance of China's opening-up. Our abundant manpower resource is an advantageous condition for China's processing trade on the international market. Now the output volume of the processing trade accounts for 48 percent of the total output of China's import and export trades. As many as 30 million people are currently engaged in China's processing trade industry and the practice has enriched many Chinese regions, and improved and revitalized many enterprises. All this has quickened China's pace into the world and made it the world's fourth largest trading nation. That said, Chinese enterprises engaged in the processing trade are mostly labor-intensive trades such as textiles, light industry and domestic electric appliances, with low technical content and the majority of trading partners being small businesses from Hong Kong, Macao and Taiwan.

Clearly, it was far from enough for China to rely solely upon the processing industry to promote her opening-up into the world. We had to move on to a higher level of exploration such as international investment, joint capital investment and cooperative development. The third large-scale importation of complete facilities was exactly such a major, focused attempt. These projects were knowledge- and capital-intensive machines and technologies characterized by large investment and high technical content handled by big enterprises. The cooperation partners in these projects were mainly global groups in the developed countries such as the USA, Japan, Germany, the UK, France, Italy and Canada. The financing of these projects involved major banking and financial organs of developed countries in the West. Dealing with these global manufacturing and financial businesses backed by over a century's operations was a huge challenge and test for China's knowledge and skills. In major contrast to our experience in doing business with smaller Hong Kong-, Macao- and Taiwan-based companies, these Western enterprises, armed with their own strong business think tanks, came with whole sets of mature standards and procedures for international cooperation. To do business with them and try to win advantageous cooperative conditions, China needed matching intelligence, knowledge and skill. Without these things, reciprocal benefits and win-win results would be unattainable. When we negotiated with Mitsubishi about co-operation in building the power plant for Baoshan Steel, we got the upper hand in the technical part of the negotiations, causing the Japanese side to protest: "Yes, you win the negotiation. But it was your national team fighting our company team." They were right. We had invited many capable experts from China's electrical power system to join our negotiating team, but Mitsubishi, as a single company, had been unable to do so. This example shows the superiority of our wide socialist cooperation. By pooling all our strengths at national level, we made our grand cooperation work. In the small and widely applied practice of "three ship-ins and one compensation," such a grand national co-operation would be neither necessary nor possible. The international cooperation ushered in with the third large-scale importation of whole equipment lines helped us expand and develop our knowledge base and impelled us to do a better job in joining the global economy.

Soon after the third round of large-scale importation of complete facilities was settled, the market-orientation reform of the Chinese economic structure kept moving on, and the old, planned economy ways for conducting large projects—including funding, construction, production management and even product marketing—were no longer appropriate. A new set of methods had to be explored and established so as to meet the requirements of the changed system. The project importation provided the impetus for exploring new methods. For instance, when the third large-scale importation of complete facilities was first initialed, it ran into a major policy change: with effect from January 1, 1981, government fund allocation for capital constructions was replaced by application for bank loans and repayment. Hence, the first challenge for these new importation projects was funding. In order to get a loan, one must have some basic capital before a bank will lend money. But where could one get the basic capital to qualify for a loan and how repay the loan over the following years? When I worked at the China National Petrochemical Company, I figured out a set of new measures in order to save eight large import projects, including four ethylene production lines. Feeling our way and learning all the time we gradually established a set of procedures suited to our socialist market economy. These procedures, such as obtaining bank consortium loans, issuing enterprise bonds, restructuring companies and going public, enabled us to work together with the large global companies. Our explorations turned out to be a trail-blazer for China to enter the international capital market more positively and to multiply the forms of her strategic investments. Without these pioneering explorations, the present investment diversification reform would have been impossible. The importation of large, complete sets of equipment has contributed significantly to acclerating reform, amassing experience and personnel development.

The third round of large-scale importation of complete facilities propelled China's modern industries, the materials and energy industries in particular, into a new stage. As the foundation for all other types of industry, the materials industry is directly tied up with the growth of economy, society and national security. From advanced weaponry made by the defense industry to light daily products used in everyday life, raw materials are essential in every part of society. They are not only the content of the productive force, but also play an essential part in its growth. Human progress is based on material innovation. Deng Xiaoping always paid attention to the basic industries of China, especially to expanding the materials industry. Even when China was suffering great difficulties, he still paid great attention to the raw and semi-finished materials industries. When meeting with army commanders maintaining martial law in Beijing on June 9, 1989, he said: "I fully support strengthening our basic industries and agriculture. Basic industries are simply raw materials, transportation, energy and a few others. We must intensify our investment in these fields. Let's persevere for 10 to 20 years, even if it means going into debt. This is also opening-up. You don't have to worry too much about this part. We will not make big blunders." The steel and petrochemical industries are the largest components of modern material industries. They symbolize the industrial modernization of a country and constitute the basis of its comprehensive national power and enterprise competitiveness. The Stone Age could produce only backward productive forces, as symbolized by slash-and-burn cultivation. The series of inventions that emerged in the Iron Age, honored by Engels as a "heroic time," were the material manifestation of historical progress. Today, we have entered the Information Age, but materials are still crucially important to us. When the China Petroleum & Chemical Corporation went public on the New York, London and Hong Kong stock exchanges, I was at a meeting in Dalian, and Phoenix TV came there to interview me. At the time NASDAQ high- and new-tech stocks were so popular in the USA that traditional manufacturing industries seemed totally doomed. But I told the interviewer that this was to misunderstand the situation and that predicting doom was incorrect. Even the best software would need a carrier and all carriers must be made with solid materials. Moreover, no matter how wonderful the Microsoft president Bill Gates made his software, he had to live, dwell in a house and ride in a car. Steel, plastic, chemical fibers and other solid materials were essential to the building of his house and car. Hardware and software always complement each other. The selection and usage of raw materials for hardware manufacturing were vitally important. China was at the intermediate stage of industrialization and would move forward on the path of new industrialization. On the one hand, we must develop new- and high-tech industry represented by electronic information, bio-engineering, and new materials. On the other, we must use new- and high-technology to transform traditional industries so as to raise their technical content. Neither type of industry, be it traditional or high-new-tech, could do without iron, steel and certain special composite materials. Top-class steel products and synthetic composite materials in particular are even more crucial to raising our life quality and creating new technologies.

In the third round of large-scale importation of complete facilities, I was involved in handling Baoshan Steel, four large ethylene lines, and Shanghai Petroleum & Chemical Plant Phase 2, all of them classed as materials industry. These imported projects have played a vital role in promoting China's material industry and advanced the level of our modern industries throughout China. Take the steel plate for automobiles for example. The steel plate used as the roof of a car is wide and must be impeccably sturdy and smooth. It should not crease under powerful impact or bending force, in order to keep the car's exterior appearance and internal quality unaffected. The off-quality of the sheet steel used meant that our former "Shanghai" sedans often corroded from the inside out and caused the paint to peel. Now the new sheet steel made by Baoshan Steel is guaranteed against rusting for 13 years. A key factor for the success of the Shenzhou V Spacecraft and Long March Rocket in launching, traveling in space and landing safely was the special heat-resistant alloy used in their materials, some of which core materials were made by Baoshan Steel.

Invariably, there are pluses and minuses in every situation. Whilst fully recognizing the great achievement of the third round of large-scale importation of complete facilities, we must also give sober thought to the errors and problems, shortcomings and mistakes, that occurred in the process, and sincerely assimilate such experiences. Of all the lessons that the importation work taught us, I believe the following three to be pre-eminent:

First, in the late 1970s, we lacked a sober understanding of China's harsh economic situation and the serious consequences of the "Cultural Revolution." Eager to go all out and accomplish big tasks quickly, the Chinese Government failed to choose the best time for its decisions. At the end of the "Cultural Revolution" period, China faced a dire situation and everything needed rebuilding. However, the Central Party leaders were focused on what China needed at the time, but failed or refused to see the other side. In 1976, the financial revenue of the entire country amounted to just 77.658 billion *yuan*, barely enough to feed her people at the time, not to mention that China was simply not equipped to carry out such major projects. The decision error resulted in unnecessary waste for China in revoking contracts, compensating foreign exporters, discontinuing capital constructions, changing land drafts, relocating equipment and demobilizing constructors and workers. The loss to China's regions and enterprises was huge. As for getting foreign loans, the work was treated in too casual a manner. Actually, infatuated with our national status of "having no foreign loans or domestic debts," we had no understanding of the outside world, not to mention a full understanding of Western capital markets. Unclear about all the conditions attached to borrowing money, we were confused about what to do once a problem emerged. It was only when China made the "adjustments" and found that signed contracts must be repaid, that we discovered that we no longer had anywhere to go to borrow the necessary funds. It was the best example of our impetuous behavior. Working in Shanghai at the time, I too felt inspired and keen to improve things fast. Aware of the local situation only, I never thought to ask about the overall situation or decisions made by the upper levels of government. Only later, when we were facing adjustment cutbacks and discontinuation, did I make myself find out about the overall situation such as the state of China's finances, physical resources and foreign loans. For the first time I discovered how little I knew about the whole situation, and began examining my blind enthusiasm. As the saying goes: "with experience comes wisdom." In the years that followed, I would always look into the macro-environment, study background trends and analyze all possible conditions before making a choice and deciding on a concrete economic issue, in order to avoid one-sided wishful thinking and actions.

Second, the scale of the importation of complete facilities was too large and the timetable too pressing. The whole equipment lines that China decided to purchase in 1978 amounted to US$ 18 billion and the initial domestic installation cost was estimated at 130 billion *yuan*. Baoshan Steel aside, these super-large projects included four large 300,000-ton ethylene lines at the same time. Leaving aside the cost of such a giant foreign purchase project, just the supply of domestic supporting facilities and construction for these production lines alone, plus later assimilation and management work were simply too much for China's national strength to handle at the time. For example, the 300,000-ton ethylene equipment imported in 1973 for Beijing Petroleum and Chemical Plant (today's Yanshan Petrochemical Corporation) failed to go into full operation for a long time because of insoluble issues of supporting parts, installation and raw materials supply. It was not for another 15 years, when China Petroleum & Chemical Corporation was founded in 1988, that the Beijing plant's ethylene line finally reached its design capacity. Even before the first imported line had been properly installed, our decision makers were eager to import four more lines simultaneously. Their hot-headed decision led to "indigestion," tremendously impacting the economic interests of our enterprises and state alike.

Third, too much focus was directed on equipment purchase rather than on subsequent assimilation and innovation. Many of the equipment technologies bought in the third round of large-scale importation we had already purchased in the second round of importation. Chinese enterprises had already purchased some crucial equipment technologies, compressors for example; but we imported them again. The 300,000-ton synthetic ammonia and the 480,000-ton or 520,000-ton urea production lines are a particular case in point: we bought 13 complete facilities in the early 1970s, a further six in the 1980s, and a further 13 in the 1990s, totaling 32 facilities. In bringing in technical equipment, no other country has ever gone in for such "importation after importation, repetition after repetition." In the late 1980s, I commented at a meeting in Urumqi about domestic production of chemical fertilizer equipment that such importation actions made those of us working in the field feel ashamed. Even so, such stupid behavior continued despite all the criticisms. The reasons behind such blunders were: 1) our importers lacked funds but foreign exporters could get support from their governments and obtain loans from their banks; 2) it was more convenient for the organizations to import whole lines of equipment, thus saving themselves the trouble of completing the installations inside China, and ensuring smooth, on-schedule installation and operation; 3) the problem in our administrative system encouraging those seeking big projects and investments. They did not have to take care of the actual management once a plant was imported and built. As for trying to make China-made facilities, that was other people's business.

Today, things are better as regards all these issues. With more domestic funding than before, China has no need to go around seeking credits and loans from foreign exporters. Our work to make more China-made equipment is even more encouraging. The core compressor of the 700,000-ton ethylene line installed in Shanghai in 2002 was manufactured by Shenyang Blower Works. It has run smoothly ever since it was installed, not one iota inferior to the imported ones. Another core element of the same production line, the cooling box splitter, was made by Hangzhou Steam Turbine Works, and it works every bit as beautifully. These important examples demonstrate that, provided we try our best to make things, we can.

Chapter IV

Making Good Use of China's Oil Resources and the Founding of China National Petrochemical Company

- A Company Reinforced by Ten Government Ministers
- How It Began?
- How to Blaze the Trail?
- From China National Petrochemical Company to China Petrochemical Corporation and Conversion into a Joint-stock Company
- Giant State-owned Enterprises Could Grow Stronger and Larger

After China's petroleum output reached 100 million tons in 1978, the vertical structure of our economic management became inadequate for effective utilization of our national oil resources, leading to major waste. China's oil consumption per US$ 1,000 of GDP not only exceeded that of the USA and Japan, but was worse even than India's. To improve this situation, to raise our economic efficiency, financial revenue and economic situation, as well as to realize the "quadrupling" of total industrial and agricultural output, the Party Central Committee and the State Council, having "thoroughly studied and with the greatest resolve," decided, in 1983, to establish a cross-departmental, cross-occupational and trans-regional large economic entity – the China National Petrochemical Company.

The growth and the expansion of this newly structured China Petrochemical Group Company (Sinopec) could be compared to a three-act play: the first act was the founding of China National Petrochemical Company; the second was the establishment of China Petrochemical Corporation; the third was its conversion to China Petroleum & Chemical Corporation according to international norms. Between March 1983 when I was transferred to Beijing to take charge of the preparatory work and my appointment as General Manager, until 1990, when I was re-assigned to become Director of the State Commission for Restructuring the Economy, I worked at Sinopec for seven and a half years, and directed the first of the three acts.

After two decades of growth, by 2003, Sinopec ranked No. 54 among the Global 500 Companies. It had the highest turnover of all Chinese enterprises, and its profits and tax reached 70.5 billion *yuan*. Today it continues to grow and has blazed quite a successful trail for the reform and the growth of China's state-owned enterprises, especially the extra-large enterprises and enterprise groups in the country.

A Company Reinforced by Ten Government Ministers

In November 1984, the second year after the founding of Sinopec, and at the invitation of the US-China Business Council, I led a Sinopec delegation to visit the USA for the first time.

Our first stop was San Francisco. The day after our arrival, we visited the Bechtel Corporation which, as the largest engineering company in the USA and in the world, was pretty proud of itself. George Shultz, the then US Secretary of State, was from this company. We were received by a company vice president, who during the course of conversation, unexpectedly asked us, which was the larger—Sinochem or Sinopec. Sinochem was the English abbreviation for China National Chemical Import & Export Company under China's Foreign Trade Ministry, while Sinopec was the English abbreviation for China National Petrochemical Company. To ask one's guests such a question was impolite in foreign affairs, but since our host had asked the question in all seriousness, we certainly could not ignore it. So the delegation secretary general, who was also head of Sinopec's foreign affairs department, replied that Sinochem was a foreign trade enterprise under the Chinese Foreign Trade Ministry, whereas Sinopec was a newly founded state enterprise at ministry-level combining both production and the trade, which was why Sinopec enjoyed the same status as China's Foreign Trade Ministry. The Bechtel Vice President nodded upon hearing the reply. Back then, Sinochem was responsible for the importing and exporting trade of China's petroleum and chemical products and so had become well known through doing business with several large American and international companies. Sinopec, by contrast, was newly founded and little known in the outside world. Sinopec's unknown status was a vivid reflection of its humble early years.

The US-China Business Council official accompanying us on our American visit realized that Bechtel's ignorance of Sinopec and its official's discourtesy stemmed from their not being adequately briefed on Sinopec's background. Apparently, the Council's official must have told our hosts more about who we were because things began changing and the reception level for us kept rising. Not only did the President and the General Managers come out to meet us, but one American company after another welcomed us and flew us to their locations in special planes. The board of directors of the Phillips Petroleum Company even sent two special planes to welcome us, and appointed a senior executive familiar with Chinese social relations, a son-in-law of the Kuomintang general Bai Chongxi, to meet us before flying us to Phillips' headquarters from our previous stop.

At Wilmington, the headquarters of DuPont, three magnates of the giant company had come out as a group to receive us. Confused by the different time zones across the USA, we were an hour late for our arrival, causing them to wait for us and delay a business trip to Mexico scheduled after meeting us. Embarrassed by our carelessness, we apologized but they told us it was fine and that they were very happy to meet our delegation. These tycoons explained that they all had a helicopter pad in front of their houses, and they could be picked up by helicopter at their own homes and flown to DuPont's special plane awaiting them at the airport to catch the flight to Mexico. We could not help but be impressed at how important time and efficiency was to them. The three tycoons sat down to meet us and invited us to visit their labs—the DuPont secret. I joked: "You know I am not a scientist and I won't discover your secrets." To which they replied: "But you have experts in the delegation." It was pretty friendly for DuPont to allow us to visit their labs; according to those accompanying us, the level of courtesy with which we were received was quite a rarity for DuPont.

At the New York headquarters of Exxon, we were received with even greater courtesy. Exxon was the largest corporation in the USA and world at the time. Its former President received us, introducing himself as soon as we were seated: "Having resigned from my position as Chairman of the Board and announced my retirement from public life, I no longer participate in social events. But because of Mr. Chen's visit, I rushed here early in the morning from my home in the suburbs to meet with you and exchange ideas." I expressed my gratitude there and then, and having exchanged greetings, we quickly entered the main discussion. I first asked him what kind of systems Exxon used and how it arranged its operating mechanisms. With Sinopec still in its infancy, we were still trying to figure out how to set up its operating systems and hoped to learn from similar large corporations overseas. He said: "To be frank, I can't really explain clearly how Exxon operates internally." He joked that "This Empire (Exxon) is too huge and too old. I can only tell you how I operate." He pressed a button on his desk and immediately a big electronic screen stretched out from the wall behind. Pointing at the screen, he explained about the Exxon oil tankers in the Pacific, Indian and Atlantic oceans, where they were moving, the tonnage of each ship—200,000 tons or 300,000 tons—and from which oil field to which refinery these ships were delivering crude. Shown clearly on the screen, the movement of the oil tankers could be controlled remotely from the large monitor. The President of Exxon said: "My main concern is crude oil supply. If supply cannot be guaranteed, everything else, including refining, chemical production and profits, will grind to a halt. This is what worries me the most." After the oil crisis of the early 1970s, big corporations like Exxon were deeply concerned about the critical issue of crude oil supply, regarding it as a crucial factor in the fate of a business. Listening to him and visiting his company dramatically widened our horizons. I felt his attitude was one of focusing on the principal issues. For a president to micro-manage such a "huge empire" would be impossible; one had to focus attention on the major issues concerning the overall situation for a company. The detail could be handled by assistants and relevant branches of the company. Exxon's scientific operating mechanism embodied the grandeur of a global corporation.

As we progressed across the USA, from DuPont to Exxon, the reception level for our delegation kept on getting higher. Bechtel had sent only a vice president to receive us, while DuPont and Exxon had been much more formal, providing us with a top-level reception. What lay behind the change in how these global companies received us? We couldn't help wondering. One day, returning to our hotel, we found a document left behind in the car by an accompanying US official. Picking it up, our interpreter discovered it was a handbook on how to host our visit. The content emphasized that Sinopec stood out from all other Chinese enterprises in that ten state leaders of minister-level sat on Sinopec's leading board. It was simply unique in China and illustrated the special importance of the newly founded company to the Chinese Government. The handbook also contained briefing notes about Sinopec's 10 minister-level leaders: company President Li Renjun was also Deputy Director of the State Planning Commission (SPC); Vice President Sun Jingwen was also Minister of the Chemical Industrial Ministry; Sun Xiaofeng was also Vice Minister of the Petroleum Ministry; Li Zhengguang was also Vice Minister of the Textiles Ministry; Xu Liangtu was also Deputy Director of the SPC; Chen Jinhua was General Manager of Sinopec and Zhang Wanxin, Zhang Haoruo, Sheng Huaren and Fei Zhirong were its Vice

General Managers. Stumbling on this handbook, we suddenly understood why our hosts were according us a higher and higher level of reception. The US-China Business Council must have sent a special notice to these host companies regarding Sinopec's background and composition, asking them to appreciate the unique status of our delegation and to receive us appropriately. Certainly, from then on we were no longer asked "which is bigger, Sinochem or Sinopec?"

How It Began?

In 1978, China's crude oil output reached 100 million tons. Therefore, how to put this resource to best use in the interests of enhancing economic efficiency and national financial revenue became a vital strategic issue for the development of the Chinese economy.

In the first half of 1981, the State Council leader several times talked about how to make full use of our oil resources, comprehensively develop our petrochemical industry, and enhance our economic efficiency. The Shanghai Finance Research Institute published an investigation report "Organizational Combination Could Enhance our Economic Efficiency Greatly" in the *Financial and Economic Bulletin*, a journal of China's Ministry of Finance. The report discussed the sad situation of petrochemical enterprises in the Gaoqiao area of Shanghai, which could not share common oil resources simply because they came under different administrations, saying that if only these Gaoqiao enterprises could somehow be unified, their potential and efficiency would be hugely increased. On July 7 that year, the State Council leader wrote an instruction comment on the issue: "We must take immediate action and make a breakthrough from one bridgehead. Let's start by unifying the enterprises in the Gaoqiao area and get some practical experience. Then we will work on the second and third cases." The enterprises in Gaoqiao at that time included refinery, chemical, chemical fiber, synthetic detergent and thermal power plants, and came under different ministries such as petroleum, chemical industry, textiles, light industry and electric power. Because of their separate administrative systems, they could not share the same raw material supplies and thus found it hard to make comprehensive and effective use of resources. Following their leader's direction, the State Council sent a joint investigation team headed by Hou Xianglin, Vice Minister of the Petroleum Ministry, to Shanghai to look into unification of the Gaoqiao plants. Having spent several days investigating the situation there, the team found all the different parties in Gaoqiao clinging to their own stands and unable to reach agreement. In late July, the State Council leader happened to be on an inspection visit of Shanghai and so made a special visit to Shanghai Refinery to hear the team's report on their work regarding plant unification there. Hou Xianglin reported to him about the team's work and about the opposed opinions of the various sides at Gaoqiao, asking whether the issue should be given further consideration since the contending locals could not reach a decision. The State Council leader replied at once: "Don't let the issue drag on any longer. It is decided that they must be united." Right there and then he put me in charge of the job. At the time, I was Deputy Secretary of Shanghai Municipal Party Committee and the Standing Vice Mayor of Shanghai City. Once appointed, I spent several months going around, talking time and again to the different sides at Gaoqiao. In November we formed the Shanghai Gaoqiao Petrochemical Company. Authorized by the State Council, the new company was the first cross-departmental, cross-occupational, economic entity to be set up in China in the 1980s. Created from the former Shanghai Refinery, Gaoqiao Chemical Plant, Shanghai No. 2 Chemical Fiber Plant, Shanghai No. 2 Synthetic Detergent Factory, Shanghai Petrochemical Research Institute, Gaoqiao Thermal Power Plant and other local plants, it set a good example for the later reorganization and unification of petrochemical enterprises in China.

While working to organize Shanghai Gaoqiao Petrochemical

Company, the Party Central Committee and the State Council started considering the overall integration of nationwide petroleum and petrochemical enterprises. In September 1981, the State Council decided to set up a planning group to work on the issue and appointed as group leader Kang Shi'en, Vice Premier of the State Council; Yang Jun from the National Science Committee and Lin Hua from the SPC were the deputy group leaders. The planning group included leading cadres from the Petroleum Ministry, Ministry of Chemical Industry, Textiles Ministry and other government branches. Following the direction of the Party Central Committee and the State Council to conduct a thoroughgoing investigation and study, the planning group circulated a draft plan for improving the efficiency of China's oil refineries, the overall utilization and promotion of China's petrochemical industry, and measures to reform its management system.

In designing the plan for best utilizing China's 100-million-ton crude oil resource, Kang Shi'en met with Sun Xiaofeng, Hou Xianglin and other leaders and experts from the Chinese Petroleum Ministry to discuss effective organization of refinery and chemical enterprises so as to comprehensively realize the goal of putting China's oil wealth to best use. Kang Shi'en pointed out that the present irrational organization must be rectified, and that all the refineries, chemical plants and chemical fiber works should be united to work together, thereby allowing them to utilize all available resource supplies, unleash their comprehensive potential and enhance their capability. Kang stressed that the core administrative structure must be reformed. For a statistical illustration of the great profits possible through enterprise integration, Kang gathered a group of petrochemical experts and technicians to make calculations and draw up a blueprint for organizational unification. To unify all China's large refineries, chemical and chemical fiber plants that used petroleum as raw material, these specialists proposed the "five integrations design," involving unified leadership, unified direction, unified marketing, unified foreign trade and unified wages. At the same time, the blueprint called for a 10-million-ton reduction in crude oil consumption, to carry out deep refining and to speed up installation of several large chemical fertilizer, ethylene and chemical fiber production facilities in order that these imported facilities could realize their potential. It also asked for greater attention on the effort to export five million tons of crude oil so as to obtain enough foreign exchange. The plan estimated that the new blueprint could lead to increased profits as high as 8.8 billion *yuan* per annum and that this figure might even go on to double. Based on the blueprint and the estimates, Kang Shi'en wrote the report "The Opinion of How to Best Utilize Our 100 Million Tons of Crude Oil." Hu Yaobang was impressed with the report and invited Kang Shi'en over to discuss the issue. Hu Yaobang ordered that Kang's report be distributed as a reference for the decision-making of the Political Bureau of the Party Central Committee. He also directed that copies be sent for information to participants in the forum of top Party secretaries of provinces, cities and autonomous regions that was being held at the time.

In his government work report at the Fourth Session of the Fifth NPC from November 30 to December 1, 1981, the State Council leader proposed ten policy points for national economic development. The third point stated: "There are fewer than 10 countries in the world that produce more than 100 million tons of crude oil annually; China is one of them. It is a huge national asset. We must make good use of this asset as it means a great deal for our drive to increase the economic efficiency of our entire society." His report analyzed the backward situation in deep processing and comprehensive utilization links, pointing out that China "lags far behind the developed industrial countries in what we can make from our crude oil resource. This is a great waste so we must work hard to reorganize and reform our current refineries and petrochemical enterprises, intensify crude oil processing and develop comprehensive crude oil utilization. Our effort will not only increase China's export values, but will also promote our development of chemical fiber, plastic and rubber products and increase market commodities for people's daily life." He emphasized: "Optimum utilization of our 100 million tons of crude oil is an important matter in enhancing China's economic efficiency, increasing our financial revenue and improving our economic conditions. Every government department and enterprise must pay high attention to the issue and cooperate fully to accomplish this vital task."

As directed by the National People's Congress, the Chinese Petroleum Ministry set up a planning team to draw up a detailed plan to optimize utilization of China's annual 100 million tons of crude oil. Analyzing the situation, the team realized that oil consumption per US$1,000 GNP was 0.31 ton in China, 0.26 ton in India and 0.17 ton in Japan, the latter figure being 47 percent less than that for China. The data pointed up the serious wastage of China's annual 100 million tons of crude oil and the bad effects it had. The planning team pinpointed five factors causing such terrible waste. Apart from fuel being burned and consumed by our oil fields directly, more important reasons were found in the refining and comprehensive usage of our petrochemical processing procedures. Under the divided administration system, regions and branches of government managed the crude oil resource separately through three ministries and 20 provinces, cities and autonomous regions. Each took what it needed so it was impossible to manage oil supply under unified planning. For example, plants under the Petroleum Ministry focused only on manufacturing fuel products, whereas plants under the Chemical Industry Ministry focused on producing petrochemical products, and those under the Ministry of Textiles were concerned only with production of chemical fibers. At Shanghai Petroleum & Chemical Plant the utilization rate of crude oil was only 26 percent. The saying "only need 2 and 3—don't need 4 and 5" referred to this wasteful situation. The "2 and 3" meant C_2 (ethylene) and C_3 (propylene) used for making chemical fibers and plastics, while "4 and 5" referred to C_4 and C_5 used for producing synthetic rubber. Since Shanghai Petroleum & Chemical Plant was concerned with producing chemical fibers only, the plant kept only "2 and 3" but threw out "4 and 5" by burning C_4 and C_5 as combined gasoline fuel. To burn off C_4 and C_5, valuable materials in chemical production, as mere fuel was a huge waste and a crying shame.

The Petroleum Ministry planning team analyzing the issue of national economic efficiency reported that efficient utilization of China's 100 million tons of crude oil per annum would greatly increase state revenue. The team cited a raft of figures to prove its point. Considering every link from production to sales, if all the petroleum and petrochemical enterprises could be united and make unified utilization of the crude oil resource, this would provide an additional 11.5 billion *yuan* to state revenue on top of the 1981 total state revenue of 117.5 billion *yuan*. The nearly 10 percent increase was no small amount. Since I did not attend the meeting to discuss the report, Sheng Huaren told me about the intense argument at the State Council meeting about the figure. When the discussion touched the topic that founding Sinopec would add 10 billion *yuan* to China's state revenue, one participant could not believe it and asserted: "That's simply impossible. It just can't be done." The State Council leader asked: "Is an eight billion increase possible then?" That person replied: "That's impossible too." "What about a five billion increase then?" "Not even five billion," came the firm reply. Finally the State Council leader firmly closed the hot debate: "We will do it even if we can only make a three billion *yuan* increase." The hot debate indicated the great conflict in people's minds and the great difficulties in the overall unification and utilization of China's petroleum and petrochemical enterprises at the time.

On January 7, 1982, immediately after the establishment of Shanghai Gaoqiao Petrochemical Company, the State Council authorized the unification of the former Nanjing Refinery, Qixiashan Chemical Fertilizer Plant, Nanjing Alkylbenzene Plant, Nanjing Chemical Plant, Zhongshan Chemical Plant, Nanjing Plastics Plant, Nanjing Changjiang Petroleum Plant and other enterprises into the new Jinling Petrochemical Company in Nanjing, Jiangsu Province. Soon, the Fushun No. 1, No.2 and No. 3 Petroleum Plants were merged with the Chemical Fiber Plant, Chemical Plastics Plant and others in Fushun, Liaoning Province, to form the new Fushun Petrochemical Company. The integrated restructuring of these plants won us experience in actual operation and prepared the Chinese public for the later establishment of the China National Petrochemical Company.

The grouping together of petrochemical plants in Gaoqiao, Nanjing, Fushun and other regions to a certain degree improved the previous wasteful administrative system characterized by multiple leaders, multiple divisions and separate managements. The unified enterprises strengthened the links between and integrated the control of production and marketing. Integration showed its superiority right from the start and clearly enhanced the economic efficiency of these plants. Encouraged by these good examples, the petrochemical plants in Tianjin, Jinzhou in Liaoning Province and other regions soon followed suit, one after another being merged into large complexes. The trend reflected that all China's regions soon recognized the superiority of unification. However, the trend also revealed the need for centralized leadership, overall planning and unified management in all these newly merged petrochemical enterprises around the country.

When the State Council leader inspected petrochemical enterprises in Liaoyang, Anshan, Dalian and other places in northeast China in August 1982, he emphasized the issue of enterprise integration. On September 18, a routine meeting of the State Council discussed the establishment of China National Petrochemical Company as well as a detailed plan for optimal utilization of our 100 million tons per annum crude oil output. In his comments on October 7 regarding the Shanghai Economic Zone and the Shanxi Energy Base, the State Council leader proposed that all important enterprises and products impacting the national economy and people's livelihood should be placed under the centralized management of the central government. Also, it was highly recommended that a sort of national group company such as a petrochemical corporation should be founded. On December 10, the Sixth Five-year Plan (1981-1985) for China's national economic and social development was passed at the Fifth Session of the Fifth NPC. One of the Plan's particular proposals was to pilot test the future reorganization and integration of all petrochemical enterprises across the country.

On February 10, 1983, the State Economic Commission, the SPC, the State Commission for Restructuring the Economy (SCRE) and the Ministry of Finance submitted a joint report to the Party Central Committee and the State Council seeking the establishment of the China National Petrochemical Company. On February 19, the Party Central Committee and the State Council issued Document No. 7; this formally approved the joint request to establish the China National Petrochemical Company, asking to centralize the leadership and management of all the refineries, petrochemical and chemical fiber plants formerly under the state ministries of petroleum, chemical industry and textiles, and to link up into a centralized China-wide system their production, material supplies, marketing, human resources, financial and property management as well as their domestic and overseas trading. Document No. 7 announced five decisions. The first was the setting up of the preparatory group for the new national petrochemical establishment headed by Li Renjun and myself. The group would be placed under the direct leadership of Kang Shi'en of the State Council. I later learned that when the central leaders were discussing the new enterprise, Comrade Ma Hong, Deputy Secretary General of the State Council, recommended

Rui Xingwen to be its General Manager and this recommendation was approved by the Party Central Committee. Rui Xingwen was the Vice Minister of the No. 7 Ministry of Machinery Industry at the time. However, for some job-related reason, the appointment did not happen. Therefore the central leaders decided instead to transfer me from Shanghai to Beijing, both to lead the new petrochemical company preparatory group and to be its General Manager. Kang Shi'en told me the reason I was nominated was mainly that I was a candidate acceptable to all sides, including the SPC, the State Economic Commission, the Ministry of Petroleum, the Ministry of Chemical Industry and the Ministry of Textiles.

In February 1983, the Organization Department of the Party Central Committee instructed me to report to my new post in Beijing. Arriving in Beijing, I asked Vice Director Zhao Zhenqing: "Why have I been asked to come?" He said: "It wasn't us. It's the central leaders who want to talk to you. Just wait." Soon the Party General Secretary Hu Yaobang wanted to speak to me. He was scheduled to go to Guangzhou that evening so he talked to me in his bedroom that afternoon. After that, the State Council leader and Kang Shi'en talked to me individually. They all stressed the very great importance the central leaders put on the founding of China National Petrochemical Company, saying they were determined to get better returns from China's annual 100-million-ton crude oil output. I remember Hu Yaobang saying: "In order to set up the national petrochemical company, we have to take away the petrochemical enterprises from our local governments. But, these enterprises are all the best plants these governments have in their regions, making them big profits. We reported to Comrade Xiaoping our decision to take over these companies, asking that a written direction be issued straight from the central leadership so that we don't have to go round trying to persuade the different localities. Comrade Xiaoping approved our request, saying 'Quite right.'" The State Council leader stressed to me that the central leaders had discussed how to realize the goal of quadrupling the gross output values of Chinese industry and agriculture by the year 2000 and believed that some super-major measures should be taken to ensure this target was achieved. Setting up the China National Petrochemical Company was one such major measure. Before concluding our conversation, he asked: "What requests do you have for taking this job? You can tell me." I replied that a technical expert working for Beijing City had been recommended to me, and though the expert himself was willing to join the new company, Beijing City government simply refused to release him. Could I have this person for the new company? He picked up the phone to call Comrade Duan Junyi who was in charge of Beijing City at the time: "You are supposed to support Chen Jinhua, aren't you? Give him the person he's asking for." Before long, Beijing City let the person come to the new company. My interview with Kang Shi'en was longer, taking half a day. Kang began by expounding on the decision-making process for establishing the new company. Then he emphasized why we must build a good structural basis so as to achieve optimum utilization of the 100 million tons of crude. He pointed to the positive significance of establishing a national petrochemical company for the efforts to correct the current economic mismanagement and to improve China's macro-economic efficiency. Kang Shi'en's talk could be summarized into four points: 1) The purpose of setting up the new China National Petrochemical Company was to ensure rational utilization of our 100-million-ton crude oil resource and to develop deep refining in order to improve our economic capability. 2) It would help accelerate the comprehensive development of our petrochemical industry in order to satisfy the needs of various sectors of the national economy and of people's livelihood. 3) Concentrating the wealth of our large and medium size enterprises to ensure central financial revenue, improving funding for enhancing profit in the macro-economy,' and concentrating all our strength in the effort to accomplish our major tasks. 4) This economic restructure would help solve our enterprise management problem of too many leaders and too many divisions. Setting up and operating the new company would help us find a new path of socialist industrial management with Chinese characteristics. Finally, Kang told me: "For the Party Central Committee and the State Council to issue a direct written decision about setting up a new state company is totally unprecedented. You should understand its importance to the central leadership. Let us work together to accomplish this task and live up to the expectations of our central leaders." After hearing from all the central leaders and realizing their determination on the decision to set up the China National Petrochemical Company, I realized the big issues behind my job transfer and felt the extremely high expectations of my new post. Without previous experience in this area, all I could do was to work hard, put my nose to the grindstone and unite everyone in the preparatory group to do a good job, so as to repay such high support. I knew the old adage "good officials don't boast," being aware that anything I expressed at that moment would be premature. I just needed to do a good job.

After more than three months of intense work, on July 4, 1983, the preparatory group for the new state enterprise convened the first meeting of general managers (factory leaders) of all the individual enterprises. The leader of the State Council and several vice premiers came to the meeting. The State Council leader addressed the meeting, emphasizing the high hopes he and other central leaders had for the new company, asking everyone to make the new company a true economic entity, not slipping back to the old path and making it another Petrochemical Ministry. Wan Li told the delegates that China's economic revitalization relied upon the development of the petrochemical industry. Much of the improvement in people's livelihood, food, clothing and daily necessities depended upon raw materials supplied by the petrochemical industry, and our present contradiction between a large population and limited arable land would also be alleviated. What did people's living standards rely on? The answer was the petrochemical industry. It might not be realistic to take all China's industries to world-leading level, but our electronics and petrochemical industries would surely make it. The new company must have modernized management. Our petrochemical industry would definitely compete with its international counterparts. After the meeting, Wan Li told me China must catch up with the Soviet Union in ethylene output by 2000. Production of ethylene, as a "building block" product in petrochemicals, represented the development level of a country and an enterprise. With access to ethylene, all kinds of materials could be synthesized. Ethylene output was a measure and symbol of the development of a country's petrochemical industry. Wan Li asked us to catch up with the Soviet Union and whether we could make it. I told him: "I don't know about the Soviet Union's ethylene output so I will need to find out about the distance between us two. But in any case, we will surely work hard to achieve this goal." After the meeting, I found that the Soviet Union's ethylene output was 2,267,000 tons in 1983, as opposed to China's output of 560,000 tons, only a quarter of the Soviet figure. We would have to quadruple our ethylene output in order to catch up by the year 2000. The gap revealed by the comparison and calculation shocked me and I felt unsure about the task. Wan Li did not check with me again on this issue, nor did I raise it with him on my own initiative. However, our later development proved that Wan Li's demand for China's ethylene output to catch up by 2000 had been a sound one, and it spurred our work dramatically. China's ethylene output in 2000 was 4.7 million tons per annum whereas that of the Russian Republic fell from 2,267,000 tons to 1,889,000 tons in 2000, just 40 percent of China's. In 2003 China's ethylene output reached 6.12 million tons while the Russian Republic's was 3.3 million tons, still trailing behind. Figures from the National Bureau of Statistics of China show that China's ethylene output ranked eighth in the world in 1982, but rose to third in 2003. Today, generally speaking, China's overall petrochemical productivity, from upstream oilfield exploration to midstream refining, and then to downstream production of synthetic fibers, plastics, synthetic rubber and major organic chemical synthesis products, plus our huge sales network, is preceded only by the USA and Japan. If the potential output of the new ethylene facilities installed in the past two years (2003-2004) is included in the calculation, China will soon surpass Japan.

China National Petrochemical Company was officially established in Beijing on July 12, 1983. Yao Yilin, a member of Political Bureau of the Party Central Committee and Vice Premier of the State Council, spoke at the inauguration ceremony on behalf of the central committee and national government. He said: "In order to realize the grand goal set by the 12th CPC National Congress to quadruple the output of our industry and agriculture by the end of the 20th century and to optimize the utilization of our annual output of 100 million tons of crude oil in the interests of greater economic efficiency, the Party Central Committee and the State Council have conducted a thorough investigation and made the major decision to merge 39 large- and medium-sized petrochemical enterprises formerly under different administrative systems and various regions, disconnecting them from the old horizontal and vertical divisions to form the largest state enterprise of petrochemical production and trading in China. This is a most significant decision." He added: "Viewed either as a long-term consideration or as a concrete action for the near future, developing our petrochemical industry will enable us to create more state revenue and savings for building the Chinese economy. The petrochemical industry is a newly emerged industry and its technological progress will spur the development of all our other industries." Now, more than 20 years on, China National Petrochemical Company did not disappoint the high expectations of the Party Central Committee and the State Council. Passing with top marks the test of optimizing China's 100 million tons of crude oil we made the contribution expected of us toward quadrupling the gross output value of our industry and agriculture by the year 2000.

The development of the China National Petrochemical Company proved the truth of the saying "the road to success is never smooth." In early 1985, the State Council wanted to transfer me away from Sinopec as First Deputy Director of the State Planning Commission. Apparently, this new appointment had been decided upon in a discussion between the State Council leader and Song Ping, Director of the SPC and the Organization Department of the Party Central Committee was already authorized to announce the new appointment. Once Li Renjun heard about it, he contested the decision fiercely and went to talk to Du Xingyuan, Secretary General of the State Council, asking the latter to convey to the State Council leader Li's strong objection to the decision. At that time Li Renjun was about to visit Singapore, but so concerned was he about my leaving Sinopec that, on the day of his departure, he called Fang Weizhong, Deputy Director of the SPC, to protest the issue. At the time, Fang was in the middle of drafting the government work report and was in frequent contact with the State Council leader. Li Renjun asked Fang Weizhong to convey his objections to the State Council leader, asking him whether the central leaders really wanted to give up 20 billion *yuan* revenue. The sum he cited was the tax and profits in 1990 that Sinopec promised the country under the "329 Plan." (Explanation of this Plan can be found on page 229) Li Renjun said that if the central leaders still wanted those 20 billion *yuan*, they must not transfer me out of Sinopec. That afternoon, I went to Beijing Airport to send off Li Renjun and he told me about his conversations with Du Xingyuan and Fang Weizhong. I laughed: "You exaggerated. I'm not that important. How could 20 billion *yuan* disappear just because I'm not there?" I also told him: "I will never lobby to be reassigned from Sinopec. Nor will I ever shirk my duty. Please feel assured about that."

Before long, Kang Shi'en talked to me formally, informing me that the central leaders had decided to send me to work on the Hong Kong and Macao Work Committee in Hong Kong and that Qiao Shi, Director of the Organization Department of the Party Central Committee, was already handling my new appointment. Shortly, Qiao Shi was appointed Chairman of the Central Commission for Discipline Inspection, so he handed on the issue of my job transfer to his replacement, Comrade Wei Jianxing. Wei went to talk to Kang Shi'en about implementing the decision to transfer me to Hong Kong, mainly so as to see who would take over my work at Sinopec. The news soon spread to Sinopec's Beijing headquarters and stirred unrest among its employees. Unclear myself about the origin and sequence of the story, in the hope of getting some clues, I went to see Comrade Li Xiannian who at the time was hospitalized in Beijing with an eye complaint. He had me sit down and asked me about the installation of the four ethylene facilities. I told him that their installation was progressing smoothly so he should rest assured. We would be sure to do a good job. Then, I asked him: "Kang Shi'en told me that the central leaders wanted to assign me to the Hong Kong and Macao Work Committee. I am not sure whether the decision has been made already or not." At this, Li Xiannian answered firmly: "Why go there? Don't go! The central leadership made the big decision to assign you to do a good job at Sinopec!" I had not proposed myself to go to Hong Kong in the first place, and so replied: "I don't object to staying in post. It was Kang Shi'en who asked me to get ready to leave Sinopec. That's why I am here to seek your advice. It is not me who's lobbied to work in Hong Kong." Li Xiannian said: "I know it wasn't you who asked to go to Hong Kong. Don't go." After this, I basically settled down and worked at Sinopec until September 1990, after Sinopec had achieved the aims of the "329 Plan" signed with the central government. After that I was appointed Director of the State Commission for Restructuring the Economy (SCRE).

During my seven and half years at Sinopec, I believe I basically fulfilled the original requirements of the Party Central Committee and the State Council. I felt I could report "mission accomplished" to the central leaders. Later, I was transferred once more from the SCRE to be Director of the SPC. Once, having finished the formal topics in a report on my work to Li Peng, I told him that Mao Zedong claimed to "repeat the movement ["Cultural Revolution"] in every seven or eight years." I had worked in Shanghai for seven and a half years (from October 1976 to March 1983), making up the first "seven or eight years." After that came Sinopec for another seven and a half years (from March 1983 to September 1990), making up the second "seven or eight years." I told Li Peng "Now that I am re-assigned from the SCRE to the SPC, I'll spend another seven and a half years while you preside over the State Council. This should count as the third 'seven or eight years.'" Li Peng laughed at this quip. I know from personal experience that it takes at least seven or eight years for any official to bring true benefit to the work he is assigned. In other words, it will take no less than seven or eight years for any cadre to manage a department or a unit well. My three "seven to eight year stints" not only enabled me to get my head down and accomplish something worthwhile, but I was also given the opportunity to acquire a great deal of knowledge and experience in these posts. All this has profited me throughout my life. I disapprove of some officials nowadays who try to get to another post after working somewhere for only a couple of years or even less than a year. They repeatedly lobby to be re-assigned, to go to a different region and a new post before they have even got their seat warm. It takes time and hard work to do anything well. Our personnel departments need time to monitor and understand a cadre. Too short a monitoring period encourages those who are eager for instant success and immediate gains, and is conducive to impetuous attitudes and work among cadres. The bad fashion of lobbying for official posts and demanding promotion results directly from the over-frequent transfer and promotion of cadres. Xinhua News Agency once reported that the average term of county party secretaries in Henan Province was a mere 18 months. What could these officials ever achieve? I often cite this example, and ask if it is right for anyone to be in a post for less than six months and then get promoted, before having even settled and found out where he is. We are materialists who must set high value on actual performance. For any official working in whatever place, department or unit, he or she must at least perform well in their assigned job before being entrusted with more important responsibilities. If we move away from real performance, we will definitely lose our criteria for judging right from wrong, and it will surely lead our work in a wrong direction.

How to Blaze the Trail?

On February 19, 1983, the Party Central Committee and the State Council stated in their Document No. 7: "The establishment of China National Petrochemical Company is a significant event in our country's economic restructuring," emphasizing that the newly founded Sinopec "is a state ministry-level economic entity different from normal government organs. Both its organizational and operating structures should be managed according to the laws of economics." The central leaders had also told me repeatedly that Sinopec should not repeat the old ways and become another Petrochemical Ministry. The leading members of the new Sinopec, including Li Renjun, Sun Jingwen, Sun Xiaofeng, Li Zhengguang, Xu Liangtu, Ma Yi (who joined the board of directors on behalf of the State Economic Commission later), Zhang Wanxin, Zhang Haoruo, Sheng Huaren, Fei Zhirong and myself all had first-hand experience and knowledge of the wasteful history of repeated splitting and putting together of departments. We were all well aware that the old way would not work, but how should we blaze a new trail? What kind of organizational and operational structure would follow the laws of economics and count as a new way? To tell the truth, we had no idea of how to follow a correct direction.

The preparatory work for getting office premises for the new Sinopec was started from scratch. As there was no place for us to work, we had to borrow one of Yanshan Petrochemical Company's office buildings at Hepingli, in the Chaoyang District of Beijing, and worked for the time being at this two-story building of only a few hundred square meters. By that time, Sinopec already had over 100-plus employees and this small building could not accommodate us all, so we had to rent a number of rooms beneath the stands of the Workers' Stadium. As our employees needed vehicles for business purposes, I borrowed an old Shanghai sedan car for them. It was under such tough conditions that Sinopec, known as the largest company in China, started its operations. Such penny-pinching is hard to imagine for many today. Some also suggested to us at the time that we should at least find a home base or build a decent "nest" (office premises) so that we would not lose face when foreign visitors arrived. But that would have been time-consuming and distracting. Our comrades at the preparatory group for Sinopec agreed that we had "no time for fine accommodation. Let's focus our energy on work. Let's do a good job first. Other things can wait."

As soon as we began our preparatory work, we encountered the immediate problem of how to take the right path. Where should we put our first step and how should we start? The Party Central Committee and the State Council had stressed that we must break down barriers between branches of government and regional divisions. So after frank discussions, we decided to start with the task of putting together all the enterprises transferred to explore a new path in these three respects:

(1) Organizational reform: Taking over the enterprises from the ministries and regions and putting them under a centralized management system. Implementing the optimized disposition of resources.

In February 1983, the Party Central Committee and the State Council had written in its approval for establishing the new Sinopec that the horizontal and vertical division of our management system (multi-headed and diversified) was the main reason for our present low efficiency and poor profitability in utilizing China's annual 100 million tons of crude oil. The current situation hampered our drive for technological reform and growth, and naturally resulted in redundant constructions and big waste. To change this bad practice, the Party Central Committee and the State Council decided to take 39 enterprises and all their subordinate plants that formerly belonged to 20 provinces, cities and autonomous regions and three state ministries and transferred them into the newly founded China National Petrochemical Company.

For the organizational reform, we decided to make our breakthrough by taking over the enterprises promised us. At the time, someone asked which would be better done first, taking over the enterprises first or building up the new company. "We don't have space to work at yet. Wouldn't it be better to build our offices first and get things set up before going around taking over the enterprises?" At a meeting of the preparatory group to discuss the work plan, I said: "Now that we are in the advantageous situation that the Party Central Committee and the State Council have just issued the decision, we'd better seize this good opportunity to take over the enterprises first. Once somebody comes out in opposition to the decision, the wind may change and we might miss our chance. So, let's strike while the iron is hot. Let's go around taking over the enterprises promised us." My viewpoint was agreed by the other members of the group. We decided to start the take-over with enterprises of the three state ministries—petroleum, chemical industry and textiles. Then, starting in early May 1983, we sent out nine teams each headed by a member of the preparatory group to the 20 provinces, cities and autonomous regions to bring their enterprises into Sinopec. Before the nine teams set out, Li Renjun and I led a team to Beijing City to try to put the central leadership's two enterprise transfer policies into concrete terms and to try to establish a pattern for other teams to follow. One of the two enterprise transfer policies issued by the central leadership in its Document No. 7 in 1983 concerned profit sharing: namely, it stipulated that the previous local government owner of a transferred enterprise is entitled to take a share of the 20 percent profits retained by the enterprise—i.e. 20 percent of the enterprise's total profits were to be shared by the enterprise and the local government that owned it before. When negotiating the handovers, we did our best to make the terms favorable to the local governments so as to help reduce resistance to the procedure. The other policy concerned the percentage of chemical products and chemical fibers—those produced after state production targets were met—that a transferred enterprise keeps back for its previous local government owner. The local governments felt that liquefied natural gas (LNG) was particularly interesting and profitable, so we let Beijing keep back about 200,000 tons of LNG a year. Once Li Renjun and I had set up the pattern of enterprise take-over in our negotiations with Beijing on the two policies, it was easier for our teams to follow the pattern when dealing with the other regions. We spent over six months in taking over 38 of the 39 enterprises promised us by the Party Central Committee and the State Council. It could be concluded that we were working in a hard and strongly determined manner. In contrast, some companies established around the same time missed their golden opportunities and failed to obtain the anticipated results.

Xinjiang was the only region that refused to turn over its petrochemical plants. The main reason was that the Party Committee Secretary of Xinjiang Uygur Autonomous Region refused to hand over the Urumqi Petrochemical General Plant and kept fighting the decision made by the central leadership. In an attempt to persuade the Xinjiang leader, I made a special trip to Xinjiang to negotiate with him. On my arrival at Urumqi, the Xinjiang capital, I went to visit Wang Enmao, the then Vice Chairman of the Chinese People's Political Consultative Conference (CPPCC), to report to him about the central leaders' decision to set up Sinopec. I explained to him that the first thing the new Sinopec wanted to do was to take over petrochemical enterprises across the country. Without accomplishing this task, we would be unable to take the next step. Of the 39 petrochemical enterprises promised Sinopec by the Party Central Committee and the State Council, only the Urumqi Petrochemical General Plant had not been handed over. I asked if he could look into the matter and give the new Sinopec some support. If we could obtain the Urumqi Petrochemical General Plant as scheduled, we would do our best to help Xinjiang in her petrochemical industry and would, as far as possible, leave as many petrochemical products as Xinjiang wished to keep. Hearing my entreaties, Comrade Wang Enmao said: "OK. I'll try to convince the Party committee of Xinjiang." The next day, the regional government of Xinjiang held a formal meeting with us to discuss the handover issue. It was presided over by Tomur Dawamat, the then Chairman of the Xinjiang regional government. At the meeting, a vice chairman of the regional government came up with all kinds of pretexts for not handing over the Urumqi Petrochemical General Plant to Sinopec. He argued: "Xinjiang is a national minority region, so we ask not to give up our own petrochemical plant." I retorted: "Ningxia is a national minority region too. If Ningxia can turn over its plants, why can't you do so too?" I told him frankly: "Don't be so arrogant. Many of the reasons you gave are just quibbles. Now that Sinopec needs cadres badly, let me go back to Beijing and ask the central leadership to get you into Sinopec. Then we'll see whose side you take." He said as soon as he heard this: "No, don't do that. Please don't do that. I'm only making suggestions. Whether Xinjiang gives you our plant will ultimately be decided by the Party Central Committee and the State Council." "But the Party Central Committee and the State Council have already announced their formal instructions," said I, "What more do you need?" So, our negotiation went on for three days, but still to no avail. So I said finally: "I'll stay put in Xinjiang until I get the Urumqi Petrochemical General Plant." I learned later that when Wang Enmao left for a meeting in Beijing he was seen off at the airport by the Xinjiang Party Committee Secretary, who told Wang about my determination to get the plant. Wang Enmao said to him: "We'd better hand over the plant. We should support Sinopec and Chen Jinhua. He may help us with our needs in the future too." Wang's advice broke the deadlock. Soon after, the handover process went through smoothly and I left for Beijing on the sixth day of my stay in Xinjiang.

Even after we had taken over the enterprises, however, some departments and regions still voiced their different opinions about the central decision. Some opposed the decision quite fiercely. While attending a meeting in Fushun in northeast China, I heard someone at the meeting challenging "when was this Sinopec set up? Our factory was founded way back in 1932." I retorted strongly: "What kind of claim is this? Fushun was under Japanese rule in 1932 when Northeastern China was controlled as the puppet Manchukuo. You don't want them to rule you again, do you? What dreadful reasoning this is! So your factory's history is longer than New China's. Do you mean our republic is not qualified to lead you?" I reacted harshly and refused to give in. Finding this argument didn't work, someone came up with another excuse and said the enterprise employees would be disgruntled once their plant was handed over. A number of comrades from the State Economic Commission were among the loudest critics and their objections affected us most seriously. It is true that our inexperience did lead to some inappropriate arrangements in enterprise management. And there were places where we did not apply the laws of economics well. However, the most fundamental point was that we firmly followed the principle of using our 100 million tons of crude oil well and we were trying our best to utilize the crude oil assets in order to improve China's economic efficiency. Nonetheless, these comrades refused to listen to us but simply disliked the fact that, in Sinopec, they had a new "mother-in-law" above them. They even questioned the necessity of establishing Sinopec. This put Sinopec in a very difficult position. Once the State

Economic Commission held a meeting to discuss the issue of whether we should give more autonomy to enterprises. Sheng Huaren attended the meeting and announced the 40 measures formulated by Sinopec for implementing the State Council's direction to expand the autonomy of the state-owned enterprises. The 40 measures stipulated detailed ways of giving more autonomy to our enterprises, but the Director of the State Economic Commission who chaired the meeting simply ignored Sheng Huaren's speech. He even said: "The worst problem is your 40 measures." Sheng Huaren returned from the meeting and told me: "He is just unreasonable. He simply refused to listen to my talk and gave his ear instead to biased words from some enterprises!" I comforted him: "Let it go. Let's follow our own way. They cannot control that many. The '329 Plan' was authorized by the State Council and we answer to the State Council only." Such was the stormy weather Sinopec had to endure in the first few years after its establishment.

(2) Enterprise reform: making contracts for production, investment and marketing for bigger contributions to the state and to the company's accumulated funds.

The takeover of enterprises was by no means the target itself, but a measure to further the national reform and to implement the systematic integration of production, material supplies, marketing, human resources, financial and property management as well as domestic and overseas trading so as to realize the goal of optimizing our annual 100 million tons of crude oil for greater profits. In those days, enterprise reform was still at an early stage of contracting, which was the initial step of Chinese-style evolutionary reform aiming to break up the existing "supply system"—a system of payment in kind by providing working personnel and their dependants with the primary necessities of life—and the practice of eating from the same big rice-pot—indiscriminate egalitarianism—throughout the country. What distinguished Sinopec from others was its higher level of contracting in its effort to guarantee a greater share of profits for the state. After turning over most of Sinopec's profits to the government, we ploughed back the profits retained by Sinopec into the enterprise accumulated funds for further renewal and construction. The last and smaller percentage of the profits going to enterprise employees served to increase their wages and improve their welfare.

In March 1984, the Central Finance and Economic Leading Group held a meeting to hear my work report about Sinopec. The meeting agreed to a proposal that, from 1985 on, Sinopec should at first be structured into an economic entity. The state would give Sinopec greater autonomous powers whilst implementing the state's guidelines, policies and plans. The leaders of the Central Finance and Economic Leading Group pointed out that the country regarded the petrochemical industry as an effective way to make money, therefore Sinopec should minimize its spending but expand and accelerate production. Once Sinopec succeeded in increasing its profits, it would provide most necessary support to the state's extremely tight finances. They asked Sinopec to try to bring its profit and tax payment up to 20 billion *yuan* by the year 1990. Then, a situation occurred where Sinopec did indeed help out the nation. One evening in March 1986, Wang Bingqian, the Minister of Finance, phoned me and said that the National People's Congress would convene soon but that the budget handled by his ministry still had a big disparity of several hundred million *yuan*. Could Sinopec lend them this amount to tide them over, on the promise of balancing the books later? I replied: "O.K. Doesn't the country expect us to provide fuel in snowy weather for the nation? Let us do so now." The next day, I consulted Sheng Huaren and we lent the needed money to the Ministry of Finance. At the same meeting convened by the Central Finance and Economic Leading Group, Sinopec was asked to design a general plan, an overall blueprint of the anticipated company structure. From the first ten days of April 1984 on, we organized a special team to find out how to design the general plan and held three forums to hear suggestions from our plant managers. We also sought advice from national ministries such as the Organization Department of the Party Central Committee, the SPC, the State Economic Commission, the State Commission for Restructuring the Economy (SCRE) and the Ministry of Finance. In the last ten days of May, Sinopec circulated "The Plan to Further Implement the Reform and Enhance our Economic Efficiency (1985-1990)." The plan, comprising "four settings, four guarantees and four covers" proposed a method whereby Sinopec made a contract with the state. The "four settings" meant that the state would set the volume of production, investment, tax types and rates, and the profit to be retained by Sinopec. The "four guarantees" meant that the state would guarantee 1) Sinopec's raw material supply, fuel, electric power and transportation; 2) essential funding for Sinopec's production; 3) centrally allocated materials and equipment; 4) the specialists required for Sinopec's production development. Finally, the "four covers" meant that Sinopec would cover responsibility for its financial management, main production output, technical renewal, original innovation and funds for trial manufacture of new products, and product quality. The ultimate target of our pledge to the nation was to accumulate a total of 30 billion *yuan* of fixed assets and contribute profit and tax total of 90 billion *yuan* in the six years from 1985 to 1990, and to achieve single year profit and tax contribution of 20 billion *yuan* in 1990. This was known to the public as the "329 Plan." Thanks to the hard work of all concerned, by 1990 Sinopec did achieve 44 billion *yuan* of total investment in fixed assets and cumulative profit and tax of 94.6 billion *yuan*. Both investment and production exceeded the targets Sinopec had pledged the nation in the contract plan six years earlier. However, because of the adjustment to the crude oil price at the time, in 1990 Sinopec fell short of its profit and tax pledge to the state, contributing only 16.75 billion *yuan* of profit and tax in that year.

At the May 23-June 20, 1984, meeting of the Central Finance and Economic Leading Group chaired by Yao Yilin, the "329 Plan" put forward by Sinopec was discussed twice. Approving our plan in principle, the Leading Group believed Sinopec had put in a great deal of work and made multiple revisions to the plan. The group leaders asked us to make additional revisions to the plan and take it to our plant managers for further discussion in August before submitting the plan to the State Council for formal ratification and our eventual implementation.

During the course of about half a year, from January to August 1984, eight successive meetings of the Central Finance and Economic Leading Group studied the performance of Sinopec, especially our contract plan on investment and production targets. This had never happened to other ministries and commissions before, which made me realize the keen expectations the Party Central Committee and the State Council had of us at Sinopec.

On October 19, 1984, the State Council approved and printed "The Plan to Further Implement the Reform and Enhance our Economic Efficiency" (the "329 Plan") presented by Sinopec in State Council Document No. 142, 1984. Before distributing our plan, the Secretary General of the State Council phoned me especially to let me know it had ratified our plan. After the issuing of State Council Document No. 142, we called a meeting attended by all our plant leaders to discuss the plan, which now had official approval from the central government. I gave a speech at the meeting and announced eight measures to implement the contract plan for real. These were: 1) adjust and strengthen all levels of management at Sinopec; 2) do a good job in technological transformation and development. Establish a strategic guideline of relying on technology to improve Sinopec's economic efficiency; 3) focus attention on the construction of priority projects; 4) intensify the creation of a talent pool to improve the quality of our employees; 5) strengthen the company operations and widen distribution of finished products; 6) expand our opening-up to the world and our cooperation with foreign enterprises; 7) implement modern modes of management and raise the level of our business operations; 8) strengthen political and ideological work throughout Sinopec. These eight measures drawn up for the implementation of the "329 Plan" were carried out in earnest and achieved pretty satisfactory results.

After fulfilling the "329 Plan," Sinopec immediately started its second contract plan—The Five-year Contract Plan of Investment and Production (1991-1995). Directed by Sheng Huaren, the second contract plan set up a "521 target," meaning that Sinopec would invest a total of 54.5 billion *yuan* over five years, handing over 20 billion *yuan* of profit and tax to the state in 1995 and realizing a total 100 billion *yuan* of profit and tax in five years. Five years later, Sinopec had made total profit and tax of 117.076 billion *yuan* in five years by the end of 1995, exceeding the contract plan target by 17 percent. We handed over profit and tax of 25 billion *yuan* in 1995, 25 percent more than the target committed to in the second contract plan. Sinopec also achieved investment of 80.4 billion *yuan* over five years, 47.5 percent higher than the pledged target. By over-achieving on every quota promised in the second five-year plan of investment and production, Sinopec further demonstrated the excellent effect of its management system and structural renewal.

(3) Reform in investment: Self-financing and pluralizing ways of investment in order to revive the eight imported production facilities including the four ethylene facilities.

One important purpose in the Party Central Committee and State Council establishing Sinopec was to have the new company put together the necessary finance to revive the 1978 importation of 10 large petrochemical facilities, in particular the four ethylene facilities. Sinopec was assigned to take care of eight of these 10 facilities. These were: the four 300,000-ton ethylene facilities, three 300,000-ton synthetic ammonia and 520,000-ton urea facilities and one 200,000-ton polyester facility that was installed at Shanghai Petroleum & Chemical Plant. The two projects not given to Sinopec were the 115,000-ton ethylene facility at Jilin Chemical Industry Corporation, which remained with the Ministry of Chemical Industry. The other was the Yizheng Chemical Fiber Plant, which remained with the Ministry of Textiles. When Sinopec got involved in the detailed negotiations for the importation of these eight production facilities, it coincided with China's central leadership's decision to rectify the national economy and to drastically reduce the importation of large production facilities. At the time, the eight facilities left with Sinopec had only a small proportion of their agreements settled and there was a long way to go before their purchase and installation were complete. The importation of the four ethylene facilities was even farther behind; most of their purchase agreements were as yet unsettled. It would take a great deal of work for Sinopec before we could revive their importation and installation.

Sinopec invested a great deal of money including large sums of foreign exchange into its work on the eight production facilities. We invested 44 billion *yuan* in the fixed assets in our first contract plan of production and investment, in the course of which over 25 billion *yuan* went into the four ethylene facilities, 56.8 percent of the total amount. The money needed for these facilities far exceeded our initial expectations both in terms of workload and responsibility. The State Council leader repeatedly asked us to do our best to complete the four large ethylene facilities. He also asked us to accompany him to the project work sites to check on the situation and seek solutions. Basically penniless at its founding, Sinopec had almost nothing to start capital construction at first. A deputy plant chief in charge of capital construction at Urumqi Petrochemical Plant challenged us openly: "Sinopec hasn't even got a pair of pants to cover its own backside. What does it have to control us?" Though the remark sounded rude, it did describe the true situation. Before 1981, China practiced the financial allocation system whereby a certain portion of the state budget every year was given to capital construction across the country. In the first instance the SPC allocated sums of money to government departments and regions, which then distributed the money among various capital constructions according to need. After 1981, China replaced the allocation system with bank loans for all projects of capital constructions. Consequently, the ministries of petroleum, chemical industry and textiles who initially imported these production facilities had their funding cut off at a stroke. Not only had they nowhere to borrow the money needed for the projects, they had no idea how to repay loans even if they could somehow obtain them. After Sinopec took over these projects, the capital construction plans for these facilites provided by their original purchasers—the three ministries—were all out of date. Nor was there as yet any new plan for where to raise the money. So Sinopec had to find a way and get money itself, in accordance with the new guideline of the Party Central Committee and the State Council that demanded "everyone must use economic means to handle economic matters." After exploring all kinds of methods, we finally decided on the following five ways to obtain money for the imported equipment.

The first and earliest method came from Li Renjun in 1985. He suggested that we use a "four-way split policy" to cooperate with local governments in raising finance. It meant that all the sides involved in the importation and construction of a production facility shared the project budget. The end products, profit, taxes and output could be shared among all sides based on their share of the costs. This method was quickly approved by the State Council leader and implemented right away. Sinopec signed agreements, one after the other, with 14 provinces, cities and autonomous regions for sharing the construction budget. We used the money collected to launch a batch of "short, smooth and fast" projects characterized by low investment, good and quick results. These small, short duration projects were made to swell Sinopec's capital accumulation for our major project constructions.

The second method was to sell petrochemical products to collect revenue. In the 1980s, petrochemical products were scarce commodities, in demand everywhere in the market. Sinopec could sell a portion of its petrochemical products to local enterprises within the annual national quota. By converting a proportion of our products into cash from buyers around the country, we would be able to collect more than two billion *yuan* a year.

The third was to "replace imported products with domestic-made products." By replacing imported petrochemical products with Sinopec's China-made products, we saved valuable foreign exchange for the country. In June 1985, we formulated a plan funded by foreign capital to intensify our plastic and synthetic fiber production in order to "replace imported products with domestic-made products" and save foreign exchange. This plan too received fast approval from the State Council.

The fourth was to issue enterprise bonds under the authorized debt quota regulated by the state. As Sinopec enjoyed a high credit standing, the distribution of Sinopec bonds went very well.

The fifth was commercial loans from overseas. Authorized by the SPC, Sinopec made successive overseas borrowings of US$ 3.04 billion, 100 million Deutschmarks and 18 billion Japanese Yen between November 1985 and March 1988. We used the loans mainly on the construction of three ethylene facilities at Daqing, Qilu and Yangtze petrochemical plants. The budget needed for the 300,000-ton ethylene facility at Shanghai was collected through other means. The State Council leader had told the Shanghai Municipal Party Committee Secretary Rui Xingwen, Shanghai's Mayor Jiang Zemin and myself to find a way of completing and commissioning Shanghai's ethylene facility as soon as possible. In May 1986, Sinopec and the Shanghai People's Government filed a joint proposal to issue enterprise bonds and take out foreign commercial loans for constructing the 300,000-ton ethylene project in Shanghai. The State Council authorized our proposal with the instruction that we should reform the capital construction management, releasing more autonomy to our plants so that they could seek loans from relevant organizations in China and abroad. Before long, I went to see the President of the Industrial Bank of Japan, San Kisaburo, whom I knew from the time we cooperated in raising finance for Shanghai Baoshan Steel. At my request, he talked to dozens of international banks and these banks formed an international loan consortium. They got us advantageous loans with low fees and good terms, which helped the smooth construction of our 300,000-ton ethylene facility in Shanghai.

Due to the huge sums involved and exchange rate fluctuation at the time, in particular with the Japanese Yen, repaying these loans posed an extremely heavy task for Sinopec. With the warm support of the Party Central Committee and the State Council, the government offered Sinopec preferential policies in the nick of time. These policies included "making best use of foreign capital, replacing imports with domestic products, removing interest on loan repayment and high price for high-cost products." Sinopec used some of the products made by the three ethylene plants of Daqing, Qilu and Yangtze to "replace imports" and used all the foreign exchange quota we had saved to repay the foreign loans. Sinopec also exported its products and put the reimbursed tax amount into loan repayment. Our products made from high-cost crude oil were allowed to sell for high prices too. All these preferential policies helped Sinopec greatly boost its loan repayment capability, enabling us to open up channels to raise foreign capital and build up a good reputation internationally.

The measures Sinopec adopted to rely upon its own strength for fundraising and capital accumulation represented an early practice of China's investment system reform. Although these measures should not be counted as the standardized investment diversification realized in China subsequently, they did bring about a tremendous change in investment channels for other enterprises. Sinopec's efforts helped transform the former state system of fund allocation, moving it into a structure whereby enterprises obtain loans, forcing them to plan their financial management carefully, save every penny of investment and pay great attention to the rate of return on investment and strengthening their repayment capability. The great change that took place in management concepts and behavior further impelled enterprise reform and laid the much-needed foundation for a modern structure of enterprise operation in the following decades.

After the four ethylene facilities at Daqing, Qilu, Yangtze and Shanghai were completed and operational, they provided Sinopec with new manufacturing capacity of 1.2 million tons of ethylene, 1.43 million tons of plastics, 140,000 tons of rubber, 680,000 tons of synthetic fibers, and 2.26 million tons of basic industrial chemical products per annum. More significantly, all four ethylene projects became important petrochemical bases in China and went from strength to strength. For example, since the initial importation and installation at Shanghai Petroleum & Chemical Plant, it has been expanded and updated four times, its ethylene output increasing from 115,000 tons to nearly one million, its plastics output from 50,000 tons to almost one million tons and its synthetic fibers and products from 40,000 tons to nearly one million tons per annum. The chicken and egg effect was remarkable—a single plant gave birth to a triple million-ton output complex.

Before Sinopec had accomplished its second contract plan of investment and production, the eight large imported facilities were successfully completed and put into production. Sinopec's capability for independent development was enhanced dramatically and the gulf between China and the top level of the world was much reduced too. Greatly pleased with the operation of our four large ethylene facilities, Li Xiannian held a special reception at the Great Hall of the People, meeting with the foreign experts who had helped build the last ethylene facility. When photographs were taken, Li Xiannian made a particular point of pulling Sun Jingwen to his side for the camera. Those of us aware of the behind-the-scenes story understood Li Xiannian's intention. As Chemical Industry Minister, Sun Jingwen had been unfairly treated when directing the negotiations for large equipment importation, being wrongly criticized for importing the petrochemical facilities at the time. In the *Biography of Sun Jingwen*, a chapter was devoted specifically to his unfair treatment over the importation. Sun Jingwen had been deeply hurt by the wrong accusation against him, which was why he was particularly happy to see the completion of these projects. Having said farewell to the foreign guests, Li Xiannian commented to us that if only the Chinese leaders had toughed it out, the suspension of these projects might have been avoided. In other words, but for all the stopping and starting on the four ethylene facilities, the plants might have been operational much sooner and already making their great contributions. As Li Xiannian had been in charge of national finance and economics for a long time, he was clear about China's reserves, what our market condition was and what was needed for people's livelihood. Agreeing with him, I said: "China is a large country with a huge population and tremendous expenditure. By tightening the belt here and there, we may be able to collect enough strength to get things done. Otherwise, if we loosen our fingers just a little, any sum of money could be spent without a cent left over. No matter how important a project is, someone can always come up with why we don't have the money or ability to do it." Li Xiannian nodded in agreement.

From China National Petrochemical Company to China Petrochemical Corporation and Conversion into a Joint-stock Company

Sinopec's growth can be divided into three major stages. Relating Sinopec's history to Wang Jiming, the current President of Sinopec, I compared the company's transformation and development over the past 20 or so years to a three-act play: the first act was the founding of China National Petrochemical Company, optimizing utilization of the 100 million tons of crude oil and implementing the contract plan for investment and production. Whilst Sinopec was making important contributions to the nation, at the same time we were accumulating strength for our own development too. The second act was the establishment of China Petrochemical Corporation, integrating upstream and downstream ends, production links, supplies and sales, and domestic and foreign trading to internationalize our operations. The third act was the restructuring of Sinopec into a joint-stock petrochemical corporation according to international norms, releasing H and A stocks on the New York, London, Hong Kong and Shanghai stock markets and going public so as to move Sinopec further towards center stage in international society. Wang Jiming agreed with my metaphor, calling it a good description that illustrated precisely Sinopec's step-by-step growth. I myself was the protagonist of Act One. Sheng Huaren, Li Yizhong and Chen Tonghai were the protagonists of the second and third acts. Building on the foundations laid in Act One, they moved China's petrochemical mission toward a higher level and a larger scale.

The second act of Sinopec's growth and reform was its restructure as a group company and integrating upstream and downstream activities, domestic and foreign trading. This part was a significant reform step in the direction of centralized integration.

In order to accelerate and perfect the development of China's socialist market economic system, to break up monopolies and promote active competition, and for faster and better development of social productive forces, the State Council decided on a strategic reorganization of the national petrochemical industry in 1998. It asked the former China National Petrochemical Company and China National Petroleum Company to swap some of their respective oil fields and refineries and to transfer petroleum companies previously led by various regions into the reorganized China Petrochemical Corporation and China National Petroleum Corporation (CNPC). After the reorganization, the two conglomerates implemented their respective integrations of upstream and downstream, domestic and foreign trade, production chain, supplies and sales, basically completing their structural centralization. In the past, the former China National Petroleum Company had generally taken care of oil fields only, but had nothing to do with the refineries and chemical engineering plants where the crude oil from their oil fields was processed and utilized. So it basically monopolized the upstream oil fields link in the chain. On the other hand, the former China National Petrochemical Company was in charge of refineries and chemical plants only, but had nothing to do with oil fields so it monopolized the downstream link of processing plants. The relationship between the two companies was non-competitive, at odds with the mechanism of active competition between enterprises, a most important part of the socialist market economy, essential to the continual strengthening of enterprises through mutual competition that would impel the development of the petrochemical cause. The reorganization broke up the division between specializations by drawing a demarcation line between north and south to form a new parallel pattern of competition between the two conglomerates. Petrochemical enterprises in southern China and in eastern China south of Beijing were transferred to Sinopec in the southern sector. Most of those in northeast China, those north of Beijing as well as some enterprises in northwest and southwest China were incorporated into CNPC in the northern sector. Since Sinopec did not have enough upstream oilfields at the beginning, the State Council decided to merge the entire New Star Petroleum Company and all its subsidiaries scattered around the country into Sinopec, in order to enhance its upstream to a certain extent. After the reorganization, Sinopec succeeded in separating its political management from enterprise management so becoming a true entity involved in business operation and market competition. The restructured Sinopec was enabled to play a new and vital role in promoting the development of the petrochemical industry, reform and opening-up practice and market competition in China.

First, Sinopec rapidly strengthened its overall capability. By the end of 2003, the total assets of the corporation amounted to 559.2 billion *yuan* and its net assets had risen to 268.1 billion *yuan*, increases of 30.8 percent and 47.6 percent respectively compared with 1998. In the year 2003, the conglomerate produced 38.16 million tons of crude oil and 5.3 billion cubic meters of natural gas, processing 124 million tons of crude oil and manufacturing 4.147 million tons of ethylene. These outputs represented growth of 8.04 percent, 30.44 percent, 54 percent and 82.86 percent respectively over the 1998 figures.

Second, Sinopec dramatically improved its profitability. In 2003, the corporation registered 466.7 billion *yuan* turnover, 70.5 billion *yuan* profit and tax, of which 28.978 billion *yuan* being profit, increases of 65.6 percent, 65.04 percent and 730.32 percent respectively over 1998.

Then, Sinopec further consolidated its marketing network and sharpened its competence. The corporation sold 75.92 million tons of refined oil in 2003, 99.8 percent more than in 1998. Its number of gas stations grew from fewer than 8,000 to 24,500, plus over 5,500 franchised gas stations. Sinopec's market control was further strengthened. Its specialized marketing network for chemical products made notable progress with improvements to its widely dispersed state. Sinopec had basically established its concept and mechanisms, oriented by market demand and guided by profit maximization.

Finally, the corporation promoted China's reforms and established the initial modern system of enterprise operation. The corporation founded the preliminary framework of a national stock-holding company, which established the system of divisional structure headed by corporate legal entity. It ensured effective operation of state assets and the realization of inflation-proofing and appreciation, accelerated the development of the main industries of petroleum and petrochemicals, and intensified the restructuring of ancillary industries by hiving off social undertaking functions from these manufacturing entities. As well as the overall restructure of the company and its conversion to a public corporation, Sinopec also took decisive downsizing action in the interests of greater efficiency, reducing its payroll numbers to 850,000 employees, from its 1.22 million peak in 2000.

Challenged by other petroleum and petrochemical industries on the domestic and international fronts, China's petroleum and chemical industries faced the highest stress of lacking crude oil and natural gas supplies. After Sinopec was founded, it stepped up its international operations in order to optimize crude oil and natural gas resources both at home and overseas and to open up the domestic and international market. As early as July 1983, when Sinopec was established, the central leadership had decided to give Sinopec the petrochemical import-export business hitherto controlled by the Foreign Trade Ministry. I was told that the China National Chemical Company, the Sinochem mentioned earlier, had also been told to prepare to join Sinopec. However, in November that year, Li Renjun and I went to talk to Zheng Tuobin, the Minister of Foreign Trade, about giving us Sinochem, but found his attitude changed. Zheng claimed that a central leader said that the reform in foreign trade would be withdrawn and hence the decision to give Sinochem to Sinopec could not be implemented. We were unsure whether the central leader's words meant that reform in foreign trade had to be reversed, nor how such a change in direction could be in line with the State Council Document No. 7, 1983, which required integration of domestic and foreign trade. We neither saw any written document of that central leader's direction nor heard it directly from that leader. It was just Zheng Tuobin who told us of it. Of course, Zheng would not make up the direction; he would not dare to do so without an actual source. But Zheng refused to give Sinochem to us and we were unable to persuade him. We reported back to the State Council, but since the direction had come from a central leader, the State Council made no comment about it and the matter was halted under such circumstances. Feeling it inadequate for a big corporation like Sinopec not to have business in the international market, we repeatedly tried to negotiate the issue. We ended up obtaining a number of small commodities such as paraffin wax, lubricating oil, etc. of less than US$10 million in total. The reform blueprint to integrate domestic and foreign trade in China was thus delayed for as long as 15 years—from 1983, the year when we went to discuss the transfer issue with the Foreign Trade Minister, until 1998, when it was finally settled with the Sinopec Group. Fifteen years were wasted in pointless waiting. I am convinced that so long as a reform involved any change to the power structure, the resistant power was tremendous. Once a government branch said nay, the whole plan might be halted. If only we could have realized integration sooner, the earlier China's petrochemical and petroleum industries would have stepped over our national borders and won business opportunities around the world. The sooner and better we could have searched for oil fields and natural gas fields and opened up their resources and markets at home and abroad. We would definitely be treading a wider path than the one we have today.

After China Petrochemical Corporation was established, it paid much more attention to exploration of upstream oil and natural gas fields and expansion of downstream market of oil products, all the while continuing its effort in developing refinery and chemical production. To solve the supply shortage and to expand the market for its products, Sinopec focused its effort primarily in four areas:

First, Sinopec continued to explore domestic resources and intensify its efforts to discover and open up oil and gas fields. According to the newest appraisal data, China has total reserves of 110 billion tons of crude oil, but of this only 13.5-16 billion tons, including 1.5 billion tons offshore, are extractable. By the end of 2002, totally 22.7 billion tons of oil reserves were verified, representing 43.4 percent of China's oil resources. Added together, the petroleum reserves in the 10 large basins and regions of Bohai Gulf, Songliao, Subei, Jianghan, Nanxiang, Sichuan, Erdos, Tarim, Zungar and the East China Sea comprise about 30 percent of China's total oil resource. Sinopec focused its immediate and near future mining exploration in three major directions—east, west and offshore China. In its effort, Sinopec cooperated successively with the American Energy Development Co., Chevron Corporation, Genting of Malaysia, the Husky Company of Canada, in such projects as risk exploration, individual well upgrading for higher output, and increasing oil extraction volume. These cooperative explorations achieved promising results. In particular, after Sinopec aligned with China National Offshore Oil Corporation, they got Shell Oil and Unocal to join them in a joint exploration of natural gas resources in the East China Sea, thus accelerating the exploration of offshore oil and gas fields in the East China Sea.

Second, Sinopec stepped up the pace of "going abroad," so as to be able to complete standardized production bases of oil products overseas as soon as possible. In this regard, despite its comparatively late start, Sinopec progressed at an impressive rate, using its superiority in aspects such as crude oil purchase, integration of upstream, midstream and downstream links, engineering, technical and labor services. Over the past few years, Sinopec has selected from a wide range of projects and participated in competitive tenders in the Middle East, West Africa, North Africa, Southeast Asia, Central Asia and Russia. By the end of 2003, Sinopec had signed and carried out eight oil and natural gas projects. These included three oilfield development projects in Algeria, Kyrgyzstan and Azerbaijan and five feasibility study projects in Indonesia, Yemen, Iran, Kyrgyzstan, and Mongolia. Some of these projects have already shown exciting signs of oil and gas deposits. In 2004, Sinopec again signed a number of major exploratory projects and its petro-engineering and technical and labor services overseas yielded good results too, with altogether 65 projects signed and carried out across 14 countries. Its teams of petro-engineers from the Zhongyuan, Shengli and other oilfields enjoy tremendous prestige in fields throughout the Middle East, Africa and elsewhere for their superb skills, fine service and steady working style. The successful upgrading of a refinery in Iran accomplished by Sinopec in 2003 was China's first large overseas petrochemical project on an EPCC (engineering, procurement, construction and commissioning) contract basis. It won wide praise from the Iranian government and enterprises.

Another major "going abroad" operation was Sinopec's work in opening up the petrochemical product market, advertising its own products and vigorously expanding its export business. China's traditional products for export included paraffin wax, refinery coke, lubricating oil base and refined oil. Owing to increased domestic demand, exports of lubricating oil base and refined oil fell. However, exports of pure caustic soda, asphalt, pure benzene, PVA, petro-mechanical and electro-mechanical equipment grew faster, and certain quantities of cracking catalyst, oil dope, molecular sieve and other products were sold overseas as well. In 2003, Sinopec exported 6.1 million tons of refined oil, a 216 percent increase on the 1998 quantity.

Third, Sinopec applied business means to guarantee domestic crude oil supply, so as to ensure petroleum security. Whilst accelerating its construction of crude oil production bases overseas, Sinopec adopted a pluralist strategy in crude oil importation. On the basis of stabilized purchase quotas from the Middle East and West Africa, Sinopec developed crude resources in the Caspian Sea area, as well as in South and North America. While rolling out its international business, Sinopec has continuously expanded its foreign operating teams and gained experience. The company is now able to develop foreign petroleum business comprehensively around the world.

Fourth and last, all the time it was exploring international business, Sinopec paid much more attention to heightening its competitiveness and control of the domestic market. In this respect, it focused on reorganizing the refined oil market and developing its marketing network. On the one hand, Sinopec supported and participated in the effort by the state to crush the smuggling of refined oil and restore order to the refined oil market. On the other hand, from the second half of 1999 on, we seized the valuable opportunity before China's accession to the World Trade Organization and the grace period to purchase massive numbers of gas stations and fuel depots by means of acquisition, stock holding, share holding, joint operation and franchised operation. Then, through the efficient renovation and new construction of gas stations, Sinopec soon built up a marketing network of refined oil in over 20 provinces (regions and cities) and established an initial, highly effective system of storage and allocation. In addition to over 5,000 franchised gas stations, the total number of Sinopec-owned gas stations grew from 8,000 in 1998 to 25,000 in 2003. Thanks to the growth of its marketing network, Sinopec experienced both dramatic changes in its refined oil marketing structure and a huge rise in its market competitiveness and control. The retail volume of Sinopec's refined oil grew from over eight million tons in 1998 to 38.85 million tons in 2003, recording 70 percent-plus increases in both retail and direct sales and representing 68 percent share of the main retail market.

The third act in Sinopec's restructuring and growth was to implement the joint-stock system from a position of strength according to international norms.

Around the time that China Petrochemical Corporation was formed, a succession of super-large enterprises controlled by Sinopec underwent conversion to joint stock structure. This was first the reorganization and going public of the Shanghai Petrochemical Corporation in 1993. Then came a succession of 17 enterprises transformed into joint stock corporations, including Zhenhai Refining and Chemical, Yizheng Chemical Fibers, Yanshan Petrochemical, Yangtze Petrochemical, Qilu Petrochemical, Shengli Daming, Zhongyuan Oil and Gas, and Jianghan Drilling. These newly formed joint stock companies raised a total in excess of 21.3 billion *yuan* on the capital market, which greatly improved the asset-liability balances of the enterprises, accelerated their internal reforms, brought on people with the necessary skills and accumulated valuable experience. All this laid a solid foundation for Sinopec's later overall structural reform into a joint stock company.

Sinopec controls more than 60 enterprises. The first batch of 17 went public a few years ago. After Sinopec was restructured into a group company, it underwent another system reform and restructured all its assets, launching an overall transformation into shareholding in

1999. The China Petroleum & Chemical Corporation was formed in February 2000. In the new shareholding corporation, the principal operations were separated from ancillary operations, fine assets from bad, and business functions from social functions. In other words, well-performing assets were transferred into the newly formed public company Sinopec, and social undertakings away from the shareholding corporation. The overall system reform of Sinopec listed totally 60 direct and holding enterprises under Sinopec, including the 17 already listed. Taking September 30, 1999 as the appraisal date, the valuation put Sinopec's gross assets at over 249.5 billion *yuan*. Its total debt was 151.3 billion *yuan*, so its net assets were 98.2 billion *yuan*, an asset/liability ratio of 60.63 percent. About 510,000 employees joined the newly formed joint stock corporation, some 42 percent of the total 1,194,000 headcount of the Sinopec Group.

After its overall restructure into a shareholding corporation, the China Petroleum & Chemical Corporation brought its management system into line with international norms by implementing a divisional system headed by the first level legal person, and setting up a governance structure of board of shareholders, board of directors, board of supervisors and various levels of managers. With the Sinopec Group as its primary shareholder, the China Petroleum & Chemical Corporation is holding-managed according to the "Company Law of the People's Republic of China," related state provisions and the standing regulations for listed companies. Sinopec Group continues its management over its unlisted enterprises and units. Successfully floated overseas in October 2000, the China Petroleum & Chemical Corporation issued totally 16.78 billion H shares at US\$ 3.462 billion. In July 2001, the corporation issued 2.8 billion A shares at 11.816 billion *yuan* in China.

The success of Sinopec's joint stock structural reform was a historical watershed for China's petrochemical industry. The event will exert a profound and far-reaching influence on both future reform and development in China and the internationalized operations of China Petroleum & Chemical Corporation. Premier Zhu Rongji and Vice Premier Wu Bangguo at the time praised it highly. The success of Sinopec's system reform into shareholding is primarily apparent in the following aspects:

One is that the reform optimized Sinopec's industrial structure as well as its assets structure. The Sinopec Group formed the rather capable China Petroleum & Chemical Corporation as its main entity on the basis of integrating its upstream, midstream and downstream enterprises. The newly formed shareholding corporation focuses its operations on exploration and development of oil and gas fields, refinery, petrochemical production and marketing. The changed asset status post-restructuring is shown in Table 4.

Table 4   **Unit: 100 million *yuan***

	China Petrochemical Corporation before the restructuring	Listed companies after the restructuring	Unlisted companies after the restructuring
Gross assets	4460.22	2532.78	1927.44
Liability	2552.89	1686.57	867.32
Ownership interests	1637.45	741.46	895.99

Two, the reform raised a great deal of funds, which significantly increased the interest of all shareholders and improved the company's asset-debt ratio. Since 1993, Sinopec Corp has raised the equivalent of about 98.4 billion *yuan* on domestic and foreign stock markets. In particular, the two major capital accumulations through the issuance of H and A shares rapidly and dramatically increased Sinopec Corp's gross and net assets. The massive injection of share capital provided the needed finance for the company's development, continual reform, and personnel reduction and outplacement. It also opened up an avenue for Sinopec's later work in the effective operation of capital, ongoing financing, purchasing fine assets and reorganizing its existing public companies.

Three, the reform brought in strategic investors and expanded Sinopec's international cooperation. Its initial release of H shares attracted for Sinopec four strategic investors—Exxon Standard Oil, Shell Oil, BP and ABB; and four financial investors—Hong Kong Henderson, Towngas, Cheung Kong Holdings and Hutchison Whampoa. Then, its release of A shares brought in nine strategic investors—Sichuan Changhong Electric, Qingdao Harbor Bureau, Ningbo Harbor Bureau, Yunnan Hongta, Sinochem, Shanghai Baoshan Steel, Wuhan Iron and Steel Works, Hangzhou Steam Turbine Co. and COSCO. The cooperation between Sinopec and these important enterprises at home and abroad helped them, in particular the big overseas corporations, to learn more about Sinopec, hence boosting confidence for cooperation, accelerating the progress of the large cooperation projects and opening up new ways of market cooperation. The expansion and acceleration of Sinopec's international cooperation also benefited Chinese in learning vanguard techniques and managerial experience from foreign countries, learning from their internationalized operations so that they could brave the challenges, cooperation and competition of economic globalization.

Four, the reform greatly clarified asset rights, improved the capital stock structure and enhanced the control and operational efficiency of state-owned capital. As the biggest shareholder of Sinopec Corp, Sinopec Group used capital as a crucial means to exercise management over Sinopec Corp and realized the fast growth of its capital and business by means of effective capital operation. Private shareholders' profit and state-owned share profit both experienced effective growth, thus enhancing the effective operation of state capital. The introduction onto the scene of foreign capital shares, national A shares and other investors enlarged the total control of state-owned capital, therefore heightening the operating efficiency of state assets. This is demonstrated in detail in Table 5:

Table 5   **Unit: 100 million *yuan***

	Before going public	After issuance of H shares	Increase over the period before going public	After issuance of A shares	Increase over the period before going public
Gross assets	2498	3409.19	36.59%	3548.71	42.18%
Ownership interest	983	1208	22.89%	1447.67	47.27%
Interest of state-owned shares out of the overall ownership interests	983	966.4	-0.17%*	1120.79	14%

*When the H shares were being issued, two percentage points of state-owned shares, or 1.678 billion shares were sold and the capital thus received was turned to the central treasury and used as social security funds, therefore the minus growth shown in the table.

After the Sinopec Group formed the China Petroleum & Chemical Corporation (Sinopec Corp) for its main operations, its non-listed units underwent changes in both living conditions and development environment, with certain deep-rooted problems that had accumulated over the years beginning to emerge. These problems were mainly redundant staff, a large amount of bad assets, overburdened social undertakings, widely dispersed industries, low competitiveness and financial difficulties. To address these problems properly, on the one hand, Sinopec Group received tremendous policy support from the state as regards land allocation, bonus distribution, tax reimbursement and other issues; on the other, Sinopec Group also intensified the reform dynamic in these units. Following the guideline of "close down and cancel a batch, reorganize and reform a batch, and strengthen and upgrade a batch," Sinopec Group worked hard to urge its non-listed units to reduce and reverse their deficits and stand on their own feet. The main measures taken by Sinopec Group to solve these problems included: 1) Cultivating into fine assets those main units in refineries, chemical plants and others that had not gone public and then, when appropriate, inserting them into the listed part of the corporation. For example, Sinopec inserted its Maoming Ethylene Works, Xi'an Petrochemical Plant, Tahe Petrochemical Plant and a number of gas stations into its listed part in Sinopec Corp in 2003. 2) Applying professional reorganization to its public and professional services in water, electricity, steam and wind power, and well-drilling, monitoring, checking and maintenance at varying levels. 3) Speeding up its withdrawal from businesses involved in non-core areas by means of reorganization, staff reduction and redeployment. By March 2004, Sinopec Group had applied such measures to 145 units involving 1.8 billion *yuan* of assets and cutting or redeploying 15,000 employees. 4) Creating favorable conditions for transferring into the wider community those units under Sinopec concerned with culture, education, health care and others operated by such social function units. Sinopec Group, as a test bed authorized by the state in 2004 for transferring, paying, solving and separating social functions from enterprises, were turning over all its elementary and middle schools as well as law enforcement agencies to the local governments. After several years of hard work, by 2003, Sinopec Group had reduced the deficit in its unlisted units sector from the original figure in excess of 10 billion *yuan* down to six billon *yuan*. The corporation hoped to achieve on average break-even by 2005.

Five, the reform into shareholding accelerated the transformation of Sinopec's systems and mechanisms, improving its operation and management of enterprises to make them more competitive. The further change of Sinopec toward a state-controlled shareholding corporation set up its initial operational framework, exercising the legal rights of investors including profiting from their investment, major decision-making and selection of managers. The China Petroleum & Chemical Corporation has built up a basic structure of a modern enterprise, a fairly standard system of corporate governance and divisional management. It has realized an integrated, concentrated system of management in such aspects as international operational strategy, major financing decision-making, fund settlement, cooperation with foreign enterprises, significant scientific research and information system. It has corrected the former bad practice of multi-layer governance, duplicated decision-making and scattered investments, and has further optimized allocation of its internal resources. The reform into a shareholding corporation allowed Sinopec to enter both domestic and foreign capital markets, placing it under the direct surveillance of the security supervisory organs, investors and news media both inside and outside the country.

The new situation has helped form a new enterprise culture in Sinopec Corp, namely, an operating concept of "competition and open-mind," an operating strategy of "resource expansion, market exploration, cost reduction, efficiency increase and prudent investment," and an operating objective of "maximizing profits for the corporation and shareholders." Also, it includes the corporation's operating mechanism of "marketization externally, integration internally," its operating rule of "standardization, strictness and honesty," and motivating mechanism of "never feeling complacent, everyone fulfilling his or her own task." As regards the corporation's operating mechanism, the key guideline is the market operating mechanism emphasizing the principles of optimum economic efficiency and maximum return on investment, encouraging the establishment of a system of effective incentivization and innovation, self-surveillance and risk control.

In line with the requirements of the new corporation system and structure, the financial system of Sinopec Corp is linked with that of international society. It has formulated a rigorous framework of financial management. By making active use of two e-commerce websites for petrochemical product sale and material acquisition as well as two e-management systems for refined oil marketing and financial management, it has launched the "Enterprise Resources Plan" (ERP).

At the same time, Sinopec Group acts actively upon the proposal for "Global Agreement" made by Mr. Kofi Annan, the former UN Secretary General. By submitting a formal pledge letter to the UN, the corporation promised to earnestly fulfill its social responsibilities and take the lead in advancing the strategy of sustainable development.

In December 2000, China formally joined the World Trade Organization. Many were worried at the time whether Sinopec and other super-large Chinese enterprises could withstand the challenges of WTO membership. The facts today prove that China's petrochemical enterprises have coped very well by properly meeting its pledge and breaking up the monopoly on importation. Surveillance by the Chinese Government has become further standardized. China's market economy is continually maturing. Foreign capital and products have further penetrated China's domestic market and Chinese private enterprises are growing more rapidly. A pluralist investment structure is taking shape. The international competitiveness of Chinese petrochemical enterprises is growing. Sinopec is greeting the challenges of the 21st century with confidence, as a major, world-class corporation.

Giant State-owned Enterprises Could Grow Stronger and Larger

The reform of China's state-owned enterprises (SOEs) has been a hot topic within China and beyond. Could the SOEs be reformed and developed, growing stronger and larger? Through the more than two decades of practice by Sinopec, we can give a definitive answer: China's SOEs, in particular the super-large enterprises and group corporations, could be reformed, developed and grow stronger and larger.

After the reform and development over the last 20 and more years, Sinopec has seen its total assets grow from 21 billion *yuan* in 1983 to 559.2 billion *yuan* in 2003, multiplying more than 26 times over. Its turnover grew from 27.3 billion *yuan* to 466.7 billion *yuan*, multiplying by a factor of 16.7. Its profit and tax was up from 10.7 billion *yuan* to 70.5 billion *yuan*, a 6.6-fold increase. Its ethylene output, an indicator of the level of a nation's petrochemical industry, increased 11-fold, from 560,000 tons a year in 1983 to 6.12 million tons in 2003. Second only to the USA and Japan in the world now, China's ethylene production will soon surpass that of Japan. Sinopec was ranked No. 54 among the Global 500 Companies in 2003. These data indicate not only that the state-owned petrochemical enterprises did keep growing larger and stronger over the past 20-plus years, but that they will continue to grow over the next 20 years as our conditions will improve.

To summarize the success of Sinopec, I believe the following practices in four aspects were of the greatest value.

(1) Insistent focus on development and persisting in growing larger and stronger

Sinopec always focused its attention and energy on development of the enterprise. It never tried to expand non-core businesses, nor got involved in bubble economic activities. I mentioned earlier that the infant Sinopec encountered repeated disturbance, with claims that it was redundant, that such a company was unnecessary and should be abolished. Particularly with a leadership changeover on completion of a term of office, or a government structural reform, someone would raise the issue of dissolving Sinopec. Some others would suggest downsizing Sinopec into a company under the leadership of a national ministry. Whenever such occasions came up, Sinopec's headquarters would seethe with rumors, employees would worry about their future and even feel depressed that their corporation was doomed. When facing such harsh situations, the members of the leading group and I sensed the acute pressure, but at the same time felt unswayed and refused to knuckle under to such charges. I never wavered in my belief that Sinopec's chance of survival depended on it succeeding. If Sinopec did a good job and developed its strength, its existence would argue for itself and no one could dissolve it. Conversely, if Sinopec failed to do well and could not develop and fulfill the task given by the central leadership, it would lose its reason for being and defeat itself. Luckily, all of our leading members of Sinopec worked hard together, making every effort to follow the guideline set by China's central leadership to establish Sinopec and make optimum use of the 100 million tons of crude oil. Our belief never wavered. We were in our prime back then, and we braced ourselves, resolving to do a good job and settle any doubts whether it was right to establish Sinopec, indeed to settle any doubts as to what kind of path China's petrochemical industry should take. We did have the aspiration to discover a brilliant path. I also believe strongly that tough conditions will temper a person; a certain degree of pressure and dispute can bring out the best in people. The disagreement was not all negative. After the China National Petrochemical Company was founded, we made up our minds to win our first battle and do a good job. To start with, we focused on the manufacturing enterprises, and made those that were producing but long unable to reach their design capacity, achieve their output targets and improve their efficiency. While implementing our first "329 Plan," we concentrated our energy on the eight imported large petrochemical facilities and a batch of projects at Luoyang, Guangzhou and Zhenhai. When we carried out the "521 Plan," we organized our second campaign to promote the petrochemical industry and build pillar projects. This time we focused on 10 major projects that included the newly built Anqing Acrylic Fibers, Fujian Oil Refinery, Liaohua Phase 2 Project, Maoming Ethylene and Jiujiang Chemical Fertilizer, and renovation work at Yanshan Petrochemical and Yangtze Petrochemical Ethylene. All these efforts demonstrated our whole-hearted pursuit of development and growth.

I learned from comrades from Jiangxi Province that when Yu Qiuli visited Jiangxi in the early 1980s, he saw that his native province had seen little improvement. Feeling deeply ashamed that he had not done much for Jiangxi when he had the wherewithal as head of the SPC, Yu Qiuli remarked to others: "I owe Jiangxi a lot!" I told Yu Qiuli: "Let me repay this debt for you." Sinopec chose Jiujiang in Jiangxi Province as the site for a chemical fertilizer plant producing 300,000 tons of synthetic ammonia and 520,000 tons of urea. Being a predominantly agricultural province, Jiangxi needed chemical fertilizer badly. The whole country should care about Jiangxi and provide it what it lacked. Comrade Wu Guanzheng, the Governor of Jiangxi Province at the time cooperated with Sinopec on the project very well. Our Jiujiang fertilizer plant was a success. Yu Qiuli was very pleased about it too.

As for our manufacturing enterprises with adequate budgets, markets, profits and competitiveness, we tried all means to intensify their technological upgrading. For example, a 300,000-ton ethylene plant could soon reach 400,000-500,000 tons after being renovated, increasing productivity by 30-50 percent. Planning, under our two contract plans, to invest 84.5 billion *yuan* over 11 years, we actually put in 121.4 billion *yuan*. History proves that such a gigantic investment plan and such fast development would simply have been impossible without the superb system and mechanism of Sinopec.

After China Petrochemical Corporation was formed and especially after it was reorganized into a shareholding corporation (Sinopec Corp), the development of China's petrochemical industry stepped onto a bigger and higher stage. Its symbolic constructions were no longer 300,000-ton ethylene plants, but 21st century, world-leading, integrated ethylene complexes producing 800,000-900,000 tons. Having reached this level, Sinopec is on a par with the advanced petrochemical enterprises around the world today.

(2) Paying full attention to core enterprise value to keep expanding our principal cause

Emphasizing development and growing stronger and larger, we still faced the issue of what to develop and how to accomplish our ambition. July 2003 was the month of Sinopec's 20th birthday. The present leading group of Sinopec held a small celebration forum, inviting Sheng Huaren, Zhang Wanxin, Fei Zhirong and myself to take part. Everyone asked me to speak first. So I talked about my deepest feelings and views during those past 20 years. "Those 20 years are but a short moment in the long river of history, merely the prime years of one human generation. However, for the Chinese petrochemical industry, it witnessed the most eventful years of its history. Led by the Central Party Committee and the State Council and supported by every side, all the employees of Sinopec made a concerted effort and worked hard to achieve a historic leap for the Chinese petrochemical industry, developing our petrochemical industry that was unknown 20 years earlier into a giant petrochemical power in the world, second only to the USA and Japan in comprehensive capability. What an extraordinary achievement this was! From among the whole process what is worth our treasuring? What successful experience should we leave for posterity?" I told everyone at the celebration gathering about a good book I had read, one that reminded me of the growth of Sinopec and somewhat resembled my feelings. It was *Good to Great* written by Jim Collins, an American. Together with a group of American scholars, Collins spent over five years reviewing the Global 500 Companies selected by the American *Fortune* magazine throughout the 30 years from 1965 to 1995. They selected the first batch of 1,435 enterprises and filtered them down to 176. Then they selected 19 of these 176 enterprises, and in the end came down to the final 11 that they believed to be the best, truly moving from being good to being great. The scholars then studied these 11 enterprises to see what enabled them to grow that well. What were the common characteristics that made them so remarkable? Using all kinds of theories and statistics to analyze these companies, the scholars finally came to a conclusion. The common feature shared by the 11 companies was that they all stick unswervingly to their core enterprise values and targets and, based on these things, they decide what to do, what not to do and what must be stopped. The behavior of the leaders of these companies all displayed the Stockdale Paradox, namely: "You must retain faith that you can prevail to greatness in the end, while retaining the discipline to confront the brutal facts of your current reality." Another common feature shared by the leaders of the 11 enterprises chosen by the author of *Good to Great* and his colleagues was that "They are all gentle and relentless, all driven by the desire and the inspiration to create outstanding achievement." They all "rely upon lofty standards, being ambitious and putting their company's benefit first." They all disliked being showy or using the mass media to boost their own image. I told the current Sinopec management that, whilst being unable to boast that Sinopec grew from being good to being great or to say that we share the same characteristics with the 11 great companies, I did know, however, that the trail we had blazed over the previous 20 years resembled many of these features, and that there was much commonality of feeling. Then, I told the younger managers of Sinopec that if they thought I was making sense, we should continue to stick firmly to our core values and targets. Sinopec must continue to put the national interest first, strive to make best use of national resources and realize the optimization of resource allocation in order to maintain the growth of China's petrochemical mission. They might encounter difficulties, setbacks, disputes and even misunderstandings in their work, but they must be able to withstand any grievance, not haggling over personal success or failure, honor or disgrace.

Now, under the new leadership, Sinopec is recording remarkable success through adhering to its principal tasks and investing into the development of its main cause. In upstream production, its total oil and gas resources have grown from over 10 billion tons when Sinopec was newly founded to over 30 billion tons. Its crude oil output has steadied and is increasing despite output from old oilfields tends to fall after years of exploitation. Its natural gas output has multiplied. In its midstream production, its crude oil processing capability has reached the total scale of Sinopec prior to the restructure, growing by an average of over 10 million tons per annum. Its ethylene output is nearly 50 percent more than the pre-reorganization figure. In its downstream production, its sales of refined oil are almost double those prior to the restructure; in particular retail sales volume has increased nearly fourfold. Sinopec's upstream, midstream and downstream production is more closely integrated than ever before. Its core operation is growing ever bigger and both its market competitiveness and anti-risk capability have been further strengthened. Sinopec is making more contributions to our country and society.

(3) Revitalizing the petrochemical cause, relying on qualified personnel and prioritizing science and technology

Twenty years ago, Sinopec proposed the policy of revitalizing the petrochemical cause, relying on qualified personnel and prioritizing science and technology. Later, we put forward the goal of competing with and taking on the world's top petrochemical companies in five aspects and 32 sub-aspects. The five aspects were overall strength, power of technical innovation, ability in market exploration, ability in business management, and capability for sustainable profit. Taking these as Sinopec's goal, we formulated policies and plans on science and technology, worked out our investment into scientific and technological research, heightening the dominance of science and technology. In the past 20 and more years, regardless of changes to Sinopec's systems and structure, its main scientific and technical research units have kept their outstanding features intact, maintaining steady, continuing progress, their personnel unshaken, spirits focused, their best experts refusing to leave. Chen Zhili, a State Council member, once went to Sinopec's science and technology research institute for inspection and investigation. Deeply impressed and greatly satisfied with what she had seen and heard, in the form of a State Council "reference document," Chen Zhili recommended to the whole country Sinopec's work in reforming its scientific research system and promoting technological progress.

For a long time, Sinopec has implemented the scientific research practice of one entity, two tiers and three systems. The one entity is to treat Sinopec as an integrated entity for formulating plans, establishing centralized decisions about strategic planning and allocating all resources. The two tiers are the research unit directly under the Sinopec headquarters and those under its enterprises. These science and technology research units carry out their research tasks and cooperate under one entity. The three systems are oil and gas exploration, crude oil processing and petrochemicals. By means of its "one-two-three" practice of scientific research, Sinopec unifies all its strength in aspects such as scientific research, design, equipment manufacture, engineering construction and product application in a sequential line of "research-design-production." Enabled by this effective structure, Sinopec researchers have solved more than 50 major technical issues, achieved over 5,200 significant research results and turned over 70 percent of these results to production in the past 20-plus years. Consequently, Sinopec has established vital technologies such as hidden land oil and gas exploration, oil recovery from high water-content areas, catalytic cracking, hydrogenation, ethylene decomposition and polypropylene technologies. This top technology capability has helped form Sinopec's technological superiority and robustness, making it a pillar in the constant development of the Chinese petrochemical industry.

Sinopec, whether we mean the early China National Petrochemical Company or the later China Petrochemical Corporation and China Petroleum & Chemical Corporation, has always emphasized the promotion and application of scientific research results and worked hard to increase the production dynamic. In the 20-plus years of its history, Sinopec has invested more than 100 billion *yuan* into the technical reformation of its old enterprises, removing obstacles and adhering with extremely remarkable success to the path of sustainable development. Sinopec applied successive technical renovations to the several 300,000-ton ethylene lines installed in the mid-1980s, raising their annual output to 720,000 tons maximum, more than doubling the original capacity. While intensifying its scientific and technical research, Sinopec Corp has adhered to two powerful guarantees. One is the financial guarantee, allowing the expenses of scientific exploration, amounting to more than three billion *yuan* a year, to be counted as direct production cost. The other is the organization or personnel guarantee. The corporation holds all kinds of high caliber training sessions and implements a reward policy and incentive mechanism to create fine working and living conditions for its professional personnel. For backbone researchers and engineers at the various technical posts and topic projects, the corporation tries every means to give them the best support and encouragement so as to motivate them with enterprise spirit and pride in achievement. By 2003, the corporation had as many as 27,800 senior engineers from various specializations, 1,641 experts in various disciplines and over 300,000 technicians of various trades and levels. It is precisely this intellectual superiority of its employees that guarantees Sinopec its overall superiority and powerful market competitiveness.

(4) Stepping up efficiency and the reform, continuing to perfect the fine mechanism of mutual interaction

As proved by both international and domestic practice, the success of an enterprise requires not only correct state policies and a fine macro-economic environment; however, two conditions are also vitally important for an enterprise in terms of its own construction. One is its efficiency, namely its strength in personnel, financial and physical resources. Without efficiency in these aspects, an enterprise will be unable to grow and do what it wishes to once it encounters a challenge or competition from formidable international rivals. The other is its mechanisms, i.e. its ability to cope with complicated and changeable situations in domestic and international markets. Only a nimble and effective mechanism structure allows an enterprise to formulate its strategies effectively, use its strength positively and appropriately, and make timely and correct predictions and judgments. Only then can an enterprise establish timely and effective measures and apply these measures flexibly to ensure the realization of expected targets.

After its restructuring and development over the last 20-plus years. Sinopec now possesses both these two conditions. In particular, since the successful floatation of China Petroleum & Chemical Corporation on the stock markets of New York, London, Hong Kong and Shanghai, its participation in the world capital market has highly promoted its effective operation. This is the role of market pressure as well as market power. The interaction of strength and structure forms a new, positive cycle. Despite the fact that world market in crude oil and petrochemical products is full of variable factors today, that crude oil is currently the most important and sensitive strategic resource in the world, that contention for oil resource amid petroleum politics, diplomacy and military power is extremely complex, nevertheless Sinopec has become a player, one with quick steps and positive reactions. It has a growing squad of professionals relentlessly accumulating experience and spreading their positive influence. Sinopec is taking an active part in global economic cooperation and competition as a newly emerging world-class corporation.

Despite the considerable gap between Sinopec and its international counterparts in the top technical indices, and though it still faces all kinds of difficulties and problems, fundamental changes have already taken place in every aspect of the corporation. Sinopec makes full use of the strengths and mechanisms shaped over the past two decades, is continuing to become more efficient through development and perfect its mechanisms through reformation, working hard to better combine the two and make them mutually enhancing in a fine interactive cycle so that Sinopec can sustain its vigor and keep heightening its superiority. Of this I am sure: Sinopec will do better and grow larger than in the past and advance China's petrochemical industry toward a new, higher stage.

Chapter V

Establishment of the Socialist Market System

- Midnight Call from the Party General Secretary
- Planned Economy: from Theory to Practice
- Market-oriented Reform Takes Hold, Advancing and Retreating Amidst Disputes
- Key and Difficult Points in Market-oriented Reform
- Successful Application of Deng Xiaoping Theory and His Riposte to Margaret Thatcher

China's market-oriented reform proceeded in incremental fashion in the process of breaking loose from the fetters and influence of the planned economy. It started in 1978 with "delegation of power" and "enlivening the economy" and expanding the operational autonomy of enterprises. It developed gradually in the process of theoretical innovation and practice, such as coming to recognize the law of values, developing the commodity economy, and the policy of taking planned economy as the main body, supplementing with market regulation, integrating planned regulation with market regulation and exploring the relations between planned and market economy. This process gave a major impetus to the development of social productivity.

Following the political turmoil of 1989, there arose a new round of disputes around reform. This, plus the disintegration of the Soviet Union and the Eastern Europe socialist block, aroused questioning and criticism of the economic reform, of market-oriented reform in particular. This brought great pressure to bear on those advocating reform. Such was the context in which I was appointed Director and Secretary of the Party Leading Group of the State Commission for Restructuring the Economy (SCRE) on August 18, 1990, where I stayed until March 1993, when I was transferred to be the Director of the State Planning Commission (SPC). This period was the most difficult time of my life. I told the central leaders that I could take neither too leftist nor too rightist a position, go neither fast nor slow. I was under enormous pressure and lost over 10kg in weight during this period.

At the beginning of 1992, Deng Xiaoping issued the speeches made during his southern China inspection tour. Reform began to sweep the length and breadth of the country like a spring breeze. The "market-oriented" reform became irreversible. The objectives of reform had become commonly recognized. The 14th CPC National Congress thus decided to build a socialist market economy.

Midnight Call from the Party General Secretary

The Fifth Session of the Seventh NPC was held in Beijing between March 20 and April 3, 1992. I represented Anhui Province at the session, and stayed at the Xiyuan Hotel. At 11 pm on the evening of April 1, Party General Secretary Jiang Zemin rang me, saying that China was at a critical moment in reform and opening-up and that all were waiting on what next step should be taken and he too was a little anxious. He asked the State Commission for Restructuring the Economy (SCRE) to prepare an in-depth study and submit a recommendation to the central authorities. I said that the situation was exactly as he surmised: all were waiting to see what attitude the central authorities would adopt and what next step to take, but there was no unanimity of opinion and there were many confused ideas. So I promised to put together some people to study the problem and submit our recommendations. The General Secretary said this would be fine, adding that he would also sleep on it.

Soon after the NPC annual session was over, on April 15, I invited the heads of economic restructuring commissions of Guangdong, Jiangsu, Shandong, Liaoning and Sichuan provinces to Beijing for a brainstorming session on the next step of reform, focusing on the relations between planning and market, as the issue was very sensitive at the time because the disputes aroused by the "June 4 Political Incident" were not over. I did not tell them about the background to the phone call from the Party General Secretary. When I was transferred to the SCRE, Li Peng, Yao Yilin and Song Ping all talked with me and I told them what I thought about reform, namely, "we can go neither too quickly nor too slowly and can take neither too leftist nor too rightist a position." That was my opinion on the reform. It was based on this understanding that I kept this forum absolutely top secret. No more than ten persons attended; no assistants, note taking or disclosure of the discussion were allowed, for fear of courting unnecessary trouble.

The forum lasted for three half-days. At the end of the forum, I filed a report based on what had been discussed and submitted it to Party General Secretary Jiang Zemin and Premier Li Peng. The report said that the participants all came from the five major provinces and that, although they represented different levels of reform and opening-up, they were unanimous that the 14th CPC National Congress would be a breakthrough in the discussion of the relationship between planning and market. The heads of the economic restructuring commissions of the five provinces deemed it necessary to clarify "building and developing a socialist market economy" based on what had been achieved in their respective areas. While we define "socialism as a system with public ownership as the foundation, the principle of to each according to his work, the nature of the state power clearly defined, and the state formulating plans and making major policies regarding the macro-economy, the market economy, being only the means and way, should only serve socialism." I filed the report on my own initiative, without consulting or letting the others go over it. It was submitted to Party General Secretary Jiang Zemin and Premier Li Peng on April 21. Attached to the report were statistical data, listing the GNP, fixed assets investment, import and export figures, foreign investment, retail sales, per capita income of urban people and per capita net income of farmers of the five provinces in 1978 and 1991, with a comparison data that served to illustrate the tremendous impact upon economic development and improvement in people's living standards. The comparison clearly demonstrated that areas employing the market mechanism well had higher indicators than those employing it less well. For details, see Table 6.

Not long before I called the forum, the SCRE had held an international workshop on the transition of economic systems, which received a paper from former US Secretary of State Dr. Henry Kissinger on April 20. His paper, "Economic Development and Political Stability," pointed out at the very start that, "In the rapidly changing world no subject is as important as this." He was referring to the theme of the workshop. He said that he fully appreciated the efforts of the Chinese Government to seize the opportunity to sponsor the workshop. He gave his views on the transition issue. First of all, he said that in discussing economic transition, most people tended to compare the "pure market system" and "pure planned economy," but in reality there were no such extreme models. He cited the USA as an example, saying that the USA was, without a doubt, the most open market economy, but the government still performed an important role in such areas as petroleum, natural gas and telecommunications. He said that an economy was mixed initially. Secondly, the transition from a relatively centralized economy to a more market-oriented economic structure was happening worldwide. He presented his views with examples citing the actual conditions and results of the transition in Central Europe, Eastern Europe, the former Soviet Union and Latin American countries. Thirdly, any country had to take into account its own particular history and cultural background in the transition. He noted that a reform plan might operate well in one country but not in another, for the clear reason that no two countries were the same. But he also held that there were indeed some points in common in the transition process. He listed seven. His

Table 6 Major economic indicators of five provinces in 1978 and 1991

	Guangdong			Jiangsu			Shandong			Liaoning			Sichuan		
	1978	1991	Growth (time)	1978	1991	Growth (time)	1978	1991	Growth (time)	1978	1991	Growth (Time)	1978	1991	Growth (Time)
GNP (billion *yuan*)	18.473	168.9	8.1	24.924	143.5	4.8	22.910	156.6	5.8	22.320	107	3.8	24.483	127.3	4.2
Fixed assets invest-ment (billion *yuan*)	2.723	45.9	15.8	2.175	20.275	8.3	2.927	39.56	12.5	2.53	30.96	11.2	2.821	27.96	8.9
Export (US$ billion)	1.388	13.688	8.9	0.418	3.461	7.3	0.83	3.83	3.6	1.52	5.77	2.8	0.019	1.319	68
Import (US$ billion)	N	8.509		N	1.043		N	1.151		0.06	0.96		0.022	0.393	
FDI (US$ billion)	(1979) 0.09143	2.583		(1979) 0.02933	0.787		(1979) 0.01276	0.468		(1979) 0.0113	0.97		Non	0.02553	
Retail sales (billion *yuan*)	9.341	85.758	8.2	10.649	66.564	5.3	10.67	66.06	5.2	8.53	51.11	5.0	10.741	162.037	14.1
Per capita income (city) (*yuan*)	N	2535.6		N	1623		361.18	1566	3.3	343.3	1542	3.5	326.04	1536.63	3.7
Per capita net income (farmer) (*yuan*)	182.3	1143	5.3	155	920.7	4.9	114.5	764	5.7	135.2	896.7	3.8	127.1	590.2	3.6

(The data were supplied by the Division of General Planning and Pilot Programs, the State Commission for Restructuring the Economy, April 18, 1992) conclusion was: "We are in an era of change. The economic activities around us are undergoing great changes, changing, although in very complex fashion, toward the market economy. It seems that leaders all over the world have arrived at the conclusion that, in general, the market provides a better basis for sustainable economic development." He pointed out: "The transition to the market economy has been extensively accepted, but the means to the end are as many as the countries attempting reforms. Obviously, there is not one way that is universally applicable. The reform must be well fitted to the economic, social and cultural context of each individual country." Concluding, Kissinger stressed: "The success of reform depends on political stability" and "in a word, economic development cannot be separated from political stability." I perused his letter and the paper. My feeling was that his views were neither politically biased nor tinged with ideology. They were very objective. Some of the important views were identical with what had been applied in the reform moves in China. I thought the paper worthy as a reference and attached the paper to the report submitted to Jiang Zemin and Li Peng.

Planned Economy: from Theory to Practice

In September 1990, when the central authorities decided to transfer me to the SCRE and issued the notice, the Commission immediately sent its Secretary General Hong Hu to pick me up from the China Petrochemical Corporation. I declined on the grounds that the official appointment had not yet been adopted by the NPC Standing Committee as normal procedures required. I asked for some briefing materials in order to prime myself for the post and then spoke with An Zhiwen (Secretary of the Party Leading Group of the SCRE) to discuss the leadership and staff members. The next day, Hong Hu brought me a batch of materials concerning the work of the Commission. Burying myself in all this, I did not know where to start. The materials included the main points of national economic reform, pilot urban reform projects, rural reform, reform of state-owned enterprises (SOEs), financial reform, reform in taxation and commercial reform. There was so much. What was the central issue? What was the key to the reform? I went over them one by one, feeling I could not see the wood for the trees. The more I read the more confused I got.

Based on my years of experience and the foci of attention at the time, I thought that the objective of reform should be to liberate and develop productive forces just as Deng Xiaoping had said. For the existing macro- and micro-economy, what was essential was to excite their vigor and vitality and introduce an effective work mechanism. But where did this vitality lie? Where did motivation lie? I recalled an experience in 1979 when working in Shanghai. It was May or June. I went to see Xue Muqiao, who had come to Shanghai from Sichuan. He told me about what he had seen during the trip and talked about the commodity economy and how local people viewed this. He said that people in the hinterland such as Sichuan in western China did not understand what the government was saying about relaxing policies and allowing the development of a commodity economy with elements of planning. However, when you got to Shanghai, whenever one talked about allowing "shipping commodities long-distance from one place to sell in another place," local people knew what the phrase meant without further explanation. They would do it quickly and well. Xue described it as commodity economy awareness. Shanghai people were capable, good at doing business and making money. That, in fact, meant that Shanghai people were highly aware of the commodity economy, were quick to seize business opportunities and knew how to exploit the market to develop the economy. When I was in Shanghai, I concurrently headed the Municipal Planning Committee. The central authorities often praised Shanghai for the good job it was doing and for fulfilling its plans well. To me, Shanghai was flexible in its planning, leaving some leeway for enterprises to arrange their production according to market demand and to carry out exchanges. All this made me feel that the vitality of an economy lies in the market. It was up to the market to liberate and develop productive forces. In my new position, in the new situation, and facing the pile of information on my desk, I decided that I should put the emphasis of reform on the market. I asked Hong Hu to have two types of material prepared—one about disputes in China over the relationship between planning and market and the other about planning and market in foreign countries.

This I did because, aside from my personal experience and feelings, there had been some backsliding in the objectives and orientation of reform and there was a heated dispute. At that time, the Third Plenary Session of the 11th Party Central Committee had restored the ideological line of "seeking truth from facts" and the Third Plenary Session of the 12th Party Central Committee had adopted the resolution on economic reform, making decisive breakthroughs in some major theoretical and institutional issues, confirming that China's socialist economy was a "planned commodity economy on the basis of public ownership" and advancing a series of new policies for developing a "socialist commodity economy." The report to the 13th CPC National Congress stressed the point that the planned socialist commodity economy should be a "system in which planning and market were intrinsically united" and that planning and market covered all society. It clearly pointed out that "market regulation is in no way going in for capitalism." On June 9, 1989, Deng Xiaoping once again stressed that "there is nothing wrong" with the principles and policies adopted since reform and opening-up, that "they will remain unchanged" and "they are not to be changed." When talking with Li Peng, Deng told him not to talk about "making planned economy the main body." All these things were evidence that the central authorities were firm in the market-oriented reform and were determined to take it deeper.

On the other hand, disputes as to the orientation and objectives of reform continued. The road of reform was rocky. Both Marxist and Western economic dogma held that socialism was incompatible with the market economy and that public ownership could not co-exist with the market economy. Such dogmatism had long fettered the people. Many theorists and officials engaged in practical work regarded planning as the fundamental characteristic of the socialist system, that the market economy was endemic to capitalism and that the market economy was associated with private ownership that was opposed to socialist public ownership. After the "June 4 Political Incident," newspapers published many articles criticizing "market-oriented reform" and the "market economy." In the earliest raising of the question, on February 22, 1990, a leading newspaper in Beijing questioned reformists: "Capitalist reform or socialist reform?" These articles had one thing in common, namely associating planning and market with the basic social system and asserting that "If we hold on to socialism, we must hold on to the planned economy" and "if we continue with reform without identifying whether it is socialism or capitalism, we would lead reform and opening-up to the evil road of capitalism." Some people even went so far as to elevate the disputes between market economy and planned economy to the level of "line struggle," saying that the disputes on the orientation and objectives of reform were "a struggle between two roads." I felt that it was a cardinal issue of right or wrong and it concerned the orientation and objectives of reform. If the issue was not resolved, the reform would end up attending only to trifles and neglecting the essentials.

On September 30, 1990, Jiang Chunze, deputy head of the Foreign Economic System Division under the SCRE and an expert in international and comparative economics, submitted some briefing materials at my instruction. Its contents included disputes and practice on planning and market in foreign countries and comments on China's planning and market; it summarized century-long disputes among the Western academic world on the main means of allocating resources, by central planning organs or by the market, starting with the Italian economist Vilfredo Pareto in 1902. The briefing also described disputes on the same subject that started in socialist countries in the late period of Soviet wartime Communism.

It showed that the economist and sociologist Pareto was the first to advance the idea of using central planning organs to replace the market in the allocation of resources. Neither he nor his followers were Marxists; nor were they Communists. They were scholars in the West studying socialist economy. At the beginning, there was no socialist system. Neither planned economy nor market economy had anything to do with a social system. The governments of Western countries drew on the lessons of two worldwide economic crises and began to explore and correct the problem of "market failure." Almost all the governments adopted the policy of government intervention in such areas as employment and taxation, exercising control over the market by employing economic resources and administrative means in order to solve the problem of medium- and long-term planning for solving social problems and to build major infrastructure projects. They even resorted to trans-national coordination. Combining the "visible hand" with the "invisible hand" began to become a universal trend for optimizing the world economic system. Since capitalist countries could use planning to make up for the drawbacks of the market, why should not socialist countries use the market mechanism to overcome the shortcomings of planning and raise the efficiency of resources allocation? The briefing showed clearly that planning was not an attribute of the socialist system; nor should the market be the monopoly of capitalism. Since capitalism could use planning, socialism could also use the market, too.

After reading the briefing, I felt the thread of my thinking was getting clearer. It reasoned things out and had a clear objective in mind. So I submitted it to the central leaders at once. After reading it, Jiang Zemin phoned me, saying: "The briefing is good. I have read it twice and instructed to have it printed for distribution among the central leaders." Li Peng instructed the group drafting the documents for the Seventh Plenary Session of the 13th Party Central Committee to make the briefing a reference material.

The relationship between planning and market was a century-old controversy. The Italian economist Pareto was one of the earliest to use mathematical tools to study economics. His analysis of economic theories had a profound influence on such theories as general equilibrium, distribution and social welfare. He published a two-volume book *Systèmes Socialistes* (*Socialist Systems*) in 1902-1903. He imagined socialism as a single unit with a single supreme planning body implementing economic plans and achieving results similar to those found in a market. He believed his hypothesis "will be proved." His follower Barone developed his hypothesis in a paper published in 1908, arriving at positive conclusions concerning the feasibility of making all economic resources owned by the public and social production planned and managed as a single unit by a single supreme planning body. The Austrian economist Ludwig von Mises published his *Economic Calculation in the Socialist Commonwealth*, designating the essential attributes of a socialist economic system to be public ownership of the means of production and central planning. But he also held that there was no way for central planning to know in advance whether production conformed to demand; neither was it possible to calculate the labor and raw materials necessary for making a product. He deemed as non-feasible Barone's presumed calculation of central planning based on market pattern, labor, means of production and other factors.

Later there was much debate in support of and in opposition to Pareto's ideas. But on both sides of the argument were experts and scholars who tried to find optimal methods of allocating resources without socio-political system or ideological associations. It was the Soviet government, especially after the death of Lenin in 1924, that put the theory into practice and associated it with a social system, hammering into shape a planned economy model. By 1929, the year of "great turn," the new economic policies stressing the role of the market had totally disappeared in Soviet Russia and were being superseded by the highly-centralized and market-excluding planned economy. Under the personal direction of Stalin, the Economics Institute of the Soviet Academy of Sciences compiled a textbook on political economics, making state ownership and planning by the central organ the most essential economic feature of socialism. The economic system lasted for over 60 years—from 1930 to 1991.

Historically and objectively speaking, the planned economy in the early period of the Soviet Union played an historic role in its industrialization, the modernization of national defense and the defeat of fascist Germany to win World War II. In contrast, the capitalist countries in the same period were plunged into grave economic crisis. Thus the new-born socialist system and the planned economy in its early period demonstrated their advantages.

According to an estimate by the American economist Abram Bergson, between 1928 and 1955, the national income of the Soviet Union grew at an annual rate of between 4.4 percent and 6.3 percent. The 1950 aggregate social product was 17.2 times higher than that of 1913, with total industrial output value 12 times higher. For the years 1929-1932 during the first five-year plan, Soviet industry grew at an average annual rate of 19.2 percent. In contrast, the total industrial output value of the USA in 1933 was 65 percent of what it had been in 1929. The corresponding figure for Britain was 86 percent; for France, 77 percent; and for Germany, 66 percent—all sharp falls. During the years 1933-1937 of the second five-year plan, the Soviet Union maintained a high growth rate of 17.8 percent, and during 1938-1940 during the third five-year plan the Soviet Union's economic growth rate remained at 13.2 percent. This rapid growth rate accelerated the pace of industrialization and rapidly changed the profile of the Soviet Union, turning Stalin's Russia from a country that "used wooden ploughs to till the land" into a Russia that "uses tractors to till the land," as Winston Churchill once said of Stalin.

While the Soviet Union was implementing a planned economy, profound changes were taking place in the world. Keynesian economics came into being and Franklin Delano Roosevelt created the "New Deal" policy. Drawing on the lessons of economic crises and borrowing achievements in theory from the academic world and from Soviet experience, capitalist countries, led by the USA, began to strengthen governmental intervention in economic operations and carry out reform in such areas as social distribution, thus overcoming anarchy in production and easing contradiction between the bourgeoisie and proletarian classes. Through correction of its internal conflicts, capitalism emerged from its two economic crises of 1929-1933 and 1937-1938 and brought its economy onto the path of development.

By contrast, the Soviets, intoxicated by the superiority of the new system, were becoming rigid in their thinking, without facing up to the drawbacks of the planned economy that were beginning to emerge. They continued to regard the market as heresy. They turned a blind eye to changes in production and market brought about by advances in science and technology and stubbornly stuck to the planned economy model. By 1958, the Soviet Union had brought into the planned economy framework and issued plan targets for 200,000 state industrial enterprises, 6,000 state farms, 5,000 technical service stations and tractor stations and 100,000 state factories and agricultural and sideline production enterprises affiliated to government institutions. Enterprises were accountable only to their superior authorities in terms of technical and economic goals. They were immune from market information, feeling no pressure from market demand. Up to 1965, before the profit-oriented reform proposed by the economist Yevsey Liberman, enterprises were issued with as many as 30 plan targets. When the reform was implemented, nine were still retained. When Premier Kosygin reported to the 21st Congress of the Soviet Communist Party in 1971, he still stressed: "The starting point of the Party Central Committee and the Soviet Government is that the mandatory plan is of major and decisive significance." "We must refute the erroneous ideas of replacing centralized planning with market regulation." Influenced by such a dogmatist attitude that flouted economic law, the Soviet Party leadership became even more rigid. Planned economy continued; production was not in line with market demand; enterprises lost their vitality; industrial technology stagnated; efficiency was low. The whole economy was on a year-on-year decline.

In 1985, Mikhail Gorbachev took over as General Secretary of the Soviet Communist Party. In face of the daily deteriorating economy, he advanced his *uskorenie* or "acceleration" strategy. Even so, he still adhered to the view that "planning remained and still remains the main lever for managing the socialist economy." While vaunting his "new thinking" slogan, he continued to regard planned economy, the quintessence of "old thinking," as the hard and fast rule and the market as "fierce floods and savage beasts." Valery Boldin, head of the Central Committee General Department, recalled in his book *Ten Years That Shook the World: The Gorbachev Era As Witnessed by His Chief of Staff* that Gorbachev would turn green at the mere mention of the word "market." One can thus picture how deeply stamped in the political economics textbook was the dogma that state ownership and planned economy managed by state organs were the fundamental attributes of socialism. It was this kind of dogmatic attitude divorced from and blind to reality that made them indecisive, thus missing the favorable opportunity for reform and leading ultimately to the decline of the Soviet economy. On December 30, 1999, the Russian President Vladimir Putin in his book *Russia at the Turn of the Millennium* analyzed the causes for the decline of the Soviet Union, pointing out that "This was our payment for putting the brakes on, even banning, the initiative and enterprise of enterprises and their personnel. Today we are reaping the bitter fruit, both material and mental, of the past decades. "

There are, of course, many factors that led to the decline of the Soviet economy, the steady drop in its people's living standards and even its disintegration. But it is undeniable that among the important reasons was the poor economic management system, the growingly rigid planned economy model that deprived the economy of vitality and misallocated resources, that ultimately led to the constant decline in productivity. In terms of the relationship between economic base and superstructure, the rigid and aging economic management system had lost its role of activating the economy and its influence on both productivity and production relations was fatal.

Market-oriented Reform Takes Hold, Advancing and Retreating Amidst Disputes

In the early post-Liberation period, China had to ape the Soviet Union, given her inexperience in building socialism, the prevailing international context and actual domestic conditions. In the First Five-year Plan period, China mainly studied Soviet experience in industry and enterprises, copying its planned economy model. The 156 complete sets of equipment given as aid by the Soviet Union were an embodiment of the basic operation of a planned economy. They yielded great results. But in the national economy as a whole, China did not copy the Soviet model wholesale. It had its own characteristics. The "Common Program" adopted at the First Plenary Session of the Chinese People's Political Consultative Conference (CPPCC) in September 1949 clearly pointed out: "The fundamental principle for the economic development of the People's Republic of China is to develop production and make the economy flourish by the co-existence of both public and private sectors to benefit both labor and management, encouraging mutual assistance between rural and urban areas and internal and external exchange." The Constitution of the People's Republic of China adopted at the First Session of the First National People's Congress in September

1954 stipulates: "The state protects the ownership of the means of production and other capital of capitalists" and "the state adopts the policy of utilizing, limiting and transforming capitalist industry and commerce and, through the management by state administrative organs, leadership of the state sector of the economy and the supervision by the workers, utilizes the positive role of capitalist industry and commerce favorable for the national economy and livelihood of the people and restricts the negative role unfavorable to the national economy and people's livelihood, encourages and directs them to transform into various forms of state capitalist economy and gradually replaces capitalist ownership with ownership by the whole people." All these were different from those of the Soviet Union. The differences were very major.

The 20th Congress of the Soviet Communist Party in 1956 exposed the shortcomings and errors in socialist construction. Mao Zedong warned China against the mistakes and shortcomings of the Soviet economy. In April 1956, he made his famous speech "On Ten Major Relationships" at the enlarged meeting of the Political Bureau of the Party Central Committee. In his speech, he summed up the experience of China in contrast to that of the Soviet Union and put forward the basic principle of mobilizing all positive factors to serve the cause of socialism and explore the road for socialist construction best suited to Chinese conditions. At the very start, he pointed out: "Particularly worthy of attention is the fact that in the Soviet Union certain defects and errors that occurred in the course of building socialism have lately come to light. Do you want to follow the detours they made? It was through drawing lessons from their experience that we avoided certain detours in the past, and there is all the more reason for us to do so now." At the Eighth National Congress of the CPC, Chen Yun, based on the thinking of Mao Zedong's "On Ten Major Relationships," elaborated on the important policy of "three main bodies and three supplements," namely, making state and collectively-operated industry and commerce the main body, supplemented by a certain amount of private business; making planned production the main body of industrial and agricultural production, supplemented by free production within the framework allowed by state plans; and making the state market the main body, supplemented by free market led by the state within a certain scope. Chen Yun's exposition reflected the spirit of "taking what had happened in the Soviet Union as a warning" and following a path best suited to Chinese conditions so as to avoid detours.

My generation all read Stalin's *Leninism*, which was held up as a classic of Marxism at the time. In this book, Stalin listed five social and economic structures in the Soviet Union, stressing "the fifth, namely the socialist structure, has become the only commanding force in the ruling position of the whole national economy." The fifth social and economic structure he referred to was socialist industrial enterprises, state farms and collective farms. Comparing Stalin's words with China's Common Program of the CPPCC, the first Constitution of China and Chen Yun's exposition, we can see the differences between China's and the Soviet Union's models of economic management. Despite the long "leftist" interference, especially the "Cultural Revolution" when the slogan "cutting the tail of capitalism" prevailed, a considerable number of private industrialists and businesses still stayed in business in the vast rural areas and medium-sized and small cities, as did trading fairs in urban and rural areas for exchanging industrial and agricultural products, and the policy was to allow them to play their supplementary roles. It was these private industries and businesses that spread quickly after reform and opening-up to ferment the urban and rural markets.

Fourteen years went by between the Third Plenary Session of the 11th Party Central Committee in December 1978 and the decision to build a socialist market economy taken by the 14th CPC National Congress in October 1992. China's economic reform was an incremental process, from inception, via development, to taking hold. I think the process can be divided into four stages:

The first stage covered the period from 1978 to September 1984. During this period, the terms "commodity economy" and "law of values" were banned and "leftist" ideas and policies still ruled. In economic management, highly centralized planning exercised rigid management over too many areas. All localities and enterprises voiced their strong demand for "delegation of power to enliven the economy." It was in such context that we saw the first evidence of emancipating the mind that sparked China's later reforms. Theoreticians were the first to recognize the fact that "commodity economy" still existed in a socialist society and still played an important role. Then the government began to delegate power, cut the areas where mandatory plans were enforced and allow the market to play its supplementary role in more areas.

In this stage, it was the "brainstorming session" called by the State Council from July to September 1978 that was the first to discuss the relationship between planning and market involved in the economic reform. Sun Yefang reiterated his "law of value first" theory; Xue Muqiao called for rectifying the situation concerning "shipping commodities long-distance from one place to sell at another place and for using the market to activate commodity circulation." Li Xiannian made a summary at the end of the session, "we must be good at managing the economy by economic means instead of eyeing the transfer of administrative powers." He stressed the necessity of respecting the autonomy of agricultural production teams and implementing the principle of "more work, more pay" and exchange of equal values.

On March 8, 1979, in his speech on planning and market, Chen Yun analyzed the defects of planning in the Soviet Union and China, saying that one of the defects had been "absence of market regulation under the socialist system, that market regulation meaning to regulate the economy by the law of values." Chen Yun put particular emphasis on the words "market regulation."

In April 1979, at the Central Work Conference, Li Xiannian, on behalf of the Party Central Committee and the State Council, pointed out "in the whole national economy it is necessary to combine planning regulation with market regulation."

In November 1979, during his meeting with Frank B. Gibney, Vice President of Encyclopedia Britannica, Deng Xiaoping put things even more clearly, when he said "It is absolutely not correct to say that market economy exists only in capitalist society and there is only capitalist market economy. Why cannot socialism engage in a market economy? It is not correct to say that we are going in for capitalism when we do so. Ours is an economy with planned economy as the main body, supplemented by market economy. But it is a socialist market economy." "Socialism can also engage in a market economy."

Deng Xiaoping, Chen Yun and Li Xiannian took deeper the idea of economic reform raised at the Third Plenary Session of the 11th Party Central Committee. These speeches gave a powerful push to the early period of economic reform. The rural reform advanced vigorously, with township and village enterprises springing up like bamboo shoots after spring rain. SOEs began to get greater autonomy in their operations; the rural and urban markets began to flourish. The Chinese economy exhibited vitality that had never been seen before.

As the urban and rural economy was coming to life, some negative aspects of the reform came to light. "Leftist" influence began to re-surface. Those who were deeply mired in "leftist" ideas, opposed to reform and enlivening the economy, and against changing the planned economy, seized on the negative aspects of the reform and began kicking up a fuss, attempting to arrest the progress of reform. During this period, one thing had the greatest impact. One leader in charge of theoretical work approved for circulation a letter to him written by five people. The letter criticized some economists for championing the role of the "law of value" and making enterprises independent economic entities, advocating that enterprise operations should mainly be regulated by the market and that the purpose of economic reform was to establish a "planned operational model on the basis of commodity economy." The writers of the letter held that the ideas advocated would "inevitably weaken the planned economy and the public ownership of socialism" and "obliterate the essential differences between socialist economy and capitalist economy." Then, in September 1982, the leading newspaper *People's Daily* published a comment article, criticizing the reform advocates for cutting back on the areas covered by mandatory plans and expanding the areas covered by indicative plans, saying that such advocacy was a negation of planned economy. The Hong Qi (Red Flag) Publishing House published a pamphlet bringing together similar articles from 1982 to 1983 with the editor's note to the foreword saying: "giving up planned economy will inevitably lead to production anarchy and sabotage the public ownership of socialism." Under the pressure of this event, the disputes in theoretical circles began to subside for a time. There were fewer articles written up by experts and scholars advocating "market-oriented reform." The operation of non-public sectors represented by Wenzhou in Zhejiang was subject to investigations and criticism. Township and village enterprises were facing a grave situation, finding it difficult to go on. These affected the progress of reform to a certain extent.

The second stage covered the period from October 1984 to the end of 1988. In October 1984, the Third Plenary Session of the 12th Party Central Committee adopted the decisions on the reform of the economic system. The decisions summed up the tremendous achievements and successful experience since the beginning of reform and opening-up and expounded a series of theoretical and practical issues, including the orientation, nature, tasks and basic policies concerning economic reform. It was a policy document on the overall reform of the economic system. Theoretically, the document made a major breakthrough, breaking away from the traditional ideas of planned economy as opposed to commodity economy, saying that the socialist planned economy was a planned commodity economy on the basis of public ownership. It also broke away from the traditional idea of putting planned economy on a par with mandatory plans, pointing out the need to progressively narrow the scope covered by mandatory plans, to expand the scope covered by indicative plans, and to make full use of economic levers and the market in regulating the economy rather than managing plans by mainly administrative means. It shattered the traditional ideas that price meant the unified price fixed by the state and that price stabilization meant making the price unchangeable, and pointed out the necessity of narrowing the scope covered by state-pegged prices and properly expanding the scope of floating prices and free prices.

History has proved that the decision of the Third Plenary Session of the 12th Party Central Committee "is the political economics that integrates the basic principles of Marxism with China's socialist practice" and "there are some remarks that our ancestors have never made; there are some new remarks," just as Deng Xiaoping put it. The series of breakthroughs, especially with regard to the relationship between planning and market, became a beacon charting the course for China's economic reform and pushed the sustained and rapid development of the economy. For the years 1984-1988, China's GNP grew by 15.2, 13.5, 8.8, 11.6 and 11.3 percent respectively year-on-year, all double-digit growth apart from in 1986, when it was 8.8 percent, but a fairly high growth rate all the same.

The third stage covered the period from 1989 to the end of 1991. This was a period of disputes, advances and retreats. In mid-May 1988, the Party Central Committee decided to complete the reforms of prices and the wages system within five years. On May 30, the Political Bureau of the Party Central Committee called an enlarged meeting, deciding to carry on with reforms of prices and the wages system. But, due to inexperience and inadequate preparation, the move touched off quite serious inflation, causing great panic in cities. There was a nationwide rush on the banks and panic buying. Prices shot up, with the Retail Price Index (RPI) in 1988 reaching 18.5 percent. In order to eliminate the negative impacts and create a favorable environment for reform, the Third Plenary Session of the 13th Party Central Committee, convened in September 1988, came out with the guiding principle of "improving the economic environment, redressing the economic order and deepening reform in an all-round manner," thus starting a new round of retrenchment. The session also adopted a draft plan for the reforms of prices and wages. But all this did not prevent the outbreak of political upheaval at the turn of spring and summer in 1989, at almost the same time as the drastic changes and transition of political power in the socialist countries of Eastern Europe and the disintegration of the Soviet Union. All the new situations in China and internationally caused great agitation and those who were not devoted to reform but clung to the planned economy attributed all the major events to the market-oriented reform. An article at the time said: "the socialist economy, in essence, is a planned economy, only needing some commodity attributes in the new stage." These people threw about criticism, saying: "To go in for market economy is to do away with public ownership, is to negate leadership by the Party and the socialist system, and to go in for capitalism." During this period, the voices criticizing market economy were growing ever louder.

Between October 10-13, 1990, more than 100 economists, well-known enterprise figures and senior government officials met in Beijing for a forum discussing theories of socialist economic reform. The forum voiced strong reactions to the integration of planned economy with market regulation, calling for the finding of precise theoretical and practical answers as soon as possible. I gave a speech at the forum, advocating "further discussions about the major topic of integrating planned economy with market regulation." Ma Hong said that this was my first time in the spotlight expressing my views since I had been appointed Director in charge of the SCRE and had asked the *People's Daily* and Xinhua News Agency to give prominent coverage.

On December 24, 1990, on the eve of the Seventh Plenary Session of the 13th Party Central Committee, Deng Xiaoping pointed out in his talks with a few responsible members of the Central Party Committee: "We must get clear theoretically that the difference between capitalism and socialism does not lie in planning or market" and "do not think that we are following the capitalist road for developing some market economy. There is nothing of the kind. Both planning and market are needed. If we do not have a market, we cannot get information from the world and that would be to resign ourselves to a backward status." These words gave a strong rebuttal to erroneous fallacies against the market-oriented reform and lent strong support to enterprises, officials and theorists in favor of reform. This proved once again that Deng Xiaoping, with his foresight and strong determination, set the reform on the right course at the critical moment when it was meeting resistance and setbacks.

The fourth stage covered the period from January 1992 to after the 14th CPC National Congress. In January-February 1992, Deng Xiaoping made a southern China inspection tour of Wuchang, Shenzhen, Zhuhai and Shanghai and issued a number of important speeches, which, with great enthusiasm, affirmed the tremendous achievements of reform and opening-up and expounded his views on a number of major theoretical issues and on the line, principles and policies of reform. He stressed that the basic line of the Party would remain unchanged for a hundred years to come. He also gave a profound exposition of the relationship between planning and market. "Whether to have more planning or more market is not the essential difference between socialism and capitalism," he said. "Planned economy does not mean socialism.

Chen Jinhua became a focus of journalists' attention when the Fifth Session of the Seventh NPC was inaugurated in March 1992.

国外经济体制研究

国家经济体制改革委员会　　　　〔总第 39 号〕
国外经济体制司 (1990) 18 号　　1990 年 10 月 14 日

外国关于计划与市场问题的争论和实践
以及对中国的计划与市场关系的评论

The SCRE's research briefing on the economic systems of foreign countries

　　关于计划与市场问题，在国际范围内已经争论了将近一个世纪。至今仍然歧见纷纭，各国的实践也在继续不断地探索。这里，从以下几个方面介绍一下争论之梗概及有关的背景材料：

　　一、从本世纪初关于未来社会资源配置方式的设想之争论到著名的 30 年代大论战。

　　二、中央计划经济体制所依据的主要经典论据及各社会主义国家关于改革模式的探讨。

In spring 1992, Deng Xiaoping made an inspection tour of Wuchang, Shenzhen, Zhuhai and Shanghai, during which he made a number of important speeches. The photo shows Deng visiting the Chinese Folk Culture Village in Shenzhen.

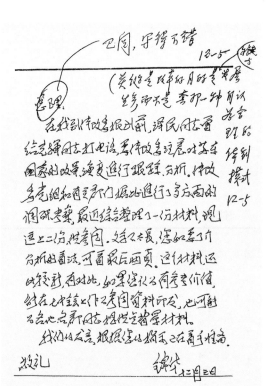

Chen Jinhua's letter to Premier Li Peng, with the latter's comments

Jiang Zemin (fifth left, front row) with the drafting group of the report to the 14th CPC National Congress (Chen Jinhua, third right)

Chen Jinhua (left), Li Peng (right) and Yao Yilin (behind Li Peng) at the National Work Conference on Economic System Reform in January 1992

Chen Jinhua (first left) giving a speech at the National Work Conference on Economic System Reform in January 1992

China's first stock exchange opened in Shanghai in December 1990. The photo shows people queuing before the door of the stock exchange.

Chen Jinhua delivering a speech at a press conference on the subject of housing reform in June 1991

Chen Jinhua at his office at the State Planning Commission, August 1996

国务院文件

State Council Document
No. 24, 1993

国发〔1993〕24 号

国务院关于坚决制止乱集资和
加强债券发行管理的通知

各省、自治区、直辖市人民政府，国务院各部委、各直属
机构：

去年以来，许多地区、部门以及企事业单位违反国家
有关规定，擅自利用发行债券等各种方式进行集资，其特
点是利率高、涉及面广、发行量大，问题相当严重。目前，
这种乱集资的状况还有进一步扩大的趋势，如不及时加以
制止，不仅扰乱金融秩序，而且还容易引发严重的社会问
题。为了制止乱集资，加强对证券市场，特别是债券发行

中共中央文件

中发〔1993〕6 号

中共中央　国务院关于当前
经济情况和加强宏观调控的意见

（1993 年 6 月 24 日）

今年以来，我国经济总的形势是好的。在邓小平同志
重要谈话和党的十四大精神鼓舞下，广大干部和群众解放
思想，抓住机遇，加快发展的热情高涨。围绕建立社会主
义市场经济体制的各项改革和对外开放不断取得新进展，
市场机制的作用进一步扩大。整个经济继续保持蓬勃发展
的势头，生产、建设、流通和对外经济技术交流全面发展。
今年一季度，国民生产总值比去年同期增长 15.1%。农业
生产虽然粮食播种面积有所减少，但夏粮总产量可望接近
或略高于去年的水平。1 至 5 月，全国乡及乡以上工业总产

Party Central Committee
Document No. 6, 1993

Zhu Rongji making a speech at the national conference on fiscal and taxation affairs in July 1993

Chen Jinhua (first right) meeting with Ivan Rybkin, Chairman of Russia's State Duma, in May 1994

Chen Jinhua giving a report at the Fifth Session of the Eighth National People's Congress, March 1997

The last load of stones is discharged into the Yangtze River to complete the damming of the river at the Three Gorges.

Capitalism also has plans. Market economy does not equate to capitalism. Socialism also has market. Planning and market are both economic means." He also said "now there are things of a rightist nature influencing us; there are also things of a 'leftist' nature influencing us. But it is the things of a 'leftist' nature that are deep-rooted. Some theorists and politicians are trying to frighten us by brandishing 'big labels.'" "It is not rightist, but 'leftist.'" "Rightism may ruin socialism and so may 'leftism.'" In his stirring speeches, Deng Xiaoping demonstrated his innovative and critical spirit, which gave another great impetus to reform.

On February 28, 1992, the Party Central Committee issued a circular on studying the important speeches of Deng Xiaoping, attempting to make the main points of the speeches known to all Party members.

On May 16, 1992, the Political Bureau of the Party Central Committee adopted the proposals on accelerating reform, expanding opening-up and striving to lift the economy to yet another new level in a better and faster manner. It was a further arrangement for implementing the spirit and the letter of Deng Xiaoping's speeches.

On June 9, 1992, Jiang Zemin made an important speech at the provincial cadre class of the Central Party School. Entitled "Get a deep understanding and implement in an all-round manner the spirit of the important speeches of Deng Xiaoping and implement economic development, reform and opening-up faster and better," the speech pointed out that the key issue in establishing a new economic system was to have a correct understanding of planning and market and their relationship and to pay more attention to and display more fully the functions of the market in the allocation of resources. After listing several versions on planning and market and on establishing a new economic system, he clearly said: "Personally, I prefer the wording 'socialist market economy.'" With this speech, Jiang made an important preparation in public opinion for the convening of the 14th CPC National Congress and the establishment of a socialist market economy. I was a member of the group drafting the report to the 14th CPC National Congress. The drafting of the report was directed by the Standing Committee of the Political Bureau of the Party Central Committee. On several occasions, Jiang Zemin called the drafting group so he could study the report. He decided that after officially setting the objective of building a socialist market economy he would give it a try at the Central Party School to test reaction. This meant soliciting opinions and pooling all knowledge and doing some preliminary work to unify thinking both inside and outside the Party.

On June 12, 1992, in discussion with Jiang Zemin, Deng Xiaoping accepted the formulation "socialist market economy," saying "in reality, that is exactly what we are doing. Shenzhen is a socialist market economy. Without market economy, without competition and without even comparison, there is no way for science and technology to develop; products will always lag behind others and this would affect consumption and foreign trade and export." He also said that the speech at the Party School might be issued for internal circulation and if reaction was good, it could be made open. This in fact fixed the theme of the 14th CPC National Congress. Later on, the Political Bureau discussed and decided to issue the draft report to the congress, to all local governments, departments and army units in order to solicit opinion. The members of the drafting group went down to provinces, autonomous regions and municipalities to hear views. I myself went to Zhejiang where, after discussion, the provincial Party Committee expressed approval. I went on to Wenzhou where the prefecture Party secretary told me they had come under great pressure, as there were many criticisms. I told him to listen to the disputes but not to argue with them, rather continue on his own road, doing more and saying less or only doing without saying anything. What was the most important was to develop the economy well and improve the living standards of the people. "By doing so, you will stand firm," I said.

In October 1992, the 14th CPC National Congress took the formal decision, putting forward in clear-cut terms that "the objective of our economic reform is to establish a socialist market economy, making it favorable for further releasing and developing productivity."

In 1993-1996, China achieved a "soft landing," thanks to macro-economic regulation. The regulation mechanism and important policies contributing to success would perfect the socialist market economy. Despite problems, the idea of keeping up with the times, an exploratory and innovative spirit, scientific attitude and participation in cooperation and competition in the economic globalization process injected new vigor and vitality into the economy and ensured that it would not go rigid or stagnate.

In September 1997, the 15th CPC National Congress took the decision to adhere to and improve the socialist market system.

In December 2001, China officially joined the World Trade Organization and accepted common international practice in world trade. This marked a major step forward in standardizing, legalizing and internationalizing China's socialist market economy.

In November 2002, the 16th CPC National Congress continued to stick to the objective of reform and put forward the people-centered scientific approach to comprehensive, harmonious and sustainable development and solidified and improved the contents of the reform.

Key and Difficult Points in Market-oriented Reform

On March 2, 1982, the State Council submitted an organizational reform plan to the Standing Committee of the Fifth NPC, proposing to set up the SCRE in order to better resolve the most difficult problems in the reform of the economic system. According to the plan, the Premier would be concurrently the Director in charge of the Commission to undertake the overall design of the structural reform. On March 8, the 22nd meeting of the Standing Committee of the Fifth NPC adopted a resolution, approving the proposal. I heard from Li Peng that Deng Xiaoping had once said that the Premier must sit on the side of reform, which was why all the premiers took up the post of Director in charge of the SCRE. From then on, the SCRE became the headquarters of the general staff for designing the reform of the economic system. During the eight years prior to my taking up the post, the SCRE had undertaken the general design of the reform according to the resolution of the NPC Standing Committee. After the political turmoil of 1989, because of the performance of a Commission-affiliated research institute, the Commission itself came in for all manner of reproach, and was thus thrown into a difficult position, with its work even coming to a standstill. After I took up the position, under the direct leadership of Jiang Zemin, Li Peng and Zhu Rongji, the work of the Commission, which had been interrupted for nearly a year, returned to normal. At that time, the Commission mainly studied the central issue of socialist market economy. In my view, the Commission should, in addition, resume its studies of reform of SOEs, joint stock conversion and the housing system, which were the focus of attention of people of all walks of life. I also thought that reform in these fields covered part of the effort to build the socialist market economy and also constituted the driving force behind efforts to build a socialist market economy.

(1) From "shattering the iron bowl" to the shift in operational mechanism

The reform of SOEs was regarded as the main and most difficult point in the reform of the economic system. After reform and opening-up, the central and local governments all formulated important policies and adopted reform measures, such as the "Law on the Industrial Enterprises Owned by the Whole People" adopted at the First Session of the Seventh National People's Congress in April 1988, which demanded that enterprises should become the main players in the market and better play their due role. But after the reform featuring delegation of power and yielding profits, SOEs met with many difficulties, unable to take new steps and become the true main players in the market.

We opined that, on the basis of work in the past, we should do some deeply penetrative and detailed work concerning the "Law on the Industrial Enterprises Owned by the Whole People," with emphasis on the shift of operational mechanism. On October 21, 1991, the SCRE submitted to Li Peng and Zhu Rongji a document on drafting detailed implementation rules for the Law. On November 8, Li Peng said in a note to the document that "I agree that Zhu Rongji and Chen Jinhua take charge of the work," adding that "ownership should be guaranteed and operational powers should be put in place." The work started at the end of November. He Guanghui, Hong Hu, Sun Yanhu and I were put in charge. Representatives from ministries and commissions of the State

Council, the Central Organizational Department, the General Political Department of the Chinese People's Liberation Army, the All-China Federation of Trade Unions and the National Federation for People with Disabilities participated in the discussion. The SCRE convened forums of officials of various provinces, municipalities and autonomous regions in charge of economic restructuring. The drafting started in October 1991 and was approved by the Party Central Committee and the State Council in July 1992, taking ten months to complete. The State Council discussed it on 17 occasions and the SCRE discussed it on 21 occasions. The draft was revised seven times. Zhu Rongji approved the work, describing it as one of the best documents concerning reform of enterprises.

The document sailed through at the 106th executive meeting of the State Council and was finally named "Regulations on the Shifting of Operational Mechanism of Industrial Enterprises Owned by the Whole People." It had 54 articles in seven chapters. Chapter II was devoted to the operational powers of enterprises, specifying that enterprises had the power in the following 14 areas: taking operational policy decisions, pricing their products and services, marketing their products, procuring materials, handling imports and exports, making investment, disposing of their funds and other assets, launching associations and acquisition, employing labor, managing personnel, distributing wages and bonuses, arranging their internal organizational setups and refusing requests for money, goods or labor service from administrative departments. It also stressed that these powers "are protected by law and no department, units or individuals are allowed to interfere with and encroach upon them." During the course of drafting the document, all departments and units concerned voiced their opinions, focusing on the powers in the 14 areas. The provisions came into conflict with the existing power pattern of the administrative departments. Some departments deemed that the delegation of power was overdone, making it difficult to manage. The departments and organizations concerned argued almost word by word on the power pattern and delegation of powers. No one was willing to let loose the rope in their hands that tied the enterprises. The drafting of the document told us that it was not enterprises that were unwilling to become the main players in the market, but it was their "superiors" that intentionally or unintentionally blocked them from doing so, asking them to obey their leadership and be subject to their management. It dawned on me that it was impossible for enterprises to enjoy full autonomy and become the main players in the market without changing the functions of governmental organs.

There was another thing that concerned the shifting of operational mechanism of enterprises. From late 1991 into 1992, a drive spread through China to shatter the "three irons"—namely, the "iron rice bowl," "iron wage" and "iron official post." The issue stirred media frenzy, causing great confusion among enterprises. In late April 1992, the China Society for the Restructuring of the Economy held its annual meeting in Wuhan. An Zhiwen asked me to address the meeting, which I did. In my speech, I said: "The shifting of operational mechanism cannot simply be construed as 'shattering the iron rice bowl, iron wage and iron post.' It is a systematic, comprehensive and matching reform, covering planning, investment, technical progress, development of new products and product pricing. If the mechanisms in these aspects are not made flexible, it will be difficult for enterprises to acquire the staying power demanded by the market even if the 'three irons' are shattered." I also said that, to shift operational mechanism, "it is, first of all, necessary to accelerate the shift of functions of governmental departments, carry out reform of government organizations to reduce administrative interference so as to create plenty of room for enterprises to maneuver. At the same time, it is necessary to accelerate the pace of cultivating the market." The Xinhua News Agency reporter attending the meeting was very sensitive, deeming it an issue of major importance and nationwide concern and reported my speech. On the next morning, the item was headline news in the newscast of the Central People's Broadcasting Station, and in the leading newspaper *People's Daily*. The reaction was good. When I met Jiang Zemin and Song Ping later, they said that my speech was correct and timely, adding that the disorderly situation should not continue.

(2) Pushing the joint stock system in the "determined try" spirit

It is already more than two decades since the start of the reform of SOEs. In terms of focus, it may be divided into three stages. The first was the stage of policy innovation, a period spanning from the early 1980s to 1992 when the joint stock reform started. During this period, the main aim was to expand autonomy and invigorate enterprises by delegating powers and yielding profits. The second stage was one of institutional innovation, from the start of the joint stock reform in 1992 to the convocation of the 16th CPC National Congress in 2002. The third stage was a stage of structural innovation, which started after the Third Plenary Session of the 16th Party Central Committee in 2003. My tenure covered mainly the second stage, which was of major importance as the reform produced a new enterprises system, namely a joint-stock-based corporation system.

The general background at that time was that, with the rapid development of the national economy and the deepening of economic restructuring, one new thing after another was coming to the fore, making the reform of enterprises even more pressing. The horitzontal links stimulated enterprises to enter into association, thus giving rise to trans-sectoral, trans-regional and trans-ownership acquisition. The drive of specialization and the division of labor gave rise to subsidiaries and branch companies. Projects launched by joint ventures required clear definition of the rights and interests of investors. Further opening-up also revealed the weakness of Chinese enterprises unable to adapt to the requirements of equity and non-equity joint ventures. Factory-like companies were unable to produce board of directors' resolutions, nor able to negotiate according to the requirements of foreign investors. Commercially, they could not carry out corresponding cooperation with foreign companies. After experiencing the first-stage exploration, confidence began to grow in the reform of enterprises, which was regarded as a key link in the reform of the entire economic system. Voices for establishing a joint stock system were getting louder but there was no unanimity on the joint stock system. In fact, there was a big dispute. Some people held that the joint stock system was the product of mass production, a sublation of the capitalist system defined by Marx; some people held that the joint stock system meant privatization, which should not be done in China. On June 23, 1992, I was invited to report on economic reform to the 20th Standing Committee meeting of the National Committee of the Seventh CPPCC. Prior to the meeting, a leader presiding over the meeting made a point of reminding me not to touch on the joint stock system. I said: "Since Deng Xiaoping has already mentioned it, it would not do for me to leave it out." So I did raise the subject, saying: "Just like securities, fund-raising by issuing stocks binds investors and forces enterprises to strive to improve management and raise economic efficiency." I also stressed: "We shall explore effective management of the stock trading market to prevent destructive acts of investment." The official presiding over the meeting kept silent after hearing this.

In his southern China inspection tour, Deng Xiaoping said: "Are securities and stock markets a good thing or bad? Do they involve danger or not? Are they exclusive to capitalism or not? Can they be applied in socialism or not? It is permissible to look at them but we must give them a determined try. If they look all right and are found correct after trying for a year or two, then give them free rein; if they are found wrong, correct them and shut them down, that's all there is to it. If we shut them down, we can do it fast or slow, or leave some remnants."

Deng Xiaoping grasped the fundamental issue of the reform and development of enterprises. Enterprises needed funds for development and for technical transformation and for enhancing their market competitiveness. It was unfeasible to make banks the only source of funds, especially for large enterprises. China must develop its capital market to satisfy the needs of enterprises. Developed countries did exactly that. The history of their development showed that the practice was maturing, safe, standard and manageable. In January 1992, I presided over a joint stock system forum convened by the SCRE in Shenzhen to look into experimenting with the joint stock system. Later on, after hearing Deng Xiaoping's speeches during his southern China inspection tour, the SCRE was determined to accelerate the study and experiments. During the following period, Jiang Zemin and Zhu Rongji telephoned me on a number of occasions, urging me to seize the time to put the reform in place. It took us six months to produce more than 30 documents by organizing 16 departments and related experts under the leadership of Sun Shuyi and coordinated by myself, He Guanghui, Liu Hongru and Hong Hu.

Before 1991, related departments carried out studies and exploration of the joint stock system and conducted preliminary experiments in selected enterprises with the support of leaders of the Party Central Committee and the State Council. But the real comprehensive and systematic reform did not start until the first half of 1992. In view of the prevailing economic and social conditions, especially the actual circumstances of SOEs, we laid down the six-point requirements, listed below, as the basic guiding thinking for pushing the joint stock reform.

One: to maintain the nature of public ownership state capital was to hold absolute or relative controlling shares, which was the orientation of reform at the time. By making state capital hold the controlling shares in joint stock companies, it showed that China was proceeding with reform that perpetuated the dominant position of public owner-ship.

Two: to adhere to the "productivity as the standard" to enable the organizational form of capital, namely, the new ownership relationship, to adapt to the production level of China so as to make it conducive to stimulating productivity.

Three: to make the related policies and regulations basically con-form to common international practice and rules in order to ensure that the reform could go ahead in a standard manner and according to law.

Four: to carry out corresponding reforms to match the system con-version, especially with regard to standard rules and regulations, the accounting system and the intermediary organizations, securities regula-tory organizations and the definition of property rights.

Five: to select trades and large backbone enterprises with a major bearing on national economic development to go ahead with the re-form so as to establish some standard models and create a better social effect.

Six: to create the conditions for large Chinese enterprises to be list-ed on stock markets overseas for the establishment of H-share market and make the rules and regulations, procedures and operations conform to international standards and requirements. At the same time, it was necessary to take further steps to standardize the rules of the A-share market through the establishment of the H-share market.

The work was one of systems engineering, involving a series of rules, systems, laws and regulations, policies and traditional concepts. In order to avoid serious frictions and clashes with the existing system, the work proceeded mainly in the following aspects:

First, while following common international practice concerning listed companies, we had to adapt it to the realities of China. For this purpose, we designed state shares and state corporate shares. At the same time, it made the following stipulations: (1) in important trades, large enterprises must realize the absolute or relative controlling position of the state shares or state corporate shares in order to maintain the dominant position of public ownership; (2) in order to prevent important trades and large and medium enterprises from running out of control and to prevent the draining of state assets, it was established that state shares and corporate shares would not be traded for the time being; (3) the setting aside of workers' shares so that the workers might participate in the operation and management of enterprises so as to demonstrate the status of workers as masters of the house; (4) the setting up of public welfare shares, that is, taking out part of the state shares and corporate shares to be used as a social security fund for retired workers; and (5) the setting up of science and technology shares to encourage innovation.

In order to reflect the basic principles of the joint stock system and safeguard the rights and interests of shareholders, we organized experiments in the trading of corporate shares and selected 15 joint stock companies to carry out stock trading.

Second, persisting in the principle of using laws and regulations as the guide, we summed up the experience and lessons of previous reforms and stressed the necessity of making the joint stock reform comply with policies and law in order to ensure standardization of the reform. To this end, we devised policies and regulations in the following aspects: (1) the standards for joint stock companies and limited liability companies; (2) measures and steps for converting enterprises into joint stock companies and the requirements for related departments; (3) accounting norms and implementation rules of joint stock and limited liability companies; (4) matching policies concerning asset appraisal, land appraisal, tax payment and materials guarantee and the establishment of intermediary organizations in such areas as accounting, law and securities; (5) procedures and methods for the trading of stocks of joint stock companies; (6) rules on the supervision and management of listed companies; (7) standard articles of association and internal rules of joint stock companies; and (8) policy connectivity after stock market listing of joint stock companies.

In the first half of 1992, we issued two comprehensive documents, two documents on standardization, 13 matching rules, four documents on intermediary organizations, two documents on accounting standards, one document on standardizing the listing on the H-share market and one document concerning post-listing policies for the H-share market.

Third, persisting in the principle of simultaneous adoption of matching and supporting measures. The work needed the cooperation and coordination of central and local governments, among State Council departments and between internal and external organizations. After a short run-in period, a group of 30 people with identical views coming from 15 State Council ministries and commissions was formed to ensure that the work was completed in a swift six-month process. These departments and units were: the SCRE, the SPC, the State Council Office for Production, the Ministry of Finance, the State Commission for Science and Technology, the Ministry of Personnel, the Ministry of Foreign Economic Relations and Trade, the People's Bank of China, the State Administration for Land Management, the State Administration for Taxation, the State Administration for Industry and Commerce, the State Administration of Foreign Exchange, the National Bureau of Statistics and the State Bureau for Material Supply.

In actual work, we paid close attention to orderly progress in a well-coordinated manner. The joint stock conversion reform touched many areas, levels and domains. Any new step required the group action of related departments. Even within a department, the work needed timely coordination so as to ensure synchronized operation. The joint stock reform took China's economic restructuring deep and stimulated the reform of the government system and financial and taxation system.

The establishment of the joint stock system involved work at all levels, including theories, laws and regulations, institutions, operational standards, recognition at home and abroad, balancing the work and interests of related departments, handling residual problems from history in enterprises, defining the functions of organizations, market operation, supervision by the state over listed enterprises and market, establishment of intermediary organizations, regulatory procedures, training of personnel familiar with stocks, securities and the market, experiments in the corporate share market, conversion of enterprises listed in the H-share market, connectivity of listing and trading, foreign affairs, supervision and consulting by the NPC and CPPCC, connectivity of policies and guidance to local departments responsible for economic restructuring. All these needed the leadership, progress monitoring and steering of the SCRE.

Fourth, persisting in investigation and study and avoiding making blunders. The work of converting enterprises into joint stock companies was to proceed from the realities of enterprises, trades and localities in order to (1) prevent the draining of state assets; (2) maintain social and enterprise stability; (3) make the work standard; (4) handle well the original rights and interests of all parties concerned; and (5) prevent problems of a political nature arising.

Thanks to persistence in these principles, the listing work proceeded surely and steadily. By the end of 2003, there were 1,287 listed companies, with a market value of 4,245.7 billion *yuan*, raising a total 1,032.8 billion *yuan*, giving a big impetus to the reform and development of enterprises and the growth of the capital market in China. The number of enterprises listed on the Hong Kong market had reached 278 by the end of May 2004, with the total market value making up 30 percent of the total in Hong Kong or as high as 50 percent if calculated by trading volume. The first group of enterprises listed overseas numbered nine, of which five achieved good performances. For details, see Table 7:

Table 7 Performance of first five of the nine enterprises listed in Hong Kong (in 100 million *yuan*)

	Total assets		Sales volume		Pre-tax profit		Net profit	
	Year for listing	2003	Year for listing	2003	Year for listing	2003	Year for listing	2003
Tsingtao Beer	26	90.02	10.48	67.14	2.6	4.26	2.25	2.45
Beiren Printing	5.46	18.93	3.85	11.05	1.11	1.02	0.84	0.96
Ma'an-shan Steel	151.29	263.55	62.39	157.40	22.98	29.88	17.58	26.59
Yizheng Chemical Fiber	102.75	120.79	62.17	103.44	10.16	2.91	8.52	2.59
Shanghai Petro-chemical	153.62	1,275.81	75.83	295.67	10.15	15.77	8.70	14.02

The establishment of the joint stock system meant a breakthrough in deepening the reform of SOEs and it laid the foundation for the establishment of a modern enterprise system. It involved the building of basic economic, political and social institutions. It showed that, under the socialist system, the joint stock system may become a form through which public ownership can be realized.

Progress in the joint stock system accelerated the pace of securing China's standing in the world market. It is a standard interface for enterprises to participate in the global economic division of labor, cooperation and competition.

The experiments in the joint stock system testified to the correctness of Deng Xiaoping's assertion that securities and stock market were not exclusive to capitalism and that they can be used and used well by socialism. Of course, due to our inexperience and urgency, what was done at the time was to convert enterprises into joint stock companies and encourage enterprises with the right conditions to get listed on the stock market. We did not anticipate what problems would occur with the stock market. In the then historical conditions, it was impossible for us to anticipate what would happen and adopt corresponding countermeasures.

(3) Housing reform

China had long been following the system of low rents and welfare distribution of housing, resulting in underdevelopment of the housing market and housing shortages whilst also stimulating a desire to occupy more and better homes, all of which gave rise to an unhealthy trend of abusing power to occupy and distribute houses inequitably, causing great social discontent. We had long been thinking about reform of the housing distribution system by commercializing it but had not dared do so for fear of failure. It was a major task for the governments at all levels to ease the strained situation in housing. When I was working in Shanghai, the Shanghai Municipal Party Committee eked out funds in 1977 and 1978 to build a million square meters of housing every year. Even so, the amount was too meager to satisfy demand. In 1979, the Municipal Party Committee wanted to build two million square meters. Though some people said this was rash, in fact, it fell far short of what was needed. Now, Shanghai is building more than 10 million square meters of housing a year and the figure has increased every year. The property market is flourishing.

I first learned the news about housing reform in a report on Deng Xiaoping's inspection of housing in Beijing's Qiansanmen area. Later on, Deng Xiaoping spelled things out clearly when he said: "Urban residents may buy houses or build their own houses. Not only new houses but also the old houses can be sold. The payment can be a lump sum or in installments over 10 or 15 years. But after the housing is allowed to be sold, the rents should also be adjusted, reflecting the prices of housing, so that people will believe it pays off to buy houses. It is, therefore, necessary to raise rents." According to the instructions by Deng Xiaoping, the State Council set up a housing reform leading group, with An Zhiwen, Chen Junsheng and Lin Hanxiong as the leaders successively. I took up the post as the leader of the group in March 1991. Liu Hongru, Liu Zhifeng and Chen Xuebin worked together with me. Not long after I took up the job of housing reform, I heard that Zhu Rongji had studied housing issues in Singapore and Hong Kong when he was Mayor of Shanghai. Later on, he made great efforts to push housing reform in Shanghai. On Singapore's experience, what impressed me most were two things. One was the housing accumulation fund and the other was that property developers had to undertake to build a certain proportion, probably 20 percent, of low-cost housing for low-income families. Later on, Shanghai took the lead to set up the housing accumulation fund. Zhu Rongji got hold of me, asking for approval of the housing reform plan. I consulted Li Peng and he agreed to release the reform scheme by the General Office of the State Council. This had a great impact in the country. All places followed Shanghai's scheme in their housing reform.

In June 1991, The Housing Reform Leading Group drafted and issued a circular on housing reform in cities and towns and held the second national housing reform conference on October 7, 1991 (World Habitat Day) to discuss the document on the housing reform in cities and towns, which was then issued by the General Office of the State Council to all localities and departments for implementation. The document made clear the objectives of the reform, the basic principles and policies. According to a survey, at that time, there were eight million urban families without houses or without adequate houses, including 500,000 whose housing averaged two square meters per person. In addition, there were 50 million square meters of dilapidated houses and 600 million square meters of makeshift houses that needed rebuilding. Every year, four million newly-weds needed housing. The key to resolving the housing problem was to accelerate the building of homes, but this building of houses had to be guided by a new mechanism rather than the old welfare distribution system. We proposed the idea of cost-sharing by the state, work units and individuals so as to motivate them to build homes. While maintaining the original investment channels, we added new channels for individuals so as to raise more funds for building homes. Such burden sharing was the outcome of pooled experience from all places over the years.

But where to effect a breakthrough in housing reform? Speeding up house building could not turn houses into a commodity. Raising rents would meet great resistance. As far as selling houses was concerned, pricing was a problem as the bearing capacity of the people had to be taken into account. Our view was that raising rents without selling homes could not achieve fast recovery of the investment; selling houses without raising rents could not form the operational mechanism of commercializing housing. The two had to go side by side. At the second national housing reform conference, we proposed to go ahead with the reform of rents, housing sales and housing construction. Welfare distribution of housing in the planned economy period had been the fundamental reason behind the shortage of workers' housing. The more homes that the government and enterprises built, the greater the service expenses and housing subsidies. The investors could hardly recoup their investment, let alone make profits, making the burden ever more heavy. On top of this, it encouraged the malpractice of "abusing power to seek housing," which affected relations between officials and people. Housing reform, therefore, should start with shifting the housing operation mechanism and achieving the commercialization of housing. Rent increases and the selling and building of houses should go hand in hand.

But from the national perspective, there should not be one unified policy and unified model. Different places should have their own ways of reform based on their individual conditions. For this reason the national housing reform conference proposed that housing reform in different places must take into account the regional disparities and bearing capacity of the local people as there were great differences in levels of economic development and consumption, housing conditions, cultural traditions and living habits and also between coastal and inland areas, between the south and the north, between big cities and smaller cities and between cities and county towns.

The establishment of housing funds was a policy we always advocated. The aim was to consolidate the funds of the original budget and enterprises for use in carrying out housing reform. But due to the balancing of the rights and interests of various departments, this work did not proceed satisfactorily. We fully supported Shanghai in setting up the housing public accumulation fund, as we deemed it an effective form for setting up the housing fund and it could help raise the paying ability of workers. We introduced the practice nationwide. After 1991, the system spread to all large and medium-sized cities. The State Council housing reform leading group issued a circular on housing fund management. The system had been proven suited to Chinese conditions and therefore got approval from governments at all levels, enterprises and the common people. After more than 10 years of accumulation, more than 70.36 million workers had housing accounts by the end of 2003, accumulating 556.3 billion *yuan*. At the same time, 234.3 billion *yuan* were issued as mortgage loans. More than 3.29 million families solved their housing problems. The practice also stimulated the building of housing and the development of housing finance.

Housing reform involved wide-ranging problems and had a major impact. In the early period, it was mainly carried out in medium-sized and small cities; it was not extended to large cities and major municipalities until it had proved successful, as housing problems in the major municipalities were quite outstanding and the workers needed to improve their housing conditions through reform. They had a sense of urgency and enthusiasm for housing reform. We discussed the Shanghai scheme with the relevant departments of the city and made it a model for other large cities to follow. The key to housing reform was to start and proceed by raising rents while selling houses, establishing housing public accumulation funds and building houses through multiple channels. At the same time, there had to be preferential policies for disadvantaged groups such as retired workers, laid-off workers and other people in receipt of government benefits. The State Council housing reform leading group heard reports from Beijing and Tianjin and relayed their scheme nationwide. By using Beijing, Tianjin and Shanghai as examples, this had a demonstration effect and got the national housing reform moving. At this time, something interesting happened. After the State Council approved the housing reform schemes of Beijing and Shanghai, all places began emulating them. But the State Council deemed it improper for it to approve every scheme and so stopped. This so irritated Nie Bichu, Mayor of Tianjin, that he rang me, saying that housing reform was a matter of major importance, concerning the immediate interests of the people. Since the State Council had approved the Beijing and Shanghai schemes why had it not approved Tianjin's? He said he could not continue as Mayor if the State Council refused approval the Tianjin housing reform scheme. He was very excited as he spoke so I had to promise to consult the State Council. I told this to the Deputy Secretary General of the State Council He Chunlin and asked the opinions of the State Council leadership. In the end, the State Council decided to approve Tianjin's housing reform scheme.

When I was working with the SPC in 1995, we set out to compile the Ninth Five-year Plan (1996-2000) and studied new growth points for the national economy. In my view, housing was the best bond between people's life and production and economic development. Later on, Zhu

Rongji rang me to say it was necessary to make the housing industry a new growth point so as to expand domestic demand. We agreed that housing was a major industry. In the past, the proportion of people's spending on housing had been about 1.9 percent, and had dropped to below 1 percent. But in foreign countries, such spending was more than 10 percent or even 20 percent. This indicated there was great potential in the housing market. If such spending were raised by even one percentage point, there would be a big market demand. The industry had a long industrial chain and could stimulate the development of iron and steel, cement, timber, chemicals, textiles, home electrical appliances and electronics and machinery. In 2003, China's consumption of iron and steel products—both home produced and imported—amounted to 270 million tons, of which half went into the construction market, the real estate industry accounting for 40 percent of that half. The practice testified to the correctness of the objectives, policies and principles set at the starting stage of housing reform. The commercialization and monetarization of housing promised a huge clustering effect to become one of the major pillar industries of the national economy. Living conditions in urban and rural areas were improved greatly.

Successful Application of Deng Xiaoping Theory and His Riposte to Margaret Thatcher

China started its phased market-oriented reform in December 1978 when the Third Plenary Session of the 11th Party Central Committee decided to grant greater management and operational autonomy to local and industrial and agricultural enterprises under the guidance of unified state plans. In October 1992, the 14th CPC National Congress officially established that the goal of economic restructuring was to build a socialist market economy. The intervening 14 years were a process of exploring ways of building the socialist market economy and a process of studying, understanding and applying Deng Xiaoping Theory.

Deng Xiaoping's courage and innovative spirit in pioneering market-oriented reform played a decisive role in directing China's reform and opening-up and its modernization drive. He dared to make breakthroughs and innovation in theory provided they conformed to the realities of China, regardless of classic dogmas in whatever country. Once he laid down his theory, he would never waver in the face of changes in the political climate or whatever disputes there might be domestically or overseas. He always held firmly to the road he pioneered and to the robustness and consistency of his theory.

In November 1979, Deng Xiaoping told Frank B. Gibney, Vice President of Encyclopedia Britannica: "Socialism can also develop the market economy." During his southern China inspection tour of Wuchang, Shenzhen, Zhuhai and Shanghai, he contended that "planning and market are not the essential differences between socialism and capitalism." He was firm and consistent in his theory of market economy. His brilliant exposition was the summation of the long practice of human society and also a correct answer to the century-old international disputes on planning and market. It was a major innovation in Marxist theory.

Thanks to the guidance of Deng Xiaoping Theory, China's economy grew at an average annual of 9.4 percent in the 25 years from 1978 to 2003. China's GDP was US$ 147.3 billion in 1978. By 2003, it had reached US$ 1,400 billion. China's import and export trade was US$ 20.6 billion in 1978, but by 2003 it had reached US$ 851.2 billion. China's foreign exchange reserves were US$ 167 million in 1978, but by 2003 they had reached US$ 403.3 billion. China ranked sixth in the world in terms of aggregate economy. According to a WTO report, China was the third largest importer and the fourth largest exporter in the world. China's comprehensive national power, status and influence have all undergone tremendous historical changes.

Alongside its economic and social development, the speed and penetration of China's marketization has intensified. Table 8 shows the degree of marketization for all types of commodities:

Table 8 Degree of marketization of commodity prices in 2002

	% of government pegged price	% of government indicative price	% of market price
Retail sales	2.6	1.3	96.1
Purchase of farm and sideline produce	2.6	2.9	94.5
Purchase of means of production	9.7	3	87.3

("Briefing on the proportion of the three types of pricing in 2002" supplied by the General Office of the State Development Planning Commission)

In 1991, the British Prime Minister Margaret Thatcher visited China. I heard from Jiang Zemin and Zhu Rongji that they were locked in great dispute with her in their discussions. Mrs. Thatcher's view was that socialism and the market economy were incompatible and that socialism could not develop a market economy, which required the building of a capitalist system and privatization. Her stubborn views might have something to do with her experience as a politician. In May 1979, Mrs. Thatcher defeated the Labor Party in elections and became Prime Minister. She left office in November 1990. Since the 1970s, Britain had suffered from the serious "British disease," with the economy in prolonged recession, inefficient nationalized industries supported by the Labor Party and an increasing fiscal deficit. When Mrs. Thatcher came to power, she adopted the proposals of F. A. Hayek and Milton Friedman to launch what was known as "the Thatcher Revolution." She asserted that monopoly of nationalized enterprises and the monopoly of trade unions were the two biggest problems for the British economy. She sold off nationalized firms to private investors. She went so far as to "privatize rain," as some people jeered. By the end of her time in office, two thirds of the nationalized companies had been sold off to private investors, involving 46 large firms and 900,000 employees. Another measure of the "revolution" was to break the power of the trade unions. In addition, the North Sea oil fields gave her regime a real prop—"God was on her side." In the vast North Sea, oil was found only in the territorial waters of Britain and Norway. During her time in power, the North Sea oil fields produced 50 million tons of oil annually (daily output in 2002 reached 2.5 million barrels—the equivalent of about 130 million tons a year). The oil revenue helped Thatcher tide over the financial difficulties and was a big prop to her reform.

Thatcher's privatization campaign tinged her view of everything and she peddled her ideas everywhere. In fact, it was a rather limited outlook. She lacked the global and historical perspective of Henry Kissinger. I have mentioned above the letter Henry Kissinger wrote me and quoted his important views, such as "reform must go ahead in keeping with the economic, social and cultural environment of a country." China's reform has proved that his views conformed to the realities of countries.

Based on available statistics, I compared China's achievements of reform with those of the "Thatcher revolution." Answers derived from practice, I believe, are likely to be the best. During her second year in power, i.e. in 1980, Mrs. Thatcher launched a privatization campaign, selling nationalized companies in space and shipbuilding. The drive gathered momentum in 1983 when she sold firms in such areas as telecoms, petroleum, iron and steel, automobile, gas, water and electricity. In 1979, the sales volume of nationalized firms accounted for 11.5 percent of Britain's GDP. By the time when she left office in 1990, nationalized businesses had been cut by 60 percent. When Mrs. Thatcher visited China in 1991, she asserted that socialism and market economy were incompatible and that a socialist market economy could never succeed. Yet, during the 12 years from 1992 to 2003—the years when China introduced the socialist market economy—China's GNP grew at an average annual of 9.7 percent. The total industrial output value of SOEs or enterprises where state shares held dominating positions grew at an average annual of 9.4 percent, far higher than in Britain.

The data show the vitality of the socialist market economy, as the state-owned or state-held industrial companies maintained the same strong growth momentum as the GNP. Production developed even faster in places that were the first to introduce the market economy. All these testify to the correctness of Deng Xiaoping's assertions: "Planning and market are both means to an end. As long as they are good for developing production, both can be used. When they serve socialism, they are socialist; when they serve capitalism, they are capitalist." The socialist system with the means of market economy helped release China's productivity and provided a sustained engine for China's development. Thatcher's views could not hold water in China. The respective developments of China and Britain show that socialism with Chinese characteristics is full of vitality and can achieve a rate of economic development far faster than Mrs. Thatcher's privatization. This comparison of facts over more than 20 years is the best answer to any argument.

In June 1992, in discussion with Jiang Zemin, Deng Xiaoping said: "Shenzhen is a socialist market economy." Shenzhen in Guangdong Province used to be a small county town. Before being made a Special Economic Zone in 1980, "it covered less than three square kilometers. It had narrow streets, the total length of roads being only about eight kilometers. There were only 100,000 square meters of buildings, the highest of which was a five-story structure. There were few factories and industrial output value was 100 million *yuan*. The GNP was a little over 200 million *yuan*. It was a less-developed county pure and simple." The Shenzhen of today is transformed. According to an official of Shenzhen City, by the end of the 20th century, an American multi-national corporation was undecided about establishing one of its R&D centers in Shenzhen, but after an on-the-spot check, it found that Shenzhen was "just like the USA," so the corporation established its R&D center there. To say that Shenzhen is the same as the USA might be an exaggeration, but Shenzhen did indeed have one of the world's best living environments. Table 9 shows the changes brought about by the socialist market economy to Shenzhen:

Table 9　Economic and social development of Shenzhen

	1980, the year Shenzhen became a Special Economic Zone	1991	2003	Growth of 2003 over 1980 (time)
Area (sq km)	2,020	2,020.5	1,952.84	
Resident population	332,900	2,385,300	5,574,100	16.74
GNP (billion *yuan*)	0.27	23.666	289.541	1,072
Total industrial output value (billion *yuan*)	0.106	31.54	561.359	5,296
Import and export (US$ billion)	0.018	19.476	117.399	6,522
Fixed assets investment (billion *yuan*)	0.138	7.936	94.91	687.7
FDI (US$ billion)	0.033	0.58	5.042	152.8
Budgetary fiscal receipts (billion *yuan*)	0.03	2.733	29.914	997
Disposable income (urban area, *yuan*)		4,563.72	25,935.84	5.68 times over 1991
Number of teachers per 10,000 people	77	45	74	
Number of hospital beds per 10,000 people	19	15	24	
Number of university students per 10,000 people	0	16	58	

There were a mere 14 years between 1978, when China introduced its reform and opening-up policy and started market-oriented reform, and 1992, when China decided to build a socialist market economy. This was just a fleeting moment in man's long history of development, just a single generation in a country with a population of 1.3 billion. What China did in this great undertaking was but one step forward. The road ahead is long. We still need to continue our exploration in order to perfect the socialist market economy.

China is changing; the world is changing. Old problems have been resolved and new ones have cropped up. There is no reason for conceit; there is no reason to stall this great reform process. Looking back, I have arrived at the following understanding and inspirations:

First, market economy is an economic development model favorable for releasing and developing productivity. The market can provide timely and extensive information; it can promote competition and activate the economy; it can lead to the optimal allocation of resources; it can improve corporate management to raise economic efficiency. The biggest flaw with planned economy is the lack of competition, vitality, work efficiency and economic results. Without the guide of the market, the allocation of resources is irrational. In a previous chapter, I cited China's iron and steel industry. In New China with the same political and social systems, steel output from 1949 to the end of 1978 was 31.75 million tons; but in the 25 years between 1979 and 2004, steel output climbed to 222.34 million tons. Steel output in 2003 was nearly seven times that of 30 years previously. The automobile industry is another case in point. Output was 149,000 units in 1978 after 30 years of development. But in the latter 25 years, that is, by the end of 2003, output had increased to 4,444,000, 30 times that of 1978. What lies behind such changes? There are many contributing factors, of course. But the most important one must be the market.

Second, market economy has some relations with ownership, but they are not absolute. Different types of ownership can all use market and take market economy as a means to develop themselves. Market economy can serve different ownerships: if placed in the service of public ownership, it is a market economy with public ownership. Of course, different ownerships differ in their management and operational mechanisms, but these are not absolute and can be changed. Public ownership may be changed and improved according to market rules. China Petrochemical Corporation is the biggest SOE, with public ownership. When founded in 1983, the total assets were 21 billion *yuan*. By 2003, its total assets reached 559.2 billion *yuan*, 26.6 times that of 20 years previously. But its public ownership has remained unchanged. This shows that state-owned enterprises and the public sector of the economy can entirely develop productivity by means of market economy whilst still retaining public ownership and can all the same enhance their influence and control power in the whole national economy.

Third, the market economy is full of vitality, but also with variables in the process of development. This, plus different understandings, especially during the transition from the planned economy to market economy, has made it necessary to study, explore and innovate all kinds of theories and to solve many problems that might crop up in practice. In carrying out reform, it is imperative to avoid too much social shock, to reduce reform cost and to take into account the bearing capacity of the people. All this has to be done in a context of no previous experience or precedent. This determines that China, in carrying out market-oriented reform, has to "feel out the stepping stones to cross the river" and must adopt the incremental method. This has been proved correct.

Fourth, the market economy is intrinsically blind, pursuing only the interests of individuals or units to the neglect of public welfare. The Chinese Government is fully aware of its drawbacks and negative effects. While displaying the positive role of market, the government formulated corresponding principles and policies to ward off drawbacks. The most important among them are persistence in the four cardinal principles, strengthening of socialist spiritual civilization, exercising of macro-economic control, strengthening of democracy and legal system, and adherence to the people-centered scientific approach to comprehensive, harmonious and sustainable development. All these measures help compensate for what market economy ignores.

Fifth, the building of a market economy must be geared to mesh with a country's political, economic and cultural development. From the mid-19th century on, China was plunged into a semi-feudal and semi-colonial state, subject to invasion and suppression by Western powers. After spending much blood, sweat and painstaking exploration, the Chinese people finally chose socialism and adapted it to actual Chinese national conditions, evolving socialism with Chinese characteristics. History has proven the correctness of that choice. Market economy, as a means, can entirely be used to realize the ideals and values of socialism and serve the efforts to create a strong country, fair society and happy people. Market economy stresses efficiency, but lacks fairness.

The Chinese Government holds that priority should be given to efficiency while giving due consideration to fairness. In its reform and development, China has simultaneously promoted both material and spiritual civilization and political civilization, displaying the essence of China's fine cultural traditions; carried out education in ethics and moral integrity, encouraging industrious labor and honest and trustworthy business operations and fighting against unlawful acts that jeopardize public interests. All these constitute major additions and improvement to the reasonable part of the market economy.

In human history, a nation or national hero of whatever historical period who acts without respect for the achievements of human civilization and common values created by man, who persists in its own way, goes to extremes and tries to wipe out other nations, can only run roughshod for a time and can never dominate the world. It is nothing but a small wave in the long river of history. This holds true politically, militarily and economically. The Chinese nation has lasted for 5,000 unbroken years through all vicissitudes, in that its culture is all-embracing, capable of absorbing all kinds of ideas and inclusive of things foreign. For New China, socialism was something foreign. Modern market economy was foreign, too. The adaptability of these concepts to Chinese conditions and their development are an inevitable choice dictated by Chinese national conditions, Chinese culture and China's philosophy.

In May 2004, Joshua Cooper Ramo, editor at large at Time Inc. and Senior Advisor to Goldman Sachs, advanced the notion of "the Beijing Consensus," which aroused wide attention. He holds that "China is pioneering a new route towards development that is based on innovation, asymmetric power, human-up development and a focus on the balance of individual rights and responsibilities," and that China is concerned "not only about economics. It is concerned about politics, quality of life, and the global balance of power. China's new development approach is driven by a desire to have equitable, peaceful high-quality growth." In a Xinhua News Agency interview, he said that "China's economy has both market and socialist elements" and "is an integration of market and socialist economies." He holds that the essence of "the Beijing Consensus" is innovation, bold experiment and defense of national interests. He also said: "Political and cultural factors are as important as economic factors in understanding 'the Beijing Consensus.'" Ramo's views aroused great debate among academic circles in China and overseas. Some agreed; some were against and some offered additions. To my mind, Ramo has grasped some of the essential factors of China's economy. The cultural factors for understanding China's socialist market economy should be the stress on adaptability, learning from the strong points of others to offset its own weaknesses and expanding its advantages to benefit both itself and others. Without knowledge of China's national conditions, its historical traditions and cultural background, a deep and informed understanding of China's major policies is impossible.

Chapter VI

Origin of the 1993 Macro-economic Control and Soft Landing

- Appointed Director in Charge of the State Planning Commission
- The Economy Overheats Again
- Preparing, Deciding, and Implementing Macroeconomic Control
- Containing Inflation to Ensure Economic and Social Stability
- Readjusting the Economic Structure and Shifting the Mode of Economic Growth
- Successful Soft Landing

China's economy was plagued with the vicious circle of "normal—overheating—adjustment—cold." This put the Chinese Government in a very difficult position. Could China escape from this vicious circle? Could it bring the economy onto the path of rapid, sustained and healthy growth? The answer was "yes," as proven by the results of China's new round of macro-economic controls.

Should a market economy need intervention by the government that safeguards the public interest? Should the socialist market economy need macro-economic controls? Can macro-economic controls be carried out in the context of socialist market economy? The practice of the 1993 macro-economic control drive also gave positive answers to these questions.

I was transferred to the position of Director in charge of the State Planning Commission (SPC) in March 1993, when the macro-economy was overheating again. Under the leadership of the Party Central Committee and the State Council, the SPC was firm in implementing the policy decision to exercise control over the macro-economy; seeking an overall balance between total supply and total demand, properly tightening fiscal and monetary policies, controlling prices, and continuing the restructuring of the economy. The flexible control and regulatory measures in line with different circumstances of economic and social development—with both development and control, both advances and retreats—succeeded in reining in inflation and ensuring sustainable and rapid growth of the economy. China succeeded in steering its overheated economy to a "soft landing" in 1996. This accumulated experience of macro-economic control under the socialist market economy.

Appointed Director in Charge of the State Planning Commission

During the second half of 1992, word began to spread that I would be transferred to the State Planning Commission (SPC). I did not pay too much attention at first. Toward the end of the year, since my work assignment was directly related to the 1993 work schedules of the SCRE, I asked Premier Li Peng about it at the end of a State Council meeting. He told me that they had indeed discussed the matter, adding that the central authorities had decided that I would remain as the head of the SCRE if Vice Premier Zou Jiahua continued his post as Director in charge of the SPC; but if Zou Jiahua would not hold the post concurrently with his Vice Premiership, then I would be appointed Director of the SPC. Not long after, the Central Work Conference was held. At a group discussion, Zhu Rongji got hold of me and told me that the central authorities had decided to appoint me Director in charge of the SPC, since Zou Jiahua would not continue in the post. He also told me that Jiang Zemin, Li Peng and himself would give full support to my work.

In March 1993, at the First Session of the Eighth National People's Congress, I was appointed Director in charge of the State Planning Commission. I was fully aware of the heavy responsibility, the complexity and difficulty of the job and the expectations of the people.

Previous holders of the post were Gao Gang, Li Fuchun, Yu Qiuli, Yao Yilin, Song Ping and Zou Jiahua. I was the seventh director in charge of the Commission. I was no comparison with the previous six in terms of seniority, work level, experience and contributions. I had served as a deputy head of the planning group under the Ministry of Light Industry, and Director (concurrently) of the Shanghai Planning Committee. I knew the complexity and difficulty of planning. The SPC is both an economic department, focusing on economy but also a major integrated department of the Party and government in managing social and economic affairs, which had to focus attention on politics and had to do well in handling relations between central and local governments, between national and local situations and between immediate and long-term interests. It had to handle very complicated economic and social issues. It was a department where social and economic conflicts converged. Many major issues could not be handled well simply from an economic perspective.

On my first day in office, I told a cadres conference that I knew that the work was heavy but I would exert myself to do the job well and hoped for the support of all members of the Commission. Since I had not handled planning work for many years, I wanted to know the actual situation and heard views from various departments. I stressed: "It is up to me to get hold of you, not for you to get hold of me." After the meeting, an acquaintance told me that people had not caught the meaning of it being for me to get hold of them and not vice versa. I told him that it was very simple. I was a new comer. I did not want to have any preconceived ideas nor did I want to exert my influence on others. I would take the initiative in getting to understand the situation, in strict compliance with the spirit of directives from the central authorities and comments from all quarters on the SPC, without any bias. I would decide for myself what to hear and what not to hear. I would refuse to be dragged into matters that had nothing to do with my job. If my mind became a receptacle for everyone's ideas, I would be at loss as to what to do and would be in a very passive position. He agreed that I was correct.

My changed role, when seen in terms of reforming the planned economy model, could actually be interpreted as changing from an engine of reform to a destination of reform. This role change happened to hit a time when China's economic reform was undergoing a fundamental turn, a moment when the planned economy would disappear forever and a socialist market economy would be officially established. I felt I had been riding a wave. In the past, I had simply issued orders about and talked about cardinal principles. Now it was my turn to action them. Trials and tribulations would be inevitable and that demanded that I would be very careful about what I said and what I did. Such a change of role from engine of reform to destination of reform was a special experience for me.

There had been much talk about the position of the SPC in 1992 when the 14th CPC National Congress decided to establish a socialist market economy. The sharpest view had come from a delegate to the NPC from a province in the western part of China, who proposed doing away with the SPC altogether. The cadres of the Commission were also thrown into confusion, not knowing what to do in the future. At the beginning of 1993, our Commission had called an executive meeting. At the meeting some people had raised the question of the "status" and "performance" of the Commission. Some recalled that, in the past, the entrance to the Commission had been all hustle and bustle, just like a market. But now, there were few people coming and that made the Commission's cadres a little isolated. When I took office, people told me about this. I told them that since the SPC had been set up by a decision of the NPC, there would not be any "status" problem. With its "status" established, it must live up to its duties and must perform them well. Only by performing its duties well, could it strengthen its position. I had always held that the transition from the planned economy to a socialist market economy in no way meant that the government would totally lose its functions in a short period of time. In going for socialist modernization China had a lot of things to do, since it had little to start out with, its territory was vast, its economic development rather uneven and there were great regional disparities in resources and growth capacity. It would still take time for the socialist market economy to establish and improve. During the process, it would be impossible to resolve many major issues without initiative, planning, encouragement and coordination of the government.

It was not long before new problems turned up for real. The macro-economy was overheating and local governments and departments were all going their own ways. Furthermore, China's market was far from being mature. The "invisible hand" was stirring up the water. But what about the "visible hand"? What should it do? Should the SPC, as an integrated economic department, do something? Could it do anything and, if so, how?

This was how things stood when I started my work as Director in charge of the State Planning Commission.

The Economy Overheats Again

China's economy had experienced several big ups and downs since the founding of New China in 1949. I consulted past fluctuations from 1953 to 1996. Over those 44 years there were five major fluctuations, four of them double digit fluctuations, and lasting between them a total of 20-plus years. Some cadres and economists termed this "*Zhe Teng*," which means "tossing and turning." The biggest fluctuation was the one that occurred between 1958 and 1962, when the difference in economic growth between the peak year and the bottom year was 51.7 percentage points. The smallest fluctuation occurred between 1992 and 1996, the difference being only 4.6 percentage points, the smallest fluctuation since the founding of New China. These violent fluctuations greatly impacted the national economy and the people's livelihood. It was a destructive impact, causing the economy to regress to such an extent that it would take years to recover. The lessons were extremely profound. For economic fluctuations over the years, see Table 10:

Table 10 The drop from peak to bottom in each fluctuation of China's economic growth

Years	Drop from peak to bottom (%)
1953-1957	9.6*
1958-1962	51.7*
1963-1968	24.2*
1969-1972	20.4*
1973-1976	11.0*
1977-1981	6.5
1982-1986	6.4
1987-1990	7.8
1992-1996	4.6

Note: Figures marked with * are drops in national income growth rate. Figures without * are drops in GDP growth rate.

What were the things in the past worth studying? What were the experiences and lessons future generations should avoid? How does one turn the lessons learned into soft strength to guide the country on to a path of healthy development? I think, the first 30 years after the founding of New China, the dominant ideology was "leftism." Leaders did not respect the objective law and lacked the spirit of seeking truth from facts, thus resulting in the blunder of opposing "anti-rashness," which resulted in the hardships wrought by the "Great Leap Forward" and the ten-year destruction of the "Cultural Revolution." Two phenomena since the 1978 introduction of reform and opening-up merit deep consideration: one is "investment thirst;" the other is "political performance effect" at the changeover of governments. These two phenomena combined and interacted with each other, giving rise to economic overheating and run-away growth, thus resulting in new and great economic fluctuations.

The term "investment thirst" was coined by the Hungarian economist János Kornai in his book *Economics of Shortage*. In this, he said that in a socialist economy, there was no enterprise or not-for-profit organization that did not want investment. "Investment thirst" was long-term and unquenchable. An investment completed may temporarily quench the thirst but soon there would be a new bout of thirst, even worse than before. This was a universal phenomenon in socialist countries. The description was very vivid. I thought it existed widely in developing countries, too and it needed comprehensive analysis from the historical perspective. If a country is to develop, to progress, construction is unavoidable. Thirst for investment is the aspiration and pursuit of growth. It has its positive aspect. It can arouse the consciousness and zeal of the people for development. The problem lies in what the thirst really means and how thirsty it is. If what is thirsted for is not correct, and if the level of thirst is out of control, it has a negative aspect. Once excessive thirst is translated into government action or becomes the objective of government driven by personal gain without correct guidance by the market and rational thinking for development, its negative effect will rapidly swell, thus touching off run-away overheated development—even going as far as to develop to the opposite of what was desired.

I have checked the relationship between past incidences of economic overheating, investment expansion and changes of government. There is, in fact, a positive correlation. Table 11 lists GNP and investment growth in the year of a change of government and for the year after. Such rises would inevitably lead to economic overheating and misallocation of resources, price rises and disorder in economic activities, which had to be reined in at great cost, in order to restore total supply and total demand to a normal and rational condition.

Table 11 Relationship between investment expansion and changeover of government

	% increase of the year over pre-changeover year		% increase of second year over change-over year	
	GDP	Invest-ment	GDP	Invest-ment
First Session of the Fifth NPC, Feb. 26-March 5, 1978	11.7	16.2	7.6	28.2
First Session of the Sixth NPC, June 6-21, 1983	10.9	16.2	15.2	28.2
First Session of the Seventh NPC, March 25-April 13, 1988	11.3	25.4	4.1	7.2
First Session of the Eighth NPC, March 15-31, 1993	13.5	61.8	12.6	30.4
First Session of the Ninth NPC, March 5-19, 1998	7.8	14.1	7.1	5.1
First Session of the 10th NPC, March 5-19, 2003	9.1	26.7		

Analysis of the data in the table shows that the "political performance effect" of the government changeover resulted in a high growth in GDP, reaching or approaching double-digit growth, in the same year and second year after the changeover of government; a rare exception was 1989, when, impacted by the political turmoil, the GDP grew only by 4.1 percent. Except for some particular years, investment growth was even higher, at least double that of GDP, to become the leading contributory factor in economic overheating.

The thing that distinguished the economic overheating of 1993 from previous incidences was its speed and strength. In 1992, China's GDP grew by 14.2 percent; total industrial output value grew by 24.7 percent; and fixed assets investment grew by 44.8 percent. The urban consumer price index (CPI) rose by 8.6 percent. The data show that 1992 economic growth was starting to show signs of overheating. However, when it came to the first half of 1993, all the indicators chalked up new records: the added value of industry showed growth of 30.2 percent; fixed assets investment showed growth of 61 percent; and the CPI of 35 major large and medium-sized cities rose by 17.4 percent, or as high as 21.6 percent for the month of June. This situation was attributable to the following factors: first, through 15 years of reform and opening-up, great changes had taken place in China's market and economic operational mechanisms, and the growth of personnel and accumulated experience created the conditions for accelerated development; secondly, through years of accumulation, economic strength had grown, especially in the eastern coastal areas, which witnessed a big influx of foreign investment and big growth in the private sector, which provided the material and financial strength for accelerating development; thirdly, Deng Xiaoping's speeches during his southern China inspection tour in early 1992 had helped remove the obstacles, both theoretical and attitudinal, which had fettered people for many years, thus exciting people's zeal for accelerating development.

In 1993, when the government was changed over following the Eighth NPC, just as I said earlier, the new government was eager to do more and better. The political performance effect spread throughout the country: a mood of major drive and fast catching-up prevailed across the land.

Preparing, Deciding and Implementing Macro-economic Control

After the first quarter of 1992, the economy continued to heat up. Acts in violation of rules, discipline and even law caused disorder on the financial market, investment to run out of control and prices to shoot up, thus interfering with and harming the overall situation of reform and opening-up. What measures should be taken to cope with such a situation? The first option was to remain calm without adopting any measures and let it run its own course. Some regarded the situation as very good and felt there was no cause for concern. Taking this non-action option might result in the problems accumulating, thus missing the best opportunities to adopt proper measures. The second option was to resort to the old ways, i.e. applying administrative means to order correction, retrenchment, stoppage of capital construction projects and down-scaling of production targets. Historical experience showed that the costs of adopting such measures were higher; plus, they were at odds with the new environment of reform and opening-up. The third option was to size up the situation and study in a timely fashion new moves to cool down the economy and steer it to an ultimate "soft landing." Whichever method, the pre-condition was to unify our thinking and enhance understanding, especially among leading cadres at all levels—at provincial and ministerial level in particular—who must all have identical views and obey orders. Under the then political and economic conditions, to do ideological and political work well and unify thinking was an important organizational guarantee for concerted action nationwide. This was China's political advantage, one enjoyed by no other country; during my meetings with political figures and economic heavy-weights of many countries in the latter half of 1996, many voiced this opinion about our macro-economic control.

In 1992, the scale of capital construction became even larger. Every local government, even townships, vied with one another to open development zones. There were construction sites everywhere and work carried on night and day. The scale of construction had gone far beyond the bearing capacity of the state and local governments. All kinds of markets had been thrown into confusion. The SPC felt that there was no alternative but to stop it. Even so, it had a lot of misgivings when coming to do so, the main worries being that "an emergency brake"—slashing back the scale of fixed assets investment and forcing a large number of projects to stop—might cause big shocks, even though to do so might yield quick results. As it involved many parties, it might leave some consequences that would become knotty problems. I had worked in local governments and enterprises. I had tasted the bitter pill with the dropping of Baoshan Steel and the four ethylene projects. It had made ideological work difficult and practical problems hard to resolve. Furthermore, it had had great negative effects on the state, enterprises and society as a whole. It had also had an adverse influence politically. So I disagreed with "emergency braking" and "universally applicable policies." Rather, I would, according to the instructions from the central authorities, seize opportunities to deepen reforms, give proper guidance to and protect the enthusiasm of the people. Different places and different industries should be treated differently so that some projects would continue and some would be abandoned. There would be both advance and retreat, all in a proper manner. This was something we had never done before and did not have the experience. We were not sure whether we could do it well or not. At that time, I worried that the economy was too overheated to cool down and if it was allowed to continue, it would result in bigger problems. At the same time I feared that the measures might be too soft to be effective and that local governments would refuse the package of measures. Such were my own misgivings, and these views were shared by many in the SPC. All hoped for some new way of controlling the overheated macro-economy without producing too much fall-out. I really felt in a pinch and was afraid of misunderstanding the instructions of Deng Xiaoping and therefore committing mistakes. As previously mentioned, neither my seniority nor my reputation would allow me to do my work poorly. Moreover, I did not have the political capital to bear such a disgrace, let alone displease all the "local officials" who would make my future work even more difficult. I had already heard about some provincial Party secretaries and governors complaining that it was I who had surveyed the problems and made the central authorities decide upon macro-economic controls. In fact, they overestimated me. Long before I was transferred to the SPC, the central authorities had already pointed to the overheated economy time and again and set about looking into control measures.

As far as I can recollect, the process of preparing, deciding on, and implementing the macro-economic controls may be summed up as the following four major steps, with some important work overlapping.

(1) Unifying thinking

As previously noted, the nation was widely divided on its understanding of the national situation that appeared after the first quarter of 1992. The focus of discussion among all cadres, especially among provincial and ministerial level cadres whom I knew, centered on three problems. One was how to size up the situation: was it overheating, actually? People in the eastern part of China held that reform and opening-up was enjoying a good momentum of development and had brought about new opportunities for development; therefore the economy was not overheated at all. On the other hand, people of central and western parts of China felt that their development had lagged behind, but that things had just turned for the better and their economy was far from being overheated. It was a question of "economic overheating in the other guy's back yard." The second was whether or not it was necessary to adopt measures and what measures to adopt? What would be the results of the measures? Would these measures affect reform and opening-up? The third problem, which was a concern to one and all and the most difficult to command, was whether or not the measures, if adopted, would affect the implementation of the spirit of the resolutions adopted by the 14th CPC National Congress and Deng Xiaoping's speeches during his southern China inspection tour, thus reversing the development trend of reform and opening-up and reducing economic growth.

The Party Central Committee and the State Council first devoted a lot of work to the three problems, so as to size up the situation. In 1992, some major economic indicators were at their highest since reform and opening-up. Yet, all places were vying with one another to "keep up with the Joneses" and to expand the scale of capital construction, resulting in a country-wide development zone fever and real estate fever. Without funds, they would set up financial institutions without approval and resort to all possible measures to raise funds. In violation of rules, banks carried out wanton inter-bank lending and borrowing, causing deposits to drop sharply and a lot of money to circulate "externally." From April 1992, the Party Central Committee and the State Council started a lot of top-down work concerning these problems.

On April 4, 1992, on the eve of his visit to Japan, Jiang Zemin wrote a letter to the other central leaders, enjoining them to be good at giving proper guidance and protection to the drives and enthusiasm of the cadres and people so that they were brought into full play. He asked the leaders to study hard how to deepen reform rather than kicking up a fuss about expanding size.

In October 1992, the central authorities called a meeting of all principal leaders of all regions and departments for the exchanging of information. Participants were briefed on the new problems arising in the macro-economy and encouraged to seize opportunities to accelerate development whilst paying close attention to problems that might arise, so as to ensure the smooth progress of reform and opening-up and economic development.

In January 1993, Deng Xiaoping said when meeting leading cadres of Shanghai: "It is essential to be steady and sure, avoiding losses, especially big losses."

In March 1993, the central authorities called a conference of provincial Party secretaries and governors to discuss how to stop wanton fund-raising and inter-bank lending and how to hold in check real estate fever and development zone fever.

On April 1, 1993, the central authorities called another meeting to brief on the economic situation. Jiang Zemin, Li Peng and Zhu Rongji made important speeches, calling on all places to interpret Deng Xiaoping's southern China speeches in a comprehensive, correct and positive manner and to persist in the principle of emancipating the mind and seeking truth from facts, taking care to draw on the lessons of the economic fluctuations in history and achieving the aim of accelerating development and doing everything possible, but meanwhile proceeding from realities and doing everything within one's capacity so as to prevent big ups and downs, and avoiding losses whilst maintaining the good momentum of economic development.

In April 1993, the State Council issued the "Circular on Resolutely Stopping Wanton Fund-Raising and Strengthening the Management of the Issue of Bonds," which was State Council Document No. 24, 1993.

The circular pointed out that many places, departments and enterprises and institutions "are raising funds by issuing bonds and other methods without authorization. Such fund-raising methods bear high interest rates, have a wide impact and the amount issued is large. The problem is very serious." The State Council decided to send out seven work groups led by leading officials of related departments to 14 provinces, autonomous regions and municipalities to check the situation.

In May 1993, the State Council issued another circular "Strictly Examine and Approve and Conscientiously Take Stock of All Kinds of Development Zones."

From May 9-11, 1993, Jiang Zemin presided over an economic work forum of six provinces and one municipality of eastern China, at which he called on them to shift their focus on accelerating development over to deepening reform, shifting mechanisms, optimizing institutions and raising efficiency. He stressed the necessity of employing economic means and legal means, supplemented by necessary administrative means, to strengthen macro-economic control and exercise effective control of economic operations so as to ease the contradictions in economic activities and strive to maintain and develop the good situation of economic operations.

On May 19, 1993, Jiang Zemin wrote to State Council leaders, urging them to seize the time to solve the most outstanding problems in the economy. Otherwise, he said, the important opportunities for solution would be gone in an instant. If the problems accumulated, they would inevitably cause big trouble.

In Xi'an, June 13-14, 1993, Jiang Zemin called an economic work forum of five provinces in Northwest China, calling on them to deploy the basic roles of the market in resource allocation and drawing attention to macro-economic regulation and control. This, he stressed, was an important part of building the socialist market economic system and also a major move in deepening the reform.

On June 24, 1993, the Party Central Committee and the State Council issued the "Proposals on the Current Economic Situation and Strengthening Macro-economic Control," which was Document No. 6 of the Central Authorities in 1993. The document outlined 16 measures for strengthening and improving macro-economic control. The document pointed out: "The current macro-economy is very tight and some contradictions and problems are continuing to develop. If opportunities are not to be seized to deepen reform and exercise macro-economic control, it would inevitably lead to a serious imbalance between social demand and social supply; inflation would be worsened; and there would even be big fluctuations in the economy that would affect social stability."

The Party Central Committee and the State Council performed well and did all that was needed to unify the thinking of the nation. I think this is manifested in the following three aspects: First, they started to get to grips with the problem very early, just as we often say "repair the house before it rains"—we need take preventive measures or tackle problems before they become really serious. From 1989 to 1992, the strength accumulated by the economic retrenchment was at bursting point; Deng Xiaoping's speeches during his southern China inspection tour and the convening of the 14th CPC National Congress had excited the enthusiasm of millions of people, heralding a new high tide of development. The Party Central Committee spotted the other side of this current in time. It started work in April 1992 and kept at it. Second, exactly enough was done. In doing business in China, the key lies with the leadership, first of all, leadership above provincial and ministerial levels. Without unanimity of thinking among officials at these levels, work would not be done well. There must be consensus among them concerning the analysis and judgment of the situation and the measures planned to deal with it. Starting from October 1992, the central authorities called a number of meetings to brief officials on the economic situation and to tell the truth to provincial and ministerial officials. Jiang Zemin went to Shanghai and Xi'an to call forums and talked with Party secretaries of provinces, municipalities and autonomous regions to discuss the situation, analyze problems and look into measures. If the leading officials at these levels got a clear understanding, it would ensure that the policies were well implemented. Third, the contents covered every aspect without one-sidedness. The 1993 economic overheating was the result of many factors, both negative and positive. It would not do to kill every factor. The central instructions and Jiang Zemin's speeches all stressed the positive, correct and comprehensive understanding of Deng Xiaoping's southern China speeches, the spirit of the 14th CPC National Congress and the necessity of providing good guidance to the initiatives of the people, protecting and deploying their enthusiasm and unifying thinking by persisting in emancipating the mind and seeking truth from facts. They stressed the importance of doing everything possible and within capacity. It was this guiding thinking that enabled the whole Party to understand and be clear about the objectives and measures for macro-economic control, and ensured that the control went smoothly.

(2) Investigation and deciding on policy

To what degree was the economy overheated? To what degree had economic disorder grown? All these needed a factual assessment. In order to get a clear idea of the real situation, the State Council executive meeting in April 1993 decided to organize seven work groups headed by the SPC and send them to 14 provinces, municipalities and autonomous regions, namely Heilongjiang, Jiangsu, Zhejiang, Shandong, Hunan, Hainan, Sichuan, Hebei, Fujian, Shanghai, Liaoning, Guangxi, Shaanxi and Guangdong to carry out investigations, look into and check on implementation of State Council Document No. 24, 1993.

When the groups returned to Beijing, I organized a meeting to hear their reports and study a report to be submitted to the State Council.

In their reports, all groups deemed the problems very serious: there was indiscriminate inter-bank borrowing and lending, and unauthorized setting up of financial institutions; there was a universal fever in the real estate industry and in the opening of development zones; there was an excessive issue of money; deposits by residents had dropped; demand was inflated; the foreign trade deficit was enlarged; and prices were going up too fast. In some provinces, the total amount of funds raised accounted for 20 percent of total bank savings. Summing up the reports from 12 provinces, the total amount of inter-bank lending had reached 312.3 billion *yuan* by the end of 1992. Inter-bank lending was large in scale and maturity terms long; the flow of funds and the purposes of those funds were irrational, resulting in a drastic expansion of fixed assets investment. Development zone fever was out of control. By the end of 1991, there were 117 development zones in the country. By the end of 1992, the number had rocketed to over 2,700—more than 20 times the total for the previous seven years. We submitted our report to the State Council on May 25, 1993. The report was entitled "Recommendations on Policies and Measures for Strictly Controlling Economic Aggregates and Strictly Implementing Macro-economic Control." At the beginning of June, the Premier's office heard the report and discussed it in depth. Then, the State Council called a meeting, presided over by Zhu Rongji, to study concrete measures. At the end of the meeting, instead of an off-the-cuff speech, Zhu Rongji offered a 13-point proposal, which he had prepared. It was a complete package of measures, especially in the financial and monetary areas and taxation, which were strongly targeted. These measures reflected mainly economic means and laid an important foundation for establishing and improving an effective mechanism for macro-economic control.

Following the meeting, I presided over a division head meeting of the SPC where we earnestly discussed Zhu's proposals. Everybody went along with Zhu's 13-point proposal and even added some specifics. I myself added three points, namely, controlling the scale of fixed assets investment, inflation, and group purchasing power. The meeting adopted my additions. The report was then revised and officially submitted to the State Council. Zhu Rongji agreed to the three additions. The 16-point proposal later on became the Central Document No. 6, 1993.

My years of experience in economic adjustment and corrections told me that Central Document No. 6 was, indeed, very good. It reflected, to a considerable degree, the maturity of the Party and the people's government in the level of macro-economic control. The document stated at the very beginning: "It is essential to get a good command of the three-point guiding principle, through which the reform spirit runs through." The document stressed that in order to make earnest efforts to seize, cherish, and use well the opportunities, it was necessary to make a start on solving the outstanding problems in the economy. The document clearly pointed out: "It is necessary to adopt a new line of thought and new methods to solve the current problems and seek a way out by accelerating the transition from the old to the new system and turning efforts to improve and strengthen macro-economic control, and to solve outstanding problems in the economy into a motive power for accelerating reform and for building a socialist market economy." The 16 measures outlined in the document were: (1) Strictly control the issuing of money so as to stabilize the financial situation; (2) resolutely correct the tendency of borrowing and lending in violation of rules; (3) employ economic levers to increase the amount of bank savings; (4) resolutely check unauthorized fund raising activities; (5) strictly control lines of credit; (6) professional banks must ensure the payment on demand of savings deposits; (7) accelerate the pace of financial reform and strengthen the central bank's ability to exercise macro financial control; (8) the reform of the investment system and the financial system must be carried out at the same time; (9) issue state treasury bonds within the prescribed time limit; (10) continue to improve the management of the issue of negotiable bonds and standardize market management; (11) improve the method of foreign exchange management to stabilize the price on the foreign exchange market; (12) strengthen overall control over the real estate market to promote its healthy development; (13) intensify tax collection and management and plug loopholes in tax exemption and reduction; (14) prioritize projects in progress and strictly control new starts; (15) actively and surely promote price reform to curtail the over-rapid rise in the general price level; and (16) strictly control the fast growth of group purchasing power. The document also predicted the possible impacts on the macro-economy and major industries. It was proved that the predictions were scientific and correct.

In order to ensure that all the measures listed in the document were well implemented in a comprehensive and effective way, when I reported to the Standing Committee of the Political Bureau of the Party Central Committee, I suggested a central economic work conference. The meeting would discuss the document and how to implement those measures. But after repeated deliberation, Jiang Zemin decided against holding the central economic work conference but to call conferences by different regions. When the document was issued, Jiang Zemin called the conferences of Northeast China, North China, Central South China and South China in Dalian and Guangzhou. I attended the two conferences. Principal leaders of the participating provinces, autonomous regions and municipalities all showed their attitudes in support of the document and all outlined their own measures to implement the document. I felt it was a good thing to hold the conferences.

As for the title of the document, there were also different considerations. At the beginning, we proposed the title "Decisions of the CPC Central Committee and the State Council on the Current Economic Situation and on Strengthening Macro-economic Control." But Li Peng and Zhu Rongji discussed it with Jiang Zemin and they agreed that the wording "decisions" was too heavy and asked us to look at it again. Some suggested the use of "circular," but they thought it too light. In the end, we decided on "proposal."

(3) The right efforts to urge implementation of the document

After issuing Document No. 6, the State Council decided to organize another seven work groups led by ministers, each group covering two provinces, autonomous regions and municipalities in order to hasten the implementation of the document. The 14 provinces, autonomous regions and municipalities were all large ones with a great bearing on the whole country. It was of utmost importance that these provinces, autonomous regions and municipalities should implement the document well. Their doing so would have a great bearing on the neighboring regions and even on the whole country. The work groups were warmly received by the various provinces, which offered good cooperation. Apart from visiting factories, construction sites, development zones and shopping centers to hear the briefings by local governments, the groups put emphasis on examining the work of local planning commissions, banks and financial affairs departments to get to know how they were implementing the Document. One province accepted the Document grudgingly and its principal leader was in low spirits. When the work group tried to make appointment for discussion, he refused on the pretext of having other activities.

In order to strengthen the implementation of No. 6 Document and to ensure that all the 16 measures were put in place, the State Council called a national financial work conference in early July 1993, and a national conference on fiscal and taxation affairs in late July, which formulated rules to be observed in implementing the Document. The financial work conference decided: to immediately stop and take careful stock of all lending and borrowing in violation of rules, and to recover all the money lent or borrowed within a prescribed time limit; that no financial institution was allowed to raise interest rates on deposits, nor allowed to engage in "savings solicitation war" by raising interest rates, nor allowed to collect kickbacks from borrowers; to immediately stop banks from injecting credit funds into economic entities they themselves operated and that banks must thoroughly separate themselves from economic entities they operated. The fiscal and taxation conference formulated rules of strict control over tax exemption and reduction, fiscal deficits and stopping the charge accounts in banks; government financial departments and their affiliated organizations were forbidden to engage in commercial financial services without the approval of the People's Bank of China and all the companies they ran were to be separated from the financial departments within a prescribed time limit.

Under the planned economy the relations between financial and monetary administration had not been rectified. When the state's budget hit difficulty, it would get an overdraft from the bank; if the banks lacked paying ability, the state would increase the issue of money, which resulted in inflation. Since reform and opening-up, advocates of reform repeatedly proposed that the central bank should maintain its independence. The SCRE also adhered to this view and accordingly designed a reform program for China's financial and monetary system. In 1991, the SCRE published the highlights of economic reform in 1992, which included the idea that the central bank must maintain its independence and that when the state budget was in difficulty, it could not overdraw from the bank or ask the bank to increase the issue of money in order to fund the fiscal deficits. When the State Council discussed the document, the Ministry of Finance and the People's Bank of China (central bank) refused to accept it. The SCRE and I became targets of criticism at the meeting. Despite this, the SCRE did not give up, holding fast to the idea that the central bank should maintain its independence, as this would be of vital importance to macro-economy and to the stability of the financial and monetary systems. Later events proved that the Commission had been right.

(4) Fine-tuning at the proper time

The macro-economic control that started in 1993 was indeed not small in strength. The 16 measures outlined in Document No. 6, and the rules set by the financial and monetary systems played a role in cutting out the ground on which the economy became overheated. The second of the 16 measures called for a resolute stop to inter-bank borrowing and lending in violation of rules, and demanded that "all banks at all levels take stock of their borrowing and lending within a prescribed time limit and recover unreasonable borrowing or lending within a prescribed time limit. Any borrowing and lending in violation of rules that fail to be recovered before August 15, or where the money had been used for other purposes in the name of borrowing must be registered sum by sum, with explanations and proposals for treatment." This was indeed a tough measure, which was termed as "Light of August 15." For the purpose of returning the borrowings in time, banks in many provinces appropriated working funds for production and reserve funds. They went so far as to resort to using the reserves on demand. Some savings bank branches even dared not open, thus causing a credit crisis.

After the Document was issued, I took a group to Jiangsu to check its implementation. On the evening of the second day after the examination work ended, the Nanjing City Party committee and government insisted on inviting me for local snacks at the Confucius Temple. To refuse their hospitality would have been too impolite, so I and my group went along. No sooner had we reached the Confucius Temple than the Party Secretary and Mayor led us to see a savings bank branch that had been shut, saying that the branch had used all its available money to repay what it had borrowed and that when savings depositors wanted to withdraw money, it had to find a pretext to refuse them. When I asked them if it was a show for our benefit, they said no and asked us to see other savings bank outlets if we did not believe them. At the dinner table, they complained again that, in order to pay back the borrowings, the city had to stop working capital loans to industrial and commercial enterprises and had to use daily cash payments to pay back their borrowings. The move was not only affecting production and market supply but also normal savings operations. When I asked how things stood in other places, they told me the situation was almost identical.

After the work group returned to Beijing, Wen Jiabao heard the report by all groups. All groups reported the situation of implementing Document 6, but did not mention specific problems. But I spoke about the problems in Nanjing. I said that the problem caused by paying back borrowings merited attention. Hearing this, Wen Jiabao said that the problem was very important and he would study it with Zhu Rongji. In the afternoon that day the General Office of the Party Central Committee phoned me, saying Zhu Rongji and Wen Jiabao would be going to Nanjing the following day and asked me to go with them. They also asked the provincial Party secretaries and governors of neighboring Anhui and Zhejiang to go to Nanjing to attend a forum.

The forum presided over by Zhu Rongji in Nanjing was very timely and very good, giving a good start for fine-tuning at proper times and proper limits in the future. The following are the original minutes of the meeting transmitted by the work groups, and show the determination of the central authorities and the extreme importance of communications on major issues.

July 29, Vice Premier Zhu Rongji heard a report from the Jiangsu Provincial Party Committee and government.

Zhu Rongji said: The 400 million *yuan* bonds that Jiangsu Province planned to issue this year will be cancelled. The projects in progress must be verified to see whether they really need money. If they really do need financial support, they will all turn to the banks for loans.

The financial difficulties in Jiangsu were caused by many factors. The disorder in the financial area is an important factor. To solve this problem, the only way out is to adopt the method of cutting out the grounds for economic overheating, in accordance with the spirit of Central Document No. 6.

First, resolutely stop indiscriminate fund-raising.

Second, stop lending and borrowing in violation of rules.

Third, resolutely implement the principle of "limiting production, reducing inventories and promoting marketing." Do not go too fast.

Fourth, resolutely control the scale of capital construction.

Fifth, the problem of financial credit. There are two channels for boosting investment to such a scale. One is illegal fund-raising and the other is lending and borrowing in violation of rules. Later on, when the national financial work conference was held, I added another point: financial departments regard budgetary funds as extra-budgetary funds and bragged about financial credit. This was also a big contributor to the expansion of capital construction.

Sixth, enterprises must be strict in observing discipline concerning liquidation. Enterprises must put their money in banks and not engage in circulation outside banks.

On the issue of bonds, please take the national situation into consideration. Bond issue plans in recent years have been too ambitious, including the nearly 100 billion *yuan* of treasury bonds. Such big amount of bonds, once put on the market, would deplete all the banks of their savings deposits. The Jiangsu provincial planning committee should counter-check their accounts with the State Planning Commission and the People's Bank to see what is necessary. If it is really necessary, the bank loan scale and fund scale will be approved. The interest rates on bank loans are lower than on bonds.

All new start-ups planned for this year are not to be started, no matter how good they are. Only if this pre-condition is met will the money needed come from banks or a small bond issue be made. Yao Zhenyan of the State Planning Commission and Jin Jiandong of the People's Bank are to organize the study on this. My personal opinion is to issue fewer bonds and expand bank loans.

In the end, Zhu Rongji agreed to increase bank loans to Jiangsu Province by four billion *yuan*.

Many years later, Jiangsu provincial Party Secretary Chen Huanyou was still grateful to me for reporting the real situation in Jiangsu. He said that, without that four billion *yuan* loan, more and more enterprises would have been forced to stop production, markets to stop operating and savings banks to shut their doors. There would have been unimaginable consequences for the whole economic operation. The "blood" in finance cannot be re-injected once the economy halts; it is like the motion of matter, where if an object loses its constant velocity, it requires redoubled efforts to re-start it. The price is very high. If the re-injection is applied before the economy stops, it would have the effect of moving "a thousand kilograms with a force of a few ounces," thus bringing the motion to normal very quickly. The truth of this was testified by Zhu Rongji's Nanjing tour and the proper fine-tuning that came later.

Containing Inflation to Ensure Economic and Social Stability

The market allocates resources mainly through price, which plays a function of transmitting information and directing allocation in the distribution and movement of social resources. In China's market-oriented reform, price reform has always been a sensitive matter concerning the whole situation of the country. China's economic reform was incremental, which, to a large extent, set great store by the effect of price reform factors, including, on the positive side, promoting production and enhancing supply and, on the negative side, causing inflation with an adverse impact on the livelihood of the people and price distortions that would disrupt normal operation.

In late 1993 and particularly in 1994, I devoted considerable energy, or my main energy, to controlling inflation. SPC Vice Directors Wang Chunzheng, Luo Zhiling, the latter being responsible for prices, and Vice Director Ma Kai, together with myself, were responsible for this difficult matter that directly concerned macro-economic control. This attracted criticism from some department directors, saying that I did not attach much attention to our specialization and did not make proper arrangements to discuss work concerning industries and enterprises, including professional planning and major projects. I did not entirely go along with this. I said that the work of the SPC was integrated and would coordinate the balance and planning of all specializations and could not be separated from specialization. If the specialization work could not be done well, there would be no foundation for balancing. But I stressed that it was up to all ministries and major companies to do the specialized work and it was up to enterprises to look after the micro-economic activities. Only such matters that had to do with balancing and coordinating the whole country were the business of the SPC. I said that China was so large and there were so many specializations that it was impossible for the Commission to attend to all matters. The emphasis of the work of the Commission was on the macro-economy, and it aimed at creating a good macro-economic environment for specialized and micro-economic activities. If the Commission was immersed in specialized areas and attending to micro-economy matters, it would drown in routine business, without the energy to manage the macro-economy or to create a good economic and social environment in the service of tens of thousands of micro-economic activities. I still hold that opinion.

For years, repeated disputes on the relations between planning and market, that is, the social results of reform, were often reflected in price fluctuations and inflation. So controlling inflation became a threshold in the process of China's market-oriented reform that had to be crossed. In my view, China's price reform was generally successful. It shed the burden of price deviating from value that had accumulated during the long years of planned economy, provided the guidance for a rational flow of resources, and promoted the growth of productivity. At the same time, China paid much attention to relative stability in prices during reform, taking great care to see that people's lives would not be much affected and that the cost of reform would be reduced so as to provide a fairly good macro-economic environment for reform. This was in sharp contrast to the "shock therapy" pursued by Russia.

The "shock therapy" reform package featuring liberalization of price and trade, privatization and control of inflation was served up in

Russia at the beginning of 1992, after the "President's Economic Work Group" headed by Yegor Gaidar came out with Russia's economic reform scheme in October 1991. The "therapy" subjected 90 percent of retail prices and 80 percent of wholesale prices to market forces rather than government control. On March 5, 1992, the decision was made to abandon basic food prices. This "shock therapy," with no careful consideration of national conditions, the bearing capacity of the people or the many problems that had accumulated during the long years of planned economy, took inflation in 1992 up to 2,500 percent and the GNP dropped by 18.5 percent. In 1993, inflation remained as high as 940 percent and the GNP dropped by 12 percent. In 1994, inflation fell to 204 percent while GNP dropped by a further 12.6 percent. Over those three years, Russia's ranking in the world economy dropped from second place to 16th. The biggest damage inflicted by the "shock therapy" on economic and social life was that people saw their life savings vanish overnight and the Ruble become worthless as legal tender. Wage earners even went bankrupt. Society was drastically shaken. The serious after-effects were not eliminated until many years later.

One of the most outstanding problems in China in 1993 was the rapid rise in prices, which aroused widespread attention. In 1992, the CPI rose by 8.6 percent over the previous year. By June 1993, the CPI had risen by 13.9 percent over the same period of 1992; by December it reached 17.3 percent and by October 1994 it was 25.2 percent higher.

In early 1994, on the eve of the NPC and CPPCC sessions, Li Peng presided over the State Council meeting to discuss his government work report. He asked me to speak first. I said that public opinion polls indicated that the most burning topic of universal concern to the people was inflation. But the local governments and related departments were still demanding to raise prices in order to increase efficiency and reduce subsidies. I proposed that there should be no price raising schemes that year, as it concerned the general situation of the country and asked all present to support my proposal and urge their affiliated units to deepen reform, improve operation and management and reduce costs. My speech expressed my burning desire at the time.

Price management has a direct bearing on each and every household. If prices were to rise, the people would blame the government, above all, the SPC. It could never shake off the blame no matter how you explained it. I feared very much that the troubles would grow and the general situation would get worse. When prices were rising, especially for grain and edible oil, which grew the fiercest and the people were panic-buying, I went to the grain depot in Xizhimen, grain shops near the Tsinghua University dorms, State No. 3 Cotton Mill residential quarters at Shilibao and the neighborhood community at Dengshikou to see what had happened and to hear comments from the sales clerks. Their worries about run-away inflation and the strong reaction of the people deeply touched me. I asked a grain shop how many times every day they replenished their grain stock. They said: three times, with the rice and flour bags piled up behind the counters to tell people that there were enough supplies to go round and there should be no stock-piling. Despite this, people would not believe it and would take home grains in bags and in hundreds of kilos. I felt the situation was very serious and should in no way be taken lightly. It allowed not the slightest neglect. In September and October 1994 when price rises were most acute, I dreamed for several nights of people panic-buying food grain. Once I even let out a tortured cry in my dream. When my wife heard it, she came and asked what had happened. I told her I had dreamed of people panic-buying food grain. This shows how great a pressure I was under at the time.

In August 1994, the Financial and Economic Sub-Committee of the NPC heard a report from the SPC. All the NPC Standing Committee members who spoke expressed their serious concern about price frenzy. Some said that if the prices were not to be controlled, they would impeach the government. After the meeting, I reported to Li Peng about the strong reaction of the NPC Financial and Economic Sub-Committee members. I said that they would not impeach Li Peng himself nor the vice premier in charge of the SPC, but myself. If impeaching me could cause prices to drop, I would be very grateful. It was out of such burning desire that, after repeated deliberations, I went to consult on the matter with Luo Zhiling who was responsible for price management. We decided to issue two circulars, urging strengthened monitoring and examination of prices of basic daily necessities and services, and the regulations on open price tags on commodities and services. I reported it to Vice Premier Zou Jiahua before the executive meeting of the SPC took the decision. He fully agreed with me. After the two documents were issued, I went around Yuquanlu Department Store and other places to see how they were being implemented and to gauge the reactions of the sales clerks. They said that open price tags were easy for departments for industry and commerce as well as ordinary people to check and supervise and they inspired confidence among consumers.

I also discussed with the People's Bank on inflation-proof savings according to the instructions by Li Peng and Zhu Rongji, so that the real income of wage earners would not be affected by currency depreciation and remain relatively stable. In discussing the inflation-proof savings structure and related weight, I repeatedly consulted the urban survey team of the National Bureau of Statistics in order to get from them original data on the income and expenditure of city residents and carefully calculate the co-efficient against inflation needed to compensate for the depreciation of the currency.

All these practical tasks were complicated and difficult and concerned the interests of the common people. It struck me deeply that I was in a dilemma in the choice between deepening reform and accelerating price reform and keeping prices relatively stable, not allowing the reform to increase the burdens on the people or to harm their interests, in particular the interests of low-income people. It required cooperation from all sides; it required proper policies and implementation schemes; it required efforts to make the "visible hand" function properly, without setting obstacles to the market at the general level while compensating for the drawbacks of the market, doing as much as possible to maintain an equitable market. Later on, thanks to the concerted efforts by the whole Party and people of the whole country, especially the Party Central Committee and the State Council, a decision was taken in 1995 to make control of inflation the first and foremost task in the state macroeconomic control. Li Peng presided over a national teleconference to check on the implementation of the policies. All this meant great support and guidance to the work of the SPC. In 1995, prices began to fall, with the CPI falling from 21.7 percent in 1994 to 14.8 percent in 1995, and down again to 6.1 percent in 1996, closer to a reasonable range.

Many years later, I made a self-appraisal of my work and felt greatly pleased. I had not forgotten the people when they were in difficulty. I had always kept in mind how to help people tide over the difficulties of currency depreciation and how to mitigate the losses caused by price hikes. Our generation had experienced years of hardships and difficulties and knew how the people struggled to live. I had the experience of working in the countryside, when I served as Deputy Party Secretary of the Dakou People's Commune of Yanshi County, Henan Province. I also worked for a number of years in a factory. I know the life of the people. Although times had changed and conditions improved, the fact that I kept the masses of the people in mind did not change. With this, China's reform measures are sure to get the full understanding and support from the people and any difficulty would be overcome. I remember that in the 1980s, Luo Gan, who was responsible for the All-China Federation of Trade Unions, organized a forum to discuss how to mobilize the workers to safeguard social stability. I said at the forum that there should be no utilitarianism vis-à-vis the common people and the workers, taking them out when needed but just ignoring them when not. That remains my view. These days, there are many articles and treatises on the differences in reform between China and Russia. I found that they missed one point, namely, the difference in the principle of reform—whether or not the reform was people-centered—which was a very fundamental difference. This is the most essential factor in the success of China's reform. China adopted an incremental path of reform, paying attention to social stability, to the protection of the people, especially the interests of vulnerable groups. This is a heritage and development in the new historical period of the fundamental purpose of serving the people always advocated by the Party. My introducing the differences between Russia's and China's reforms is for the precise purpose of stressing the importance of the principle of reform. Having the common people at heart, the reform would be correctly orientated and there would be the sources of strength. Otherwise, the reform would lose popular support, go off track, and even end in failure.

One of the major activities in the process of price reform or one of the prominent features was the dual-track price system. It started in 1982 and ended in.1996, lasting for 14 years. This was a big issue during my term at the SPC. Joseph E. Stiglitz, Nobel economics laureate and former Senior Vice President and Chief Economist of the World Bank, spoke highly of the transitional system to the market economy, saying that this was Chinese wisdom and that such a wise transitional method could both push reform and develop production, avoiding too big a shock to society. Facts have proved just that. Another big matter was the integration of foreign exchange rates. At first, Zhu Rongji asked me to take the lead in looking into this and to put forward recommendations. Later on, the study project was moved to the People's Bank of China for continued investigation and implementation.

The dual-track price system was a major move for that stage of price reform. Since supply and demand of some basic manufactured goods were thrown into serious imbalance and the then macro-economic environment did not allow big price adjustments, the state, in order to solve the outstanding problems of market demand, adopted both planned management and market regulation over the market system and prices of some products in that particular period.

Dual-track pricing started with petroleum and was later extended to almost all capital goods and some important consumer goods. In 1982, with the approval of the State Council, oilfields were allowed to sell and export the crude they produced in excess of the contracted quotas at international prices. The Daqing Oilfield sold above-production-quota crude at 644 *yuan* per ton, higher than the normal price of 544 *yuan*. Other oilfields sold their above-quota crude for 532 *yuan* per ton following the example of Shengli Oilfield. The differential income was earmarked for use as exploration and development funds to make up for shortfalls. In May 1984, the State Council issued interim rules on further expanding the autonomy of SOEs, allowing enterprises to fix their product prices at 20 percent higher than the state pegged prices. In January 1985, according to the instructions of the State Council, the State Price Administration and the State Material Supply Bureau issued a circular concerning the relaxation of the prices for manufactured capital goods, allowing manufacturers to sell part of their products, extending the scope of direct sale for all products, with the proportion of products whose prices are regulated by the market increasing steadily. According to a survey by the Institute of State Price Administration conducted in 17 provinces, municipalities and autonomous regions, the amount of capital goods purchased by enterprises at the plan price accounted for 44 percent (or 28 percent in value) of all needs. Among them, the amount of coal covered by the plan price was 45.4 percent; of steel, 29.7 percent; of timber, 21.7 percent; and of cement, 15.5 percent. This marked the start of the dual-track pricing, that is, the co-existence of plan prices and non-plan prices.

The system developed rapidly in 1985-1987 and was at its peak in the years 1988-1990. The price hikes were very severe. By the end of March 1989, the market price of coal was 149 percent higher than the plan price; that of crude oil, 213 percent; steel, 105 percent; timber, 112 percent; copper, 150 percent; and aluminum, 124 percent. The situation eased a little as supply and demand eased off after the corrections of 1990. After Deng Xiaoping made his famous southern China inspection tour speeches, the pace of reform picked up and the state let go of the prices of most products, subjecting them to market forces. After 1993 and 1994, the dual-track prices of such major capital goods as iron and steel, machinery, coal and crude oil were merged. By 1996, dual-track pricing had totally disappeared. The system became history.

The dual-track system—adding market price to the plan price— played both positive and negative roles. In the early period, it played a big positive role but, as time went on, its negative effects began to show.

Looking back, the positive role of dual-track pricing manifested itself in the following: (1) it was conducive to liberating and developing productive forces, invigorating enterprise activities and increasing the efficient supply of products. Enterprises could arrange their own operational activities after fulfilling state plans. However, since only the surplus above state-set quotas was subject to market forces, the market regulation was in reality a kind of "marginal regulation." Relatively speaking, only marginal interest was what enterprises pursued of their own accord, therefore, marginal price naturally became the orientation for enterprises pursuing their own interests. The system enlivened the activities of enterprises, invigorated the national economy and promoted industrial restructuring, thus injecting renewed vigor and vitality into the national economy. To a certain extent, the system satisfied market demand and balanced the interests of the state, enterprises and individuals; (2) it opened up a channel for the growth and development of the markets for manufactured goods and capital goods. This transitional way accelerated the growth of the capital goods market; (3) it stimulated the development of township and village enterprises (TVEs). Under the planned system, TVEs could hardly get the materials allocated by state plans. But dual-track pricing increased the channels of goods supply. With money, TVEs could buy the production materials they urgently needed, thus giving an impetus to the development of TVEs; (4) it breached the plan price system and accelerated its disintegration, thus playing a positive role in stimulating the transition from the plan price system to the market price system.

The negative side of the system lies in the following: its features determined its transitional nature. In the span of a few short years, the system revealed its drawbacks and shortcomings both in theory and in practice. It aroused wide criticism. (1) It gave rise in effect to two markets, disrupting the unity of market and the state plans. Plans for allocating production materials could not be fulfilled; (2) it damaged the sameness of value criterion, resulting in the same amount of money having different purchasing power on the two markets, making it difficult to make an objective assessment of economic efficiency of enterprises; (3) the two markets were guided by different rules, thus jeopardizing fairness in competition and resulting in market disorder. The players on the two markets had different capacities and the disparities between the two prices were too great, thus inducing reselling and speculation for exorbitant profits and provided a breeding ground for abuse of power for personal gain, bribery, corruption and other malpractices. The direct consequences of dual-track pricing stimulated price hikes in some products. After the introduction of dual pricing, the portion covered by state plans was reduced year by year, and the price level outside plans shot up due to material shortages. All this became an important factor affecting price stability and even causing inflation.

But when viewed as a whole, the positive and progressive effects outweighed the negative. In the transition from the planned economy to market economy, dual-track pricing was inevitable in the planning, material allocation and investment systems. Dual-track pricing mirrored the changeover of these systems. Thanks to the introduction of the dual-track pricing, we realized the coordination and simultaneous progress of price reform and the reform of the whole national economy. It acted as a bridge in the transition from the planned price system to the market price system.

Readjusting the Economic Structure and Shifting the Mode of Economic Growth

The macro-economic control of 1993-1996 was different from any adjustment and correction in the past. It did not demand one-sided retrenchment. On the contrary, the control and regulation were made into a positive means of effecting both advance and retreat, both development and retrenchment according to different circumstances of economic and social development. There was no "one clear-cut," i.e. the same policy universally applied to all. It was neither impartial nor fair to say "the SPC is effective in applying the brakes but not in starting up." In truth, the SPC did act ineffectively in starting up in some cases, and there were also times when it was unable to apply the brakes. But in general and in most cases, both starting up and braking were effective. The Commission safeguarded the general interests of the state.

The scale of investment in capital construction after 1993 proves that the SPC was not just interested in and effective at applying the brakes. Table 12 shows the growth of fixed assets investment in the years 1993-1996.

Table 12

Year	Investment (unit: 1 billion *yuan*)	Growth over previous year (%)	Investment rate (%)
1993	1,307.2	61.7	37.74
1994	1,704.2	30.37	36.45
1995	2,001.9	17.47	34.23
1996	2,291.3	14.46	33.75

Fixed assets investment in the four years of macro-economic control from 1993 to 1996 all experienced double-digit growth. It was 75.3 percent increase in 1996 over that of 1993. The year-on-year range of growth tended to be reasonable. The annual drop of one to two percentage points in investment rate was appropriate, making it possible to reduce the scale of investment and maintain a fairly reasonable rate of growth, thus playing an important role in easing the total demand and supply situation.

Even more importantly, great changes took place in the investment structure. Lagging agriculture, energy and infrastructure had long remained a "bottleneck" of China's economic development. In 1993, when the macro-economic control started, the state began to increase input into these areas in a planned manner. Some projects that had been dreamed of by generations of people actually started, reached a peak or were completed. Central investment in water projects increased at an average annual rate of 42 percent. Grain production, where output had long lingered around 400-450 million tons stopped stagnating and reached an annual output of 500 million tons. The Beijing-Kowloon Railway was opened to traffic. The Three Gorges Project completed the damming of the Yangtze, and the Xiaolangdi Project completed the damming of the Yellow River in 1997. In November that year, on my way to attend the celebrations for the damming of the Yangtze, I said to Jiang Zemin that the damming of the Yangtze and the Yellow River was a great historical coincidence, a double-happiness for the Chinese nation, a thousand-year rarity. But it was a pity that we had not made enough publicity and that many people were unaware of it. Jiang Zemin said: "That is right. There should be good publicity."

The 1993 macro-economic control not only helped improve the structure of the national economy but also significantly boosted our economic aggregates and integrated national power. The data are shown in Table 13.

Table 13　Major growth indicators of the national economy, 1992-1996

Indicator	Unit	1992	1996	% growth of 1996 over 1992
GDP	1 billion *yuan*	2,663.8	6,788.5	54.8
Fixed assets investment	Ditto	808	2,297.4	184.3
Consumer retail sales	Ditto	1,099.4	2,477.4	125.3
Total imports and exports	1 billion US dollars	165.5	289.9	75.1
Of which, exports	Ditto	84.9	151.1	77.8
imports	Ditto	80.6	138.8	72.3
Fiscal revenue	1 billion *yuan*	348.3	740.8	112.7
FDI employed	1 billion US dollars	11	41.7	279.1
Foreign exchange reserves	Ditto	19.4	105	440.3
New housing in urban and rural areas	1 million sq. m.	860	1,220	42.4
Per capita living space in urban areas	Sq. m.	14.8	17	14.9

Per capita living space in rural areas	Sq. m.	18.9	21.7	14.9
Per capita disposable income in cities and towns	*Yuan*	2,027	4,839	29.5
Per capita net income of rural families	Ditto	784	1,926	24.4
Grain output	1 million tons	442.66	504.54	14
Raw coal output	Ditto	1,120	1,400	25.2
Steel output	Ditto	80.94	101.24	25.1
Shaped steel output	Ditto	66.97	93.38	39.4
Ethylene	Ditto	2	3.04	51.7
Integrated circuits	Ditto	160.99	3,889.87	2,316.2
Chemical fiber	Ditto	2.13	3.75	76.2
Color tv	1 million sets	13.33	25.38	90.4
Air conditioner	1 million sets	1.58	7.86	397.5
Power generating capacity added	1 million kilo-watt	13.79	17.41	26.3
New railways in operation	km	1,057	2,171	105.3
New roads added	Ditto	4,458	10,179	128.3
Of which, freeways	Ditto		1,443	
Fixed phone users	1 million	11.47	54.95	379.1
Mobile phone users	Ditto	0.18	6.85	3,773.8

Note: GDP, per capita disposable income of urban families and per capita net income of rural families are computed in comparable prices.

The SPC always held that it was necessary to see the outstanding problems in our national economic development and, when things were good, it was even more necessary to address the extensive tendency in economic development and to stress the need to shift the mode of economic growth, changing from extensive operation to intensive operation, making great efforts to adjust the product mix, conserve energy, reduce raw material consumption and to improve the quality of economic growth. In August 1997, the SPC held a conference in Beidaihe to discuss and launch the work of shifting the mode of economic growth. At the end of the conference, Li Peng and Zhu Rongji and other vice premiers met with the participants, drawing their attention to the importance of shifting the economic growth mode and calling on all places to implement the spirit of the conference and to improve the quality of economic growth. At the meeting I made a report entitled "Really Push the Shift in the Mode of Economic Growth." In this, I stressed the necessity of changing our concepts. The history of world economic development showed that it was an objective law to rely on the progress of science and technology and to follow the path of intensive operation. It was, therefore, necessary to understand this law deeply and do the work early in order to gain the initiative and make progress. Otherwise, one would inevitably be kicked out of competition. I also stressed the necessity of coming to grips with the shift in two aspects simultaneously and that the shift in the economic system was predicated on change in the economic growth mode. It was therefore necessary to remove all obstacles to economic growth and, through shifting the growth mode, advance and enrich the contents of economic system reform. Thirdly, I stressed the necessity of giving full play to the role of market mechanisms and achieving optimization of resources allocation by relying on market competition and the "survival of the fittest" principle. The fourth point I stressed was that we must make great efforts to adjust the structure. I said that it was necessary to make a strategic adjustment with regard to the industrial structure, product mix, organizational setup of enterprises and the deployment of regional productivity so as to promote the optimization and upgrading of our economic structure. My fifth point was that we must really rely on the progress of science and technology. I stressed the necessity of intensifying technology development and extension, and speeding up the commercialization and industrialization of achievements in science and technology in order to improve the technological levels of industries. My sixth point was the need to formulate and implement correct economic policies, encouraging intensive operation, limiting and eliminating extensive operation by fully employing such economic levers and means as price, taxation, credit, interest rate, interest discount and depreciation so as to create a good policy environment for shifting the mode of economic growth.

At that time, the Mayor of Shanghai Xu Kuangdi was also in Beidaihe. When he heard about the meeting, he remarked to me that the SPC had really come to the point: "leading the cow by the halter." I said that extensive operation was characteristic of developing economies in their high-speed development and that, given the great trend of economic globalization, the rapid spread of information and technology and our advantage as a late-comer, it was possible for us to shorten the period of extensive operation so as to avoid detours and spend less on "tuition." I too held that the success of China's modernization mission depended, to a large extent, on the result of this work.

I repeated my views at the national economic conference on November 23 of the same year. I pinpointed the most outstanding problem in all areas of economic operation as being the autarkic economic structure featuring "big and all-inclusive," "small and all-inclusive," overlapping construction at low levels, serious waste and poor economic results. I gave a detailed analysis of the actual situations in various industries and enterprises, drawing their attention to the gaps between them and advanced international levels and proposed recommendations for fundamental changes. When seen today, these problems still remain the major ones that concern the whole situation of our national economic development and future prospects. It is a pity that these problems keep recurring time and again, whenever the opportunity arises. China must make a lasting breakthrough if the market economy in China is to grow mature.

I also believed it necessary to make shifting from extensive to intensive operation a priority in all business operations and make it a universal guiding principle. Now, when China's aggregate economy exceeds US$1 trillion, the pressure brought about by extensive operation on the resources and environment as a result of wasteful consumption of human and financial resources, fuel, raw materials and all other production activities has become too heavy for society to bear. In order to push the shift in economic growth mode and to conserve energy, the SPC, after years of preparation, produced "The Law of the People's Republic of China on the Conservation of Energy (draft) and submitted it to the NPC Standing Committee for deliberation in the first half of 1997. On November 1, 1997, I made an explanation of the law at the 28th meeting of the Eighth NPC Standing Committee. At the very start, I said: "Conserving energy is an important measure for rational and effective energy utilization, for easing the strain on energy supply, for raising economic efficiency and for protecting the environment. It is a long-term strategic principle to make great efforts to conserve energy and raise the level of the utilization of energy." In my explanation, I also stressed: "Our energy utilization rate is only 30 percent, 10-20 percentage points lower than that of developed countries and our unit energy consumption of major products is between 30 percent and 80 percent higher than that of developed countries." The energy conservation law has 42 articles in six chapters, making specific provisions concerning the scope of adjustment, management energy conservation, rational use of energy, technology for conserving energy and legal liabilities. The NPC Standing Committee adopted the law at its 28th meeting. But the implementation of the law, just as I pointed out before, would be cast aside whenever the situation improved and when we talk about development. This remains a major issue that limits China's economic and social development today. It is, therefore, necessary to strengthen the enforcement and implementation of the law and to intensify education and training of cadres and business managers so that they understand that energy conservation is a principle set in stone.

Successful Soft Landing

Between 1993, when the central authorities decided to exercise control over the macro-economy by producing 16 measures, to 1996, China succeeded in curtailing inflation while maintaining a sustained and rapid economic growth. Compared with the previous year, the GDP in 1996 grew by 9.7 percent and industrial added value by 12.5 percent; the CPI rose by 6.1 percent; fixed assets investment by 14.8 percent, and money supply (in a narrow sense) rose by 18.9 percent; the foreign trade surplus came to US$12.2 billion; the registered unemployment rate in cities and towns was three percent. The situation improved further in 1997, when the GDP grew by 8.8 percent; fixed assets investment increased by 8.5 percent; the CPI rose by 2.8 percent; the foreign trade surplus reached US$40.3 billion and foreign exchange reserves increased to US$133.9 billion. The economic performance indicated that China had brought the economy into an orbit of sustainable, rapid and healthy development. Chinese and foreign media commented that China had succeeded in achieving a "soft landing." With great improvements in the macro-economy, China was able to resist effectively the Asian financial crisis and, under the situation of stagnation of the global economy, persisted in not devaluing the Renminbi, thus making a positive contribution to the recovery of the world economy and winning widespread approval from the international community. The Nobel Economics Laureate Merton Miller commented: "Nothing can hurt the public more than inflation. The Chinese Government is pursuing a right policy to curtail inflation. Soft landing is a significant achievement and should merit great attention in the other parts of the world."

Economic "soft landing" was advanced by an American professor in 1985. In the mid-1980s, some foreign economists borrowed the phrase to describe the change of economic operation from an abnormal state to a normal state. They held that "soft landing" was an ideal objective in the changing economy, but also a difficult one to achieve. China's success in solving the dilemma of curtailing inflation while maintaining economic growth aroused widespread attention and approval from the world. Toward the end of 1996, when I visited Britain, France and the Netherlands, meeting and talking with their financial officials and bank governors, they all showed great interest in China's "soft landing," leaving me with a deep and unforgettable impression.

More than a decade has passed since the macro-economic control started in 1993. Its achievements have been proven in practice. Now when I look back, I think there are eight points that merit summing up.

(1) There must be state macro-economic control in developing the socialist market economy. The development histories and realities of all countries show that no economy with absolute freedom and no government intervention exists in the world, only that the government intervention is different in content, form and degree. The Nobel Economic Laureate Paul Samuelson once stressed there were three major roles that government can play in the market economy: to correct market failure, regulate distribution and take care of all social groups, especially the interests of vulnerable groups in order to reduce unemployment and stabilize society. China's socialist market economy has yet to mature and it is necessary to see both the positive side of the market in resource allocation as well as its blind and unfair side and its absence of function in regulating the interests of the general public and the long-term interests. China's socialist market economy is integrated with the basic socialist

economic system. If they integrate well, they can give play to both the advantages of the market and the superiority of the socialist system. Only by doing so, will it be possible for us to find the proper point of integration in handling the relations between economy and social development, between market mechanism and macro-economic control, between long-term objective and current tasks, between local and general interests, between efficiency and equity; to avoid the blindness and limitations brought about by absolute market freedom; and to promote a comprehensive, coordinated and sustainable economic development. This was an innovation in theory and also an innovation in practice. It is a positive exploration in the human development mode.

(2) It is essential to formulate and keep to the correct guiding principle of macro-economic control. At the very start of cooling the economic overheating, the Party Central Committee and the State Council stressed positive, comprehensive and correct understanding of the spirit of Deng Xiaoping's southern China inspection tour speeches and to persist in emancipating the mind and seeking truth from facts; to protect, guide and display the initiatives of the people; to correctly handle the relations between reform, development and stability and achieve the objectives of both accelerating development as far as possible and proceeding from reality, and doing everything within our capacity; to make the steps sure and steady and to avoid losses, especially big losses. These guiding principles were well targeted at the reality of economic overheating; they were also the summation of historical experience to avoid repeating the one-sided retrenchment of the past.

(3) Size up the situation well and correctly fix the main objectives for macro-economic control. In economic and social development, the total supply and total demand are always changing. If the conflict between them is too big or too drastic, it will result in overheated or overcooled economy. There are many contributory factors to the overlarge contradiction and they need timely studying and analyzing and

arriving at correct conclusions. The 1992 economic overheating mainly featured development zone fever, real estate fever, indiscriminate fund-raising and inter-bank borrowing and lending, and a disorderly financial market. So it was a correct option in 1993 to start with correction of the financial order so as to arrest the momentum of economic overheating. When the effects of economic overheating were transmitted into prices, causing serious inflation, the emphasis of macro-economic control in 1994 was shifted to curtailing inflation by increasing supply and containing overheated demand, using a combination of measures such as price, taxation, credit, interest rates and exchange rates, so as to strike a basic balance between total demand and total supply, thus bringing down prices step by step.

(4) Institute properly tight financial and monetary policies. The 1993 macro-economic control was different from the "emergency brake" applied in the past. This time, we did not introduce excessively tight policies nor did we resort to overall control and correction. Instead, we paid attention to structural adjustment under the condition of general balance. There were both startups and cutbacks; there were both advances and retreats, giving more attention to maintaining a sustained, rapid and healthy development. The introduction of the properly tight financial and monetary policies helped maintain a proper growth of investment demand and consumption demand and continued to provide effective supply and improve the economic structure, thus both reining in inflation and avoiding big fluctuations in economic growth.

(5) Accelerate structural adjustment and promote structural optimization. The emphasis of the work was put on agriculture, infrastructure and the weak links in the basic industries. In agriculture, we introduced the policies of protecting arable land, increasing investment and raising the prices of agricultural products to stimulate agricultural production and supply, thus lightening the pressure of inflation. In

energy, transportation, telecommunications and other infrastructure areas, we strengthened the weak links to remove "bottlenecks." In industry, we adjusted the product mix and, as regards products for which there was no market demand, exercised the policy of "restricting production, cutting inventories and promoting sales" so as to encourage them to supply goods really needed by the market.

(6) Strengthen dynamic monitoring and forecasting of macro-economic operations, controlling the strength of macro-economic regulation. Careful observation and analysis of the operation of economic and social development required a whole set of comprehensive, systematic and accurate data so as to arrive at an accurate judgment and, on this basis, to apply appropriate fine-tuning. In analyzing the macro-economic indicators, emphasis should be put on money supply, scale of fixed assets investment and investment structure and CPI, studying their relations to see their impacts during and after the period.

(7) In the reform of the political system, especially with the assessment of the performances of cadres and their promotions and demotions, we must implement the scientific approach to development put forward by the Third Plenary Session of the 16th Party Central Committee and the "people-first" principle and eschew making economic growth rate and investment expansion the main criteria. We should do everything possible to prevent the "investment thirst" syndrome and government changeover effect. We should correctly give play to the government changeover effect to avoid big economic fluctuations.

(8) It is necessary to carry out in-depth investigations, and study and pool the wisdom of the people in formulating macro-economic control policies. After policies are formulated and put into implementation, we must objectively observe the actual results, paying attention to problems that might crop up and adopting timely measures for correction and improvement. To make the policy decision process more democratic and scientific is a whole process of policy decision taking,

implementation, feedback and improvement. The 1993 macro-economic control was successful in that the leadership set great store by this experience.

The macro-economic control that started in 1993 was practiced in the context of introducing the socialist market economy. In general, I think it was a success. It took us only a little over three years to bring the overheated economy back to normal and achieve a "soft landing." It was really great. Comparing it with 1988-1990, we can see the differences. The 1988-1990 economic adjustment brought GNP growth down drastically—from 11.3 percent to 3.8 percent, a drop of 7.5 percentage points in three years. It was too big a fluctuation. In the 1993 adjustment, however, the economic growth rate dropped from 14.2 percent in 1992 to 9.6 percent in 1996, a fall of 4.6 percentage points in four years, much milder than the previous retrenchment. More importantly, when the economic growth dropped to 3.8 percent in 1990, the economy became overcooled, resulting in inadequate supply and shortages of commodities, higher unemployment and reduction in revenue, thus weakening the strength of the macro-economy, affecting sustainable development and increasing the negative effect in economic circulation. Obviously, the 1988-1990 retrenchments were not viable. I said to Jiang Zemin once that we should strive for 20-30 years of stable growth and for this purpose we should set our eye on the quality of growth, harmonious economic and social development and the increase in employment and revenue. When China's aggregate economy reached 10 trillion *yuan*, the quality of economic growth would become the paramount issue. In 1996, China's GNP reached 6.7885 trillion *yuan*, 940.7 billion more than in the previous year. In the same year, fixed assets investment reached 2.2947 trillion *yuan*, with the input/output ratio being 2.44:1. By 2003, China's GNP reached 11.6898 trillion *yuan*, 1.1726 trillion more than in the previous year. Fixed assets investment in the year was 5.5118 trillion *yuan*, with the input/output ratio expanded to 4.7:1. If the newly added working capital were added, the input/output radio would be even bigger. For every five *yuan* of input, there would be only one *yuan* of output. This was the quintessence of extensive operation and such a growth mode would obviously not last long. So I suggested putting the emphasis of work on quality and efficiency, with the annual growth rate kept at about six percent within a range allowing movement of a few percentage points. If the ceiling and floor were exceeded, this would bring about all kinds of problems and negative effects. Of course, it is an ideal model. It is hard to operate. A high-ranking official once told me that Jiang Zemin had mentioned my views on a number of occasions.

Of course, the 1993-1996 macro-economic control was not perfect. There was much room for improvement. For instance, what does "properly tight financial and monetary policies" mean? How proper should they be? How long should they last? And how to control them? All these need continued study and practice. After I left my post, I exchanged views with a responsible official and asked him whether there was any connection between the post-1998 deflation and the "properly tight financial and monetary policies" of 1993? What were their relations? Where did the problem lie? I think there are some relationships. The "properly tight financial and monetary policies" of 1993 lasted too long and were not relaxed at the proper time, thus leaving some deflationary impact later on. This, I said, merited reflection and assimilating lessons from. I also think that China's financial reform, the systems of financial organizations, financial regulation and the quality of the people in the financial area could not meet the requirements for building the socialist market economy. This is the most difficult area in the economic reform, an area urgently in need of a breakthrough. Of course, human history is a history of development, a history of constant exploration and advance. During the course of exploration, blunders in judgment or setbacks are inevitable. What is important is to learn from past lessons and to avoid rigidity in thinking and complacency in action, not to mention getting drunk on success. Only by this attitude, can we find a more reasonable path and get closer to reality step by step. Difficulties and setbacks can never obstruct the general trend of forward development.

In 1997, the World Bank issued a full-length report *China 2020: Development Challenges in the New Century*. The report said: "Currently China is experiencing two changeovers, changeover from the command economy to a market economy and the changeover from rural and agricultural society to urban and industrial society. The success China has achieved in the two changeovers has caught extensive attention. China has become a country with the fastest economic growth in the world. Since 1978, its per capita income has more than quadrupled. In just one generation, China has achieved successes that took other countries several centuries to achieve. This is the most attractive development in our times in a country whose population exceeds the combined total of Africa and Latin America." After China achieved "soft landing" in 1996, China's economic and social development began to enter into a new round of sustainable, rapid and healthy development. The achievements in all areas fully testify to the objectivity and correctness of the comments by the World Bank.

Chapter VII

Four Inspection Tours as a Standing Committee Member of the Ninth National Committee of the CPPCC and My Four Visits to Africa

- CPPCC Membership Was My Long-standing Wish
- Inspection Tours for CPPCC Standing Committee Members Are a High-level Form of Participation in the Discussion and Administration of State Affairs
- International Activities of the China Economic and Social Council
- My Four Visits to Africa

Towards the end of 1997 and at the beginning of 1998, I was summoned twice by Comrade Hu Jintao. His first talk with me took place at the Jingxi Guesthouse during a plenary session of the Party Central Committee convened to discuss matters concerning the election of the 15th Party Central Committee. Comrade Hu Jintao said to me that since I was already over the age limit, I would not be nominated as a candidate for membership of the 15th Party Central Committee. I told him I fully agreed, adding that I was mentally prepared for this. I also said that this was a good practice, and that, in view of the fact the ruling parties in the socialist countries had all along failed to solve the problem of succession, this CPC practice would be beneficial in ensuring a long period of stability in China and also have a favorable impact on socialist parties in other countries. I expressed the hope that the Party would persist in this practice so that it would provide an institutional guarantee for political stability, economic development and policy continuity in China. He went on to enquire whether I had any preferences as regards my future arrangements, adding that the central authorities had not yet made a decision on the matter and that I might give it some thought and tell him my ideas if I had any. I told him that I had none, but would follow whatever arrangement the central authorities would make for me. The second talk took place in his office, focusing on matters concerning the election of the Standing Committee of the Ninth National People's Congress (NPC) and of the Ninth National Committee of the Chinese People's Political Consultative Conference (CPPCC). He told me that the central authorities had decided to nominate me as a candidate for vice chairmanship of the National Committee of the Ninth CPPCC. I responded that I was willing to work there.

To my mind, the CPPCC is an organization of the united front in China where the cream of all walks of life in the country is concentrated. Many prominent figures among its members have always commanded my admiration. Working in the CPPCC, I would be able to hear their insightful ideas first-hand, and I would cherish this valuable opportunity to learn and work.

On March 14, 1998, at a plenary meeting of the First Session of the Ninth National Committee of the CPPCC, its chairman and vice chairmen were elected. I became one of its vice chairmen by 1,862 votes.

CPPCC Membership Was My Long-standing Wish

I agreed to work in the CPPCC largely because of my long years' admiration for this organization. Its National Committee is made up of representative figures of various political parties, people's organizations, ethnic minorities and professions, who are highly accomplished, prestigious and influential. When I worked in the State Commission for Restructuring the Economy (SCRE) and later the State Planning Commission (SPC), I was always impressed by the journal of the CP-PCC National Committee carrying excerpts of its members' speeches at its sessions. For learning about social conditions and public opinions, acquiring knowledge and broadening horizons, I found many of their addresses insightful and helpful to those holding leading posts and engaged in practical work.

After I came to the CPPCC National Committee, I was all the more impressed by the deliberative plenary meetings during its annual sessions. Many addresses contained clear-cut and sharp views. Some members came from the front line of educational, health and social work. Their discussions of social problems were based on data and just grounds and were powerful, striking deep chords with people. Some speakers came from the fields of natural and social sciences and engineering. Their addresses dealt with international advanced theories and technologies, identified the gap between China and the advanced international level and indicated the future direction in which China should move; thus they were knowledgeable, informative and enlightening and at the same time inspirational. Members from the world of literature and the arts spoke in praise of new people and new things while criticizing social maladies, showing their conscience and compassions for the morality of the nation. I was intensely interested in these addresses, finding them enlightening, informative, provoking and helpful to the improvement of work. I tried hard not to miss the deliberative plenary meetings to hear their addresses because such meetings were occasions for CPPCC members to air their views and make proposals on state affairs and also a good opportunity for me to expand the range of my knowledge.

Prior to the convocation of the Ninth National Committee of the CPPCC, when I was still working in the SPC, Zhu Xun, then Secretary General of the outgoing National Committee, telephoned saying that he would brief me on the CPPCC staff apartment buildings, implying that he wanted to ask for additional financial allocation from the SPC. I said there was no rush and that the matter could be discussed after I went to the CPPCC. He said no because that would be too late. I thought to myself that he must be afraid I would no longer be able to help solve this problem once I was in the CPPCC and relieved of my powers, as a popular saying goes: "Powers expire with the office." So I agreed to hear a report from the General Office of the CPPCC National Committee in my capacity as Director in charge of the SPC. I think that probably was the first and only occasion for a director of the SPC to hear a report from the General Office of the CPPCC National Committee. Zhu Xun, Zheng Wantong, his designated successor on the new National Committee, Sun Huaishan and others were present while on the SPC side were Chen Tonghai, Vice Director of the Commission in charge of capital construction, the head of the Investment Department, and others.

The visitors told me that because of funding shortages over the successive years, the CPPCC National Committee had a backlog of problems in providing housing for its staff. In the case of the leading cadres at the level of bureau director and above, among its staff and the various non-Communist parties the per-capita floor space was only 25 square meters, which was too low. Housing accommodation for the cadres of ministerial status among the non-Communist parties, numbering more than 20, had not been satisfactorily solved despite attempts to do so. The housing investment allocated by the SPC from 1981 to 1997, ranged from 2.5 million to 10 million *yuan* per annum, which the visitors described as only a "drop in the ocean." With the housing shortage becoming increasingly acute, staff complaints had grown louder. This had become a demoralizing factor. The visitors asked for 200 million *yuan* of investment in housing in order to solve the problem. During the ensuing discussions, I spoke first. I said that the CPPCC National Committee was an organization of the united front in China, with a concentration of representative figures from various political parties, people's organizations, ethnic minorities and professions. I went on that it had wide influence and played a major role in national political life and the central authorities had repeatedly emphasized the need to attach importance to its important role and bring it into fuller play by doing a good job of the united front work in the new period. The various non-Communist parties all played a role in state affairs of China and were an important component part of the socialist political system with Chinese characteristics. Therefore, I said, it was essential to provide necessary working and living conditions for them in the spirit of "treating each other with all sincerity and sharing weal and woe." Good arrangements should be made in this respect even if it meant corresponding cuts in other respects, I concluded. I had asked Vice Director Chen Tonghai beforehand to help solve the problem, so after I finished, he expressed his agreement, stating that he would try his best to satisfy their needs. Luckily, it was the beginning of the year and the SPC still had some money at its disposal. After making readjustments in various quarters, the Commission finally agreed to allocate the requested sum of 200 million *yuan*, paid in two installments over a period of two years, that is, 100 million *yuan* a year. People in the General Office of the CP-PCC National Committee were overjoyed at the prospect of solving at once all the problems that had piled up over the years, including housing for the ministerial-level cadres of the non-Communist parties, staff apartment buildings and purchase of a large number of cars for office use. Thereafter, I twice approached Vice Director Jiang Weixin of the SPC for help in improving the office facilities of the CPPCC National Committee, to the delight of its staff.

While I was the Director in charge of the SPC, I received a letter from Ms. Lei Jieqiong saying that the China Association for Promoting Democracy, of which she was a founding member, had been sharing an office building with other organizations and wanted to build a separate building since the original arrangement could no longer meet their needs. She asked the SPC to help make necessary arrangements with the funding. I had always held her in high esteem. I first got to know her name even before the founding of the People's Republic of China in 1949, when I was working in Shanghai. She had been a member of the Shanghai Peace Petition Delegation to petition the Kuomintang Government in Nanjing and was beaten up and injured by KMT secret agents at Xiaguan. She was an American-educated intellectual. Her cooperation with the CPC dated back to the most difficult years of the War of Resistance against Japanese Aggression, sharing weal and woe with it and making important contributions to the Chinese revolution and construction. I said to myself that she would not have written this letter unless the situation had been dire. So I asked Song Mi, head of the Commission's Investment Department, to come to see me. I told her to work out a way with the people from the China Association for Promoting Democracy, which she did. After the office building was eventually completed, Ms. Lei Jieqiong wrote to express her satisfaction and thanks. She would often bring up this subject when we later met. I said to her: "Elder Sister, please don't talk about the matter any more. I feel embarrassed. This is something we should have taken the initiative to do in the first place. Sorry for the neglect." Later, I asked myself, are such things difficult? They are, to some extent, but not necessarily a mission impossible. They are certainly not as easy as "breaking off a twig," but neither are they as humanly impossible as "clasping Mt. Tai under the arm and leaping over the North Sea with it." The crucial thing is how we prioritize them in our work. Where there is a will, there is a way. The Chinese Communist Party is committed to a policy of "long-term coexistence, mutual supervision, sincere treatment with each other and the sharing of weal and woe" in relationships with the non-Communist parties, but this needs to be implemented through specific work. I explained this point to the cadres of the Commission, adding that it would be a most effective way to implement the principle of the CPC Central Committee through our concrete work. We would achieve good results if we took such matters to heart, I added.

I heard that Li Ruihuan, then a senior Party leader and Chairman of the CPPCC National Committee, had a famous saying. He said that the attitude of quite a few comrades toward the CPPCC could best be summed up thus: "When they are in office, they have powers but not the will; after they come to the CPPCC, they want to help, but do not have the powers any more." I think his saying contrasts vividly how those in power feel before and after they come to the CPPCC. Visiting various parts of the country on fact-finding tours in my CPPCC capacity, local committees would sometimes ask leaders of local planning commissions to attend some functions. On such occasions I would often quote Li Ruihuan's saying to them: "You indeed have powers now, but if you do not have the will, and if some day you happen to sit on the CPPCC committee when the term of the current government ends, then you would find yourself in a powerless position even if you want to do something for the CPPCC committee." "It wouldn't hurt you to take such matters to heart. There's nothing wrong with you if you are a bit generous when you still have powers to help. Do not ignore people just because you have powers. Be considerate when occasion requires. In fact, it is also a matter of allocation. The national resources are there, and some organizations must not be allowed to possess too much and have too affluent a life while others, without access to such resources, have a tough time. This is not fair in terms of political culture. As far as the essence of socialism is concerned, we should all aim at equitable distribution."

Inspection Tours for CPPCC Standing Committee Members Are a High-level Form of Participation in the Discussion and Administration of State Affairs

The preface to the "Common Program of the Chinese People's Political Consultative Conference," adopted at the First Plenary Session of the CPPCC on September 29, 1949, said: "The Chinese People's Political Consultative Conference, comprising representatives of the Chinese Communist Party, the various democratic parties, people's organizations, localities, the Chinese People's Liberation Army, the various minority nationalities, overseas Chinese and other democratic patriots, is a form of organization of the people's democratic united front. Representing the will of the people of the whole country, it hereby proclaims the founding of the People's Republic of China and forms their own central government." In his inaugural speech at the CPPCC session, Mao Zedong said the CPPCC "bears the nature of representing the people of the whole country and has won their confidence and support. Therefore, it proclaims itself to perform the functions and powers of the National People's Congress." He also stated in the speech: "Our work will go down in the annals of history of humankind and will demonstrate that the Chinese, making up one quarter of the total human population, from now on have stood up."

The First Session of the First National People's Congress was held in Beijing from September 15 to 28, 1954. It adopted the "Constitution of the People's Republic of China" and the organic laws of the NPC, the State Council, the people's courts and the people's procuratorates.

On December 21, 1954, the First Session of the Second National Committee of the CPPCC was convened in Beijing. In his political report, Zhou Enlai, Vice Chairman of the CPPCC National Committee, pointed out: "With the convocation of the NPC, the CPPCC has lost its function as an organ of state power performing in an acting capacity the functions and powers of the NPC, but still retains its inherent role for the united front, that is, shedding its acting role while retaining its inherent role." The CPPCC used to have the nature of an organ of state power, with the power to elect and participate in a government and perform the functions and powers of the NPC, but after the convocation of the NPC, it had its functions and nature redefined as "conducting political consultation and exercising democratic supervision." Then, in March 1994, an amendment to the Charter of the CPPCC National Committee was adopted at the Second Session of the Eighth CPPCC National Committee, adding "discussion and participation in state affairs" to its principal functions. From then on, the functions of the CP-PCC have been defined as "conducting political consultation, exercising democratic supervision, and participating in the discussion and management of state affairs."

In the opinion of Aristotle, the best form of government was the republic. According to modern political science, a government should be made up by the masses of people and the elite of society. A modern state, whether under the system of a national people's congress or a parliament, whether it mono-cameral or bi-cameral, generally employs democratic forms of various kinds to elect people's deputies and choose representatives of various walks of life. In some cases, respected prominent figures who have made real contributions to society may be selected not through general elections, but their achievements and contributions to the country and society, and the esteem in which they are held by people and society are also a kind of popular will. The CP-PCC National Committee is made up of members who are prominent figures selected by the various political parties, people's organizations, ethnic minorities and professions. Once selected this way, they shoulder responsibilities, political, moral and professional, for representing their respective political parties, people's organizations, ethnic groups and professions, playing a major role in participating in state affairs and enjoying wide respect both in China and abroad. Although this kind of selection is not general election as such, it nevertheless involves consultations among the political parties. Moreover, the CPPCC members are respected, highly positioned and highly accomplished, and their work, achievements and influence make them worthy of representing the circles from which they come and constitute a kind of popular basis. So it cannot be said that without general election the CPPCC is not broadly representative.

In November 2002, I went to Japan for a meeting. After the meeting the host arranged a visit to Mt. Fuj and I visited a kimono museum at the foot of the mountain. On display were various styles of kimonos in different woven fabrics and decorated with a variety of patterns. The 91-year-old museum owner enjoyed a high reputation in Japan and abroad. He had come especially from Tokyo early that morning to show me around the museum. I was impressed by his hospitality. Before we said our goodbyes he asked me hesitantly and slightly apologetically: what kind of a post is a vice chairman of the CPPCC? I saw that the old gentleman was very sincere, so I did not resort to a diplomatic answer, but answered him with the same degree of candor. I said that the CPPCC National Committee is made up of noted personages from the CPC, non-Communist parties, people's organizations, ethnic minorities and professions, is an organization for the united front as well as an important institution for multi-party cooperation and political consultation led by the CPC; it is an important form of socialist democracy in the political life of China. I further told him that it did not have legislative or executive functions, but it carried out political consultation, democratic supervision and discussion and administration of state affairs over major state issues and important principles and policies. Then I gave him an analogy to illustrate the post of a CPPCC vice chairman. Admitting that the analogy may not be completely appropriate, I said that its vice chairmen, as far as their personal achievements, social status, prestige and influence are concerned, were somewhat similar to vice speakers of the Senate in Japan. Hearing that, he said he saw the point and thanked me for my patient explanation. This shows that candid communication is necessary among countries with different forms of government, for only this can help build a relationship of mutual understanding and trust.

The CPPCC Charter states: "Participation in the discussion and management of state affairs includes investigation and study of major issues in the political, economic, cultural and social life and other issues of common interest to the people, and reflection of public sentiments and demands through consultation and discussion, reports of investigations, resolutions, acts and other forms of comments and proposals to the Chinese Communist Party and state organs." Discussion and participation in state affairs may take a variety of forms, and from my own experience I feel the inspection tours by its Standing Committee members should be a high-level activity. Each such tour draws Standing Committee members and members of the National Committee, who, in the spirit of "working around the central task and serving the overall situation," set a subject which has a bearing on the overall situation. At the end of a tour, they present a formal study report to the Standing Committee of the CPPCC National Committee. At the same time, a report is sent to the CPC Central Committee and the State Council as a result of a specific activity of discussion and participation in state affairs.

During my five-year term on the Ninth CPPCC National Committee, starting from 1999, I led such inspection tours for four consecutive years to do field investigations on the country's central work in the current year.

The first inspection tour, in 1999, was on state-owned enterprises (SOEs). In early 1999, the Party Central Committee decided that the theme of its next plenary session would be SOE restructuring. At a meeting of the CPPCC chairman and vice chairmen, it was decided that the next meeting of the Standing Committee would discuss SOE restructuring in order to implement the guidelines of the Party Central Committee's plenary session. Li Ruihuan nominated me to lead an inspection tour for Standing Committee members, whose task was to produce a study report on the topic as a preparation for the projected Standing Committee meeting.

From July 20 to August 1, 1999, I led the inspection tour to Liaoning Province where SOEs were concentrated. We were briefed by the Liaoning Provincial Government and city governments of Shenyang, Benxi, Fushun, Liaoyang, Anshan and Dalian. We made field trips to 11 enterprises, including Jinbei Automotive Shareholding Corporation (Limited) of the First Automotive Group, the Northeast China Pharmaceutical Group Company, the Northeast China Transmission and Transformer Equipment Group Company, the Benxi Iron and Steel (Group) Company (Limited), Fushun Petrochemical Company, Liaoyang Petrochemical Fiber Company, Anshan Iron and Steel (Group) Company, New Dalian Shipyard, Dalian Chemical Industry Company and the Daxian Group. On July 29, before winding up its study, we met with leaders of the province to exchange views and reached consensus.

After the tour, an inspection report was produced on SOE restructuring in Liaoning and its progress in the three-year program for relieving the difficulties of SOEs. On behalf of the tour delegation, I delivered the report to the meeting of the CPPCC National Committee's Standing Committee. The report fully affirmed progress in these respects made by Liaoning Province, the cities and SOEs we had inspected, highlighting their successful practices and making suggestions. It concluded: SOEs in Liaoning should, above all, further emancipate their minds and change their concepts; it was essential for them to speed up their efforts to become market-oriented by establishing an operating mechanism, a technical innovation mechanism and a distribution mechanism compatible with a market economy; the government should persist in its focus on the larger SOEs with a view to making them stronger, and effectively implement the strategy of forming giant corporations and groups, which was necessitated by the local industrial pattern; and it was necessary to intensify the reform of the property rights system within a group, improve its governance and speed up its technological transformation. The tour recommended: 1, Liaoning Province should take technological transformation as the inevitable path to reinvigorate its industry and become more competitive; 2, it should take the market as the guide so as to successfully identify projects for upgrading enterprises; 3, it should set its sights on advanced standards when choosing technologies in order to start from a high level; 4, it should attach importance to the transformation of the technological equipment of major industries with a view to improving the level of the industry as a whole; 5, it should encourage the integration of production, education and research and give fuller play to the initiative of various quarters.

I was invited to give an impromptu speech when we visited the New Dalian Shipyard. I said I was very pleased to see the five super oil tankers of 300,000 tons each it was building for Iran. I recalled that more than a century previously, at the height of the Westernization

Movement in China, our forerunners set the goal of a rich country and a strong army with sturdy ships and powerful guns. Generation after generation of people had surged forward, wave upon wave, to fight for this lofty goal, shedding their blood or even laying down their lives. As they fell, more people had taken their place. From Li Hongzhang, Zuo Zongtang, Zhang Zhidong to Shen Baozhen, they had devoted their energies to the establishment of modern industry in China, especially the shipbuilding industry, and their spirit of perseverance was still shining today. But in the old China, their ambitions could not possibly be realized. Only after the founding of the People's Republic of China and under the leadership of the Chinese Communist Party, the ambition for "sturdy ships and powerful guns" had been realized, thanks to the efforts of two generations of people. I said that the oil tankers of that capacity represented the current top international shipbuilding level. They had undertaken the hull design, construction and equipment manufacturing or purchase. I told the audience that I was gladdened and made proud by their achievements and thanked them for their contributions to the country's prosperity.

The second tour, in 2000, was on the work of readjusting the economic structure. From July 21 to August 2, 2000, I led an inspection tour for members of the CPPCC National Committee's Standing Committee to Shandong Province, which was quite representative of the whole country due to its fairly complete range of economic structure.

Shandong was an economically strong province, among China's front-runners in terms of aggregate economic volume and growth rate. It was one of the faster developing provinces in the coastal areas, especially in areas north of the Yangtze River, registering marked improvements in people's living standards in both urban and rural areas. It used to be known for its size of population and natural resources. Now it has basically turned into a large and economically strong province too. We held that Shandong should, building on the achievements already made, give full play to the role of market mechanism, shape an environment for equitable competition to encourage superior enterprises to prosper, and make real efforts to lead the local authorities and enterprises onto the path of shifting the focus of their work to the improvement of the quality and efficiency of the economic growth by striking the right balance between growth rate and efficiency, quantity and quality, and scale and structure. The readjustment of the economic structure should aim at raising the proportion of tertiary industry, especially modern service industry, such as tourism, information consultancy, logistics, banking, insurance, technical service, community service and various kinds of intermediary services, which should be the focal areas to be encouraged in readjustment efforts. We emphasized that these areas promised the greatest potential for creating jobs in the future and offered immense scope for speeding up development. Therefore, greater efforts and policy incentives should be made to expand these areas. Governments at various levels should remove as soon as possible the access barriers based on ownership, administrative regions and industries so as to allow different legitimate enterprises to access the market. The growth of tertiary industry and the process of urbanization should supplement each other. Urbanization meant not only an increase in the number and size of cities, but also, and more importantly, the need to establish and improve city functions. To speed up urbanization, the emphasis was to speed up the construction of a market system. Comrade Wang Leyi, a national model worker, had been invited to more than 10 provinces to advise on the industrialized operation of agriculture. He told me and others in the tour that the root cause of the failure in many localities to start such operations or to do them well was the fact that in the absence of a sound market, there were bottlenecks in distribution and that local towns did not have the function of helping farmers open up markets.

Tertiary industry only accounted for 33 percent of China's national economy, almost 30 percentage points lower than the world average of 62 percent. The figures for the United States, Western Europe and other advanced countries were all between 70 percent and 80 percent. Tertiary industry is the industry that employs the largest number of workers. China was not well developed economically and was under great employment pressure. The moment the subject of creating new jobs came up, people immediately thought of opening new plants. But the point was—how could there be so many plants to run? For a time industrialized countries did run many plants, but they were unsustainable, so labor was shifted to tertiary industry instead and as a result tertiary industry grew very quickly. Building new plants everywhere would deplete natural resources and pollute the environment—this was the lesson of the developed countries. While we were in Shandong, we hammered the point that Shandong was a big province, with a 90 million population, so it would have no future without developing tertiary industry.

We recommended that in the course of readjusting the economic structure, the government should define its function as giving guidance, offering incentives, coordinating and serving. Firstly, it should do a good job of economic development forecasting and draw up plans that would serve as guidance in enterprise development. Secondly, it should make market rules for ensuring equitable competition so as to create a good market environment for independent operations of enterprises and common development of multiple economic sectors. Thirdly, it should employ government finance and other public resources to develop the infrastructure and public services as conditions for enterprise growth. Fourthly, the readjustment of the economic structure should suit the local conditions, trying to do certain things and refraining from others. Enterprises should not only study the domestic market but also pay attention to the international market. It was necessary in the planning stage to identify local comparative market strengths in order to make best use of the favorable conditions and avoid the unfavorable ones.

We also suggested that local governments below the provincial level should handle three aspects well in this work. Firstly, trying to do certain things and refraining from others. They should not have the vain hope of attempting everything, nor the impulse of following suit as soon they spotted someone else doing something new; rather, these local governments should proceed from local natural resources and market conditions, giving prominence to priorities and local characteristics. Secondly, they should build a technological innovation mechanism, so that new products are developed continuously. Thirdly, they should pay attention to discovering case study examples and using them to broaden the horizons of other enterprises. We stressed that one case in point was Shandong's approach to spreading the industrialized operation of agriculture—having the market lead the way, having leading enterprises set an example and having science and technology supply the driving force.

In particular, the inspection party emphasized that the slogan of "being the first to realize modernization" should not be raised casually, and that correct explanations on this point were necessary. Modernization as a goal we strive for was a process of development and change, its content in particular changing with the emergence and fast development of a new economy. We should keep up with the trends of the world economy and scientific and technological development and make timely adjustments and supplements to the content of modernization. Modernization in a true sense was all-round modernization embracing science and technology, culture, ideology, education and other areas, with a developed economy, advanced politics and social progress, and, in particular, it entailed institutional innovations. If the stress was only on aggregate economic volume, per-capita GNP and several other economic indicators, without due attention to the transformation of institutions and mechanisms, advanced science, technology and education, as well as soft power such as ideology, morality and other aspects of the spiritual realm, then this brand of modernization would not be a true modernization nor a modernization in the scientific sense. We further pointed out that sole emphasis on aggregate economic volume or per-capita GNP would easily lead to the undesirable tendency among locali-ties of vying with each other for high growth rates at all costs, abetting the tendency toward boasting and exaggeration. We had suffered too much from such things in the past. A county or a county-level city does not exist in isolation; it could hardly claim to be able to realize mod-ernization ahead of others without major changes in the surrounding environment.

The third inspection tour, in 2001, was on the issue of reinvigorat-ing the major technological equipment manufacturing industry. At several sessions since the First Session of the Ninth CPPCC National Committee, a number of CPPCC members had made 14 proposals concerning China's major technological equipment industry, urging the government to attach importance to this issue. It was decided at a meeting of the Standing Committee in 2001 that I lead an inspection tour on how to reinvigorate this branch of industry. From September 1 to 12, we inspected Liaoning and Heilongjiang provinces, where major manufacturers of technological equipment were concentrated. Our tour consisted of 11 members of the Standing Committee of the National Committee and three National Committee members. This high-level group included two former secretaries of provincial CPC committees, five former ministers, six former vice ministers, and one academician of the Chinese Academy of Engineering.

We visited 13 key leading enterprises covering heavy machinery, shipbuilding, iron and steel, power and other industries. We found that since the beginning of the reform and opening-up process, especially since the 1990s, these enterprises had made breakthroughs in manage-ment, product development, market opening-up and technological transformation, becoming shining lights in China's technological equipment manufacturing industry. For example, the 600,000 KW large-scale thermal power generating units produced by the Harbin Power Station Equipment Group Company and its 700,000 KW large-scale hydropower generating units for the Three Gorges project; the thermal-walled hydrogenation reactor of the 1,000-ton class and the 300MW nuclear reactor pressurized container produced by the First Heavy-Duty Machinery Group Company; the 1,700mm large-scale continuous casting and rolling equipment independently developed by the Anshan Iron and Steel Group Company; the 300,000-ton super-large oil tankers built by the New Dalian Shipyard and its fifth-generation semi-submersible offshore oil rigs; the fifth-generation high-speed roll-on roll-off ships for dual use produced by the Dalian Shipyard; the cracking air compressors for large petrochemical installations produced by the Shenyang Blower Works; and important parts for F class gas turbines, which the No. 410 Plant produced for GE.

Members of the inspection tour were intensely impressed by what they saw in these enterprises. They became more aware that major equipment manufacturing was of extreme importance to the national welfare and people's livelihood, economic development and national security. Many such enterprises were a very important branch of the country's industry even in peacetime. In participating in the cooperation and competition of economic globalization, China needed to rely on these enterprises to meet the challenges from the developed countries. In the eventuality of a changed international environment threatening China's security, they would be all the more important to the country as a pillar of national defense. We all agreed that the issue of major equipment was of utmost importance. After discussion among ourselves, we wrote a report to the Party Central Committee and the State Council, entitled "Ten Recommendations Concerning the Reinvigoration of the Equipment Manufacturing Industry." We suggested that a "Specialized Plan for Reinvigorating the Equipment Manufacturing Industry" be drawn up as soon as possible, with guiding principle, development strategy, goals, focal areas, steps and matching policies; that the formulation of the "Plan for Major National Technological Equipment Development and Manufacture during the Tenth Five-Year Plan Period" be speeded up, supporting basic research in major technological equipment and the development of commonly used technologies, and encouraging the approach characterized by digesting and assimilating imported technologies, emphasizing improvement and innovation and acquiring as soon as possible China's own intellectual property rights.

The report suggested intensified efforts to map out and implement strategies in response to China's accession to the World Trade Organization (WTO). It was essential to increase input into research in technological equipment and technological transformation. The key to invigorating China's equipment manufacturing industry was to support the technological progress and innovation of enterprises. The state should, by setting up a technological development fund for industries, support the establishment of a technological innovation system with enterprises as the main body and combining production, education and research.

It also suggested that:

The state should speed up the reform aimed at transforming the VAT system from the present production-based model to a consumption-based model, so as to make Chinese-made technological equipment more competitive in domestic and foreign markets. It should, in line with international practice and the principle of national treatment, revise the current practice of offering tax exemptions to imported machinery and electrical equipment in support of equitable competition by Chinese-made technological equipment.

The state should make the equipment manufacturing enterprises a focal area of its credit and funding support. It was essential to set up major technological equipment seller's credit or buyer's credit for encouraging Chinese and foreign users to buy Chinese-made equipment. These enterprises should have priority in going public.

Problems left over from the process of converting debt into equity should be handled appropriately.

The state should work vigorously to push forward the formation of a group of large engineering corporations embracing users and manufacturers and combining technological design, system integration, general project engineering contracting and whole-process service. Such corporations were expected to use Chinese-made major technological equipment as far as possible.

The social security should offer a preferential policy of a transitional nature.

There should be early formulation of specialized regulations on reinvigorating the major technological equipment industry and the drafting of "Rules on State Major Technological Equipment Work" which would specify various supportive policies.

The State Council should set up a regular inter-agency coordinating mechanism, with the responsibilities of the coordinating and other departments clearly defined and a joint meeting held at fixed or non-fixed internals to study problems.

I sent a copy of the report to Comrade Wei Jianxing (then a member of the Standing Committee of the CPC Central Committee), who had once worked in a similar plant. He knew the issue, so when I discussed it with him I asked him to keep an eye on its progress and put his weight behind it. Concerning some individual important matters we had encountered during the tour, I talked over them with Comrade Cao Gangchuan (then chief of armaments in the People's Liberation Army), asking him to look into and help solve them.

At the Shenyang Blower Works I was particularly happy to see the cracking air compressors it was producing for the 700,000-ton ethylene installation at the Shanghai Petrochemical Company (Ltd). Its director, Su Yongqiang, told me that one unit was undergoing test running at the plant while another had been shipped to Shanghai and after being adjusted and tested, had reached the advanced international standards of comparable foreign products. He said their products were one third the cost of similar foreign products. I recalled with Chairman Xiao of the CPPCC Liaoning Committee and the Secretary of the Shenyang Party Committee, who accompanied me on the tour of the plant, that I had been involved in this ever since the importation of complete sets of technology and equipment in 1972. At that time, I told them, China imported from abroad the technology and equipment of cracking air compressors for 115,000-ton ethylene installations in the hope that this would help China build and develop the equipment some day. More than 20 years had passed, but China continued to buy them in from abroad. A lingering question in my mind had always been: "Could China build them? How can we possibly go on buying in like this?" Seeing their products, I was overjoyed. I told them it was my birthday and I took this good news as my birthday present. I emphasized that now that China was able to produce cracking air compressors of the 700,000-ton class, nothing would get in the way of developing the petrochemical industry.

The fourth inspection tour, in 2002, was on how China's automotive industry should meet post-WTO-accession challenges.

From September 2 to 13, 2002, I led a CPPCC inspection tour, which inspected the Shanghai Automotive Group and the Dongfeng Automotive Group general corporations. The First Automotive Group presented the inspection group with briefing documents on the subject. The inspection group gave full affirmation of the various measures taken by the three groups for meeting the post-WTO-accession challenges. It was satisfied that these measures were quite adequate and that these groups had taken the initiative in handling the matter.

Chen Jinhua (third left, front row) presiding over the Second Plenary Meeting of the Fourth Session of the Ninth CPPCC National Committee in March 2001

Chen Jinhua (first left) inspecting the Second Automotive Group in September 2002

Chen Jinhua (second left) at the inaugural meeting of the China Economic and Social Council. Seated from the right are Hu Qili, Chen Junsheng, Ye Xuanping, Chen Jinhua and Zheng Wantong.

In July 2001, a memorandum on cooperation was signed with the French Economic and Social Council.

Chen Jinhua (second left) talking to local press in Bucharest after attending the IAESCSI meeting

In talks with the delegation of the Algerian ESC, June 2003

Chen Jinhua and President Chiluba of Zambia in talks, December 1998

Chen Jinhua and President Nujoma of Namibia in talks, December 1998

Meeting Prime Minister Emane of Gabon

In July 1976, the Tanzam Railway linking Tanzania and Zambia was completed. Picture shows Chinese, Tanzanian and Zambian workers laying track.

Deng Xiaoping discussing with Yuan Baohua (first left, front row) on the subject of enterprise management in China in March 1980. First left on back row is Zhang Yanning.

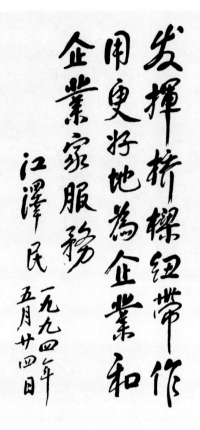

An inscription written by Jiang Zemin for the CEMA/CEDA to encourage them to better serve enterprises and enterprise directors

UN Secretary General Kofi Annan's letter of thanks

19 February 2002

Dear Mr. Chen,

I would like to express my appreciation to you for co-hosting, with the United Nations, the "Chinese Business in the New World" forum in support of the Global Compact.

The fact that so many people participated in the event - business leaders from China and other countries, as well as prominent academics and heads of civil society organizations - showed not only the relevance of the subject, but also the fine organizational work carried out by you and your colleagues. Your own opening address, setting out your strong commitment to the Compact, also contributed greatly to the success of the gathering.

Thank you again for the support provided by the China Enterprise Confederation. I hope others in China and elsewhere will follow this fine example.

Yours sincerely,

Kofi A. Annan

Mr. Jinhau Chen
President
China Enterprise Confederation
Beijing

Representatives of the Ministry of Labor and Social Security, All-China Federation of Trade Unions and the CEC meeting in Nanjing to implement the laws on labor and trade unions, November 2001. Wei Jianxing is fourth from right. Chen Jinhua is third from right.

Premier Zhu Rongji (first left) talking with CEC leaders and others Yuan Baohua (second left), Chen Jinhua (fifth left), Li Rongrong (third left) and Zhang Yanning (fourth left) in October 1999

Chen Jinhua (first right) feting WEF Chairman Prof. Schwab at the Chinese Enterprise Summit in 2001

Chen Jinhua (left) meeting Mr. Imada, Kei-danren Chairman

Chen Jinhua meeting Yasuhiro Nakasone and other Japanese dignitaries when visiting Japan to celebrate the 30th anniversary of the normalization of Sino-Japanese diplomatic relations

Among the members of the inspection party were He Guangyuan, former Minister of the No. 1 Ministry of Machinery Industry, which administered the automotive industry, former principal Party and government leaders of the areas in which the major automotive companies were located, such as Lu Rongjing, He Zhukang, Ye Liansong, Zhang Boxing and Li Youwei, and automotive experts. They all knew the subject very well. At the end of the tour, we put forward the following seven proposals:

One: it was necessary to have a clear understanding of the direction in which the automotive industry was moving. As tariffs on imported automotive products would gradually fall during the transition period following WTO accession and quotas for imported parts increase, the Chinese automotive industry would face an ever-growing challenge. We should keep a cool head in the face of the current brisk production and sales and avoid blind expansion by building or expanding low-level assembly lines. We should have a correct appraisal of the situation, fully tapping the potential of existing enterprises and selecting several sound enterprises on which to concentrate resources so as to strengthen and enlarge them.

Two: it was necessary to formulate and implement at an early date policies and measures for guiding the development of the automotive industry. The state should come up with a set of comprehensive and complete policies and administrative rules in keeping with post-WTO-accession requirements, in order to guide the harmonious development of production, marketing and services.

Three: it was necessary to streamline the administrative functions of the government and establish a scientific motor vehicles administrative system. At the time, there were overlapping and ill-defined functions among government departments and a multiple leadership resulting in contradictory policies, and both the enterprises and users complained loudly about such phenomena in the administration. The inspection group suggested to the State Council that it pay attention to this problem and to undertake the coordination necessary to rationalize administrative functions vis-à-vis automotive products so that a unified and coordinated administrative system would be established. It was necessary to draw on common international practices and formulate a roads and vehicles law and other related laws and regulations in the effort to establish a scientific administrative system over vehicles in accordance with law.

Four: it was necessary to accelerate the pace of Chinese enterprises in improving their technological development and innovation capabilities. China's automotive industry must have independent R&D capabilities, its own intellectual property rights and brand names if it wanted to gain the initiative for development in competition in the wake of the country's WTO accession and make China a leading automotive manufacturer in the world. The report suggested that China should formulate preferential policies, compatible with WTO rules and in reference to the preferential tariffs for localization of auto parts, to support Chinese enterprises in developing products with independent intellectual property rights.

Five: it was necessary to expand the automotive service trade, encompassing marketing, leasing, credit, insurance, used car sales, maintenance service, dealing in auto parts, car remodeling, information services, car logistics and other areas. As a downstream industry of the automotive industry, the automotive service trade is an important pillar for the development of the automotive industry and an important area for extending the industrial chain, stimulating the macro-economy and creating new jobs. Studies showed that the gap between China and the developed countries was even wider in the automotive service trade than in manufacturing and that there was an even greater potential for development. It suggested that the government organize enterprises and relevant quarters to study this issue fully, map out measures, start and speed up the building of an automotive service trade system in China and expand the areas of this trade.

Six: it was necessary to speed up the building of an auto parts system. The strategic goal of the country's auto industry development was to become a major manufacturing country with a complete industrial chain, not a big assembling country. Parts were the foundation of the auto industry and the building of a high-level auto parts manufacturing system was an important condition for realizing this goal.

Seven: it was necessary to help the First Automotive Group and the Dongfeng Automotive Group in their efforts to shed the functions of running social facilities. The state and local financial departments should make active efforts to help them in reducing their burdens so that they would be able to advance unencumbered.

On June 15, 1979, Deng Xiaoping, in his capacity as Chairman of the Fifth CPPCC National Committee, delivered an opening address to its second session. In the address, "The United Front and the Tasks of the People's Political Consultative Conference in the New Period," he said: "To achieve China's socialist modernization, it continues to be necessary for the participants in the CPPCC to hold consultations and discussions on the nation's general principles, its political life and the social and economic questions related to modernization. It is still necessary for them to exercise supervision over each other and over the enforcement of the Constitution and law." The fruitful results of the four inspection tours for standing committee members organized by the Ninth CPPCC National Committee were evidence that such tours were a good form of CPPCC carrying out consultations and discussions on economic and social issues. In reviewing these four tours, I feel that such tours demonstrate their advantages and roles in the following four areas:

One: this form is beneficial to bringing the political and professional advantages of the CPPCC into play.

The CPPCC National Committee, by including in such tours those standing committee members who are former leaders of provinces and ministries, entrepreneurs and experts, is able to combine the strong points of various quarters and pool wisdom from all directions, so as to raise the quality of its participation in the discussion and administration of state affairs. The four tours I led included former provincial Party secretaries, ex-governors, ex-ministers, ex-vice ministers, and well-known entrepreneurs, academicians of the Chinese Academy of Engineering; and experts and academics in areas relevant to the subjects under study. Some of these standing committee members had long years of experience in leading a variety of government economic departments and industrial branches while others were highly accomplished in their professions, enjoying fame in China and abroad. Hence, an inspection tour thus composed would benefit from their backgrounds when conducting a study of major economic and social questions and problems in industrial management. Their views were to the point and convincing. The study findings were analytical, contained original views and made recommendations. I had known many standing committee members over long years and had been impressed by their mastery of policies and practical ability. After being retired from active leading posts on grounds of age, their experience and knowledge would go to waste if not put to proper use. Participation in inspection tours gave them an opportunity they valued highly. During the tours, they listened attentively, took notes and expressed original views in discussion and summing-up sessions. This fully demonstrated the strength of the CPPCC as a pool of brainpower and raised the level of its participation in the discussion and administration of state affairs by contributing ideas.

Two: it is beneficial to promoting implementation of the central work of the Party and government.

The subject of such inspection tours and the areas it covered were usually chosen to tie up closely with the central task the Party Central

Committee had set for the current year, so it was able to serve the overall situation and was highly relevant to the central task. The Party Central Committee, in deciding on a central task, had both the immediate consideration of solving outstanding contradictions in the light of current circumstances and a long-term view that took the overall situation into account. Generally speaking, it is not difficult to focus on a single major issue related to the central task. What is difficult is to consider all aspects of an issue carefully and make all-round arrangements so as to avoid one-sidedness. This requires strategic planning in the course of carrying out the central task. To do this, we must have a correct understanding of the principles and policies of the central authorities and show sound judgment in studying a complex situation and grasping the nub of a matter. Those ex-ministers, ex-provincial Party secretaries and ex-governors among the standing committee members are equal to these requirements on the account of their long years of past experience in leading posts. They are able to form sound judgments and make correct recommendations when they size up the progress of the central task and the implementation of policies in the course of inspection tours, rather than limiting their discussions to matters at issue or expressing views that lose sight of the overall situation.

Three: inviting the participation of relevant officials from competent departments benefits direct communication and CPPCC involvement in the administration of state affairs.

After the CPPCC National Committee forms an inspection tour, it first of all invites leaders of the government departments concerned to brief its members on the background, relevant policies and outstanding current problems related to the subject of the study. All the tour members attend such briefing sessions and discuss and exchange views with the speakers as part of their preparation before the tour. The inspection tour also invites relevant leaders of the competent departments under the State Council, banks and, in some cases, experts from research institutions, to follow its program. One advantage of this kind of composition is to facilitate communications with policy-making departments and research institutions and full exchange of views before, during and after the study, making it easy to reach a consensus of views and to follow up on them. The inspection tours on the reinvigoration of the major equipment manufacturing industry and the auto industry strategy in the wake of WTO accession both invited the State Development Planning Commission (new name for the State Planning Commission) and the State Economic and Trade Commission to send competent directors or vice directors on the field studies. The latter provided information to the inspection groups whenever necessary, including plans under way and to be implemented. They were able to hear at first hand the views of standing committee members and also those of local governments and enterprises. Such direct communications at multiple levels are helpful to government departments in many ways in improving work, making a good job of planning and studying policies and implementation measures.

Four: direct communication with local governments and enterprises helps decision-making departments grasp the situation on the ground and improve the quality of their decisions and helps local governments implement central government tasks.

The first thing the inspection tours did on arrival was to hear a report from the government of the province or city. As the CPPCC is in a fairly impartial position, local governments and enterprises normally do not hesitate to speak the truth, which is especially important on sensitive issues. For example, the goal of lifting SOEs out of difficulty in three years and related policies proved difficult and encountered quite a few practical problems in the course of implementation. The representatives of enterprises were reluctant to tell the true situation, still less to express differing views. We encouraged them to speak the truth, to tell us about problems. After hearing what they said, the leaders from the ministries and provincial and city governments accompanying the tour all found it well said, saying it would help them know the true situation and improve their work.

Practice is the sole criterion for judging the truth. Looking back to the findings of the four inspection tours, the problems they raised and the recommendations made, whether the viewpoint on all-round economic development and economic readjustment, or focal issues like the reinvigorating of major equipment manufacturing industry, enterprise reform and transformation and the auto industry response to WTO accession, were all to the point, correct and still viable, and compatible with the points presently emphasized by the central authorities, having being tested in practice over these years. By acting upon our recommendations, both the decision-making and implementing departments and units would avoid many detours and make fewer errors, thus reducing losses. These recommendations reflected the standards of the ex-provincial Party secretaries, ex-provincial governors, ex-ministers and professionals, and showed that the form and make-up of inspection tours could fully deploy the strengths of the CPPCC and help raise the quality of its participation in the discussion and administration of state affairs.

International Activities of the China Economic and Social Council (CESC)

In terms of political status, nature, functions and influence, the CP-PCC National Committee can find parallel organizations only in the Fatherland Reunification Front of the Democratic People's Republic of Korea and the Vietnam Fatherland Front. The national political organizations in other countries, apart from the governments, are mainly congresses, with lower and upper houses, and they have parallel relations with the Standing Committee of China's NPC on a bilateral and multilateral basis. Parliaments of foreign countries have occasional contacts with the CPPCC National Committee, but these contacts usually have the nature of goodwill visits, without involving political cooperation or working exchanges.

Since the beginning of reform and opening-up, China has conducted pan-directional, multi-level foreign exchanges, so the scope and channels of such exchanges have kept expanding. Against this background, the CPPCC National Committee has also become increasingly active in international activities, making friends with many organizations and individuals. A notable organization is the International Association of Economic and Social Councils and Similar Institutions (IAESCSI).

In 1995, Zhu Xun, Secretary General of the CPPCC National Committee, went as an observer to the Association's Fourth International

Meeting, held in Lisbon, Portugal. In 1997, Qian Zhengying, Vice Chairwoman of the CPPCC National Committee, went as an observer to the Association's Fifth International Meeting, held in Venezuela.

Economic and social councils and similar institutions were founded in various countries after the end of the Second World War. They enjoy a fairly high status and exert major influence in French- and Spanish-speaking countries in Europe, Africa and Latin America. The one in France has the nickname "Third Parliament." Most of such councils and similar institutions are consultative institutions on economic and social affairs in their own countries, and at the same time have consulting and supervisory functions, enjoying a fairly high position in their countries. In July 1999, at its Sixth International Meeting, held in Mauritius, the IAESCSI was officially inaugurated as an international body corporate. Hu Qili, CPPCC Vice Chairman, led its delegation to the meeting and the CPPCC became a founding member of the IAESCSI and sat on its first Board of Management.

The objective of the IAESCSI is to promote dialogue and exchanges among its members and, at a wider level, to encourage dialogue between economic and social partners around the world. It has a chairman, general assembly, management board and executive secretary. The IAESCSI's chairman is the chairman of the economic and social council of the country chosen to host the international meeting, which is held every two years. The general assembly is held once a year. The management board is the governing board of the IAESCSI and its members are elected at the general assembly for a term of two years.

The full members of the IAESCSI are economic and social councils of more than 30 countries, including South Africa, Algeria, Argentina, Belgium, Benin, Burkina Faso, Cameroon, China, Côte d'Ivoire, Curaçao, Finland, France, Gabon, Greece, Guinea, Hungary, Italy, Lebanon, Luxembourg, Mali, Morocco, Mauritius, the Netherlands, Portugal, Romania and Senegal. The Social Coordinating Council of Macau, the Economic and Social Council of the European Union and the African League of Economic and Social Councils are affiliate members. The Third Management Board is composed of the representatives of the economic and social councils of 13 countries—Algeria, Benin, Guinea, Brazil, China, France, Gabon, Spain, Luxembourg, the Netherlands, Portugal, Tunisia and Côte d'Ivoire. The Economic and Social Council of the European Union and the African League of Economic and Social Councils are affiliated members of the Management Board. By July 2001, total membership of the IAESCSI exceeded 50, as its influence expanded.

Having taken part in bilateral activities with economic and social councils and in the activities of the IAESCSI, Qian Zhengying and I both felt that economic and social councils and the CPPCC National Committee were not on corresponding levels. Economic and social councils vary from country to country, with France's Economic and Social Council being called the "Third Parliament," yet in most countries they have a status between the national level and the ministerial level, so their political status, authority and prestige cannot be mentioned in the same breath as the CPPCC National Committee, which, being a national-level political organization, would create protocol problems when engaged in contacts with economic and social councils of other countries. Considering that the IAESCSI is an important organization, with more than 50 members, had already established close ties with us, and that it can play a role in representing the civic society in pushing forward the multi-polarization trend of today's world, the CPPCC National Committee decided to establish the China Economic and Social Council for the purpose of conducting bilateral and multilateral cooperation with the IAESCSI.

On July 2, 2001, the China Economic and Social Council (CESC) was officially established. I was elected its president, with Zheng Wantong, Fang Weizhong, Chen Bangzhu, Liu Zhongde, Wang Senhao,

Tian Zengpei and Zhang Guoxiang as its vice presidents, Wang Shenghong as its secretary general, and Bao Daochong and others as deputy secretaries general.

The statute of the CESC states that its aim is to "play a role in research, consulting and service, and support the country's reform, opening-up and economic and social development. Internally, it works to unite and join hands with various economic and social circles in the study and discussion of major issues in the country's economic, social and other fields, making recommendations and airing views in the service of the country's economic construction and social development; externally, it works to promote exchanges and cooperation with the IAESCSI and its member organizations and economic and social councils of various countries in general, to present the policies of China's economic and social development, to assimilate and draw on advanced foreign experience, and, at a wider level, to promote dialogue with economic and social partners of various countries around the world so as to contribute to the world's economic and social development."

On the same day as the CESC was founded, Li Ruihuan, when meeting with the delegates to the inaugural meeting, said: "Since its founding, New China has scored tremendous achievements in various development and social programs, but it is still at a comparatively low stage of development and needs to cooperate well with various countries in the world and constantly assimilate and draw on all achievements of the humankind's civilization. It is necessary to have an all-round knowledge of conditions both in China and elsewhere in the world. If we only study China while leaving aside the world, we would fall behind the tides of the world; if we study only the world while ignoring China, we would divorce ourselves from the conditions in China. It is essential to combine the study of China with that of the world, with a special focus on strategic issues having a long-term bearing on the overall situation." His speech indicated the clear direction for the work of the CESC.

Soon after the founding of the CESC, in July 2001, I signed a protocol on cooperation between the CESC and the French Economic and Social Council with the latter's president, Jack Derman, at The Hague, the Netherlands.

France was the pioneer country in founding economic and social councils and exerts major influence in terms of the IAESCSI's role and its relationship with the CESC. The French Economic and Social Council can be dated back to a mid-19th-century school of thought, which advocated organized representative institutions for all economic and social actors. After the First World War, various chambers of commerce demanded the formation of an organization capable of shouldering this task. In 1919, the "Labor-Economic Council" was founded. The National Economic Council, founded in 1925, was consolidated when it won legal recognition in 1936. The Constitution of the Fourth Republic in 1946 mandated the creation of an economic council and guaranteed the independence of this representative institution from the government and parliament. The clause on the economic and social council in the October 4, 1958 Constitution of the Fifth Republic was similar to that on the economic council in the 1946 Constitution. Since then, the French Economic and Social Council has had a secure place among French state offices and has played an ever-growing role. This is how what is termed the "Third Parliament" came into being.

It has 231council members divided into 18 groups and serving a term of five years. Some 70 percent of the council, i.e., 163 members, are designated by their organizations as follows: 69 are directly elected by trade unions in the private and public sector; 65 by chambers of private industrial, commercial and handicraft industrial enterprises, as well as farming and self-employed representative organizations; 19 by cooperatives and mutual-aid societies, and ten by family associations. The remaining 30 percent of the council, i.e. 68 members, are appointed by the government. Of these, 17 are selected on the basis of recommendations by relevant consultative organizations, from among state enterprises, associations and expatriate French; nine are appointed after consulting the most qualified professional groups in overseas provinces and territories; two are picked from the savings and real estate sectors and appointed by administrative decree; 40 are senior members of economic, social, scientific and cultural circles and are also appointed by the Cabinet administrative decree. Its composition ensures that the council represents the overall interests of the various economic and social communities across the country. It keeps close and constant contacts with the 26 regional councils in metropolitan France, overseas provinces and territories and with the Economic and Social Council under the European Council in Brussels.

It has two major functions: to promote dialogue among different social and professional strata of diverse interests; and to advise the government and participate in the making of economic and social policies. The French government is obliged to solicit its opinions about state plans and motions it is going to table before the National Assembly. At the same time, it may consult it on any other issues or motions in the economic and social areas. When necessary, it may invoke the law of emergency procedure under which the Economic and Social Council must present its report within one month. The latter should also present regular reports on current economic and social situations.

Unlike many other government consultative bodies, the French Economic and Social Council has the right to present its views on any issues within the domain of its functions. Its opinions, reports and studies, once adopted, are sent to the Premier immediately. In this way the government keeps informed of the positions of various social and professional groups on major issues related to economic and social policies. The views of the council are also sent to the National Assembly, which often has specialized committees to hear the council's reports before meeting in full session. French newspapers and audio-video media often report on the council's activities and its meetings.

I took part in a number of multilateral and bilateral activities of economic and social councils. From these activities I feel that the economic and social councils and their functions are a product of the attempt of industrialized countries to deal with a multitude of economic and social conflicts and a dialogue mechanism in the past century, especially since the Second World War for coordinating the interests of various interest groups, so that different social and interest groups can communicate, hold dialogue and consultations in a timely manner to reconcile contradictions and avoid antagonism, live in harmony and promote social stability and a coordinated economic and social development. It should be said that it is a kind of democratization of social and political life, a progressive practice that complies with trends and popular wishes, and a successful experience. A major reason why economic crises did not touch off general social crises in the form of social revolutions in the developed countries in the West, as some people had anticipated, is that these countries have taken pains to harmonize class and labor relations through organizations like the economic and social councils.

As the economy and society have developed in China, more and more social problems have accumulated. Participation in these activities to learn and assimilate the experience of foreign countries is to meet the needs of China's development and is an important aspect of China's efforts to strengthen its soft power. However, many of our departments and local governments in China have yet to recognize this point and governments still prefer to handle matters themselves when things happen, because they do not have sufficient confidence in others. Thus, the local governments and Party committees are exposed in the front line with no room for maneuver. The CPPCC National Committee takes advantage of this channel to learn the successful practices of other countries and study various contradictions in China in the course of its economic and social development in order to make suggestions to the government. Of course, we also present our own good experiences to foreign countries in two-way exchanges.

After I was elected President of the China Economic and Social Council, I became more involved in foreign exchanges, notably bilateral and multilateral meetings.

In July 2001, the Seventh International Meeting of the IAESCSI was held in The Hague, the Netherlands, with the theme "Balancing globalization: essential for the vulnerable." In my address to the roundtable conference, I said: "The theme of this meeting reflects the common concerns of people today about the numerous economic and social problems stemming from economic globalization. It also expresses their wish to promote, through dialogue, rational practices, to avoid and overcome irrational, negative factors, and to work together to promote the sound development of economic globalization to make it pursue good and shun harm in the interest of the well being of humanity. International organizations and governments of various countries should work together to build an international environment where the whole society is able to share the fruits of globalization and achieve common prosperity." I then proposed five suggestions: firstly, to cancel or mitigate the debts of poor and vulnerable countries; secondly, that developed countries should open their markets to the strong products from such countries; thirdly, to strengthen intellectual support to such countries so as to build their capacities for participating in globalization; fourthly, that international organizations should pay attention to the interests-related demands of these countries and take them into consideration; and, fifthly, that developing countries should strengthen mutual dialogue and efforts to learn from, exchange and cooperate with each other and support each other so as to jointly meet the challenges. Delegates from the EU's Economic and Social Council and from Gabon quoted me in their speeches and called on the international community to pay attention to and protect the interests of developing countries and to establish a mechanism for protecting the interests of the vulnerable.

During my stay in The Hague, one thing left a deep impression on me. I was staying in the house where Li Hongzhang (a late-19th century influential Chinese official in charge of China's foreign affairs) had once stayed. It was spacious, but the temperature was above 30^0C. Despite this, the Dutch stuck to their practice of not installing air conditioners in the rooms for fear of damaging them. When they installed a ceiling fan, they made sure that it was located in a spot that would not damage the property. The house faced the sea and a century later, it was still well preserved. The Netherlands is committed to sustainable development and its people take good care of nature. They follow the concept of trying to preserve nature as it is and take practical steps to do so. I saw few man-made lawns along the streets, but natural shrubs and grass that had been left intact. There was no littering. This was a money-saving way to keep the environment beautiful. By contrast, we in China talk about sustainable development more often than others, but when it comes to practice, things are done in a slipshod manner, either without considering costs or neglecting the management of completed projects. This is indeed not a good practice. We must do more than we talk and focus on management and on educating people in the need to cultivate good habits.

In June 2002, I led a CESC delegation to the Third General Assembly of the IAESCSI held in Bucharest, Romania. The theme of the meeting was fighting poverty through sustainable development, towards a purposeful and phased partnership. In his address to the meeting, Romania's President Iliescu pointed out that the international community should adopt measures and try through democratic means to reduce social polarization and ensure citizens' rights.

Through panel discussions and informal contacts, I felt that a number of European countries, through long years of explorations and practice, had accumulated much successful experience in formulating and implementing social policies. For example, for the employment issue, the European Union has established a fairly complete system of services for employment through a variety of forms, including intermittent employment, flexible employment (varied and widely flexible forms of employment in terms of time, income, location and other aspects), part-time employment and temporary employment. The President of the Greek ESC told me that at first all the EU countries except France approved flexible employment. France had stuck to its eight-hour working day at the insistence of their trade unions, but had later realized there were not enough jobs and switched to flexible employment. Back in China, I suggested to people of the National Development and Reform Commission (new name for the State Development Planning Commission) that China should vigorously push flexible employment so that more people could be employed. Some people can earn enough to support themselves by working only one or two hours a day while others need work only half a day, so not all people have to work an eight-hour day.

Economic development and social development are mutually reinforcing. Without the support of economic development, social development would be an empty phrase. Without the safeguard of social development, economic development would lose its foundation and motivation. Economic development must be matched by systematic and sound social policies. By social policies we mean a series of norms, measures, decrees, regulations, etc., which are based on the principle of justice, taking as their main objectives the solution of social problems, guarantee of social security, and improvement of social environment and the well-being of the society as a whole, and which are formulated and implemented mainly through state legislation and administrative intervention. The level of a country's social policies is an indicator of a sound society and a measure of social civilization. China has a pressing need to strengthen the study of social policies for the purpose of maintaining social stability and promoting social progress.

In June 2003, the IAESCSI held its eighth meeting in Algiers. I was invited to make a presentation titled "Sustainable Development and Anti-Poverty in China." I stated that the Chinese delegation was very happy to join other delegations in discussing the important subject of eradicating poverty through sustainable development. My speech was as follows:

> The "Fighting Poverty by Promoting Sustainable Development— towards a New Partnership Approach" and the "Algeria Declaration" drafted by the working group basically reflect the views of the developed and developing countries in the IAESCSI, and represent the voice of the IAESCSI. The Chinese delegation hereby expresses its endorsement. Countries vary in national conditions and practices and the results they have achieved in sustainable development and poverty reduction are not identical either. I avail myself of this opportunity to present to you China's work in sustainable development and poverty alleviation.
>
> As known to all, the issues of sustainable development and poverty are often intertwined. In China, the difficult and focal areas in dealing with the two problems are mainly concentrated in the western parts of the country. With poor natural conditions and a relatively backward economy, these areas are China's focal areas for ecological improvement and poverty alleviation. At present, China still has 30 million poor rural residents who do not have enough to eat and wear without help and about 80 percent of them live in the western regions.
>
> Since 2000, the Chinese Government has increased its support to the western areas in investment projects, tax policies and financial transfer payments, providing a strong impetus to local development. In the years 2000, 2001 and 2002, local GDP grew by 8.5, 8.7 and 9.9 percent respectively, as against 7.2 percent in 1999.
>
> We have given prominence to sustainable development throughout the process of developing the western regions. The Chinese Government has carried out in a planned way the project of converting land for for-

estry and pasture by providing free grain, tree saplings and allowances to farmers.

Another important work is to improve infrastructure, such as energy, transport and telecommunications sectors as well as education, science and health, so as to build up sustainability for future economic and social development. In the past three years, the government has arranged a number of key construction projects every year, including highways, railways and power stations. The well-known Three Gorges hydro project is located in the mid-western part of the country.

China will continue to take the sustainable development and anti-poverty as an important strategic task in the 21st century and persistent in doing this work well. It will continue to shift the pattern of economic growth to the path of new-type industrialization, and gradually build a land- and water-saving eco-farming system, an energy- and materials-saving industrial system and a highly efficient, energy-saving comprehensive transportation system. It will push the construction of the eco-environment in an all-round way, including the construction of a number of eco-function conservation areas in the source areas of the Yangtze and Yellow rivers and other areas—expanding the scope of converting land for forestry and pasture, encouraging rotational grazing for pastoral improvement, strengthening the protection of the land, wetland and marine life and restoring ecological functions and biodiversity. It will quicken the development of environmental protection related industry, improve the technological ability of sustainable development, and try to combine the construction of the ecological environment with industrial development and regional economic development in an effort to speed up the economic and social development of poor areas.

Sustainable development and anti-poverty are the major common task that countries around the world face today. China has done some work in this respect, but its task remains arduous. It will continue to further cooperate and coordinate with the international community, expand mutually beneficial cooperation and adequately publicize the spirit of the IAESCSI Algiers Meeting. Developed countries should discharge their due obligations and responsibilities, showing concern for the difficult situation in developing countries and actively and effectively providing funds and technical support to build the capabilities of developing countries for sustainable development and anti-poverty. China is willing to join hands with various countries of the world to push the world in the direction of balanced, stable and sustainable development and strive together for the building of a peaceful, developed and harmonious "global village."

My participation in multilateral and bilateral activities of the IAESCSI has made me aware that participation in such organizations and exchanges with foreign countries on economic and social programs will be very helpful to China in solving current and future problems. In such exchanges and cooperation, our country emphasizes the construction of hardware and focuses on engineering and natural sciences while generally speaking, social fields—theories, systems, policies and methodologies for dealing with social problems—do not receive adequate attention or get listed on the agenda. In fact, such fields are equally important to the stability, progress and prosperity of a country and that is why developed countries have regarded them as part of their soft power. There is a pressing need for us to raise our awareness and set out to study ways to address this problem at an early date. If we fail to arrive at a correct understanding or solve the problem before it is too late, we would be diverted and pay the price.

My Four Visits to Africa

I made four visits to Africa, two of them to North Africa, the other two to Sub-Saharan (or Black) Africa. My Sub-Saharan tours took me to Namibia, Zambia, Benin, Mali, Guinea, Gabon and South Africa and on my outward and return journeys I also passed through Mauritania, Cameroon, Ethiopia, Kenya and Tanzania. Here I will focus on my visits to Sub-Saharan Africa.

In October 1998, staff of the Foreign Affairs Bureau of the CPPCC National Committee asked me whether I would like to lead a delegation to Namibia, Zambia and Benin. I agreed readily, since visiting Africa had been a long-cherished wish of mine. Back in the 1950s, I had read *Inside Africa* by an American author named John Gunther and had been fascinated by his description of the social systems, tribal life, customs and landscapes. I also read Hemingway's *Green Hills of Africa*, with all its beautiful descriptions of the continent. During the 1950s and 1960s, national liberation movements surged across Africa and the many African leaders who visited China at the time left a deep impression on me. It was with these memories that I set foot on African soil. The three countries I was going to visit had belonged to different suzerain states and there were no direct air links between them, so we had to make repeated detours, with a total of 36 take-offs and landings. Without such firsthand experience, one cannot fully appreciate the fact that control by the former suzerain states over their former colonies could be so profound and far-reaching.

The total area of Africa is 30.3 million sq. km., more than three times the size of China. Its total population is 760 million people. A 1979 study of the United Nations Development Program said that its idle land was enough to feed both its own population and that of Western Europe and that its existing fertile land, even without reclaiming a single additional acre, was capable of producing 130 times its current yield. It boasted 40 percent of the world's exploitable water resources, the overwhelming majority of the world's diamonds and chromium (for making stainless steel), 50 percent of its gold, 40 percent of its silver, 90 percent of its cobalt, eight percent of its petroleum and 12 percent of its natural gas. A U.S. research institution once stated—without taking the trouble to mask its intention—that Africa had all the minerals America could need in wartime and peacetime. No other continent has such a wealth and diversity of natural resources as Africa. Africa is the flattest of all continents apart from Antarctica. Its total GNP was no more than US$400 billion but its total foreign debts were as high as US$340.5 billion. According to a U.S. estimate, its annual interest payment on foreign debts accounted for 237 percent of its export revenues or 327 percent if South Africa was not included. According to the rankings of the International Monetary Fund, eight of the world's ten poorest countries are in Africa.

Many of the materials I read said that one could not claim to have been to Africa unless one had gone to Sub-Saharan Africa. I find this true. Forty-eight of Africa's 53 countries are concentrated in that part of Africa, with a total area of 22 million sq. km., twice the size of China or 72.6 percent of the total area of Africa, and with a population of 600 million accounting for 78.6 percent of the total population of Africa. According to statistics from the World Bank in 2003, the population of Sub-Saharan Africa accounted for 11 percent of world population, but only one percent in terms of world GDP. With the exception of seven countries where the situation was a little better, all other 41 countries in this region registered an average per capita GNP of US$ 0.77 a day. In July 2004, Jeffrey Sacks, special advisor to Kofi Annan, the then U.N. Secretary General, declared openly that the total foreign debts incurred by the Sub-Saharan countries had reached US$ 201 billion and that these countries had no ability at all to bear them. War, famine, poverty, hunger and other sufferings are a perpetual scourge to the old people, women and children there. It pains my heart when I see such scenes on television.

Namibia, Zambia and Benin all lie south of the Sahara Desert. Namibia and Zambia are in southern Africa, near South Africa. Benin is in western Africa. Before departure, we were briefed on Africa and were vaccinated against a number of epidemic diseases. Once we got there, I found that epidemics were not as terrible as some people had described. I have been to Africa four times, but am I not still in good health? Why do some people paint so terrible a picture of Africa? I think that either they have not been there themselves and are just parroting what others have told them, or that they are unwilling to go there themselves and so deliberately exaggerate conditions there. Actually Africa is worth going to. It promises great prospects to those who, with just a bit of boldness that can hardly be called adventurism, will be able to start and expand their businesses. People there, from statesmen to common folks, are warm and friendly to the Chinese, an increasingly rare phenomenon elsewhere.

The delegation of the CPPCC National Committee I led paid a goodwill visit to Namibia, Zambia and Benin from November 26 to December 17, 1998. It had been invited by Namibia's National Council, Zambia's National Assembly and Benin's Economic and Social Council. It was the first high-level CPPCC delegation to southern and western Africa since the Eighth National Committee of the CPPCC. The three countries attached importance to our visit, according us a warm, friendly and high-level welcome. The presidents of the three countries met with all members of my delegation. President Nujoma of Namibia, after meeting the delegation, invited us to a roast duck dinner he hosted in a restaurant and went out the way to ask the general secretary of the ruling party to keep us company. President Chiluba of Zambia had a separate meeting with me after meeting the full delegation. We visited the Mukuni Village and the Maramba Cultural Village, both steeped in the traditions of Black Africa, Nchanga Open Pit—the well-known copper mine, and the Chambishi copper mine which a Chinese company had bought, and a textile mill and hospital built with Chinese assistance.

In our visits to the three countries, we acted in the spirit of "doing more work, promoting friendship and increasing cooperation." We briefed our hosts on the 15th CPC National Congress and China's progress in reform and opening-up, economic construction and social development; made a presentation of the system of multi-party cooperation and political consultation under the leadership of the CPC and the important role of the CPPCC in the political, economic and social life of China; and highlighted China's independent peaceful foreign policy, emphasizing that China attached importance to developing its relations with African countries and was willing to work with the three countries and other African countries to develop bilateral relations and Sino-African relations oriented toward the 21st century on the basis of the principles of equality, mutual benefit and common development.

While we were in Namibia, President Nujoma spoke warmly of the friendly and cooperative relations between the two countries, especially the growth of economic and trade relations. He stated that the relations between the two ruling parties were sincere. Namibia was eager to seek south-south dialogue and cooperation with Asia, in particular with China, which he termed Namibia's most reliable friend. Facts had shown them that to learn from China and persist in the policy of independence and self-reliance was the only correct way out for Africa. In his private talks with me he expressed his mistrust of the World Bank. I felt that these small countries, which had been subject to aggression and bullying from major Western countries, were still wary of them and this wariness died hard.

In Zambia, President Chiluba expressed his satisfaction at relations both between the two countries and the two parties and his appreciation of China's support to Zambia in the latter's most difficult period, especially in its struggle for national independence. China had since continued to give tremendous support in the railway, highway, agriculture, textiles industry, telecommunications, broadcasting, health, education and military fields. He said that the Zambian government was very happy that China had bought the Chambishi copper mine (the copper content of Zambian copper ores is as high as six percent— more than 10 times higher than Chinese ores) and that it would provide legal and other guarantees for China's equitable and legitimate benefits. He expressed his sincere hope that more Chinese entrepreneurs would come to his country to open up markets. He also said that the disintegration of the Soviet Union had resulted in an imbalance in the world, and that Africa was very much neglected in the affairs of the United Nations and international affairs in general. The West now had nothing to worry about and neglected Africa even more. He hoped that China would exert its important influence so that Africa would have genuine peace, stability and development. Speaking of the CPPCC National Committee, he said this broadly representative organization reflected the wisdom of the Chinese people and the visit to Zambia by the CPPCC delegation was an important step for strengthening relations between the two countries. He added that Zambia was a member of the British Commonwealth and used to follow the British example; now it was time to look east and learn from Chinese experience.

In Chambishi, a leader of the copper mine told me about progress made in the preparations to restore production following its purchase by China, and I went down the pit to see the workface and equipment. I told the Chinese experts and miners working there that their work was a response to the Chinese Government's call for opening up two markets, Chinese and foreign, and utilizing two kinds of resources, Chinese and international, and thus had a great and far-reaching significance. I emphasized that, in running a joint equity mine in a foreign country, they should not aim just to obtain resources, but, more importantly, to develop friendly and cooperative relations between the two countries to the benefit of both. At the same time, they should learn to operate in a foreign country and train personnel as part of the effort to meet the challenge of globalization.

In Benin, President Kerekou said the Benin-China friendship was a genuine one. He said that Western countries also provided assistance to his country, but they did so with their own agenda while China's assistance was sincerely intended to help Benin in its development; that the people of Benin saw this, for example in the textile mill, hospital, stadium and government office projects built with Chinese assistance. The president said that his country was small and poor, but had its dignity; it was not a slave to money.

At present, although China and African countries have established what is called "all-weather" friendly and cooperative relations based on mutual trust and support, their economic and trade relations still lag behind the political relations. Africa is an important continent where big powers will vie for natural resources and markets in the 21st century. According to data of the Organization of Petroleum Exporting Countries, Africa's proven oil reserves are 93.55 billion barrels, accounting for nearly 8.8 percent of the world's proven reserves. Major Western oil companies already have a considerable investment there while China has just begun. We should further expand our cooperative operations in Africa as we have done in Sudan. The Chinese Government should provide support to enterprises in terms of law, banking, insurance, shipping and other necessary conditions for their development in Africa. When foreign companies do business in China, banks, insurance and marine shipping companies invariably follow promptly to open up their operations at the same time; they also organize chambers for self-regulation and invite legal consultants to protect their rights and interests. In China, the diplomatic mission of a home country provides diplomatic protection for the commercial activities of such enterprises through bilateral or multilateral contacts. These are internationally accepted practices. China should do the same if it wants Chinese enterprises to operate in foreign countries. At present, China's trade and economic contacts with African countries are basically official ties, handled by the commercial and economic sections in the Chinese embassies while commercial operations in a true sense have just begun. Most operators in the latter category there are small private and individual businesses and some of these personnel are deficient in business ethics and other aspects and have had a negative impact among local people. Such problems should arouse our high attention and require serious efforts to address.

From July 1 to July 13, 2000, I paid my third visit to Africa, which took me to Guinea, Mali and South Africa. I also attended the second meeting of the Management Board and the first General Assembly of the IAESCSI held in Libreville, capital of Gabon. Our delegation received a warm, friendly, and high-level welcome. President Conte and Prime Minister Sidini of Guinea, President Konare and Prime Minister Sidibe of Mali, Vice President Ndinge and Prime Minister Ntoutoume-Emane of Gabon met with the delegation. During our stay in these countries we visited major projects built with Chinese assistance and Chinese-foreign joint ventures.

This visit was an important diplomatic move on the part of the CPPCC National Committee aimed at promoting China's understanding, friendship and bilateral relations with Guinea, Mali and Gabon. In his meeting with the delegation, President Conte of Guinea said that the peoples of Guinea and China were brothers, and that, in the course of Guinea's development, friendship and cooperation between the two countries must on no account be neglected. He added that the great Chinese people were Guinea's friends, that China had made tangible contributions to Guinea's economic development, and that the new presidential house, agricultural projects and Chinese companies operating in Guinea were welcomed by both the government and people of Guinea.

In Mali, President Konare told me that, in the four decades or more since the establishment of diplomatic relations between Mali and China, cooperation between the two countries in industrial, agricultural, military, health, sports, youth and other areas had kept growing and had achieved positive results. Mali had become China's special partner for friendly cooperation among African countries.

In southern Mali, we visited a tribe with a history of over a thousand years. We were ushered into a VIP room, which was actually a room of about a dozen square meters, with several raw ox hides on the dirt floor serving as cushions. The chief wore a white cotton robe, and sported a sickle-shaped object on his shoulder, which he said, upon my query, was his symbol of power. When asked his age, he told me that he was 73, adding without being prodded that he was about to hand over his power. Asked who was going to succeed him and he said it was his elder son. I asked whether the villagers would agree and he replied that it would be no problem, adding that his words counted. Then, he offered to show us around a "modern mosque," a dried clay structure less than 100 square meters in area. By "modern," they meant it had electric light. Our hosts told us that this tribal village was a tourist attraction. Everywhere on the surface of its dirt roads was a kind of black fermented food drying in the sun, sending out an unpleasant odor. I was deeply struck by the local scarcity of goods. It seemed that the biggest and most pressing problem facing Africa was to provide enough food and clothing to local population and work for development.

In Gabon, Vice President Ndinge greeted us on behalf of the president, who was absent on a foreign tour. He emphasized the importance of friendly cooperation with China, which had helped build the building of the National Assembly and would continue to build one for the Senate. He called China a "friend in need" and a "true and lasting friend." After the meeting, we made a special trip to a tourist attraction marking the Equator, which crosses northern Gabon, about three hours' drive from Libreville. The vegetation and natural scenery were very beautiful, with forest coverage exceeding 80 percent. An hour or so after our motorcade had left the capital, we began to see noticeable differences between town and the countryside. This part of the country had no access to electricity and the houses were shanties. On our arrival, a short man came over and directed the cars to park. He offered to tell us what to see and complained that the unavailability of water and electricity had hampered tourism. I thought he had a point there, but because of his small stature, I was confused about whether he was a boy or an adult and asked about his age. The Chinese ambassador in the group helped phrase my words into the local language. He stared at me blankly for a long time before saying he did not know. After a while, he said he was born in 1958. If this were true, that would make him 42 years old in 2000. I thought to myself this man probably had no schooling so had trouble with numbers.

We left many places with an impression of urban and rural poverty, blank faces, slow working and loose social fabric.

There is a wide difference between North Africa and Sub-Saharan Africa. Countries in Sub-Saharan Africa also vary widely. In Benin, we visited the "Gate of No Return," where we saw a site of slave trade in former days. This is what we were told: black slaves were gathered under a big tree, tied and blindfolded, and forced to walk around the tree 20 times until they were totally disoriented. Then they were led to the ships for slave trading. There was an office near the dock, where the slaves were weighed. Slave traffickers put the ideal weight of a slave at 140 lb. Those who were over-weight or under-weight, and particularly those with disease, were pushed into the Atlantic through a door of the office. Till this day, there is no exact figure of the total number of slaves sold. According to one source I read, between the 16th and 19th centuries, the number of slaves shipped to the Americas ranged between 10 and 15 million. If those shipped to Europe and other places were included, some historians put the total number at 50 million. We visited a plantation not far from the "Gate of No Return" once owned by a Portuguese colonial official. When the people of Benin rose to drive out the colonialists, this planter took away everything he could and set fire to everything he could not. A resident journalist of the *Los Angeles Times* stationed in Sub-Saharan Africa wrote a book on Africans, in which he commented that Portugal stood for all the evils of colonialism, and that it had sucked dry its two biggest colonies in Africa until they were as dry as a dead cow, leaving nothing behind except the certainty of economic calamity. What I saw in Benin proved he was not overstating the situation. Bloody and barbaric rule, ruthless plunder and the roots of insoluble troubles and seeds of division and hatred that they left behind once they were forced out—all this explains the turmoil in many places. In 1494, the Pope, in order to mediate the scramble for land between the Spanish and Portuguese empires, proposed a line between the North and South Poles, the areas west of the line to come under the sphere of Spain and those east of the line to come under Portugal. His proposal was final. Those lands unlucky enough to be in the eastern portion and become Portuguese colonies thus suffered even greater hardships.

My four visits to Africa are an unforgettable page in my experience. In the 12 countries I visited, I had meetings with presidents, vice presidents, prime ministers, senate and national assembly speakers, foreign ministers and heads of national economic and social councils, as well as a great number of other dignitaries. The sites I visited included factories, mines, hospitals, construction sites, farms, national forest parks and tribal villages. I came into contact with tribal chiefs, grass-roots leaders, workers and men in the streets. Africa has left me with mixed impressions—it is the cradle of mankind, a continent extremely rich in natural resources, a continent which has survived untold hardships and calamities, a continent where the rich have wide expanses of land while the poor are totally landless, and a continent promising great hope yet still facing a rough path ahead. Admittedly, my African studies are not deep; nevertheless, they are firsthand observations. I still have confidence in Africa. I firmly believe that Africa will become better off in the future. However, at the same time I feel its road of development will be a long one. This reminds me of a line from Qu Yuan, a famous Chinese poet more than two thousand years ago—"Long as the way is, I will keep on searching above and below." Indeed, the African people's search for the road of development will be long.

The following is my four-point impression of my four visits to Africa:

One: the peoples of various African countries are full of friendly feelings for the Chinese people and have eager expectations of them.

Friendly ties between Africa and China date back to early days. Six hundred years ago, the famous Chinese navigator Zheng He led a commercial fleet to Kenya on the east African coast and beyond. China and African countries respected and supported each other in the independence movements for national liberation and the reconstruction after becoming independent during the last century. As a young student, I took part in mass rallies in response to the late Chinese leader Chairman Mao Zedong when he issued statements in support of Africa. I was also among the throngs lining the streets to greet visiting leaders of

African anti-colonial movements for national liberation. In 1971, the U.N. General Assembly adopted a resolution for restoring the rightful seat of the People's Republic of China in the U.N. Heading the list of the sponsors were Albania and Algeria, (popularly known in China as the "Two A's"), the second of the "A's" being an African state. Making up one third of all votes in the U.N., African countries have stood on China's side all along in the restoration of the latter's seat in the U.N., in its successive struggles for persisting in the "one China" principle, against the attempts for Taiwan and Tibet independence and against the attempts of Western countries to interfere in China's domestic affairs under the pretext of human rights. They have thus given China strong political and moral support. Such support has stood the test of the changing international situations and political turmoil in various countries.

I covered a total distance of well over 10,000 kilometers during my travels in Africa. Wherever I went, whether in town or countryside, in capitals or border tribal villages, I was greeted by warm and friendly faces. This was no accident. Once we went to the world-famous Victoria Falls in Livingstone in the company of the deputy speaker of Zambia. On November 16, 1855, the British explorer Livingstone got there as the first white man to see the falls and he named them after the reigning British Queen. The falls are located on the middle reaches of the Zambezi River, on the border between Zambia and Zimbabwe. They are over 1,700 m across and 108 m at the highest point. The average maximum flow in high water season (March to May) is 7,640 cu. m. per second and only 250 cu. m. per second in low water season (October to November). In the high water season, the spray rises as high as 300 m and the roaring waters can be heard 60 km away. We went in early December, still the low water season, and the falls on the Zambian side of the border had all but dried up. To have a full view of the falls we needed to go to the Zimbabwe side, but we had no Zimbabwean visas.

At this point, the Zambian deputy speaker traveling with us, without telling us his intention, went over to the other side and told the frontier control officials there that we were guests from faraway China, Africa's best friends, friends in need, who were always supportive of Africa in the struggle for national independence and national construction. He explained our problems to them, asking them to do us a favor by allowing us to go over to their side without visas. This would be a gesture of repayment of kindness on the part of Africa to Chinese friends, he added. Without asking for directives from their superiors or requiring us to go through any formalities, they let us cross the border to view the falls. We were very happy that we were able to enjoy the fruits of Sino-African friendship.

Two: the prerequisite for African development is political stability and domestic peace.

There are 53 countries in Africa and they vary greatly in the level of development, owing not only to their natural endowment, but also to the human environment, the most important of which is peace and political stability. Without peace, there will be nothing else to speak of; without political stability, nothing can be done. The sufferings that domestic turmoil and wars bring to the people are the most horrifying scenes on earth. In 1415, the Portuguese set foot on the African continent for the first time, marking the beginning of colonial rule by Western powers in Africa. In order to delineate their spheres of influence, they drew several dozen straight lines to arbitrarily divide the continent into colonies and protectorates under different suzerain states, artificially grouping tribes which hitherto had no common bonds while in some cases separating the same tribes. The root causes of today's incessant tribal feuds and wars date back to those days. Traveling in Africa, one may encounter such odd examples: two adjacent countries, separated almost only by a road, have no direct air links with each other simply because they once belonged to different suzerain states and one has to detour via the airport of a third country that used to have the same suzerain state. We were also told that some countries still had no direct international telephone services with each other but had to go via London, Paris, Rome, Lisbon or Madrid, depending on which suzerain state they had formerly had. Such an absurd state of affairs is still taken for granted in some African countries.

Algeria and Tunisia are neighbors. Algeria is a big country in Africa, 2.38 million sq. km. in area, with a 30-million-plus population and rich natural resources. On the other hand, its neighbor, Tunisia, is a small country, with a population fewer than 10 million, and only 160,000 sq. km. in area. Moreover, it is poor in natural resources. I visited both countries but saw an obvious gap between them. In Algeria, Algiers and Constantine provinces had an unstable political situation and a stagnant economy and were slow in recovering from the damage done by the domestic turmoil of a few years earlier. In Algiers you found few signs of the prosperity that once made this city famous after France established its provisional capital there during the Second World War. But when we arrived at Tunisia, we saw a different picture. It had been politically stable and developed economically over the past decades and its cities were prosperous. Its Mediterranean coastline had become a tourist Mecca frequented by foreign tourists, presenting a scene of tranquility and affluence hard to distinguish from European countries on the Mediterranean. From the different situations in these two neighboring countries, I felt the importance and value of peace and a stable political situation. Africa needs development, but, above all, it needs peace and social stability.

Three: it is essential for a country to proceed from its national conditions in choosing a road of development.

The surging movements for national liberation and independence in Africa during the 1950s and 1960s wrought changes to the African scene and to the world in general, bringing earth-shaking changes to the international pattern. One African country after another became independent and these newly independent countries all faced tasks of construction and development. As a reaction to the ruthless rule and plunder by Western powers over a long period of time, the newly independent African countries hated and were opposed to these colonial rulers and, with a few exceptions, most countries drove them away, seeing this as a historical inevitability left to them. They turned eastwards for help, placing their hopes on the socialist Soviet Union. It should be said the leaders of the newly independent African countries were all political elite, with great ideals of transforming the world and helping the people, and enjoyed high prestige as they had led the people in a protracted and dauntless struggle culminating in the overthrow of colonial rule. However, they were inexperienced in running and building their states and did not have a thorough understanding of national conditions, especially with regard to such questions as what social development stage their countries were in and what policies they needed. Over-eager to develop the economy and change the backwardness of their countries, they emulated and even copied Soviet experience by promoting state-owned factories and collective farms on a large scale. Such rash and ultra-Leftist policies were ill suited to their economic base and caused the productive forces to fall rather than advancing them, with the result that the economy declined year by year. This aroused dissatisfaction among the people, which in turn led the ruling parties to intensify their political control and suppress the enthusiasm of the masses and the enterprises, which in turn resulted in continued deterioration of the economy. Such a vicious cycle caused economic and social problems to snowball. With the disintegration of the Soviet Union towards the end of 1991, the very survival of those countries that had learned from the Soviet political and economic model came under great threat. Stage directed by Western countries, many countries, in a break with their past practices and jumping from one extreme to the other, introduced a multi-party system and privatization. As a result, there were a multitude of political parties in a country, with several dozen or even a hundred parties in one small country, and they engaged in partisan strife, resulting in political turmoil, deteriorating economy and worsening poverty.

The road of development trodden by Africa stirs people to deep reflection. It shows that a country must proceed from its own national conditions in choosing its road of development, analyze and understand correctly the historical stage it is in and formulate corresponding policies. Policies, if over-impetuous or ultra-Leftist, would lead only to a drop in the productive forces, dissatisfaction among the people and ultimately the loss of the means to build a beautiful country. Once out of power, one's ideals, no matter how fine, would be in vain. Julius Nyerere, the former President of Tanzania, dubbed "Africa's sage" and "Conscience of Black Africa," was a respected political leader who enjoyed a special place in the 1960s and 1970s. He rightly proposed focusing domestic efforts on attacking the "three enemies of poverty, ignorance and epidemic," stating that he would let others land on the moon while his country must strive for grain self-sufficiency. Yet this great man was an idealist and did not practice what he had preached, turning his ideals into rainbows. He revoked all incentives, making everyone with an annual income in excess of US$ 30,000 to pay income tax at 95 percent, and nationalizing all land property valued at more than US$ 14,000. During his 30 years in office, he changed none of his theories of government. He openly declared that if anybody thought that Tanzania's economic difficulties would cause him to change his pet policies of *ujamaa* and self-reliance, that person was dreaming. "*Ujamaa*" is a Swahili word meaning communal. It is not clear whether *ujamaa* was borrowed from China's people's communes. In his famous Arusha Declaration made in January 1967, he expounded his ideas on socialism and self-reliance, which were the epitome of his policy ideas. However, facts are ruthless. Whoever runs counter to the law of historical development must pay the price. Zanzibar, part of Tanzania, was once the most prosperous part of Africa, but now conditions are bad, power blackouts are frequent and stores are empty. His ultra-Leftist policies were seriously detached from Tanzania's realities and went beyond the limit of what people could accept. Tragedy was bound to happen.

In my talks with leaders of the countries I visited, they all said that their countries had gone off-course by learning from the Soviet Union in the past, nor was it right later to make a U-turn to learn from the West. They said that such reversals from left to right brought a great deal of suffering and made them realize that they would do better to follow China's example in proceeding from national conditions when formulating down-to-earth policies and pushing development in active and steady steps. I said that China too had suffered a great deal before realizing the importance of seeking truth from facts and seeing the point that rash and ultra-Leftist policies spoilt things rather than achieving their intended goals. "Let's learn from each other," I said.

African leaders visiting China are all praises for its development and very interested in its experience. In May 2000, a Zambian Parliamentary Delegation visited China at the invitation of the CPPCC National Committee. The two sides held talks after the delegation returned to Beijing at the end of its tour, which had taken in Shanghai, Hangzhou and Wenzhou. The head of the delegation put this question to me: Why is everybody in China so enthusiastic about production and work? I replied that I was very happy that China had left such an impression on the speaker. I then listed some points. Firstly, everybody was busy with work mainly because people wanted to live a good life after going through hardships over a long period. They turned their desire for a good life into action, so they supported the government wholeheartedly by running the economy successfully. Secondly, government policies and all other measures were designed to stimulate production, support people's production and encourage people to work for a better life. In appointing and appraising officials, the Chinese Government measured what they have done for the people. Thirdly, the ruling Communist Party played a role of core leadership in all the activities of the people and the government. Pre-Liberation China used to be described as quicksand—its people yet to be awakened, and its officials corrupt. This, plus foreign aggression and plunder made the Chinese economy backward for a long time and caused untold sufferings to the people. It was thanks to the long ideological education and organizational work done among the people by the Chinese Communist Party and its leaders Mao Zedong, Zhou Enlai and Deng Xiaoping that this state of affairs was gradually changed and the country kept improving. There was nothing profound about it. After hearing what I said, the Speaker commented that that might be the case, adding that Africa needed to do the same.

Four: there is a wide scope for China's cooperation with Africa.

Since its founding, New China, despite its limited resources, has given various forms of assistance within its capability to newly independent African countries, assistance which was sincere, unselfish and without strings attached. Such assistance covers railways, highways, textile mills, sugar refineries, hospitals, stadiums, office buildings and other physical facilities, but also involves a large number of medical teams which serve remote poor areas, treating local people on their doorstep. In Mali, I made a special visit to see a hospital built with Chinese assistance in a province. Its three-story building is the best structure locally, equipped with a complete range of equipment and staffed with Chinese doctors, nurses and administrators. When I toured the wards, I saw some penniless patients. I asked the head of the hospital whether it charged patients and was told that most patients were too poor to pay, but the hospital had never rejected any patient on that account. The hospitals built with Chinese assistance and Chinese medical teams have won public praise.

Since sending its first medical team to Algeria in 1963 at the invitation of the latter, China's medical teams have maintained a presence in Africa for over 40 years. Incomplete statistics show that by the end of 2003, China had sent medical teams to 47 African countries, which accounted for 89 percent of all the countries in Africa; a cumulative number of 15,000 medical personnel/times, accounting for 83 percent of the total, who treated 180 million patients, accounting for 71 percent of the total treated. China had signed governmental agreements with 34 African countries on sending medical teams to their countries, involving about 880 medical personnel. These African countries accounted for 83 percent of the total recipient countries and the personnel figure accounted for 80 percent of total personnel dispatched. Presidential and cavalier medals were awarded to 363 Chinese medical personnel. Twenty died on post. They will always be remembered for their contributions to the Sino-African friendship.

Some medical teams are general while others are specialist. They combine Western and Chinese schools of medicine. Their members are mainly clinicians, but also include personnel in quarantine, medicine inspection, disease control, health, equipment maintenance and other general services. In most cases, they are middle-rank or senior professionals, between 30 and 50 years of age. With a determination to live up to the expectations of the motherland and in the spirit of internationalism and patriotism, they work in extremely difficult conditions and in close cooperation with local staff and have treated large numbers of common and recurrent diseases and cured quite a few complex and difficult cases. They have thus saved many critically ill patients. They have imparted their knowledge to local staff without reservation by inspecting wards together, forming joint operating teams in addition to giving lectures and organizing training sessions. They have trained 3,000 primary and intermediate medical personnel for African countries and given in-service training to tens of thousands of local medical and nursing personnel. Their expertise and professional ethics have won high praise from the leaders and people of the countries in which they work. Apart from sending medical teams, China has also built 43 hospitals, clinics and health centers in 26 countries. Such assistance in medical skills has made a major contribution to promoting friendship and cooperation between China and the recipient countries and improving health in the recipient countries. Working hard and even giving up lives, the Chinese medical teams have won warm welcome and wide acclaim from the governments and peoples of the recipient countries. Chinese medical teams are examples of China's long cooperation with numerous developing countries. China has no parallel in the world in the number of medical personnel sent, of the countries covered and the provision of medical and technical services.

China also attaches great importance to cooperation with African countries in agricultural technology. Incomplete statistics show that, since the 1960s, it has implemented close to 200 agricultural projects in 40 African countries, covering agricultural technical experimentation stations, extension stations and a number of sizeable farms. Altogether it has sent 10,000 agricultural technicians, who have reclaimed and worked close to 70,000 hectares of land, registering good harvests of rice over large tracts and good sugar cane production so that the countries concerned have become self-sufficient in sugar production. Since the late 1970s especially, China has helped build a number of sizeable farms, playing a major role in relieving local grain shortage and contributing to the economic growth of the recipient countries. While I was in Guinea, I could not find time to go to a farm, so I asked its director to come to my hotel instead. He told me that the local land was fertile, the climate good and that the crops had a high yield. But he found the local farmers unwilling to learn new farming techniques because they preferred to stick to the traditions, and so they were still poor. It seems to me that the solution lies not in agricultural techniques per se, but in rapidly finding a social system and working mechanism capable of promoting agricultural production and social progress.

The tangible Chinese assistance brings benefits to wide social sections of the recipient countries. Local people praise China's selfless assistance from the bottom of their hearts. Leaders of various African countries have expressed the hope that such assistance will continue. I believe it is worth doing even if it costs more than it pays in an economic sense. It is a great cooperative cause as it sets its sights on the people and the future. Of course, as situations change, the content and forms of cooperation must change accordingly. Investment, trade, joint equities and cooperative production should gradually become important forms. Zhu Rongji made this point when he was visiting Africa as Chinese Premier. The government leaders and business leaders of the African countries I visited all told me they agreed with Zhu Rongji's thinking, but that they also hoped China would continue the past forms of assistance, which had been proved effective. In my view, a change in the forms of assistance is inevitable. A complete continuation of the past practices would be difficult to sustain for the Chinese side, but would also be no good to the recipient countries, especially in the case of free granting of industrial plant, because to do so would only encourage equalitarian practices, compromise independent operating and economic accounting of enterprises and discourage their efforts to improve management and competitiveness.

The most important thing for enabling Chinese enterprises to set up businesses overseas is, I think, for the Chinese Government to provide necessary conditions for doing so, especially in Africa and other economically less developed countries. It needs to do a wide range of things, from providing legal protection by Chinese embassies and consulates general, setting up banking and insurance offices, sending lawyers or cooperating with local lawyers, to opening air routes. On their part, enterprises should organize themselves into chambers for better self-regulation. These are all common international practices. Western enterprises coming to China for business have, without exception, adopted them. I visited the Chinese shopping areas in Namibia and Benin. The owners come from China's Liaoning Province, dealing in textiles and handicrafts. They told me that business was easy, only that whenever disputes arose, they had nowhere to seek help so had to settle in private by "gray methods." This may serve the purpose of small businesses, but with big enterprises and a legitimate market economy, it is totally irrelevant. They need open, legitimate and legal services and protection, which is beyond the reach of enterprises alone, but should be done with government planning, support and encouragement.

Africa is richly endowed, has a vast market and the governments and people of African countries are friendly to China. Going to do business there promises broad prospects. People should be prepared to endure hardship and display a pioneering spirit in business. I visited a port in Cameroon in the company of the Chinese ambassador to that country. I saw pile upon pile of superior logs. The ambassador told me that the two countries had reached an agreement under which an economically developed prefecture-level city in China was to set up a development zone. For that purpose, that city and the province administering it had sent some personnel on a field trip, but nothing had been heard from them since their return to China. After repeated enquiries from the embassy, the city responded with further questions. In my opinion, such problems could be solved. Had the partner been a developed country, they would not have posed such questions. Now they pointed to this or that problem, but the real reason was that they were not willing to work in hard conditions. On my return to China, I personally discussed the matter with the leaders of that province and the department concerned, explaining to them that this cooperation would be beneficial to both sides. They would not tell me to my face that they were against it, but actually they were not of a mind to go through with it.

Another example is cooling ointment (balm). It is a very common small commodity in China, but is widely welcome in Africa. The extent of its popularity in Africa is unbelievable. If someone gets in trouble in Africa, a gift of balm will work wonders and the trouble is over. Its effect is more magical than even the ads claim. Yet, it is in short supply in Africa. Why not produce it jointly in Africa? Even if it cannot be produced in Africa at present, is it possible to send the ingredients in bulk and repackage them locally, along the Coca-Cola model?

Africa is weighed down by historical legacy and current odds. Its quest for a road of development has been long and arduous. But this vast continent, while subject to untold human sufferings, is also richly endowed and promises a vast market. It is full of challenges to business starters, but replete with opportunities for success too. What counts is human effort. If people can take good advantage of friendly ties, start from joint development of resources and markets, with win-win as the aim, then Sino-African cooperation will have bright prospects.

Chapter VIII

Origins of the China Enterprise Confederation and Evolution of Its Functions

- China Enterprise Management Association Established for Learning Advanced Foreign Experience
- From China Enterprise Management Association to China Enterprise Confederation
- Participating on Behalf of Enterprises in the National Tripartite Mechanism for Coordinating Labor Relations
- Participating in the International Labor Conference and International Organization of Employers on Behalf of Chinese Employers
- Cooperation and Contacts with Famous International Organizations
- China's Urgent Need of Standard and Mature Social Intermediary Organizations

The China Enterprise Confederation (CEC) is the biggest social body in China's business world, comprising 30 national trade associations as collective members, 47 collective members from various provinces, autonomous regions and municipalities directly under the Central Government, 260 collective enterprise members from major cities, grouping a total of 545,000 enterprises, in addition to a further 4,500-plus members in directly-affiliated enterprises. Its member enterprises span all sectors, from state ownership, mixed ownership and private, to Sino-foreign joint-equity ventures.

In April 1999, I was on a business trip to Changsha in Hunan Province when Comrade Yuan Baohua called me, saying that he had decided not to serve any longer as President of the China Enterprise Confederation (CEC)/China Enterprise Directors Association (CEDA) and was recommending me for the post. He added that Zhu Rongji had agreed. This came as a total surprise. Yuan Baohua was widely revered for his seniority in Chinese economic circles, especially in the world of industry. He had been on the team led by Zhou Enlai and Li Fuchun negotiating with the government of the Soviet Union on the latter's assistance to China's First Five-year Plan (1953-1957). I had known him for several decades and esteemed him as an elder brother. Now that he was calling me in person and had secured agreement from Zhu Rongji, I said nothing except that I would follow their decision.

Back in Beijing, I went to see Yuan Baohua. He gave a detailed account of the CEC setup, work and personnel. He said that because of his advanced age, he had been searching for someone to succeed him, at first, from among leading officials of the State Economic Commission and industrial and communications departments, but without success. Then he suddenly hit on my name, he said, and secured Zhu Rongji's approval of his choice. I told him that when I retired from active service in the State Planning Commission, I had told myself not to take on any new assignments. But now that he and Comrade Zhu Rongji wanted me to take this job, I promised him I would work with Zhang Yanning (the then Director General of CEC) and we would try our best to push forward the work he had pioneered.

China Enterprise Management Association Established for Learning Advanced Foreign Experience

Towards the end of 1978, the State Economic Commission sent China's first economic delegation to Japan in nearly 30 years in order to study economic and enterprise management. Its principal members were its leader Yuan Baohua (Vice Chairman of the State Economic Commission), its advisor Deng Liqun (Vice President of the Chinese Academy of Social Sciences), deputy leaders Xu Liangtu (Vice Chairman of the State Economic Commission) and Ye Lin (Vice Chairman of the Beijing Municipal Revolutionary Committee), its Secretary General Zhang Yanning (a commissioner of the State Economic Commission and bureau director general). Its members included Song Jiwen (Vice Minister of Light Industry), Zhang Huaisan (Vice Minister of the Tianjin Municipal Revolutionary Committee), Zhou Bi (Director of the industrial and communications office of the Shanghai Municipal Revolutionary Committee) and Ma Hong (Director of the Industrial Economy Institute of the Chinese Academy of Social Sciences). The delegation's report to the State Council on its study findings suggested that China should follow Japan's example of bringing the role of associations into play in its economic development and form a China

Enterprise Management Association to study enterprise management systems and methods in China and abroad, sum up, exchange and extend related experience, train enterprise management personnel, collect information and data and carry out exchanges at an international level. It should comprise relevant industrial departments, industrial and mining enterprises, research institutions and institutions of higher learning and operate under the guidance of the State Economic Commission. In March 1979, with the approval of Vice Premiers Li Xiannian and Yu Qiuli, the China Enterprise Management Association was formed, with the State Economic Commission, the Chinese Academy of Social Sciences, the People's University of China, and Beijing, Shanghai, Tianjin, Liaoning and other provinces as joint sponsors. CEMA was China's first social-economic body at the national level in the early days of the country's reform and opening-up.

On March 3, 1979, the inaugural meeting of the CEMA was held in Beijing. Vice Premier Kang Shi'en addressed the meeting. Its first board of directors was elected through consultations. It had 55 directors, 34 of whom were executive directors. The CEMA President was Yuan Baohua, its Advisor, Deng Liqun. Its vice presidents were Ye Lin, Sun Youyu, Ma Hong, Xue Renzong, Chen Yu, Deng Cunlun, Zhang Huaisan, Zhou Bi and Hu Linyun. Its Secretary General was Zhang Yanning and its deputy secretaries general were Xue Baoding, Ji Chongwei, Kang Xinhao, Yin Chonghua and Li Zhanxiang.

On April 22, 1984, the CEMA ninth annual meeting/the inaugural meeting of the China Enterprise Directors Association (CEDA) was held. Party and state leaders Zhao Ziyang, Li Peng, Yao Yilin, Tian Jiyun and Bo Yibo attended the meeting. Yuan Baohua became the honorary director general of the first board of directors of the CEDA, Zhu Rongji, Ms. Hao Jianxiu, Sheng Shuren and Ms. Zeng Zhi, its advisors. Its President was Zhang Yanning (concurrently Director General), its Executive Vice President Sha Ye, its vice presidents Ma Shengli and others.

As China introduced the reform and opening-up program, the Party Central Committee and the State Council attached even greater attention to enterprise management. In March 1980, Katsuji Kawamata, a Vice Chairman of the Japan Productivity Center and President of the Nissan Motor Company, Ltd., led a delegation to China at the invitation of the CEMA. In his meeting with the Japanese delegation, Deng Xiaoping said that Sino-Japanese cooperation should not limit itself to business, but should extend to exchange of experience: that what China lacked most at present was production management expertise. Management was a science too, indeed a more comprehensive science, and China was too shaky in this regard. China should learn from Japan in science and technology, but even more so in enterprise management, which was more important than doing business.

Following the guidelines of Deng Xiaoping, the Party Central Committee and the State Council, soon after its founding the CEMA started many-faceted work in studying enterprise management, vigorously pushing forward the modernization of enterprise management in China.

(1) Studying and extending modern enterprise management

It conducted investigations and studies into hot and difficult spots in the reform process, with a view to providing policy recommendations to the government and research achievements to enterprises. Its main work included:

Assisting the government in conducting pilot projects in the Capital Iron and Steel Company and seven other enterprises regarding the expansion of their decision-making power; it conducted pilot projects regarding modern management in 300 enterprises across the country, in which the "18 Methods of Modern Management" and "Experience of 224 Typical Enterprises in Switching Mechanism" were popularized.

Directed by Yuan Baohua, it held national seminars on modern enterprise management for many years running, and formulated and implemented the "Outline of Enterprise Management Modernization" during the Seventh and Eighth Five-year Plan Periods; it participated in the investigation and studies organized by the legislature and the government in connection with the formulation of the "Enterprise Law," "Labor Law," "Township Enterprise Law," "Labor and Employment Security Law" and "Regulations on Transforming Enterprise Operation Mechanism in the Industrial Enterprises of the Ownership of the Whole People."

It undertook the "Studies on the Competitiveness of Large Chinese Enterprises" and the "Studies on the Operation and Management Modes of Chinese Enterprises" commissioned by the State Natural Sciences Fund; it participated in studies on modern enterprise systems, a project organized by the central authorities, and drafted study reports on some parts; and it completed a project jointly conducted with the United Nations Center for Regional Development regarding the management rationalization of Chinese enterprises.

It institutionalized the national annual review of innovation achievements regarding enterprise management.

It pioneered 1,000-enterprise surveys and, from 1998 on, published the annual "Chinese Enterprise Development Report" based on these surveys for distribution in China and abroad.

Starting from 1997, it undertook various assignments as and when required by the Enterprise Research Center of the State Economic and Trade Commission.

(2) Providing intellectual support to enterprises

From March 1987 to March 1999, it offered various forms of training classes, television and correspondence lectures and other forms of training to train middle-rank and senior managerial personnel for enterprises, with a total attendance of more than 300,000 people/times.

Among these were: 34 national training classes, a task entrusted by the former State Economic Commission, for local economic commission chairmen; 13 national workshops for officials engaged in economic restructuring, a task entrusted by the former SCRE; 14 seminars for young plant directors (managers), held in cooperation with the Youth League Central Committee; more than 500 short training courses on various subjects; sponsored more than 2,000 young and middle-aged managerial cadres (senior management cadres in provincial economic commissions and Party committees overseeing local industries) for advanced studies abroad; and held TV and correspondence lectures on operations and management in modern enterprises, in cooperation with the Labor and Personnel Management School of the People's University and China Central Television, which was attended by more than 26,000 students across the country.

In 1998, in accordance with a directive from Premier Zhu Rongji, it cooperated with the Hong Kong General Chamber of Commerce in staging three seminars on the utilization of foreign funds in the transformation of SOEs in the mainland of China.

Between 1984 and 1994, it organized six China-EC Management Institute EMBA classes jointly sponsored by China's State Economic Commission and the European Community, graduating 249 students.

(3) Training enterprise directors and expanding their ranks

Since 1995, every April 21 has been "National Enterprise Directors' Day," on which enterprise directors of diverse ownerships in different parts of the country gather to hold dialogue, exchanges and seminars or to discuss cooperation.

A total of 162 enterprises were cited as national outstanding enterprises (Golden Horse Prize) and 196 enterprise directors, as national outstanding enterprise directors (Golden Globe Prize).

China's first management consulting company was set up in 1984 and it completed the first management consulting study since the beginning of the reform and opening-up program. It trained the country's earliest management consulting professionals, published *Enterprise Management Consulting* (a textbook for trial use), *Theory of Management Consulting and Methods* and other relevant books, and provided consulting service to 297 enterprises. It ran 47 training classes for 25,000 consulting professionals/times (including 10 international training classes with an attendance of nearly 500 persons/times). Starting from 1987, the work of certifying senior consultants for Chinese enterprises was carried out.

CEMA provided more than 70,000 items of market information to entrepreneurs every year and edited and published 1,300 titles, including *Encyclopedia of Chinese Enterprises*, *Textbook for Updating Management Knowledge of Enterprise Operators* and *A General Survey of Chinese Enterprises*, as its intellectual service to enterprise directors at different levels.

Starting from 1981, it cooperated with the World Economic Forum in holding the annual "China Enterprise Summit." Chinese leaders Jiang Zemin, Li Peng, Zhu Rongji, Wu Bangguo, Huang Ju, Wan Li, Gu Mu and Tian Jiyun attended such forums on different occasions. The event is a platform for dialogue, exchange and cooperation between Chinese and foreign entrepreneurs.

Each year it holds a meeting on China's economic policies and major industry development forecasts, a Sino-Japanese industrial seminar, a Sino-Japanese enterprise management workshop, a selection of top ten news items concerning Chinese enterprises, and issuing new records achieved by Chinese enterprises.

In February 1987, with the approval of the People's Bank of China, an Enterprise Management Science Fund was set up, with Yuan Baohua as its president.

From China Enterprise Management Association to China Enterprise Confederation

In April 1998, in accordance with the decision of the CEMA Board of Directors and with the approval of the State Council, the CEMA was renamed the China Enterprise Confederation (CEC), with corresponding adjustments and additions to its work. These adjustments, made in the spirit of advancing with the times, aimed to adapt the functions of an intermediary organization to the market economy. Specifically, the following factors were taken into consideration:

One: the adjustments were conducive to developing social intermediary organizations in response to the call of the 15th National Congress of the CPC and promoting the conglomeration and growth of enterprises;

Two: they were conducive to expanding the service scope of the CEC and its representation and coverage. Through its efforts over many years, the CEMA had formed a fairly systematic organizational network across the country and a fairly complete range of service functions, laying down the organizational and working foundation for turning into a confederation, which operates at a higher level and with greater service functions.

Three: they were conducive to protecting the interests of the enterprises and enterprise operators as a whole. After adopting a new name, the confederation has further strengthened its integrity as an organization of enterprises representing their overall interests; they were conducive to performing its intermediary role and implementing the laws, regulations and policies regarding enterprises and enterprise operators, to encouraging enterprises to discipline themselves while protecting the lawful rights and interests of enterprises and enterprise operators, and to transmitting the voices of enterprises and enterprise directors, enabling the CEC to become a true bridge between the government and enterprises.

Four: it serves as an organization of Chinese employers in participating in the activities of International Labor Organization (ILO) and, as the representative of employers in the tripartite coordinating mechanism, in legislation concerning labor and in the coordination and settlement of labor disputes. Also in that capacity, it carries out exchange and cooperation at an international level, and forges closer ties with the ILO, the International Organization of Employers and other related international organizations.

On May 31, 1999, the CEC/CEDA decided, by letter, on the resignation of Yuan Baohua from the presidency of both organizations, to be succeeded by myself in both capacities. It was also agreed that Yuan Baohua became their Honorary President. The Honorary Presidency was created at my suggestion after consulting Zhang Yanning. I said on the occasion that Yuan Baohua had founded the CEC, enjoyed high prestige in China's economic and industrial community and deserved the post as its Honorary President. This would also enable the CEC to benefit from his continued attention, guidance and support, I added.

On June 5, the CEC Sixth Board of Directors held the fourth meeting of its executive board at which it heard a report on the results of the proceedings for replacing its president by letter. It also examined and adopted a plan for CEC capacity building.

The four-plus years between April 1999, when the CEMA was re-named the CEC, and September 2003, when its Seventh Board of Directors was elected, constituted a period of transformation and fast growth for the CEC. In keeping with the progress of the country's reform and opening-up and modernization and sticking to its objective of serving enterprises and enterprise directors, it smoothly effected the switch from the CEMA to the CEC, establishing its status as an organization representing enterprise operators (employers), readjusting its service functions and expanding its areas of service.

In its membership composition, it switched from its past focus on SOEs to all types of ownership, with special emphasis on opening to enterprises of mixed ownership and private ownership, so as to broaden the basis of membership. While serving large enterprises, it worked energetically to serve middle-sized and small ones too. Now half of the 4,500 directly affiliated member enterprises are non-SOEs. Of its executive directors, those from enterprises make up a sizeable proportion. It is a rule that those from enterprises make up the overwhelming majority of CEC vice presidents. The CEC sees to it that it gives full play to the role of the enterprises serving as vice presidents, executive directors and directors in various activities. It also strengthens ties, exchanges and cooperation with enterprise confederations in various provinces, municipalities under the Central Government, autonomous regions and in major cities, in an effort to make the system of enterprise confederations work more coherently.

The major work and activities of the CEC after its establishment are outlined below:

1.   On August 3, 2001, China officially set up a tripartite (government, enterprise organization and trade union) conference system for coordinating labor relations, with the CEC designated the representative organization of the Chinese enterprises in the national tripartite

mechanism, which jointly worked out and implemented the guidelines on the work of establishing and improving the tripartite mechanism for coordinating labor relations. On its part, the CEC issued a circular on the focal points of the work of province-level enterprise confederations/enterprise directors associations on the building of a tripartite mechanism. At present, such a mechanism has been built at the provincial level across the country and the work is extending to cities (prefectures) and counties (districts) in most provinces. Such a mechanism has also been established in specialized fields in some localities. The tripartite mechanism is headed for gradual institutionalization and standardization.

2. On June 2, 2003, the General Council of the International Organization of Employers (IOE) adopted a resolution unanimously recognizing the China Enterprise Confederation as China's only representative organization of employers at the national level and accepting it as a full member.

3. It took an active part in the formulation of laws and regulations concerning labor relations, contributing suggestions and opinions to laws on labor, trade unions, and administrative approval, and regulations on the prohibition of use of child labor, and joining other organizations in drafting the rules on collective contracts and regulations on the management of part-time labor arbitrators.

4. It has established ties with most members of the IOE. It is in quite close contact with employer organizations in Japan, Republic of Korea, Norway, Australia, New Zealand, Singapore and Malaysia.

5. In 2000, the "Management Year" designated by the State Economic and Trade Commission, the CEC proposed ways to deepen enterprise reform and development and attain the goal of helping SOEs out of difficulties within three years. It prepared a study on the ways to extricate large and medium-sized SOEs out of difficulties in three years and, after winning favorable comments from Premier Zhu Rongji

and Vice Premier Wu Bangguo, was reprinted in the *Economic Daily*, the *China Enterprise News* and the magazine *Management in China and Abroad*.

6. In 2002, in the wake of China's accession to the WTO, it launched a WTO-related professionals training project and presented a number of studies to the Party Central Committee, the State Council and the State Economic and Trade Commission, on such issues as mastering WTO rules, the post-accession reform of administrative management system of the Chinese Government and its streamlining, and progress in building a modern enterprise system.

7. It released a list of China's top 500 enterprises for 2002, 2003 and 2004, along with the world's top 500 for comparison, with an analysis of indicators to show the strengths, improvements and deficiencies of Chinese enterprises and suggestions for improvements. The move was in response to the central authorities' call for forging a number of big companies and enterprise groups possessing brand names, independent intellectual property rights and strength in their main lines of business and core capabilities. It was also a follow-up on the guidelines issued by the State Economic and Trade Commission and six other ministries on developing internationally competitive large enterprises. The annual release of the top 500 Chinese enterprises has become a famous CEC brand, one designed to encourage Chinese enterprises to grow bigger and stronger in the course of learning from the world's top 500.

8. It commended and publicized success stories of 134 entrepreneurs. Among them were Xie Qihua (Baoshan Steel), Zhang Ruimin (Hai'er), Ma Fucai (PetroChina), Wei Liucheng (CNOOC), Liu Jie (Anshan Iron and Steel), Miao Wei (No. 2 Automotive Group), Zhu Yanfeng (No. 1 Automotive Group) and Lu Guanqiu (Wanxiang Group).

9. It launched, in cooperation with the China Medical Fund, a

health service program for enterprise directors.

10. It released the rules of self-discipline for honest business, urging enterprises to discipline themselves and conduct open and equitable competition in business operations while earnestly discharging social responsibilities.

11. It actively responded to the call for a Global Compact from UN Secretary General Kofi Annan made at the World Economic Forum, urging enterprises to discharge their social responsibilities. He wrote a letter to me to express his appreciation of the CEC work in support of the Global Compact. In October 2004, he had a seminar with Chinese enterprise leaders in Beijing at which they exchanged ideas on how to further the work in this respect.

12. It cooperated with the World Business Council for Sustainable Development and the government of the Netherlands in carrying out studies on enterprise sustainable development and clean production. CEC set up its Business Council for Sustainable Development.

13. It organized the First China Employer Forum, Private Entrepreneurs Forum, Conference of Enterprise Management Innovations and Sino-Korean High-Level Financial and Economic Summit, as it expanded cooperation with Chinese and foreign partners in its new areas of operations.

14. On September 15, 2003, it held its Seventh National Conference of Representatives at which the Seventh CEC Board of Directors was elected. On February 20, 2004, its executive council adopted the outline of the work of the CEC Board of Directors between 2003 and 2008.

The above focal work of the CEC reflected the switch of functions from CEMA to CEC. In its early days the CEMA did a great deal of work in implementing directives from the Party Central Committee, the State Council and Deng Xiaoping on strengthening enterprise management by focusing on SOE management improvement and achieved extensive results. Its efforts were warmly welcomed by enterprises. After the founding of the CEC, this work remained as one of its basic tasks. In an effort to keep up with the advance of times, the CEC took the initiative to adapt itself to China's socialist market economy that was in the process of continuous improvement, and initiated work related to the macro-economy. It was aware of the need to start intermediary service to enterprises after the separation of government administration from enterprise management by serving as a bridge linking government and enterprises and linking enterprises and society at large. It worked energetically to help solve problems common to enterprises, something which individual enterprises or sectors were unable to do on their own. The CEC represented Chinese employers at an international level, made friends and promoted cooperation, safeguarded the lawful rights and interests of Chinese employers and better served Chinese enterprises and enterprise directors.

Participating on Behalf of Enterprises in the National Tripartite Mechanism for Coordinating Labor Relations

The tripartite mechanism originated in Western market economy countries between the late-19th and early-20th centuries. Through consultations and mediation among government, employers and workers over labor relations issues, it aimed to ease acute conflicts between labor and management, promote democratization and protect the lawful rights and interests of both enterprises and workers, so as to ultimately achieve the purpose of developing the economy and promoting social stability. The founding of the International Labor Organization (ILO) in 1919 was an important mark of the official formation and growth of the tripartite mechanism. In 1983, China formally resumed its activities in the ILO. Since then, China has sent a tripartite delegation to the International Labor Conference every year. Comprising the Labor and Social Security Ministry, the All-China Federation of Trade Unions and the China Enterprise Confederation, the Chinese delegation was actively involved in work regarding the formulation and revision of international labor standards and conventions. In 1990, China officially ratified the ILO Convention 144 Concerning Tripartite Consultations to Promote the Implementation of International Labor Standards and started the operation of the tripartite mechanism for coordinating labor relations in China.

With the establishment of a socialist market economy in China, profound changes have taken place in the field of labor relations, notably, daily-increasing labor disputes and sharpening contradictions in labor relations. While 12,368 cases of labor disputes were registered at various levels across the country in 1993, the figure rose to 184,000 cases involving 610,000 people in 2003, respectively 15.6 times and 17.1 times higher than 10 years previously. The establishment of harmonious and stable labor relations had become a major issue bearing on social stability and economic development and in urgent need of tripartite mechanism comprising government, trade unions and employer organizations. In January 1998, the State Economic and Trade Commission officially entrusted the CEDA with the responsibility of representing it in regular work of coordinating labor relations in enterprises and legislation on labor, handling of labor disputes in enterprises and contacts with the International Organization of Employers. In August 2001, drawing on the successful practices of Western market economy countries and with the approval of the Party Central Committee and the State Council, a national tripartite mechanism for coordinating labor relations, comprising the Labor and Social Security Ministry, the All-China Federation of Trade Unions and the China Enterprise Directors Association, was formally established and launched.

In November 2001, these and several other organizations held a meeting in Nanjing to exchange experience in implementing in an all-round way the labor law and the trade union law and promoting collective contracts and labor contract. These organizations were the Labor and Social Security Ministry, the State Economic and Trade Commission, the All-China Federation of Trade Unions, and CEC/CEDA. Wei Jianxing addressed the meeting. A written address from Wu Bangguo was delivered. Leaders of the sponsor organizations also spoke. The

Nanjing meeting was a major event following the establishment of the tripartite mechanism. I attended the meeting and heard that some local enterprise confederations did not pay enough attention to this matter. I immediately discussed ways of improving the situation with Chen Lantong and other attendees from the CEC. I asked them to call Zhang Yanning, who was presiding over a meeting of enterprise confederation secretaries general in Northeast China, telling him to work out ways to implement the guidelines of the Nanjing meeting and bring the confederations' work up to standard. I held that the tripartite mechanism was a mature experience of the countries with a developed market economy in handling labor relations. Now China had decided to do the same and charged the CEC with the task of representing the employers. This was faith placed in the CEC by the state and the CEC should discharge its responsibility well. At a subsequent meeting in Qingdao attended by secretaries general of local enterprise confederations, I sent out a strong message to them. I said that now the state had decided to establish the tripartite mechanism and made the CEC the representative of enterprises, how could they fail to pay enough attention to this work? If they went on like that without making efforts, then I would bypass the confederation of their province and pick another enterprise organization instead. My words shook up the local confederation leaders and they quickly changed their attitudes after the meeting.

On August 6, 2003, a two-day national meeting opened in Zhuhai to exchange experience in pushing the work of tripartite mechanism for coordinating labor relations. More than 180 delegates attended the meeting. They were chairmen and vice chairmen of the mechanism in various provinces, municipalities directly under the Central Government, autonomous regions, cities with independent budgetary status, the Xinjiang Production and Construction Corps and the national construction industry. Speakers at the meeting included Wang Dongjin, Vice Minister of Labor and Social Security, Sun Baoshu, Vice President of the All-China Federation of Trade Unions, and Chen Lantong, Vice President of the CEC. Representatives of Beijing, Hebei, Jiangsu, Zhejiang, Anhui, Fujian and Guangdong as well as the national construction industry made presentations on their experience in the work. The meeting further promoted the work of establishing the tripartite mechanism.

From April 28 to 30, 2004, the "China Employment Forum" was held in Beijing, with China's Ministry of Labor and Social Security and the ILO as the sponsors and assisted by the All-China Federation of Trade Unions and the CEC. Its theme was "Globalization, Structural Adjustments and Employment Advancement." Huang Ju, a member of the Standing Committee of the Political Bureau of the CPC Central Committee and Vice Premier, addressed the meeting. Zheng Silin, Minister of Labor and Social Security, and the ILO Director General made keynote speeches. The forum heard speeches from leaders of the Ministry of Labor and Social Security, the All-China Federation of Trade Unions, the CEC and the Chinese Permanent Mission to the UN Office at Geneva. Among the more than 620 delegates were representatives of China's National Development and Reform Commission and the Ministry of Finance, the labor departments of Singapore and other countries, ILO experts and consultants, representatives of related international organizations, government delegations of 27 countries and regions, as well as Chinese and foreign experts, scholars and business leaders.

The CEC strengthened guidance over and ties with local enterprise confederations with the aim of actively encouraging them to improve their organization building and participate in the tripartite mechanism. At present, this mechanism has been established in 30 out of the 31 province-level administrative divisions (excluding Tibet) across the country. In 16 provinces, the CEC/CEDA is the sole representative of enterprises while in another 11 the enterprises are represented by provincial economic and trade commissions and enterprise management associations jointly. In Ningxia and Xinjiang, the economic and trade commissions are the representatives of enterprises and in Hainan enterprises are jointly represented by the enterprise directors association and the general chamber of commerce. Out of the 402 prefecture-level cities across the country, 261, or 64.9 percent of the total, have the tripartite mechanism. Pilot programs at the county-level cities have already been completed.

With the establishment of the tripartite mechanism, the CEC took an active part in the formulation and revision of relevant laws and regulations as the representative of the employers. From 2001 till up to now, it drew up and issued documents, including the provisional regulations on the management of part-time labor mediators, regulations on collective contracts, rules on minimum pay; it issued jointly with other organizations documents including a circular on further strengthening the work of handling labor disputes, a circular on further promoting the system of equal consultation and collective contracts, a circular on strengthening and coordinating supervision by labor departments and supervision by trade unions over the implementation of the laws related to labor security, guidelines on establishing and perfecting the tripartite mechanism for labor relations, opinions concerning the issues related to the building of the ranks of part-time labor mediators and a circular on the issues related to the assessment of work ability; and it was involved in the revision of relevant laws, regulations and rules, including the provisions banning the use of child labor, the Social Security Law (draft), the interpretations (II) of the Supreme People's Court on the laws applicable to cases of labor disputes and a circular on implementing the provisions concerning collective contracts.

In accordance with the work arrangements of the national tripartite coordinating mechanism, the CEC also carried out in a planned way investigation, studies and field trips on labor relations, focusing on such issues as labor disputes in China and ways to deal with them, labor relations in Chinese enterprises and recommendations for measures to deal with them, the need for protecting the personal rights and interests of enterprise operators and corporate social responsibilities. It also studied legal aspects related to employment, pay and labor relations in enterprises.

In order to meet the needs of work in the tripartite mechanism, the CEC also held various kinds of seminars to train personnel. It launched a training program on the tripartite mechanism and employers; held a series of seminars in cooperation with the ILO, such as an international seminar on the subject, an international seminar on globalization and China's labor relations and enterprise opportunities and challenges, gender equality and employer work coordination meetings, an international seminar on occupational safety and health, an international seminar on HIV prevention in workplaces, and an international seminar on changes in human resources; held a seminar in cooperation with the Norwegian Employers Organization on tripartite mechanism and collective bargaining, and a seminar on labor relations; and held in cooperation with the United Nations Development Program a seminar on sustainable development, a forum on social responsibilities of Chinese enterprises in the 21st century, and a seminar on clean production.

I was quite keen on the tripartite mechanism. The fact that cases of labor disputes in China rose 15-fold in a 10-year period was a signal deserving our high attention. If labor relations are not handled well, it will inevitably have an adverse impact on economic development and social stability. As things stand now, whenever a problem arises in labor relations, like loss of jobs and complaints about pay, a local government is invariably in the first line of handling it, leaving no leeway for negotiation. If and when the contradiction sharpens, police and armed police force are used to maintain order. In my view, this is not the best approach. Democratic methods should be promoted in the settlement of problems in labor relations, as in other fields, i.e., dialogue on an equal footing and democratic consultations rather than force. This is a world trend representing social progress. The fact that the tripartite mechanism has received high attention in developed countries and is in use there shows that it goes with this tide and proves its viability in solving problems. In the interests of the effort to build a harmonious society, China must follow this road. It is an inevitable trend and nobody must go against it.

Participating in the International Labor Conference and International Organization of Employers on Behalf of Chinese Employers

China was a founding member of the ILO and became one of its 10 permanent members in 1944. After the People's Republic of China was founded, the Taiwan authorities continued to occupy China's seat in the ILO. With the adoption of Resolution 396 at the 26th UN General Assembly in October 1971, the PRC resumed its legitimate rights in the UN. On November 16 the same year, the governing council of the International Labor Office, in accordance with UN Resolution 396, decided at its 184th meeting to restore the legitimate right of the PRC, expel the representative of the Taiwan authorities and invite New China to participate in ILO activities. However, China at that time did not have sufficient understanding of the ILO, believing it was an organization "preaching class reconciliation and practicing reformism in the service of capitalism and the imperialist policy of infiltration and expansion." Moreover, the ILO unreasonably wanted New China to pay the membership arrears owed by the Taiwan authorities and the arrears since 1971. In September 1977, the Chinese Government sent a note to the Director General of the ILO, stating that China would not consider participating in ILO activities for a period of time to come, nor discharge any duty, nor consider paying so-called membership dues. In February 1978, the 205th session of the ILO Governing Council adopted a recommendation designating China as a non-functioning member, which was adopted at the 64th International Labor Conference held the same year. ILO Director General Francis Blanchard held the view that China should participate in ILO activities and tried to convince various quarters of his point. He expressed through diplomatic channels his hope that China would participate in ILO activities. In his letter to the Chinese Government he said that the ILO would not be broadly representative until China joined it. As a result of repeated consultations and after the ILO decided to cancel the so-called "arrears" owed by China and to restore China's voting right, the Chinese Government decided to resume its ILO seat. At the 69th International Labor Conference in 1983, China resumed its activities in the ILO and its status as a permanent member of the International Labor Organization was restored.

The International Labor Conference is held every year, attended by a tripartite delegation of the government, the employers' organization and the trade union of a member state as well as representatives of other international organizations and non-governmental organizations. It is held in Geneva, where the ILO is based, and it usually lasts one to two months. Normally a Chinese delegation is led by the minister or a vice minister of the Ministry of Labor and Social Security, a member of the secretariat or a vice president of the All-China Federation of Trade Unions, and a vice president or director general of the CEC.

The International Labor Conference has more than ten permanent committees and technical committees, in which tripartite representatives of governments, employer organizations and trade unions of all member states conduct full discussions and consultations and exchange views. Seeking common ground while reserving differences, they try to reach consensus through consultation and the conventions, recommendations, protocols and resolutions thus made are the formal documents of the ILO for guiding its member states in the legislation and practice in the field of labor. By the end of 2003, the ILO had adopted a total of 185 international labor conventions and 194 recommendations, the most important of which are the eight core conventions, namely, Forced Labor (1930), Freedom of Association and Protection of the Right to Organize (1948), Right to Organize and Collective Bargaining (1949), Equal Remuneration (1951), Abolition of Forced Labor (1957), Discrimination (Employment and Occupation) (1958), Minimum Age Convention (1973) and Elimination of the Worst Forms of Child Labor (1999). By 2004, China had ratified 22 international conventions, one of which is ILO Convention 144, which ILO adopted in 1976 and China ratified in 1990. Concerning tripartite consultations to promote the implementation of international labor standards, it requires the ratifying parties to undertake to operate procedures which ensure effective consultations with respect to matters concerning the activities of the ILO between representatives of government, of employers and of workers.

The Governing Body of the International Labor Office is composed of members representing governments, employers and workers. As a permanent member of the UN Security Council China is per se a government member of the ILO Governing Body. A Chinese worker representative was once a deputy worker member but later failed to be re-elected. He was re-elected eventually. For a long period, New China did not have an employer seat, due to the fact that to stand for election one must first be a member of the International Organization of Employers. For many years the seat due to China had been occupied by Taiwan's organization of employers whose official name contains the wording "Republic of China." In its participation in UN activities China has always upheld the principle that Taiwan has no right to represent China and must change its name. Through repeated work, including diplomatic struggle, the CEC officially joined the International

Organization of Employers and became an employer member of the ILO in 2003, only after Taiwan's employer organization was renamed Taipei China: Chinese Federation of Industries.

On April 25, 2003, the IOE decided to accept the CEC as its member and indicated that, with effect from January 2003, it had changed the name of Taiwan's organization of employers into Taipei China: Chinese Federation of Industries in its internal use. On June 19, it sent a letter to the CEC confirming that the CEC had become its full member. In fact, it added, its website had made adjustments as early as January 2003. The letter stated that the CEC is China's sole representative in the secretariat of the IOE, the Employers Group of the Council of the International Labor Office and in all ILO activities—including in the case of the Hong Kong Employers Federation, which is invited to participate in relevant activities on the nomination by the CEC. This point was made very clear in the 1999 resolution.

After becoming an IOE member, the CEC actively engaged in related activities.

a)   Becoming a co-founder of the Asia-Pacific Federation of Employers and taking an active part in its activities

The Asia-Pacific Federation of Employers is composed of the national employers' organizations of countries covered by the ILO Regional Office for Asia and Pacific. Its main objective is to promote mutual understanding and cooperation among its members in labor, economic and social policies and worker-employer relations. As a founding member, the CEC has always taken an active part in its work, strengthened exchanges with other employers' organizations in the region and promoted bilateral and multilateral cooperation in the context of China's efforts to promote friendship and cooperation with other Asian and Pacific countries.

b)   Attending the Asia-Pacific High-Level Employers Meetings

In October 2000, Zhang Yanning and Chen Ying, Director General and Deputy Director General respectively of the CEC, attended the fifth session of the Asia-Pacific High-Level Employers Meeting in Singapore, during which they exchanged experience with leaders of other national employers organizations, briefed each other on labor practice in their respective countries and explored possibilities of strengthening ties between them. In December 2003, Chen Lantong, Vice President of the CEC, attended its sixth session in Dacca, Bangladesh, having dialogue and exchange of views with other delegates on how the regional employers' organization should meet the challenges of globalization and encourage the social responsibility of enterprises.

c)　Attending IOE council meetings

In 2003 and 2004, the CEC attended the sessions of the General Council of the IOE as a full member during the International Labor Conference. The agenda of the IOE council meeting for 2004 included: ratifying the summary of the IOE council meeting for 2003, listening to the executive committee's report on activities for 2003, reviewing the "Strategic Framework of the IOE 2004-2009," approving the financial report for 2003, approving the budget for 2005, approving resolutions on membership matters, amending the IOE statutes, as well as elections of executive committee members, regional vice presidents, treasurers and vice treasurers.

d)　Back in China, it has carried out capability building and professional activities in keeping with its due rights and obligations flowing from its membership of the IOE.

Cooperation and Contacts with Famous International Organizations

(1) Cooperation with the World Economic Forum

The World Economic Forum was originally called the European Management Forum. It established a cooperative relationship with the China Enterprise Management Association more than 20 years ago through the introduction of Qian Junrui of the Chinese Academy of Social Sciences. Our cooperation mainly covers two items: holding the Chinese Enterprise Summit in Beijing and organizing Chinese business leaders to attend the annual meeting of the World Economic Forum in Davos, Switzerland.

The Chinese Enterprise Summit was launched in 1981 and attracts hundreds of famous Chinese and foreign business leaders, senior officials and academics each year. The Chinese Government gives special attention and support to it and each year a Chinese state leader comes to address the summit and meet the delegates. The summit is a venue for foreign business leaders to know more about China and seek investment opportunities; it helps make them more confident of their trade and investment in China. It is also an occasion for Chinese business leaders to know more about the world, make acquaintance with foreign business leaders and make their debuts in the world arena. This annual event has an ever-widening appeal to Chinese and foreign business leaders and is becoming an important platform for wide exchanges and co-operation.

Usually two Chinese delegations attend the annual Davos meeting. One is a government delegation led by the Premier or a Vice Premier of the State Council or other senior government officials, who deliver a keynote address to the meeting and preside over the China Day, during which foreign participants are invited to meetings, dialogues and dinners with the Chinese Government Delegation. The other is a Chinese enterprise leaders' delegation organized by the CEC. I went to Davos first as leader of the Chinese Government Delegation and later as head of an enterprise leaders' delegation.

The annual meetings mainly focus on trends in economic globalization and various views. Their participants are mostly political leaders of various countries and leaders of trans-national companies. Chinese enterprise leaders find themselves a little out of place. Moreover, because of the long distance, language issues and the timing (usually around the Chinese New Year holiday period), Chinese enterprise leaders generally are not keen to participate. I have talked about these obstacles to Professor Schwab, chairman of the WEF, who indicated that improvements would be possible. But actually there have been no significant improvements so the Davos forum still is not attractive to Chinese enterprise leaders. I am in favor of Chinese enterprise leaders, especially those of the younger generation, taking an active part in these two events, so as to understand the outside world, follow new market trends and acquire new knowledge and information. These two events can serve as a springboard to those enterprises that wish to go international.

(2) China Employers' Forum

The China Employers' Forum is an annual large-scale international forum hosted by the CEC. Its objective is to provide a platform for exchanges between Chinese and foreign enterprises and employers, a bridge between enterprises and government, information necessary for

Chinese enterprises in improving their competitiveness on the domestic and international markets, to protect the legitimate rights and interests of enterprises and employers and to raise the profile of Chinese employers at home and abroad. It invites leaders of relevant Chinese government departments, ILO, IOE, trans-national companies and famous Chinese enterprises and economists to make presentations on topics and share ideas on hot or difficult issues of common interest to enterprises and employers. Its participants are mainly senior managers of enterprises and enterprise groups and prominent public figures.

(3) Cooperation with the Japan Business Federation

The Japan Business Federation (Keidanren) is the biggest federation of enterprises in Japan. Its chair is held by the most prominent Japanese business leader, who was nicknamed the financial "emperor" during the days of fast economic growth in Japan.

In 1996, President of the China Enterprise Management Association, Yuan Baohua, and the President of the Japan Federation of Employers' Associations (Nikkeiren), Jiro Nemoto, agreed to establish the annual "China-Japan Industrial Seminar," to be held on a chosen subject, the venue alternating between China and Japan. This is a meeting and exchange of visits by high-level Chinese and Japanese business leaders. In 2002, the Japan Federation of Employers' Associations was incorporated into Keidanren. When I was visiting Japan that year, the new Keidanren Chairman Hiroshi Okuda, who was President of Toyota Motors, solicited my views about our future cooperation. I said that CEC and Keidanren were each the biggest and most important federation of economic organizations in our respective countries and that developing cooperative relations between them would play a positive role in increasing friendly ties between our two peoples and promoting economic and trade cooperation between our two countries. The Chinese side proposed that its cooperative relations with Nikkeiren would become one with Keidanren and that the two sides would continue to hold the China-Japan Industrial Seminar, which had already been held six times. Chairman Okuda agreed.

In 2003, the seminar was held in Suzhou, Jiangsu Province. Chairman Okuda led a delegation to it. I asked him whether he had been to the city before and he replied that he had visited as a tourist many years previously and that the main attraction he had visited was the Hanshan Temple. The temple is famous in its own right, but its fame is spread far and wide by a Tang Dynasty poem describing the ringing of its bell at midnight. Since this poem by Zhang Ji was included in a Japanese textbook, many older-generation Japanese have read it. I told Chairman Okuda that the current abbot of the temple was an accomplished calligrapher and that I would ask him to write out the poem on scroll. Okuda was delighted at this. Subsequently I had the calligraphic work mounted and sent to him. I believe that for the friendship between the Chinese and Japanese peoples to be carried on for posterity, a wide foundation must be built for friendship among non-governmental circles in the two countries. Late Chinese leaders such as Zhou Enlai, Deng Xiaoping and Liao Chengzhi, made friends with many Japanese, including prominent financial leaders, who later played an important role in the normalization of Sino-Japanese diplomatic relations and in economic and trade cooperation between the two countries. In March 1984, Deng Xiaoping, when meeting Japan's Prime Minister Yasuhiro Nakasone, said words to the effect that the two countries' leaders had made a far-sighted decision in Tokyo a year earlier, that Sino-Japanese ties should be viewed and developed from a long-term perspective; first, from the perspective of the 21st century and thence continued into the 22nd and 23rd centuries and for posterity. This matter is more important than any other issues between the two countries, he added. When I was in Japan in 2002, I quoted these words of Deng Xiaoping on different occasions. The financial and economic leaders to whom I spoke all responded approvingly. I hold the view that this work should be continued without interruption by making many friends in all Japanese social strata, especially among the younger generations, to make Sino-Japanese friendship play a new role in the new historical period.

The year 2002 marked the 30th anniversary of the normalization of Sino-Japanese diplomatic relations. My visit to Japan was part of the celebrations. I saw that some Japanese friends who had done so much for Sino-Japanese friendship had reached old age, and they were worried at the paucity of successors. In Osaka I asked the chairman of the local Japan-China Friendship Association about how it was faring and was told that the phrase "good old days" was not enough to describe the current sorry state of Sino-Japanese friendship activities at non-governmental level, with no successors to carry on the work. He said it was a pressing task to carry out work among young people in a way attractive to them, adding that Sino-Japanese friendship should be rooted in non-governmental circles and young people. I think he was right. China should take the initiative and do painstaking work, overcoming interference and sabotage by right-wing forces in Japan and reaching out to different Japanese social strata, especially to the young, so that the Chinese and Japanese will truly live in friendship from generation to generation.

(4) Cooperation with the World Business Council for Sustainable Development (WBCSD)

The World Business Council for Sustainable Development was created by such well-known multi-nationals as Shell, BP, GM and Toyota. Its objective is to promote closer cooperation, dialogue and exchanges among enterprises, governments and other social organizations dedicated to sustainable development and to push efforts to seriously practice the concept of sustainable development in enterprises. The WBCSD had long hoped to start cooperation with and have a branch in China, but nothing had come of it. Later I wrote a letter to Premier Wen Jiabao in which I said that this matter had to do with China's image and the social responsibilities of enterprises. I further told him that the chairman of Shell had written to me many times, asking me to push it in China, but I could not account for myself because a solution had eluded me despite trying for a long time. I suggested to Premier Wen that the matter receive adequate attention. Premier Wen forwarded my letter to the Ministry of Civil Affairs for handling and soon the necessary procedures involved were completed. The CEC formally set up its Business Council for Sustainable Development.

In addition, the CEC has cooperated with the Norwegian Chamber of Commerce and Industry for many years. The two sides hold training programs on worker-employer relations, human resources, enterprise management and other issues every year and organize Chinese enterprise directors to Norway on field trips.

(5) China-Korea Financial and Economic Summit

The China-Korea Financial and Economic Summit is a meeting of senior business leaders of China and the Republic of Korea jointly sponsored by the CEC and the Federation of Korean Industries (FKI).

The first such meeting was held in Seoul, Republic of Korea from June 15 to 20, 2004, where I led the 29-member CEC delegation. It focused on the economic restructuring and industrial cooperation between the two countries. The participants had discussions and dialogue on issues such as the direction of industrial cooperation and effort to promote a free trade area, China's reform and opening-up and China-Korea enterprise cooperation. The Korean side attached importance to this meeting and the Korean Vice Premier Lee Hun-Jai (Acting Premier) met with me and some senior members of the CEC delegation. During the meeting he asked me why the CEC and FKI, two important organizations, had not forged cooperative relations until many years after the establishment of diplomatic relations between the two countries. I quoted a Chinese saying "regrets at not having met earlier" to describe our feelings about this belatedness, but I was quick to add that nevertheless we had a good outcome. He smiled in agreement.

The CEC delegation visited the Pohang Iron and Steel, the SK Group and other large Korean enterprises where we discussed matters related to cooperation. The visit left a deep impression on me.

China's Urgent Need of Standard and Mature Social Intermediary Organizations

The perfection of a socialist market economy ultimately depends on two factors: enterprises being truly the main operators of the market, and the transformation of government functions. The course of the growth and maturing of these two factors must be accompanied by the emergence of standard intermediary service organizations tailored to their tasks. All mature market economy countries have a full range of intermediaries covering law, finance, auditing and various industrial associations, which provide a platform for effective cooperation between government and enterprises, ensuring independent operating of enterprises free from interference while effectively supervising enterprises in discharging their social responsibilities without doing damage to public interests.

The main function of an industrial association is: externally, to advocate legitimate rights and interests and, internally, to exercise sector-specific self-discipline so as to ensure fair, equitable and orderly competition. Under the conditions of the socialist market economy, enterprises need to go through industrial associations to protect the interests of their own enterprises and of the industry as a whole and to solve problems in market competition and related economic and social problems, such as pricing, market share, technical standards, through coordination and consultation to strike a balance between interests.

China has 362 trade associations registered with the Ministry of Civil Affairs: 206 in industry, 67 in commerce and logistics, and 74 in other areas. Owing to historical reasons, they are usually attached to the relevant government departments and some are even an extension of administrative agencies or their subordinate offices. As far as their functions are concerned, they are far from being a true intermediary service organization under the socialist market economy. The 15th National Congress of the CPC set the task of developing social intermediary organizations, but the results of its implementation are by no means satisfactory. Judging by mature market economy countries worldwide, an industrial association generally has three kinds of function: a) providing various kinds of services to its member enterprises, such as information, consultancy, training, etc.; b) coordinating—it carries out consultation and coordination to iron out differences and promote development when tension arises among its member enterprises or with outside organization; c) serving as a bridge between industry and government and between industry and society at large, with the emphasis on relaying government views to the enterprises and transmitting the demands of enterprises to the government. As a federation of various industrial associations, the CEC needs to do a good job of developing social intermediary organizations. On the other hand, the governments at various levels need to energetically advocate this work and the industrial associations to intensify their work. The goal is to bring, within ten years or so, the social intermediary organizations in China up to the level roughly commensurate with the socialist market economy.

The Smoking Gear Trade Association of Wenzhou in Zhejiang Province is one of the few industrial associations in China that have done superior work. The city is a major lighter producer, exporting 600 million lighters annually, which account for about 70 percent of the global metal lighters market. One third of its exports go to EU countries. In May 2002, the EU initiated anti-dumping procedures against Chinese lighters. As individual enterprises were too weak to act on their own, it was left to the Smoking Gear Trade Association to answer the lawsuit promptly. In July, it organized Dahu and 14 other local leading producers to answer the suit. Using WTO rules, it hired experienced lawyers from France and Belgium to file a "non-industrial injury appeal." In September, EU officials went to Wenzhou a number of times to make on-the-spot investigations to verify all the financial, marketing and cost accounts of the enterprises involved. In July 2003, the EU decided to terminate the anti-dumping investigation procedure. The Chinese side won the case as the other side withdrew the lawsuit unconditionally. What the Wenzhou Smoking Gear Trade Association did can be done by other associations.

The majority of China's industrial associations have done a poor or inadequate job. An example is the recent loss of an anti-dumping case brought by a small US enterprise with only about 700 workers against leading Chinese color television producers such as Changhong, Konka, TCL and Prima. With the imposition of anti-dumping tariffs ranging from 5.22 to 78.45 percent, China's export of color televisions suffered a great blow. In retrospect, the relevant departments concluded that the defeat was attributable, among other things, to the absence of a strong industrial association familiar with international trade rules and capable of effectively organizing and coordinating its member enterprises.

Industrial associations are a kind of mechanism for realizing economic democratization. Democracy is an important hallmark of modern economy and without it, an enterprise cannot stimulate its creativeness, mobilize the enthusiasm of its workers or improve its competitiveness. An industrial association can help an enterprise expand democracy and improve its position to meet competition and challenges. The examples above illustrate the importance of strengthening economic democracy. It is essential for China to intensify the reform of industrial associations, speed up the transformation of their functions and improve their style of work. It is necessary for the associations to rely on enterprises, display economic democracy and do a good job of strengthening their functions as intermediary organizations in providing services, coordinating and serving as a bridge, so as to provide better services in the country's effort to perfect the socialist market system and in the efforts of enterprises to participate in cooperation and competition amidst economic globalization.

Chapter IX

Boao Forum for Asia and Chief Delegate of the Chinese Government

- From the Manila Proposal to the Boao Forum for Asia Declaration
- "The Gods in Heaven Sent Down Dongyu Island."
- Four Annual Conferences Spread Boao's Fame Far and Wide
- The Future of Asia and Its Regional Economic Cooperation

A non-governmental, non-profit, self-financing organization, the Boao Forum for Asia (BFA) is the only international organization to be established and permanently located in China registered under Chinese law. It aims to provide a high-level interactive platform for state leaders, business people and academics of the countries of Asia to share their views on economic development, population, environment and other pressing Asian issues. The BFA is committed to the task of promoting, on the basis of dialogue, mutual understanding and cooperation among the Asian countries. At the same time, the Forum is open to the world, welcoming officials, business people and academics from around the world to participate in its activities, helping enhance discussion, exchange and cooperation between Asia and the rest of the world as well.

Preparatory work started in 1998 and the BFA was formally inaugurated in 2001. Including the inaugural conference, by the end of 2004, the BFA had held altogether four conferences, and its influence around Asia and the world had greatly grown.

In 2001, the relevant parties recommended me as China's Chief Delegate to the Forum, to undertake all its construction work and to coordinate all the various services promised by China as the host country. I was told to fulfill all the pledges made by the Chinese Government to the Forum to help ensure its normal operation. After my retirement from the post of Vice Chairman of the CPPCC in 2003, Jiang Zemin wanted me to continue my work as China's Chief Delegate to the BFA and coordinate the various tasks shouldered by the Chinese Government. By working together with a wide variety of contacts and communicating with all the public figures through my work at BFA, I conclude that the BFA has been a significant platform for dialogue. As an important communications channel in the era of economic globalization, the BFA definitely has a most promising role to play in promoting regional cooperation in Asia.

From the Manila Proposal to the Boao Forum for Asia Declaration

In September 1998, Jiang Xiaosong, Chairman of the Hainan Boao Investment Holdings Co., Ltd. invited the former Australian Prime Minister Bob Hawke and the former Japanese Prime Minister Morihiro Hosokawa to Manila for a meeting with President Fidel Ramos of the Philippines to discuss the establishment of an "Asian Forum." Prior to this, in July 1997, Jiang Xiaosong, Hawke and Hosokawa had already had a brainstorming meeting at Boao, on the island province of Hainan, about setting up an Asian Forum. Later, because certain reasons prevented Morihiro Hosokawa from further involvement in preparations for the forum, the Chinese Ambassador to Japan, Chen Jian, was asked to visit Yasuhiro Nakasone, a former Japanese Prime Minister, to see if he could join the forum work. Mr. Nakasone accepted the invitation, and became Japan's official representative at the inaugural conference of the BFA.

Around the time when Ramos, Hawke and Hosokawa met in Manila, the Asian financial crisis was escalating fast. The financial markets experienced fierce turbulence and the Asian economies were facing an unprecedented crisis. Feeling keenly the urgent pressure caused by the Asian financial crisis, Ramos, Hawke, Hosokawa and others were emphatic about the importance of studying and learning from the experience of the World Economic Forum at Davos. They proposed the formal setting up of a similar forum for Asia to discuss vital issues of Asian development, particularly in view of the current financial crisis. The new forum for Asia would invite the leading figures from the worlds of politics, business and academe in Asia to engage in dialogue and offer ideas for Asian governments and enterprises through communication and deliberation. Having reached agreement at their Manila meeting, they held a press conference in Manila and issued the "Manila Proposal." In this they pointed out that the Asian countries needed to strengthen their regional economic coordination and cooperation in the face of the huge opportunities and challenges engendered by today's global economy. The cooperation would enable these countries to safeguard regional economic security, maintain and further promote the benefits to the region. The Asian region lacked a sense of organization when compared with the European Union and North America in setting up and expanding their free trading zones. The proposed "Asian Forum" would be a non-governmental, non-profit international organization with permanent headquarters whose operation would be supported by a specially established fund, serving the purpose of providing a high-level platform for dialogue among politicians, business people and academics from around Asia. It would concentrate on such issues as economic development, population and environment in the Asian region and it was the sincere wish of the forum organizers that it would promote mutual understanding and cooperation on the basis of dialogue and communication.

After the "Manila Proposal" was published, its drafters had Bob Hawke write letters to China's President Jiang Zemin and Governor Wang Xiaofeng of Hainan Province, suggesting the official founding of the "Asian Forum." They also proposed that the new Forum for Asia should be based in Boao Town in Qionghai City, Hainan Province.

After the Manila meeting, Jiang Xiaosong came to see me at my

CPPCC office, asking me to preside over the preparatory work for the new "Asian Forum" and to be China's chief delegate to the Forum. I replied that the issue must first be decided by the Party Central Committee; if the central leadership approved my being involved, I would then talk to him about the issue. This was my first meeting with Jiang Xiaosong. I told him that if things worked out and I really started working with him, it must be an interesting coincidence of fate.

After the smashing of the Gang of Four in 1976, I went to work at Shanghai as the Deputy Secretary of Shanghai Municipal Party Committee, the Executive Vice Mayor, the Director of Shanghai Planning Committee and concurrently Director of the Labor and Salary Commission under the Shanghai Party Committee (Shanghai was the only provincial level administration to have such a commission). Every Chinese New Year between 1977 and 1979, hundreds of thousands of urban educated youths sent down to the countryside but back in the city for the Chinese New Year holiday, would plead outside the Shanghai municipal government offices asking to be allowed to return home to Shanghai. After the holiday season of 1979, because these young people's repeated pleadings had not been properly dealt with, over 100,000 of them besieged the offices of the Shanghai government on the Bund for two or three days, refusing to leave. The huge crowds paralyzed the traffic of downtown Shanghai. Mobilizing all its police to try to control the situation, the Shanghai government still found it hard to maintain order. Eventually, the city had to redeploy its firefighters to help defend the government building on the Bund. On the evening when the gathering was at its largest, some young people went to sit on the northbound railroad track, claiming they wanted to go to Beijing with their petition. The Shanghai Party and government leaders, Peng Chong, Wang Yiping, Han Zheyi and I got not a wink of sleep that whole night, keeping in telephone contact with Beijing to ask how we should deal with the young people's request. Later, the central leadership decided on a policy to let children take over their parents' posts in the city so these former urban youths could return to Shanghai. Gradually the problem was settled. Jiang Xiaosong's father was Jiang Junchao, a famous film director in the Shanghai Film Studios. His mother was Bai Yang, a famous movie star. Jiang Xiaosong had been living in a village in Anhui Province for a while and was qualified to return to Shanghai in line with the replacement policy. But both his parents were renowned figures in the film world so he could not step into the job of either of his parents. One day I was chairing a meeting of the Labor and Salary Commission to discuss the replacement policy. The office manager of the commission reported on how the work was progressing and cited the example of Jiang Xiaosong. How, he asked, was Bai Yang's son to substitute for his mother as a film star? I said that the main gist of the state policy was to vacate precious employment positions so as to provide jobs for the returning youths. It was not that a child must do exactly what his or her parent had been doing. We should, therefore, grant Jiang Xiaosong's request to replace his mother in Shanghai. Hence Bai Yang retired from the film studio and her son Xiaosong returned to Shanghai and was employed at the studio.

Shanghai had hundreds of thousands of educated youths sent to live in the rural areas as far away as Xinjiang, Heilongjiang, Yunnan and Guizhou. The close-by provinces included Anhui and Zhejiang. I saw some of their letters pleading to return to Shanghai. Some letters enclosed pictures too. What touched me the most were the pictures sent by a group of youths sent to live in Xinjiang. They sent pictures of their dwellings there. These were but waist-deep pits dug into the ground and then covered with a few tree branches that could hardly block strong winds, heavy rain or blizzards. Their living conditions were so poor. Seeing those pictures, I felt greatly disturbed and a deep sympathy for these young people. After the Third Plenary Session of the 11th Central Committee of the CPC, our national Party and government led by Deng Xiaoping performed a great many good and important acts. Among these were the actions to help several millions of former urban youths to return to their home cities and restore the university and college entrance examination. It changed the fate of several million educated youths and united them with their families. It should be counted as the greatest good deed of all and one of the most popular acts of kindness. Jiang Xiaosong was one of those millions of urban youths who were able to return home. I told Jiang Xiaosong that I had presided over the issue of returning home for hundreds of thousands of Shanghai youths but his name was the only one I had heard. Isn't it a sort of coincidence of fate! He nodded repeatedly "It is fate. It is fate."

After the Manila meeting and the numerous consultations by the sides concerned, Ramos and Hawke visited Beijing in October 1999, where they formally told the Chinese leaders about their blueprint for the "Asian Forum" and asked for their support. They expressed their hope that the Chinese leaders could participate in the work of the forum. Comrade Hu Jintao met them and, on behalf of the Chinese Government, announced that China agreed to lend support to and participate in work for the BFA because China had all along supported regional economic cooperation in Asia and advocated multi-level and multi-domain dialogue. Hu Jintao also suggested that the forum organizers consult the various Asian countries about it. Hence, they entrusted the Chinese side to send a questionnaire letter to 26 Asian countries as well as special envoys to a number of countries to hear their opinions on the topic. The work turned out to be warmly supported by all these countries, unanimously approving the suggestion to establish a Forum for Asia. Therefore, the preparatory work for the new Forum for Asia was officially launched.

In November 2000, the preparatory group for the Boao Forum for Asia held a meeting of experts from 24 Asian countries. The meeting discussed and passed five important foundation documents including

"The Asian Forum Declaration (Draft)."

In January 2001, the *People's Daily* invited me to an international forum in Sanya, Hainan Province. After the forum was over, I accepted the offer by the Hainan Provincial leaders to visit Boao on my way back. On the evening of my arrival at Boao, the comrades of Hainan Province and the Ministry of Foreign Affairs reported to me about the expert meeting and gave me a set of meeting documents. There I met Ajit Singh from Malaysia who had been invited to Boao as candidate for the post of Secretary General of the new forum. I read all the meeting documents I was given but was not clear why they hoped to get me involved in the forum work, nor how it was linked with Jiang Xiaosong's earlier visit to my office. The next morning I had a short meeting with Fu Ying Director of the Asian Affairs Department of the Ministry of Foreign Affairs, Chen Ci Director of the Overseas Chinese and Foreign Affairs Office and Liu Qi Director of the Planning Department of Hainan Province. I told them my feeling about the meeting documents and asked them seriously: "Why are you reporting to me about the work on the Asian Forum and giving me all the documents? What kind of role do you want me to play in it? Do you want me to join the forum as a representative like all the others sent by their own countries, or do you want me to undertake the hosting work by the Chinese Government?" I asked them to find out from their superiors and then let me know, but they did not supply the answer I was owed. It was not until the eve of Chinese New Year in February 2001 that I saw the report from Hainan Provincial government to the Party Central Committee suggesting that I should be China's official representative at the Forum for Asia. The request was checked and verified by our Ministry of Foreign Affairs and then approved by Li Ruihuan and Qian Qichen. Only then did I come to see what role I was expected to play. I was appointed as Chief Delegate of China to the Boao Forum for Asia as well undertaking all the facility construction and coordinating all sorts of services to be provided by the host country, in fulfillment of the promises made by the Chinese Government to the Forum and to ensure its proper operation. I heard later that I had been one of three candidates and was the final choice for the job after rounds of discussions among the various parties.

The Boao Forum for Asia (BFA), sponsored by 26 Asian countries, was officially founded on February 26, 2001. Before the inaugural conference a preparatory committee meeting was held, led by Fidel Ramos, Bob Hawke, Yasuhiro Nakasone and myself. Twenty-six countries were represented at the inaugural conference—Australia, Bangladesh, Brunei, Cambodia, China, India, Indonesia, Iran, Japan, Kazakhstan, Kyrgyzstan, Laos, Malaysia, Mongolia, Myanmar, Nepal, Pakistan, the Philippines, South Korea, Singapore, Sri Lanka, Tajikistan, Thailand, Turkmenistan, Uzbekistan and Vietnam. The conference passed the "Declaration of the Boao Forum for Asia."

The Declaration consists of "Foreword," "Vision," "Mission" and "Strategy." It declares openly and directly: "At the beginning of the new millennium, we have gathered here in Boao, Hainan Province in the People's Republic of China to review the economic and social challenges facing Asia. We recognize the importance of developing Asian perspectives on emerging issues and challenges facing Asia. We further recognize the need for sustained efforts to promote greater interdependence and economic integration of the region." The Declaration states that its members are "firmly convinced that through dialogue, coordination and cooperation amongst the countries of Asia, new Asian perspectives will emerge to cement and deepen economic ties, enhance trade and investment within the region and the world at large." Therefore, they proposed seven strategies in the Declaration. These were: Convene conferences, seminars and workshops on a regular basis, to discuss important issues relating to Asian development, trade, investment and environmental protection; complement the regional initiatives underway to intensify collaboration between the governments and business communities on trade and investment matters; serve as an early warning system for the business communities on the impact of global trade and investment liberalization measures; identify and disseminate information on emerging business and investment opportunities; serve as a clearing-house for promoting joint ventures between business communities operating in Asia; undertake feasibility studies and provide consultancy services to business communities and governments; and become a global center for research and graduate training to equip business communities with better management and technological capabilities. These seven strategies indicated that the Asian member countries of the Forum paid great attention to the economic and social issues ignited by the Asian financial crisis. The Declaration solemnly declared: "The Boao Forum for Asia is established under the laws of the People's Republic of China and will be permanently located in Boao, Hainan Province, China."

The important political figures attending inaugural conference of the Boao Forum for Asia included President Jiang Zemin of China, King Mahendra of Nepal, Premier Mahadier of Malaysia, Vice Premier Qian Qichen of China and Vice Premier Nguyen Manh Cam of Vietnam. Apart from Ramos, Hawke and Nakasone, other former prominent politicians included Farooq Leghari (former President of Pakistan), Kirti Nidhi Bista (former Prime Minister of Nepal), Punsalmaa Ochirbat (former Prime Minister of Mongolia), Sergey Terechshenko (former Prime Minister of Kazakhstan) and Lee Soo Sung (former Premier of South Korea). On behalf of the Chinese Government, President Jiang Zemin of China gave a speech of congratulation on the founding of Boao Forum for Asia. He pointed out: "The birth of the Boao Forum for Asia reflects the desire of the Asian countries to conduct dialogue and seek cooperation for a common development in the wider context of globalization which this era calls for." He said: "As the host country,

China will continue to provide support for the healthy growth of our Forum for Asia." Jiang Zemin inscribed a poem to express his joy at the significant event as well: "Fresh is the scenery of Wanquan; wide is the water, pure the evening breeze. Multiple sages arrive from around the world; Boao looks more pleasant."

Two years later, on January 24, 2003, Jiang Zemin met with Fidel Ramos and other board directors of the Boao Forum. He told them that the founding of the Forum displayed the confidence of Asians that they could do things well. He added that the people of Asia should aspire to build Asia into a better place, and that the Forum and various forms of cooperative mechanism could contribute to this goal. He also told them: "Personally, I have very high expectations for the Forum and wish to see it grow and expand until it becomes a highly active organization in Asia." At the time, I was in Europe attending an international conference on sustainable development, so could not get back in time for the meeting. In that year I would leave my post at the CPPCC. Jiang Zemin said to the BFA Secretary General Long Yongtu and the Ministry of Foreign Affairs: "Even though Chen Jinhua will relinquish the post of Vice Chairman for the next session of the CPPCC, he will continue his job as our chief delegate at the Boao Forum. The job is still his. He is qualified." Hence, my activity at Boao continued.

"The Gods in Heaven Sent Down Dongyu Island."

Hainan Island lies in a central position relative to countries of East Asia, South Asia and Southeast Asia. More than 20 countries and regions can be reached within three hours flying time from Hainan.

The water city of Boao Aquapolis is located on the east coast of Hainan Island between Haikou and Sanya. Three rivers (the Wanquan, the Longgun and the Jiuqu) converge at Boao before flowing into the sea. On the eastern edge of Boao stretches Jade Belt Beach, a long sandy beach extolled in *Guinness World Records*. The sand bar separates the sea and the river, with the vast South China Sea to one side and the sparkling Wanquan River to the other. Rivers, lakes, sea, and cold and hot springs merge into a dreamy landscape of rolling hills and meandering mountains. Tropical forest, farmland and rural cottages enhance each other's beauty, creating a beautiful magical picture. Blessed with the best-protected natural ecology, Boao is praised by experts as the best-preserved virgin estuary of its kind in the world. The selection of Boao as the permanent venue of the Forum for Asia reflects man's ideal of humankind and nature in harmonious coexistence. Boao is a work of magic combining the natural landscape of Asia and modern civilization.

To meet the needs of the Forum, the Boao Aquapolis was planned to be built on an area of 41.8 sq. km. including 8.5 sq. km. of water.

A four stage rolling program of construction was planned. The construction plan was not verified and approved even when the BFA was officially established. In the summer of 2001, invited by Hainan Boao Investment Holdings Co. Ltd., I chaired a meeting of Chinese experts to seek their suggestions about the plan for the Boao Aquapolis. Afterward, Du Qinglin, the then Secretary of Hainan Provincial Party Committee, and I sat down to discuss the project and all its work with the Boao Investment Holdings Co. Ltd, the COSCO Group Co. and the leaders of the competent departments in Hainan provincial government. However, these parties argued heatedly over the topic and failed to reach agreement. Finally, Li Wei, President of the Hainan Golden Coast Lawton Group said that we should first of all settle the area with the local government. Feeling that his opinion hit the nail on the head, I echoed his suggestion right away and asked Du Qinglin to decide on the issue with the Provincial Governor Wang Xiaofeng as soon as possible. Before long, following the direction of Wang Xiaofeng, the Hainan provincial government officially authorized "special planning region" status for the 41.8 sq. km. area of the Boao Aquapolis. Dongyu Island, within the area, has a more level surface area, so Phase 2 of the Aquapolis Project was focused on Dongyu Island, and was started officially once approval was received. I spoke at the meeting, declaring that to judge from the prevailing situation, it would need about three years to iron out all the controversial issues before the construction of Phase 2 could really take off. Events later proved my estimate correct.

Before then, Phase 1 had seen the completion of the Golden Coast Hot Spring Hotel (a super five-star hotel), the Jinjiang Hot Spring Hotel, the Blue Seashore Villa and an open, membrane-roof auditorium plus all the ancillary facilities. The Phase 1 buildings had basically met the requirements of the BFA inaugural conference.

The first annual conference of the BFA took place in April 2002. As it happened, the number of participants swelled way beyond the original estimate. At the time accommodation at Boao could only meet the needs of some 1,000 guests but the number of people invited to the first annual conference ended up as 1,800-2,000. Including staff, the total number of people at the site reached 3,000, way beyond what Boao's facilities could handle. Furthermore, the situation was exacerbated by the conference's organizational chaos. Of all those who were unhappy about the conditions of the first annual conference, the Hong Kong representatives were the vociferous, making numerous criticisms about the reception arrangements. That said, all other aspects of the conference, such as the topics, its keynote speeches—in particular the speech from Zhu Rongji—and other speakers' talks on various topics, were uniformly excellent, and widely praised for their focus and high quality, both by those actually attending the conference and by those who had only read about them. Zhu Rongji apologized to the meeting representatives for the inadequacy of the preparatory work, promising that reception arrangements for the next annual conference would definitely be better than for the first.

After the first annual conference of BFA was over, I called a meeting with the leading members of the Chinese government branches, regional officials and enterprises involved in the project to make a searching review of the experiences and lessons of the conference. After the review meeting, I wrote a report personally to Jiang Zemin, Zhu Rongji, Li Ruihuan and Qian Qichen, with a comprehensive analysis of the various aspects of the first BFA Annual Conference 2002, elaborating on successes, faults and suggestions for future work. After that, I spent a great deal of time and energy supervising and coordinating the construction of Phase 2 on Dongyu Island. I was determined to handle the facilities well and improve the services at future conferences to ensure that Zhu Rongji's pledge to participants at the first annual conference would be substantiated.

That year, I traveled to Hainan four times to discuss and coordinate the construction of Phase 2 with the Hainan Party committee and provincial government, the COSCO Group Co., the Boao Investment Holdings Co. Ltd., Qionghai city and other parties. The construction units of Hainan Province, the COSCO Group Co. and others responsible for Phase 2 gave up their holiday time even during the Chinese New Year, braving the cold, wet weather on the worksite day and night. Their action fully displayed the spirit of the Chinese people living up to their word and fulfilling their promises. From laying the foundation in July 2001 to completion in April 2003, Phase 2 took only one year and nine months to complete the building of the International Conference Center, the Sofitel Grand Hotel, the golf course, the BFA office building, the south main expressway and three large bridges, not to mention all the associated power and water supplies, post and telecommunication facilities, sewage treatment plant and green zones. Dongyu Island, the focus of Phase 2, had originally been an undeveloped island with rural land and jungle. The virgin land was inhabited by some 200 farming households mainly engaged in fishing and other productive activities. The completion of Phase 2 worked a dramatic transformation of Dongyu Island, turning it into a modern international conference center, a leisure paradise, a fully equipped, marvelously furnished showplace. In my time I have been to the World Economic Forum, the European Forum, the Pacific Basin Forum and other major forums around the world, but I am convinced that none can match the overall level of the BFA with respect to physical facilities and ecological environment. The BFA has created a world-class platform for dialogue among Asian countries both in its facilities and its ecological environment.

The second annual conference of the BFA was held in November 2003. The Chairman of the World Economic Forum, Professor Schwab, attended at our invitation and visited Beijing after the end of the conference. When I hosted a welcome banquet in his honor, he was full of praise for the facilities of Boao. He kept saying how unbelievable it was to build such an excellent conference center in such a short time and how really great it was. I have no idea where he had learned that I was in charge of coordinating the construction undertaken by China. At the banquet he asked me suddenly: "Mr. Chen, could you help me make Davos as attractive as Boao?" I replied: "Thank you. But I am getting old and could no longer undertake such a task." Although it might have been just a polite pleasantry on the part of Professor Schwab, his praise revealed a truth nonetheless. The physical facilities at Davos, such as its conference center, guest accommodation and infrastructure, for example roads, were indeed far behind those of Boao.

The construction of the Boao Aquapolis took eight years in all, from the official launch of Phase 1 in January 1996 to the completion of Phase 2 in April 2003. Among the projects involved, the construction on Dongyu Island took one year and nine months with a total investment of about three billion *yuan*. It transformed a small fishing village unknown on the map into the famous showplace of an international forum venue, winning increasing fame in Asia and the rest of the world. The transformation was just incredible. Sheng Huaren once told me about a conversation with the Speaker of the Indian Parliament when he escorted the latter on a tour of Shanghai in early 2002. Visiting Lujiazui in Pudong, his Indian guest sighed that he had been to Shanghai just a few years earlier, when the development of Pudong was just starting and the Lujiazui financial zone did not even exist. All of a sudden everything had popped up. It was really as if "the gods in heaven had put Lujiazui there!" Hence, when I spoke at the coordinating meeting to inspect the completion of Boao Phase 2 project undertaken by China, I borrowed the comment of the Indian guest and said: "Now it is really appropriate for us to say 'the gods in heaven sent down Dongyu Island !'"

The physical construction and related infrastructure of the BFA was initially undertaken by the Boao Investment Holdings Co. Ltd. Then the construction was carried out mainly by Hainan Province and the

COSCO Group Co. All these parties helped China keep her solemn pledge as host of the BFA. The Chinese central and local governments and the enterprises involved in its construction made a giant contribution. The main builders were Hainan Province and the COSCO Group Co. Their excellent after-sales service improves year after year. It has won wide praise from the Boao board and the politicians, businessmen and academics of all the countries participating in the Forum. I am filled with sincere respect for their outstanding work.

Four Annual Conferences Spread Boao's Fame Far and Wide

The inaugural conference of the Boao Forum for Asia was launched on February 26, 2001. This was the first major conference convened by Boao and I have already referred to it. The birth of the BFA aroused wide attention internationally. After the press conference held before the inauguration, reporters from CNN overtook me, asking for an interview. They asked me directly whether the founding of the Boao Forum was aimed at the USA. To this challenge I replied: "The Boao Forum for Asia Declaration states explicitly that the BFA is a dialogue platform for Asian countries to discuss their issues of development. It is open and welcomes all countries from around the world, including the USA, to join us to exchange ideas and talk about the issues concerning Asia and the world." I went on: "Pressed by rapid economic globalization, Europe, the Americas and Africa have all intensified their forms of regional economic cooperation. Asia will certainly follow this trend and communicate among ourselves about our regional economic development so as to promote our own development and prosperity and meet the challenges of economic globalization. Could we say that for the countries of Europe, the Americas and Africa to discuss their regional economic cooperation is aimed at the USA?" "Of course not. Obviously your question is wide of the mark," I told them. They fell quiet.

The first annual conference of the BFA was held in April 2002. Its theme was "New Century, New Challenge and New Asia—Asian Economic Development and Cooperation." Premier Zhu Rongji of China, Prime Minister Junichiro Koizumi of Japan, Premier Thaksin Shinawatra of Thailand, Premier Lee Han-Dong of South Korea as well as Tung Cheehwa, Chief Executive of Hong Kong and Edmund Ho Hau Wah, Chief Executive of Macau and a dozen former political figures from various Asian countries were present at the conference. More than 1,800 representatives from several multinational corporations, large enterprises and many experts attended the conference. Prior to the annual conference, I was attending another meeting in Guangdong Province, right after which I was scheduled to go straight to Boao. I was sitting on the rostrum with Li Changchun who was the Guangdong Party Secretary at the time. Phone calls kept coming from Hainan urging me to rush to Boao, where urgent matters were waiting on my decision. This illustrates the chaotic situation on the eve of the first annual conference of the Boao Forum.

In his speech at the first annual conference, Zhu Rongji said that regional cooperation among Asian countries was lagging behind compared with that of Europe and North America. So he made suggestions of how to promote economic cooperation in Asia: 1) Take economic cooperation as the key point to develop an all-out cooperation step by step. 2) Start from existing channels of cooperation to keep expanding its scope. 3) Further develop bilateral cooperation and strengthen the foundation of regional cooperation. 4) Implement an open cooperative relation in Asia. In conclusion, Zhu Rongji said: "The Asian people are industrious, ingenious and striving constantly for the self-improvement. These were the magic qualities of our glorious achievements in the past and they will usher in an even brighter tomorrow for Asia. China is willing to work together with all the other Asian countries to open up a glorious future for a new era of Asia!" Zhu Rongji's speech and his responses to questions raised afterwards were a splendid highlight of this session, praised by all sides.

Premier Thaksin of Thailand made a keynote speech on the theme of "Asian Economic Cooperation and Development." He elaborated the relationship between the Asian Cooperation Forum advocated by the Thai government and the Forum for Asia at Boao, saying that the two forums formed a mechanism of two parallel tracks—the Asian Cooperation Forum on one track and the Boao Forum for Asia on the other. As non-governmental organs, they would complement each other as partners greatly needed among the countries of Asia. Both forums would become great mechanisms for the Asian countries to seek opportunities, build up mutual trust and remove existing barriers.

Prime Minister Junichiro Koizumi of Japan made a keynote speech on the theme "The New Millennium and Asia—Challenge and Opportunity." He started his speech by citing the history of the eminent Chinese monk Jianzhen of the Tang Dynasty who sailed east to Japan. Jianzhen's five attempts to sail to Japan had all ended in failure, but his sixth voyage, setting sail from Sanya in Hainan, had been successful. Prime Minister Koizumi said: "It is precisely because of this background that Hainan Province is a most suitable place for us to discuss the future of Asia in the new century." "The three values of freedom, diversification and openness," he continued, "are the main strength propelling the peace and progress of Asia. Firstly, it is recognized that freedom means democracy and human rights politically and the growth of market economy socially. Secondly, the development of Asian countries has been realized under a highly diversified background. Thirdly, cooperation in Asia should not focus only on our own households behind closed doors. Instead, it should be open to other areas of the world." His speech also stressed, "China's vigorous economic growth will offer challenges as well as opportunities for Japan. It will provide huge opportunities for the world economy. Japan and China can work to strengthen their bilateral and complementary economic relationship."

Premier Lee Han-Dong of South Korea elaborated on four issues in his keynote speech, "New Century: Asia's Economic Development and Future Cooperation in the 21st Century": "1) Strengthening regional trade and cooperated investment. 2) Intensifying cooperation and ensuring the stability of finance and foreign currency markets in the region. 3) Further driving cooperation in the realms of culture, education and technological exchange. 4) Heightening cooperation and eliminating poverty." Lee Han-Dong emphasized, "The Asian countries must exchange experience and cooperate with one another to form a tighter framework of regional economic cooperation, which has never been needed as badly as it is needed today. If Asia hopes to become a thriving region in the 21st century, this will be the fateful key."

The second annual conference of the BFA was convened on October 31, 2003. It had originally been scheduled for April 2003 but was postponed because of SARS outbreaks in China and some other countries and regions. The theme of the second conference of BFA was "Asia Searching for Win-Win: Cooperation to Promote Progress." The honored guests arriving at the conference included Premier Wen Jiabao of China, President Musharraf of Pakistan, Premier Goh Chok Tong of Singapore and a number of former government leaders from various countries as well as Tung Cheehwa and Edmund Ho Hau Wah. Also attending the conference were ministers of several countries, representatives of international organizations, Nobel Prize winners, renowned entrepreneurs and experts.

Wen Jiabao made the keynote speech at the second annual BFA conference. He expounded China's position and opinion on the topics of "maintaining peace and stability," "promoting development and prosperity," "strengthening regional cooperation and communication" and "facing the world, opening up and cooperating." He made four suggestions for Asia to achieve "Win-Win." Everyone attending the conference reacted warmly to Wen Jiabao's speech, expressing their satisfaction with its content. At the banquet dinner that evening, Wen Jiabao gave an impromptu speech. He said that Boao had originally been a fishing village, a small town. However, closely embracing the ocean, and with the broad capacity of the ocean, it absorbed different opinions and ideas. His analogy beautifully unified the geography of Boao with the objectives of the Boao Forum for Asia. His comparison of broad mind and embracing oceans was erudite and full of meaning, warmly applauded by Chinese and foreign guests.

President Musharraf of Pakistan gave a speech entitled "Drive Forward Trade and Economic Cooperation Between Pakistan and Other Asian Countries," in which he expressed opinions on "the challenge of globalization," "Asian cooperation" and "investment in Pakistan." In respect of "Asian cooperation," he made five important points: 1) comprehensive and integrated exchange; 2) establishing a cooperative economy; 3) strengthening Asian values; 4) alleviating tension and peaceful solutions to political conflicts; 5) sharing scientific and technical results.

Premier Goh Chok Tong of Singapore gave a speech entitled "Asia—Catalyst of World Globalization," in which he expounded five ideas—"Asia—a new center of growth," "three challenges," "structural reform and its extension," "regional integration" and "global integration and its catalyst." He concluded with this proposition: "Along with Asia's rising, the Asian region will face high pressures and tension emerging within and between countries. Asia will become a powerful catalyst in the liberalization of world trade. By keeping an open world system and persisting in policy reform at home, pushing for further integration of the Asian region and letting it play a constructive role in WTO, APEC and ASEM, Asia will become a great propelling force in the construction of the new economic mansion of the world." Furthermore, he also emphasized that China would "play a crucial role" in the whole process.

The conference also held specific sessions on topics such as "Economic Globalization and Industrial Labor Division," "Arrangements for Regional Free Trade and Closer Economic Cooperation of Asia," "Seeking a New Breakthrough in Financial Cooperation in Asia," "The Accelerated Catching-up and Cooperation of the IT Industry in Asia," "The Reforming Power of the Mass Media: Balance Between Power and Responsibility," "Energy, Environment and Sustainable Development" and "The Peaceful Rise of China." The speakers and audiences enjoyed lectures, dialogues and discussions at these subject sessions. Because they touched the key concerns of all Asian countries, these discussions were highly popular with conference delegates.

Thanks to the timely completion of Phase 2 on Dongyu Island, plus good control over participant numbers and an improved reception service, the second annual conference of BFA was a great success, winning favorable comment from all sides.

From the second annual conference in 2003 on, the China Reform and Development Forum (CRDFC) and the Secretariat of the BFA co-hosted "The Forum on China's Peaceful Rise," still at the Boao conference venue. Managed by Zheng Bijian, it invited important government leaders, diplomats, academics and other famous international figures to discuss the peaceful rise of China and related topics. It has attracted many prominent figures from China, Asia and the rest of the world to Boao, and is having an increasingly wider influence.

The third annual conference of the BFA was held on April 24, 2004. As it could not be decided which Chinese leader would be present until less than a month before the start of the conference, many important invited guests were waiting to see. The forum secretariat was very anxious about this and asked me to help confirm the issue as quickly as I could. I wrote to President Hu Jintao to invite him to attend the conference and give the keynote speech at the conference. He agreed quickly and the news was announced by the spokesperson of the Ministry of Foreign Affairs. The third annual conference soon became widely subscribed to.

President Hu Jintao of China gave the keynote speech at the opening ceremony of the third annual conference of the BFA. He began by presenting the achievements made by China over the previous 25 years, since implementing the reform and opening-up policy. Then he stated: "China is a member of the Asian family. Her development is closely linked with the prosperity of Asia. China has already and will continue to bring about positive influence for the development of Asia." He elaborated further about the positive influence, citing "China's development has brought forth important opportunities for the development of Asia," "China's development has promoted the peace and stability of Asia" and "China's development has poured new vigor into the regional cooperation of Asia." He emphasized: "China will take positive measures in the following aspects to enhance her cooperation with other Asian countries: 1) Strengthen good neighbor relationship and mutual political trust. 2) Explore and deepen bilateral economic cooperation. 3) Intensify the process of regional economic integration. China hoped to discuss with the other Asian countries different forms of free trade arrangement until a free trade cooperation network of Asia is formed. 4) Promote cultural and personnel exchanges. 5) Advance dialogue about security and military exchanges." Finally, Hu Jintao announced: "The development of China is bound up with Asia. Asia's prosperity needs China as well. China will stick to the path of peaceful development, lift up the banner of peace, growth and cooperation so we can create a new phase of Asian revival and make even greater contributions to the lofty cause of human peace and development." After the speech, he answered questions from conference delegates. The speech and question and answer session were warmly received and highly praised by all sides. During the noon break, Hu Jintao quietly visited the surrounding area of Boao Water City accompanied by only one guard. He expressed satisfaction with both the facilities and the conference services of Boao.

During the annual conference and topic sessions, government ministers of China, Japan, the Philippines, New Zealand, Australia and South Korea all gave speeches. Excellent speeches were made too by entrepreneurs from global and Asian companies including BMW Group, Royal Philips Electronics, South Korea's Tristar, China's Sinopec, Taiwan's Semiconductor Manufacturing Co (TSMC), and UPS; also by the president of Hong Kong Hang Lung Group, and representatives of the World Bank, Asian Development Bank, People's Bank of China, China Construction Bank and China Development Bank. Well-known experts and scholars including Zheng Bijian, Wu Jianmin and Luo Qi gave special lectures, making many valuable suggestions about China's peaceful rise, Asia's development and cooperation between Asia and the other areas of the world.

The four BFA conferences received warm commendation from many countries, especially those in Asia. The then Secretary General of the United Nations, Kofi Annan wrote in his letter to BFA: "The founding of the Boao Forum for Asia has proven the belief that only by the joint effort of all countries in the world, can issues of global concern be dealt with in a positive fashion."

Fidel Ramos stated: "Asia has many forums, but none of them can match the BFA in intellectual and diplomatic experience." He added that the BFA had already become the forum where Asian matters were discussed by the whole world.

Bob Hawke commented: "Our greatest satisfaction is that we were able to create a major dialogue platform to benefit the lives of more than half the world's population."

Yasuhiro Nakasone said: "The ocean here is azure blue. The forest here is lush green. The people of Boao are honest and warm. I hope the inauguration of Boao Forum for Asia will be the starting line for Asia to leap into the 21st century."

Kim Dae-jung of South Korea said: "Compared with the continents of Europe or America, the integration of our economy and society is still less than satisfactory. I believe that the Boao Forum for Asia will play a significant role in improving matters."

President Musharraf of Pakistan remarked: "Through its work to advance economic exchange and cooperation among the Asian countries and around the world, the BFA will safeguard the interests of the Asian people enormously."

President Nazarbayev of Kazakhstan said: "The BFA will become the force to impel and solve the social, economic, political and other problems between Asian countries."

The words by these leaders from the United Nations, Southeast Asia, Northeast Asia, South Asia and Central Asia represented the common aspirations and heartfelt wishes of the Asian nations. The Chinese officials, entrepreneurs, scholars and I shared the same impression in our conversations. We all agree that these aspirations are being turned into positive actions and lofty sense of missions warmly embraced by all the countries and regions of Asia.

The Future of Asia and Its Regional Economic Cooperation

As we entered the new millennium, all countries were speeding up their efforts toward regional economic cooperation in response to the opportunities and challenges flowing from economic globalization.

Europe has been in the front rank in this aspect. Cooperation within the European Union and use of the Euro has widened and deepened. The Euro, the unified currency of the EU, was officially adopted on January 1, 1999. On May 1, 2004, the EU expanded by taking into membership 10 more countries, including Poland and the Czech Republic. The first draft of the European Union Constitution was passed on June 17, 2004. Now the EU consists of 25 member nations with a population totaling 450 million and overall territory reaching four million square km. At US$ 10 trillion, its overall GDP equals the power of USA. They are realizing the dream predicted by the famous French writer Victor Hugo, more than 100 years ago: "All European countries, with no need to discard your varied characteristics and shiny individuality, will all fuse into a unity of a higher, ideal level."

The Americas and Africa have also established their own unifying associations, drawn up timetables and stepped up the pace in conducting regional economic cooperation.

It is true that Asia has several regional cooperative mechanisms in place too. These include the Association of Southeast Asian Nations (ASEAN) comprised of 10 member nations, the "10+3" (Conference of the 10 countries under ASEAN plus leaders of the three countries of China, Japan and Korea), and the Shanghai Cooperative Organization. However, just as the leaders of several Asian countries have pointed out, compared with the Americas, Europe and Africa, regional associations in Asia lag behind somewhat. With an area of 44 million square km—29.4 percent of all the land territory on the earth—the space occupied by Asia is 10 times that of the 25 countries of the EU. Asia's total population of 3.87 billion people represents 60 percent of the world population. Blessed with regions of rich and diverse natural resources and endowment, Asia's reserves of crude oil, tin, magnesite and iron ore all rank No. 1 in the world. Half of the world's deposits of petroleum, coal, uranium and water are in Asia. Its outputs of paddy rice, natural rubber, quinine, pepper, sesame seed, desiccated coconut and tea represent between 80 percent and 90 percent of the total global output of these commodities.

Although Asia has rich deposits, huge human resource and a vast market, the majority of her resources and finished products are sold to the Americas and Europe. Compared with regional trade in the rest of the world, which has average level of 45 percent, in Asia the ratio of regional trade is way lower. This situation indicates that there is still great scope for regional cooperation in Asia as well as broad prospects for development.

In pushing for Asian regional economic cooperation, it is certainly important to point to the resources, the complementary markets and reciprocal benefits and the huge profit that regional cooperation could bring to the continent. However, people must also recognize and pay full attention to the different historical traditions and cultures existing in Asia. The great gulf existing among the histories, cultures, ethnic groups and religions as well as development of economies and societies on this continent means that any effort to push for economic cooperation in the Asian region must start from increased communication and mutual understanding, from promoting of common recognition through dialogue, before acceptable ways of cooperation can be accepted by two or more sides. It will need gradually involving wide participation of governments and individuals, and multiple driving mechanisms for discussions among governments, enterprises and academics on an equal footing. Among these driving mechanisms, the BFA could act as an important platform. Its openness, non-governmental and not for profit nature, its public, democratic and free dialoguing style could help mutual understanding and pooling of knowledge for Asia to explore all kinds of ways for regional cooperation. I believe this tendency is crystal clear for everyone to see. And it is surely achievable through our work. In the near future, I am sure that regional cooperation in Asia will grow, just like that of the European Union, from small to large, from weak to strong, continuing to mature. Asia's tomorrow will surely become more magnificent.

Chapter X

Recalling the Visits to China of Russian, Japanese, Cuban and American State Leaders

- Yeltsin's Eagerness to Meet Deng Xiaoping
- Morihiro Hosokawa's Hopes for a Pair of Crested Ibises for Japan
- Castro Full of Praise for China's Socialist Cause
- Al Gore's Enthusiasm for IT and Environmental Protection

A formal protocol of the Chinese Government in the past was to appoint a state minister to accompany foreign heads of state or government leaders when they visited China. This protocol was an expression of the top-level reception accorded to the distinguished guests. It was also a convenient way for us to enhance the friendship between China and the foreign country during its leader's visit to China. My feeling about the arrangement is that being escort to such guests was a positive and significant job.

While I was the director of the State Commission for Restructuring the Economy (SCRE) and of the State Planning Commission (SPC) I was appointed many times to this job of accompanying foreign state leaders on their trips around China. The foreign leaders I escorted during their visits included Boris Yeltsin, President of the Russian Federation, Morihiro Hosokawa, Prime Minister of Japan, Fidel Castro, President of Cuba and Al Gore, Vice President of the USA, as well as the premiers of Italy and of Russia. By staying close to these foreign statesmen, I had the chance to see at close hand their varied temperaments, particular perspectives and interesting personalities.

Yeltsin's Eagerness to Meet Deng Xiaoping

President Yeltsin of the Russian Federation visited China for the first time in December 1992. I was appointed leader of the accompanying group representing the Chinese Government during his visit and welcomed President Yeltsin at the airport on behalf of President Yang Shangkun. Yeltsin got off the plane and we conversed briefly while he took a short rest in the airport VIP Room. He asked me: "Are you the Director of the SCRE?" I replied yes. "How is it? Is the job difficult?" I told him that the overall situation of China was doing well and that once the macro-economy had improved, it had become much easier for government departments to do their jobs. The brief conversation President Yeltsin had with me was not just diplomatic courtesy. The kind tone of his inquiry gave me a warm sense of his kind attitude.

Our motorcade left the airport and the President started looking around repeatedly. I sensed he was not just enjoying the scenery through the car window but seemed to be waiting for something to happen. But he said nothing; nor was it appropriate for me to inquire about his behavior. Once our motorcade arrived at Jiuxianqiao a team of motorcycle escorts appeared either side of our motorcade, at which President Yeltsin seemed to settle down and asked where we were. I told him this was Jiuxianqiao, the point at which we entered the city of

Beijing, and the point at which the Chinese guard of honor started to escort his delegation. I realized that Yeltsin set great store by show and the level of treatment accorded him. But it might also be the Russian diplomatic style.

After our motorcade passed Jiuxianqiao, Yeltsin asked me: "As Director of the SCRE, what are your views about the reforms in China and in Russia?" I replied: "I have not studied the situation of the Russian reform, so I can only comment on the reform in our own country." "Sure. I'd be very glad of the chance to hear about China's reform today." I said: "Up to now, I should say that, in general, the economic restructuring process is going on well. Our economy continues to grow. The people's livelihood is improving and our society is stable. Personally, I feel that the reason why China's economic restructuring has gone so well so far is mainly that we have highlighted three issues in our reform. First, China started the reform from our actual national conditions. We are making our reform in an evolutionary and gradual way directed by our market. We value the reform experiences of other countries but we do not imitate their processes. We base our decisions on the national conditions of China. Our biggest national conditions are our one billion-plus population, our underdeveloped economy and the low income level of our people. We pay particular attention to the social effects of reform, emphasizing that the reform must benefit the majority of the people. If a reform must cause a stir in society, it must be bearable for the majority of the people. China had a system of universally low wages, so our people are very vulnerable to any major inflation. We pay a great deal of attention to our price reform and try our best to solve problems caused by price rises in people's daily life. Second, China has persisted in handling well the relationship between reform, development and social stability. China keeps carrying out new reform measures to promote development. At the same time, we are also very careful about social stability. If a nation's economic, political and social environment is unstable, then nothing can be accomplished. The vital lesson from the "Cultural Revolution" was that it caused social instability, meaning our economy failed to develop properly and people's lives could not improve. Now we want to reform, develop and move forward, so we know our social stability is the prerequisite for everything. Deng Xiaoping said that if people take to the streets parading and petitioning every day, China would have no energy left for construction. All the reform measures we have adopted over these years have been based on the premise of social stability. Finally, during the process of our reform, we organize our government officials, enterprise representatives, experts and scholars to participate in formulating plans and studying the related policies. The advantage of doing so is to bring together the know-how of people from different sides and discuss various views so they can mutually compensate for each other's insufficiencies. For instance, government officials have a better understanding of the overall situation of the country, but may be burdened by bureaucracy and feel reluctant to change the existing power pattern. The enterprise representatives are mostly concerned about the market and their own profits, and their views may benefit reform and development but may also have their limitations. The experts and scholars are good with concepts and theories but may not be clear about the actual conditions. When mulling over the reform measures, the Chinese Government gathers all these three kinds of people to hear their different perspectives. It will help the decision-makers to consider the interests of different social strata and groups so as to avoid one-sidedness." I was talking about China but I was actually comparing our reform measures with those of Russia. Although I was very indirect in my explanation, Yeltsin might still understand what I was implying. After hearing what I said, he fell silent for a while. Then, he commented that my opinion did make sense.

When our motorcade was approaching Tiananmen Square, I told

Yeltsin that the center of Beijing—Tiananmen Square—was right ahead. He started to focus his attention on Tiananmen. In a short while, he told me: "I have another issue to talk to you about." "OK." "I would like to see Deng Xiaoping. Will you arrange it for me?" I said: "Now Deng Xiaoping has announced his full withdrawal from the public. He no longer meets any foreign guests." Refusing to give up, Yeltsin explained that he wanted to see Deng Xiaoping, even for just a few minutes to express his respect for Deng. He said the relationship between China and Russia was unique. Since he was so sincere in his request I could tell him I would convey his request to the Chinese leadership. After we arrived at the Diaoyutai State Guesthouse, I told the Foreign Minister Qian Qichen of Yeltsin's request, reporting that I had said no to him politely but he simply would not give up. Which was why I had to tell him that I would convey his request to my superiors. Qian Qichen said that the Russian Foreign Minister had also asked him the same thing. I said: "OK, so now I have reported his request to you." Later, President Yang Shangkun asked me what Yeltsin thought about his visit to China. I said he had asked about China's reform and that I had explained it to him, but that then he had asked very eagerly to meet with Deng Xiaoping. That evening, Yang Shangkun hosted a welcome banquet for President Yeltsin at the Great Hall of the People. Before it started and while people were walking into the banquet hall, Yeltsin pulled Yang Shangkun aside and asked if he might see Deng Xiaoping to express his respects, if only for a few minutes. Yang Shangkun, just as I had felt, could not make any promises either. It turned out that Yeltsin did not succeed in meeting Deng Xiaoping during his stay in China.

The next day, General Secretary Jiang Zemin gave a dinner for President Yeltsin at the Diaoyutai State Guesthouse and the Russian President was full of praise for the dish named "Buddha Tempted to Jump the Wall." Jiang Zemin told him: "Since you are going to Shenzhen soon, I will tell Shenzhen to cook the same dish for you when you get there. They make it even better." Jiang Zemin told me to take care of his offer so I told the Protocol Department of the Foreign Affairs Ministry to notify Shenzhen about the issue.

I accompanied President Yeltsin on visits to the Great Wall and the Forbidden City. As a young man, Yeltsin had majored in architecture and was deeply interested in what he saw. On the Great Wall, he noticed the jointing mortar of the bricks and asked what it was. "How come the bricks are still so well bonded after all these centuries?" I told him that, according to the experts, very strong bonding mixture of glutinous rice, tung-oil and lime was used. When we visited the Forbidden City, Yeltsin asked about its architectural design, the construction materials and other aspects about the imperial palace. It really corroborated an old Chinese saying—"Talk shows what a man does."

Early in the morning of the third day of Yeltsin's visit, his advisor informed me that the President would not go to Shenzhen as scheduled because of something back at home. I remarked: "But the Shenzhen schedule was set long ago. Everything is already arranged." However, Yeltsin's advisor insisted that things back home prevented him from going. I could do nothing to change their minds. Soon after breakfast, Yeltsin came over to talk with me. I asked him if he had slept well and he replied that he had slept very well. Then he explained that he had things at home so he could not go to Shenzhen as originally scheduled. I said Shenzhen was a window on and a test bed of China's reform and opening-up policy and there would be exciting new things for him to see there. Moreover, everyone there was expecting him. But he persisted in saying he really could not go this time and would wait for another opportunity to see Shenzhen. As it was not appropriate for me to demand what was so urgent back in Russia, I could only say that we hoped the president would find another opportunity to visit Shenzhen. President Yeltsin then volunteered that there had been an "earthquake" at home, that some people back in Russia were plotting a coup, and he had no alternative but to dash home. Later I learned the actual reason was that some in his circle did not want him to see the exciting window of China's reform. They felt uneasy about Yeltsin seeing the brilliant achievements and experience of China's reform and opening-up to the world and so used a domestic report as a pretext for obstructing his visit to Shenzhen and interrupting his schedule.

Morihiro Hosokawa's Hopes for a Pair of Crested Ibises for Japan

Prime Minister Morihiro Hosokawa of Japan visited China at the invitation of Premier Li Peng on March 19, 1994. When discussing plans for receiving for the Japanese Prime Minister, China learned that Japan was hesitating about finalizing a batch of loans to China under its "Overseas Economic Cooperation Fund" (i.e. Japanese government Yen loan). Since I headed the SPC that was in charge of this realm, the Chinese leaders appointed me to lead the group accompanying Mr. Hosokawa during his visit to China, in the hope that I could help persuade the Japanese Prime Minister to finalize the loans as soon as possible.

When I joined the discussions about the detailed reception plan for Prime Minister Hosokawa, someone in the reception group mentioned that he had another objective for visiting China this time: Japan was very eager to obtain a pair of crested ibises from China. The crested ibis is an extremely rare and very beautiful species of bird, a species enjoying the top category of protection in China. In the past, crested ibises were found in many places including China, Russia, the Korean Peninsula and Japan. However, owing to climactic changes over recent years, only a very few crested ibises survive in the Hanzhong area of Shaanxi Province. When Jiang Zemin visited Japan in 1992, he had given a pair of crested ibises to Japan as a gift. Unfortunately, one of the pair had died so no breeding had been possible. It is said that the Japanese love the crested ibis with a passion. The saber feather on the Japanese emperor's sword preserved in Kyoto's Imperial Palace was a crested ibis feather. When a crested ibis was laying eggs, NHK, Japan's public broadcaster, actually televised the process in its entirety. Apparently, before leaving for China, Mr. Hosokawa had said that if he could obtain a pair of the ibises from the host country, he could claim to have accomplished his mission in China. Because of this, after discussion, China, as host, decided to present Japan with another pair of crested ibises on the occasion of Hosokawa's visit, and asked me to handle it. I went to talk to Xu Youfang, Forestry Minister at the time. I told him: "The Japanese Prime Minister will visit China and he dearly wishes to receive a pair of crested ibises. A meeting today has decided to satisfy his wish. Could you prepare the gift for our nation?" He agreed and promised to get the birds ready.

The main purpose of Prime Minister Hosokawa's visit to China was to discuss cooperation on environmental protection between China and Japan. As a result of the visit, the two states signed the "Cooperation Treaty of the Environmental Protection Agreement" on March 20, 1994. At the same time, the Japanese side sincerely hoped to receive a pair of crested ibises from China. The meeting between the leaders of the two countries was going well and Hosokawa was very pleased with his visit. When he visited a farm produce market at North Taipingzhuang in Beijing, Hosokawa saw fresh watermelons for sale. He remarked that in Japan watermelons were not yet ready for market, so he was admiring and praising the watermelons right there. Happy to have his melons so praised, the farmer selected two big ones from his pile and presented them to the Japanese Prime Minister. It was "common man diplomacy" and the TV reporters loved the picture. So Mr. Hosokawa, holding the two watermelons, smiled happily into the reporters' cameras.

As regards the Japanese loans under its "Overseas Economic Cooperation Fund," I found a chance to raise the topic with Hosokawa in my capacity of Director of the SPC, and asked: "As the Prime Minister may be aware, I head up the State Planning Commission. Loans are arranged by our Commission for our country every year. We have already finalized our annual plan for this year except for loans from your country's Overseas Economic Cooperation Fund, so I hope that the Japanese side will be able to settle this issue as soon as possible." He replied: "This issue has aroused various kinds of opinions in Japan. As our parliament has conflicting views on the subject, our government cannot simply ignore opposing opinions. We need more time to work on it." I said: "I see. I hope the Prime Minister might help speed up this issue so that it can be finalized soon. It would be a significant action for the friendly cooperation between our two countries." After completing my escorting duties, I told the comrades working on the issue in our Commission: "I did what I could, but I feel it is hard for Morihiro Hosokawa to get any substantial result. Let's follow our own timetable now and not wait any longer; otherwise it may delay our own schedule. The bureaucratic system and administrative procedures in Japan are very long drawn out. Once a thing has been decided, it's very hard to change. Added to which, some Japanese politicians hostile toward China always try to use the Overseas Economic Cooperation Fund loans to make trouble or complicate situations. What's more, Morihiro Hosokawa is one of the few prime ministers in the post-World War II period not to be head of the Liberal Democratic Party too. As a political 'lame duck' in Japan, he can hardly achieve anything substantial on this matter."

Castro Full of Praise for China's Socialist Cause

To the majority of people in the world, Fidel Castro, President of Cuba, is an extraordinarily famous figure, an object of admiration and mystery at the same time. To many in Latin America and around the world, Castro is a hero. He visited China in November 1995 and I accompanied him during his trip through China. During more than eight days in close contact with him, I experienced his leader's magnanimity and charisma, his serious and wise work style, his resolute character and the humane personality beneath his dignified appearance and demeanor.

About a month or so before President Castro's visit to China, I had accompanied Premier Li Peng on a visit to Mexico in October 1995. On our arrival, our Mexican hosts arranged for us to go to Cancun, the famous tourist resort and once venue for the South-South Summit Conference. Cancun was only a 30-minute flight across the Caribbean from Cuba. We felt it inappropriate for a Chinese leader to pass by Cuba's door without paying a call, so, from Cancun, Li Peng sought direction from the Chinese leadership. After getting the go-ahead to cross the Caribbean and pay a visit to Cuba, we met with President Castro at Havana Airport where he and his party and national leaders of Cuba received us in an extremely simple reception room. Li Peng briefed

Castro about the domestic situation in China and repeated his invitation to come to China, asking if he could decide on a time to visit. The President said it had long been his wish to visit China. He had no problem about deciding on a date but knew how busy all the Chinese leaders were. Li Peng listed to Castro all the main activities for the Chinese leaders in the near future and suggested that the best time would be after the Chinese National Economic Work Conference, since all the major Chinese leaders would be in Beijing at the time to meet him. Castro agreed to this idea right there and then. When asked whether China should arrange the plane to fly him to Beijing, he replied that there was no need, since Cuba still owned two Soviet-made Il-62 "grandpa planes." Our meeting with Castro and his comrades at Havana Airport was very brief but the atmosphere was intimate and without polite empty talk. This was the first time I saw Fidel Castro close up.

After further discussions between the diplomatic services of the two countries, President Jiang Zemin sent an official invitation, and on November 29, 1995, Fidel Castro stepped onto Chinese soil for the first time, making an official state visit to China. The visit schedule was originally set for a week but it was stretched to eight days because of the full program. To my great excitement, the Party Central Committee appointed me to head the escorting group for Castro. I was to accompany him throughout his journey to Beijing, Xi'an, Shanghai, Shenzhen and Guangzhou.

At about four in the afternoon of November 29, President Castro's special plane arrived at Beijing's Capital Airport. I walked up to welcome him to China on behalf of President Jiang Zemin and Premier Li Peng. After a short rest at the airport, I accompanied him on the drive to the Diaoyutai State Guesthouse. As soon as he sat down in the car, he asked me anxiously: "What time is sunset in Beijing?" Not understanding what he meant, I said casually that sunset would be soon, in half an hour or so. Then, he asked how long it would take to drive from the airport to Tiananmen and I suddenly realized that he wanted to see Tiananmen before night fell. I told him the ride would probably take about 20 minutes before our cars would pass Tiananmen, before it got dark for sure.

In the car, I said to President Castro: "You are welcome to take your time to visit China. We hope you will see more places. As you may be aware, we have arranged several places for you to visit, but please let us know if you have any other requests we don't know about. We will certainly make the necessary arrangements." He said he was happy with the arrangements and had no other requests. Later, Castro asked me about my thoughts on Japanese agriculture, in particular about their rice production and government subsidies to it. Since I knew only the general situation of Japanese agriculture, I said that agricultural production in Japan was very developed, but since the great majority of the votes for Japan's ruling Liberal Democratic Party came from their rural areas, the Japanese government made great efforts and adopted many measures to protect rice production in particular. I told the President that this was as much as I could tell him, since I was not too clear about the details. If needed, I could find him more specific information about the issue. He replied that was unnecessary. He was just being curious.

When our motorcade passed Tiananmen Square, Castro pressed his face to the window glass, gazing longingly at the Tiananmen Gate. His eyes clung to Tiananmen for a long time and then he fell into deep thought.

When the motorcade passed by the SPC office building, I pointed it out to him and told him this was where I worked. He commented that planning for a nation was particularly important and was very busy work. "You don't have to accompany me here all the time. Just concentrate on your own job and I will look for your help whenever I need to." I assured him he need not worry: "The Party Central Committee

Chen Jinhua (first left) and Jiang Xiaosong (first right) with President Fidel Ramos of the Philippines and his wife at the Boao Forum, February 2001

Chen Jinhua with President Fidel Ramos (second right) of the Philippines, former Australian Prime Minister Bob Hawke (second left) and former Japanese Prime Minister Yasuhiro Nakasone (first right) at the founding ceremony of the Boao Forum

Jiang Zemin with representatives of other countries to the founding ceremony of the BFA (Chen Jinhua, first right)

Chen Jinhua, Wang Xiaofeng (first right) and others discuss the plans for the Boao Aquapolis.

Chen Jinhua accompanies Zhu Rongji on his meeting with personages from the industrial and commercial circles of Hong Kong and Macau to the first annual conference of the BFA.

Chen Jinhua and Wang Xiaofeng (second right) at the construction site of Dongyu Island

Hu Jintao delivering the keynote speech at the opening ceremony for the BFA annual conference 2004

Wen Jiabao (fifth left) with government leaders from various countries at the BFA annual conference 2003 (Chen Jinhua, first right)

Chen Jinhua (right) talking with Long Yongtu, Secretary General of the BFA, during the annual conference in February 2001

Chen Jinhua (first right) accompanies Russian President Boris Yeltsin on a visit to the Monument to the People's Heroes in Tiananmen Square.

Chen Jinhua (first right) accompanies Boris Yeltsin and his party on a sightseeing visit to the Great Wall at Badaling.

Morihiro Hosokawa (center) holds up a watermelon presented to him by a Chinese farmer by way of "ordinary people diplomacy."

Chinese President Jiang Zemin and Cuban President Fidel Castro toast the signing of three agreements on economic and trade cooperation between China and Cuba. (Chen Jinhua, center)

Chen Jinhua accompanies Fidel Castro on a visit to the Terracotta Warriors Museum in Xi'an.

Chen Jinhua accompanies Fidel Castro on a sightseeing visit to the Great Wall.

Chen Jinhua welcoming US Vice President Al Gore to China at Beijing Capital Airport

has entrusted me to accompany you for your trip and to take prompt care of your needs. Just let me know whatever you wish to see and know. My duties for the week at the Commission have already been taken care of." Hearing my reply, he said repeatedly: "That's good. That's good."

The next day, President Jiang Zemin and President Castro held a formal talk at the Great Hall of the People and a small-scope discussion was held before the formal talk. The talk went very well as both sides completely shared the same viewpoints. The officials of the two countries expressed their satisfaction with the talk during which both sides introduced their respective domestic situations, expressing their perspective and stance toward international issues that concerned them. Castro talked about the international grain trade, saying that the price of rice on the world market was rising sharply and that a major factor in the rocketing price was China's purchasing on the world market. "China earns a great amount of foreign currency with your huge exports of commodities. So China can buy a lot of grain on the international market. Since you import a gigantic amount, the price of rice has been driven up dramatically since China has started buying it. Cuba, by contrast, has no foreign currency and we cannot afford to purchase grain once the rice price is driven too high. Our children will starve without the grain we need to buy from abroad." In the car, after the talk, I explained to him more about China's grain importing. "You talked about the international grain market, the rising price and our buying of rice. Your opinion was sound and excellent, but I just want to tell you more about the issue. Basically, China relies on herself to feed her people. We are about 97 percent self-sufficient in grain supply, so our grain imports account for only one percent to three percent of our national grain consumption. Moreover, most of this small percentage was purchased mainly because of the conditions set by nations such as the USA, Canada and Australia which required China to buy large amounts of their grain products as the exchange in bilateral deals." After hearing my explanation, Castro nodded to indicate that he understood what I explained.

After the formal talk, I sensed Castro's great concern for grain production all the time. Once, he asked about China's automobile output and told me: "China should not put her main effort into the automobile industry, but should develop her system of public transport. Once the number of cars grows, they will occupy lots of space in roads and parking. Instead, China would do better to prioritize the task of feeding her large population and to treasure her arable land as a long-term asset." Although his advice had its limitations, his sincere advice was based upon a correct stand that we must value our arable land and try our best to develop our public transport. He was definitely right. I believe his advice must have been what he felt keenly as the result of his observations during his stay. When he visited Xi'an, the local government arranged a visit to a peasant's household following a visit to the Terracotta Warriors Museum. Chosen and prepared in advance, this was quite a well-off household, owning a television and other modern appliances. Castro asked the host a series of questions: how many members were there in his family? How much land did his family have? What was the annual grain yield from the land they had contracted from the village? Was the harvested grain enough to feed his family? Did they sell any? Feeling quite satisfied with the replies, Castro left that peasant household. En route, however, he suddenly asked the car to stop and walked straight into another peasant's house without consulting anyone. Unprepared for the visit, the peasant host of the second family was asked the same questions. It happened that the second household was similar to the first well-off one arranged by the local government. In fact, these villages were all doing well since they were in the vicinity of the Terracotta Warriors Museum. Besides cultivating their pieces of farmland, they also made money from the thriving tourist business. Most of them had a rather decent life. From Castro's inquiries, I felt he was conducting an investigation. He wanted to verify, with his own eyes at grassroots level, what he had been told by the Chinese leaders in Beijing. By comparing the policies and measures he heard at the top level with his own findings at the basic level, he wanted to judge whether the top and the bottom were consistent and what the actual situation was.

One of President Castro's attractive traits was that he listened to presentations very carefully and asked questions earnestly. He would recalculate all the figures he was given, first converting them into US dollars to judge whether or not they were expensive and then comparing them to prices on the Cuban market. Deeply concerned about the investment and the construction of the Three Gorges Project on the Yangtze River, he asked me for details of the investment into the huge dam. How much would each unit of electricity cost once the hydropower station started operation? What was the cost in US dollars? As soon as I answered a question, he would calculate the number mentally and then told me the result of his number comparison. He felt that the cost of the Three Gorges electricity sounded reasonable. Castro's working style and method impressed me greatly. I realized more keenly how hard it was for him to run Cuba under the long-term blockade by the USA. Castro told me that Cuba was a small country and her limited arable land must satisfy both the need to feed her people and the pressure to make foreign currency to pay for imports. Therefore, the Cubans must be very careful to use their land sensibly. Basically, they used one-third of their land to grow grain, one-third to grow sugar cane and one-third to grow tobacco. Cuban sugar was world-famous and Cuban cigars were the best in the world too. The sugar and cigars, however, were destined mainly for export. Even under such extremely difficult circumstances, the Cubans still persisted in carrying out the socialist distribution principle. They stressed taking care of the weak groups and tried to meet the needs of the elderly, children and patients with their limited food. In 1996, the UN convened the Social Development Summit Conference in Copenhagen to discuss global social issues such as employment, anti-poverty, health care and education. Leaders from more than 100 countries attended, including Premier Li Peng. I went with him as the head of the Chinese delegation. The conference stipulated that no one's talk must exceed seven minutes. Most of the state leaders received polite applause before and after making their speeches. However, President Castro's seven-minute talk was interrupted by no fewer than 10 explosions of applause and the conference hall was filled with thundering cheers. The numbers of Cuban teachers, doctors and hospital beds per thousand people, as Castro cited in his speech, all exceeded those of the USA. He stated that the American government neglected its own poor, so what right did it have to lecture other countries on this and that! The American government had better put its own house in order first!

On December 1, I accompanied President Castro on a sightseeing visit to the Great Wall and gave him a roast duck dinner at Quanjude Roast Duck Restaurant. The head chef gave him an on-the-spot demonstration of preparing the duck. He invited Castro to sign his name on the duck and then put it into an oven to roast. In a short while, the succulent roast duck with Fidel Castro's signature was served up. Extremely happy about it, Castro felt greatly satisfied and ate a lot. I chatted with him while we ate the duck. I asked him what was in his mind when he led a band of revolutionary youths to attack the Moncada Barracks in July 1953. Did he imagine that he would one day eat roast duck in Beijing over 40 years later? He said he did not think of anything at that moment, being focused solely on the objective of overthrowing the reactionary Batista regime. I also asked him whether he had read Chairman Mao Zedong's works on guerilla warfare while leading the revolutionary movement in the Sierra Maestra. He said he could not obtain the works then and it was only after the success of the Cuban

Revolution that he was able to read Chairman Mao's work published in Spanish. Had he been able to read Chairman Mao's works in the Sierra Maestra, the Cuban Revolution might have won sooner, he claimed. I told him I had read his famous self-defense in court, "History will absolve me." Greatly surprised, he asked me how this speech had got published in China. I told him I had read it in the *People's Daily*, which had printed the full text of his self-defense at the time. Then I asked him about Che Guevara. He said Guevara was originally a doctor, a wonderful man full of noble ideals. Guevara was Castro's comrade-in-arms and once held the posts of President of the Central Bank of Cuba and Industry Minister. Like Castro, Guevara is regarded as a hero by many countries and peoples.

When President Castro was in Beijing, we arranged for him to pay his respects at the Monument to the People's Heroes and to honor the remains of Chairman Mao Zedong. He walked slowly toward Chairman Mao's crystal sarcophagus and stood there for a long time, paying homage to Chairman Mao with the deepest reverence. When we talked about the Chairman, Castro was extremely sincere and told me he had the highest respect for him, saying that Chairman Mao had always stood by the side of oppressed nations and peoples, offering the most sincere and selfless support to their national liberation and independence movements. He told me several times that the behavior of the Soviet Union and the Communist Party of the Soviet Union had been full of national self interest, caring only about their own advantage, and showing indifference to others. Cuba had suffered greatly from this. Those lessons had sunk in deep.

We were flying to Xi'an. As soon as the plane took off, Castro called over his young assistant and asked him to provide a detailed background briefing on Xi'an, the city he was to visit, covering history, geography, people, etc. That young assistant, probably in his early 30s at the time, was very capable. He opened up his laptop and reported to

Castro about Xi'an and Shaanxi Province in which it is located. Castro listened to his assistant and asked questions, repeating some important facts to memorize them, so that he could talk to his local hosts after landing. Then, he asked me to make use of our time on the plane to talk about the experience of China's economic development to José Luis Rodríguez Garcia, Vice President of Cuba's Council of Ministers and Minister of the Economic Planning Ministry. I said I could not really lecture Mr. Rodríguez about our experience, but I could relate what we had done. Whenever China and Cuba held formal talks, Castro dominated most of the talk from the Cuban side; his entourage could hardly get a word in. So right from the start we never arranged separate meetings for our two countries' ministerial counterparts. Hence this special discussion between myself and Mr. Rodríguez had to be an ad hoc arrangement. I sat facing Mr. Rodríguez over another table in the cabin. What Mr. Rodríguez showed great concern about during our talk was how to control inflation whilst preventing the economy from shrinking. At that time, Cuba had a double-digit inflation rate, which was causing his government great anxiety. At the time China's macro-economic regulation had done well and seen initial success. The "soft landing" of China's economy was also starting to show results. I told Mr. Rodríguez how China had achieved the "soft landing" and emphasized to him the importance of keeping overall quantitative balance between overall supply and demand. I advised him to watch the currency supply and try to keep control at an appropriate level, and to heighten price management in accordance with legal measures. The effort to control inflation did not mean tightening up on one side only: it was necessary to treat both the symptom and its causes, to regulate the situation comprehensively. Economic, legal and necessary administrative methods should be adopted for the macro-economic regulations and controls, tightening up those that needed tightening and letting others grow that should grow, and taking the opportunity to rectify unreasonable structures. Thus, the state could control prices whilst increasing the efficient supply capability so the economy could maintain rapid growth at the same time. Mr. Rodríguez listened to me very earnestly, asking for details from time to time and noting down important data and measures I cited. He remarked repeatedly: "China is a big country with complex conditions. But you people have been able to achieve economic growth as well as control of inflation while developing your economy. It is truly marvelous! Through seeing everything here with our own eyes, we feel even more keenly that China's path is a correct path."

When President Castro visited Shanghai, he stayed in the presidential suite at the Jinjiang Tower Hotel. Someone told me that Latin Americans loved vintage osmanthus wine made in Beijing and that went for Castro too. I said that was no problem, as we would give him a case of osmanthus wine. I asked my assistants to buy this particular wine in Shanghai but we failed to find any, so I phoned Beijing to ask the Sinopec staff to help me. They bought the case of wine and sent it to Shanghai that very evening. I also selected and bought a 100-piece set of Western-style tableware in Jingdezhen blue-and-white porcelain as my personal gift to President Castro. On the evening before we were to leave Shanghai, I went to Castro's hotel room and said: "I have accompanied you all the way during your visit. Our next stop is Shenzhen and Guangzhou, and you will leave China from there. That is why I want to give you some personal souvenir. Not knowing what you like, and knowing that even if I ask you won't tell me, I have chosen a 100-piece set of Western-style tableware in Jingdezhen blue-and-white porcelain. I hope you will like this memento." Castro was very happy with it. He thanked me and said he would store away the valuable set of porcelain when he got back, and that when I visited Cuba, he would invite me to his home and entertain me using this set of tableware. I said: "That's wonderful. I will definitely come and visit you in Cuba."

On December 7, our second day in Shenzhen, Castro visited the

Chinese Nationality Park by arranged schedule. The Park management had imposed a slight control over the number of visitors and selected 3,000 people to come that day for security reasons. Somehow, the news got out that Castro was to visit the park and a large crowd started to gather there. There was a sea of people, old and young, men and women, an estimated ten thousand at least. They were very well behaved, enthusiastic but polite. Everyone was cheering heartily for Castro, jumping up and down with joy. The scene touched Castro deeply. He told me he had been to many countries and experienced many welcomes from massed crowds, but had never seen one as touching as that day, with everyone cheering, enthusiastic, natural and well behaved. He was greatly moved. I saw a young man, in his early 20s to judge from his appearance, jumping up and down in excitement. I asked him: "Do you know who this is?" The young man answered as if Castro was one of his own family: "He is our Old Ka!" I asked again: "What do you think of him?" "He is a hero who dares to challenge the Yanks!" I asked the young man what his job was and he replied that he was a taxi driver. This event revealed the lofty image Castro has in the minds of the Chinese.

The warm support Castro received from the public reminded me of another occasion I witnessed. In the mid-1990s, the central leadership sent me to visit Brazil and then Chile. In a museum on Latin American history and culture at San Diego in Chile, I saw a display of famous national heroes of Latin American countries in the past centuries. Castro's picture was high among them. I knew that all the governments of the Latin American countries practiced capitalism so they certainly disapproved of socialism. The reason they respected Castro was not from a shared ideology, but because of admiration for their hero. They respected Castro for his personal charisma, his firm stand to keep state independence and national dignity, his passion for his people and his courage in the face of super powers and oppression.

At the end of Castro's visit to Shenzhen, President Jiang Zemin made a special visit to Shenzhen to meet him again. He accompanied Castro on a visit to a local bicycle factory and hosted a dinner for him again. At that time, Cuba was suffering from economic difficulties so their government could not repay the several hundred million US dollars Cuba owed China. Castro's delegation asked if they could delay the loan repayment. Jiang Zemin asked my opinion and I said the two sides had discussed the matter already and we had also got approval from the State Council about our opinion. Cuba could not repay the loan anyhow and it was not that we would be unable to survive without having that sum right there and then. We could postpone the deadline for their debt repayment. So Jiang Zemin told Castro: "I have discussed the issue with Director Chen. We agree to your request to postpone the repayment." Jiang Zemin also assured Castro that he could tell me all his requests during the remainder of his visit.

At the end of Castro's visit to Shenzhen, Guangzhou's White Swan Hotel sent a motorcade to drive him and his delegation to Guangzhou. He spent one night at the White Swan Hotel and left for home the next day. On our way from downtown Guangzhou to the airport, I congratulated President Castro on his successful visit to China. His talks with the Chinese leaders had gone very well; the cities he had visited all represented something special about China; Jiang Zemin had made a special trip from Beijing to Shenzhen to meet with him for the second time, something that had never happened before with a foreign head of state. I added that, because of the limited time, he might still have things to say and that if he had any important suggestions, I could convey them to our central leaders on his behalf. Having pondered my request for his suggestions for a while, Castro answered that he really could not think of anything more to say. He was very pleased with his visit to China since it had given him the valuable opportunity to see for himself the tremendous progress China had made. Everywhere in

China he had seen vitality and vigor and he keenly felt the prosperity of socialist China. China had given him hope, given him stronger confidence in socialism. Next, he mentioned the importance of youth work. He said that while China had eight democratic parties, Cuba had none. Nevertheless, Cuba had public organizations to provide a channel for the government to communicate directly with young people, including middle school students. He said he needed to go back to Cuba quickly to attend the soon to be held Convention of Middle School Students. He emphasized: "The young people are active in their thoughts and are often impressionable. To communicate with them frequently is vitally important. We must listen to their opinions and ideas as much as possible, the university students in particular. The victory of socialism ultimately depends on them. Only when they accept, understand and practice the socialist system, is there hope for the socialist cause. Whenever the Cuban government makes a major decision, we always tell our young people about it, discussing and communicating with them." I answered: "You are right. After China implemented the reform and opening-up policy, we rather eased up on youth work and their minds were confused for a while. After the political turmoil of 1989, Deng Xiaoping and our Party Central Committee came to realize the problem. Many measures have been adopted to strengthen political work among our students, particularly among university students. Personally, I feel there is still a long way to go even though the situation has now improved." Castro agreed and told me he had always paid special attention to student work. After seeing him off at the airport, I passed Castro's advice to Dai Bingguo, the Vice Minister of the International Liaison Department of the CPC, asking him specifically to relay Castro's advice, word for word, in his report to the Central Party Committee.

Of all the foreign leaders I have accompanied during their visits to China, the one that touched me most deeply was Fidel Castro. I saw in him a great leader of a small country. I came to realize how an outstanding statesman with historical perspective and world vision could come from any country, be it small or large.

Al Gore's Enthusiasm for IT and Environmental Protection

In March 1997, Al Gore the then Vice President of the USA, visited China at the invitation of Premier Li Peng. At the time, there was frequent friction between China and the USA on trade. Both the American government and people were making an issue of their trade deficit with China: feeling that the USA was suffering big losses in its trade with China, they wanted China to expand her imports from the USA or reduce her exports to the USA. In his talk with Vice President Gore, the Chinese Vice Premier Zhu Rongji pointed out that the main reason for the big American trade deficit was that the two countries did not have an equal trading relationship: the USA wanted China to import more American products, but refused to export especially high and new technologies to China. "We can import only Californian oranges or apples all the time, right?" Al Gore could not come up with an answer to the question. Also raising the issue when talking with Al Gore, Li Peng said: "Director Chen Jinhua of our State Planning Commission is accompanying you during your visit in China. He can tell you more details about the issue." Premier Li Peng meant for me to try to persuade Al Gore on the issue. Later, I did talk to the Vice President about the US trade deficit with China, but he chose to keep silent, saying only that different sides have different stands. I felt that his real interests did not lie in this field.

During Vice President Gore's visit, he showed more interest in China's information technology: he presided over the Information Highway Project sponsored by the Clinton government. His scheduled visits in Beijing, including high schools, forums and seminars, were all related to the subject of information technology. As Vice President of the USA, this field was his main focus of attention: he was not interested in any discussion about the US-China trade deficit.

Al Gore cared about the issue of environmental protection also. During his visit to Xi'an, Gore mentioned that he had heard about the bleakness of China's northwestern area, and asked if it had been caused by man-made destruction such as wars. I told him it was true that destruction from wars during the past centuries, people's neglect of the natural environment, excessive deforestation in certain regions and failure to conserve water and soil had all contributed to the deterioration of the environment in that area. However, viewed from a comprehensive perspective, none of these were the root reasons. The primary reason for the bleakness of China's northwestern area was the ecological transformation caused by global climate change. The continuous stretches of Gobi, and the desert spreading for thousands, tens of thousands, even hundreds of thousands of square kilometers across China's northwest had been formed by years of scarce rainfall, lack of moisture and sunshine evaporation. Human damage could not have caused such huge areas of Gobi and desertification. But it was true that excessive tree felling and destruction might have been partially responsible for the environmental deterioration. Take Xi'an for example. In the past, it used to have eight torrential rivers. The largest was the Wei River and this was still the main water resource for Xi'an residents. Excessive tree cutting and other human excesses had affected the surrounding environment of Xi'an and the people there were paying a heavy price for it. These were all painful lessons for us. Al Gore listened to me, eventually commenting: "Yours is a scientists' viewpoint." I replied: "I am not a scientist, but I believe these views make sense."

Today, we pay a great attention to environmental protection so that our living environment will not continue to deteriorate, and hoped that our efforts might at last reverse the horrifying tide. Environmental deterioration in a specific region will expand and eventually affect a wider range. It is not an easy task for mankind to transform the desert. Without water, there can be no greening of the deserts. Several years ago at a conference on developing China's western regions, I made two points. The first was that the most critical issue to developing our Northwest was water. A fundamental condition of successfully opening up our western regions was for people to stop increasing their water usage and stop wasting water resources. Fail to treasure water or to ruin water resources would not only put an end to any hope of developing China's West, but would also have long-term adverse consequences. The other point was that we must inherit the Yan'an Spirit in our effort to open up the West. Putting out the hand for more money from central government would not work. These two points might have sounded untimely and offensive to some comrades. But it was and remains my firm belief that I was right to say so.

图书在版编目（CIP）数据

亲历中国改革：陈锦华国事忆述：英文/陈锦华著.
—北京：外文出版社，2008
ISBN 978-7-119-05191-8
I. 亲…　II. 陈…　III. 经济史—中国—现代—英文
IV. F129.7
中国版本图书馆CIP数据核字（2008）第012300号

英文翻译：王明杰　　纪　华　　王宗引　　金绍卿
英文审定：Sue Duncan　　贺　军
责任编辑：刘芳念
装帧设计：蔡　荣
印刷监制：韩少乙

亲历中国改革：陈锦华国事忆述

陈锦华　著

©2008　外文出版社
出版发行：
外文出版社（中国北京百万庄大街24号）
邮政编码：100037
http://www.flp.com.cn
电　　话：008610-68320579（总编室）
　　　　　008610-68995852（发行部）
　　　　　008610-68327750（版权部）
制　　版：
北京维诺传媒文化有限公司
印　　制：
北京外文印刷厂
开　　本：640mm×960mm 1/16　印张：35
2008年第1版第1次印刷
（英）
ISBN 978-7-119-05191-8
15000（精）
11-E-3815S

2